WITH THE EYES OF FAITH

WITH THE EYES OF FAITH is one of the volumes in a series, IMPACT BOOKS, designed to bring to the modern reader the significant achievements of scholars, both Catholic and non-Catholic, in the fields of Scripture, Theology, Philosophy, Mathematics, History, and the Physical and Social Sciences. Among the titles in the series are:

What Is Philosophy? By Dietrich von Hildebrand
Modern Ethical Theories by James McGlynn, S.J., and Jules Toner, S.J.
The School Examined: An Essay on the Curriculum by Vincent Smith
Catholic Thought in Crisis by Rev. Peter Riga
Contraception and the Natural Law by Germain Grisez
Introducing the Old Testament by Frederick L. Moriarty, S.J.
This Good News: An Introduction to the Catholic Theology of the New Testament by Quentin Quesnell, S.J.
Maturing in Christ: St. Paul's Program for Growth in Christ by George Montague, S.M.
Seven Books of Wisdom by Roland Murphy, O.Carm.
God and Contemporary Man: Reflections of a Christian Philosopher by Robert J. Kreyche
The Word Dwells Among Us by William E. Lynch, C.M.
New Testament Essays by Raymond E. Brown, S.S.

With
THE EYES
of
FAITH

John L. Murphy

THE BRUCE PUBLISHING COMPANY
MILWAUKEE

NIHIL OBSTAT:

JOHN E. TWOMEY, S.T.L., PH.D.
Censor librorum

IMPRIMATUR:

✠ ROMAN R. ATKIELSKI
Auxiliary Bishop of Milwaukee

October 11, 1965

Library of Congress Catalog Card Number: 65–27903

© 1966 THE BRUCE PUBLISHING COMPANY
MADE IN THE UNITED STATES OF AMERICA

TO
A. AND R. JONES
FRIENDS

Preface

The title of this volume has been chosen in order to single out in fitting manner the general content of its chapters. It is really a collection of essays on the overall topic of faith and reason, and the relationship which exists between them. Because of this, I have borrowed the title from the article of Pierre Rousselot, "Les yeux de la foi." This now famous article appeared in the *Recherches de science religieuse* in 1910. It has been read and reread, praised and attacked; both the author and his followers have attempted to clarify its thought. Through it all, however, we must admit that what Rousselot had to say has done more to stimulate thought and discussion on this topic than perhaps anything else written in the present century. He did not solve all the problems, but his activity has served as a leaven in the bread, and his influence has spread accordingly.

Except for the Introduction, which has been written for the present book, the other chapters appeared, in slightly different form, in a number of periodicals between 1961 and 1963. Editing them for book form has meant mixing them up here and there, rearranging the order at times; I have also made use of the opportunity to clarify my thought or to alter it on those points where I thought it advisable. In general, however, the original articles have remained substantially intact. I would like to express my gratitude to the publishers of the following periodicals for permission to reprint the articles here:

The American Ecclesiastical Review, Washington, D. C.:
"Modern Man and God," 144 (1961), 244–271.
"Modernism and the Teaching of Schleiermacher," 144 (1961), 377–397; 145 (1961), 15–38.

viii   Preface

"Faith and Reason in the Teaching of Kierkegaard," 145
(1961), 233–265.
"Unwritten Traditions at Trent," 146 (1962), 233–263.
"Two Theories of Faith," 147 (1962), 14–36.
"A Rationalist Defense of Christianity," 148 (1963), 217–235;
315–336. (Most of this article is presented in the Appendix;
some sections, however, have been joined to the other
articles.)
Proceedings: The Catholic Theological Society of America, 1962:
(The Seventeenth Annual Convention, June 25–28, 1962, held
at Pittsburgh, Pennsylvania.)
"Can Historical Method Prove Christ's Divinity?" pp. 3–64.
Theological Studies, Woodstock, Md.:
"The Influence of Bishop Butler on Religious Thought," 24
(1963), 361–401.

I would also like to take this opportunity to thank Reverend
Ronald O. Crewe and Mr. Donald J. Buzanowski for their generous
assistance in preparing these essays for publication.

In an age in which the theological world is struggling both to
free itself from the overly rationalistic spirit of the past few centuries and to keep from falling into any pit of antirationalism or
subjectivism, these varied topics may prove helpful if brought
together in book form. This was the publisher's thought, at any
rate, and I do hope it is justified.

Faith and reason are important to our age, and we need to
discuss their relationship. The two are closely allied, but they
must not be confused. While it is true that we extol the power
of human reason, the Christian also realizes that for him the
greatest enlightenment comes not from his own native powers but
from that divine gift which opens the door to reality much more
effectively, and which enables him to see the world and human
existence more clearly with the eyes of faith.

JOHN L. MURPHY

St. Francis Seminary
Milwaukee, Wisconsin

Introduction

Of all the topics which have concerned modern religious thought since the time of the Reformation, none is more basic than that of faith. It is easily enough seen how Luther's insistence upon salvation by faith *alone* would bring this subject to the fore, but it was at the hands of the Rationalists of the seventeenth and eighteenth centuries that the notion of faith suffered the most. Luther's faith was essentially vital and supernatural; it was an acceptance of Christ as Redeemer, involving a total commitment of the individual to Him, and it included the acceptance of the message, the doctrine which Christ proclaimed. The faith of the sixteenth-century Lutheran was far from a creedless faith; the same was true of the Swiss reformers. As Dillenberger-Welch wrote, ". . . the issues of the sixteenth century concerned justification, and such doctrines as the Incarnation and the Trinity were largely taken as part of the received faith which needed no reformation."[1] The *Catechism* of Luther and the *Institutes* of Calvin bear eloquent testimony to this doctrinal aspect of the Reformation faith.

Even the debated matter of justification did not depart from the essential concern for revealed truth. What was debated was the *manner* in which the individual is justified through Christ, and the *means* by which this is accomplished. The eventual response of the Council of Trent has not always been appreciated, either by Catholics or non-Catholics, but it proclaims a faith which stands at the very beginning of man's salvation — the "foundation and root of all justification," as the Council phrases it.[2] This is not the faith of a cold intellectual assent that many have associated with Catholic belief, but rather a full, personal response to God's call, in which there is human activity, but the activity proper to one who reacts to the initial call of God: "Justification must begin with God's call, a call which they do not merit. . . . The result is that, when God touches the heart of man with the illumination of the Holy Spirit, the man who accepts that inspiration certainly does something, since he could reject it; on the other hand, by his own free will, without God's grace, he could not take one step toward justice in God's sight."[3]

What may have resulted from the early debates of the Reformation era is the tendency to pass over too quickly, in Catholic circles, the prime importance of faith. Luther and Calvin both found in the concept of justification by faith a point of departure for their religious thinking. The Catholic reaction has only too frequently been a tendency to overemphasize other important elements in the total view of justification, but at the cost of an adequate presentation of the role of faith. The continued insistence on the fact that man is not saved by faith alone has not always been balanced with the Tridentine insistence upon faith as the foundation and root of justification; and the rejection of the Reformers' explanation of the effect of the sacraments as coming from faith alone may have led many to neglect insisting upon the fact that the fruitful reception of the sacraments demands faith. While the *ex opere operato* effects can be present with merely the intention of the minister and recipient, faith is not to be ignored in the presentation of sacramental theology. As the *Constitution on the Liturgy* points out: "The sacraments not only presuppose faith, but by words and objects they also nourish, strengthen, and express it: that is why they are called 'sacraments of faith.' "[4]

REEVALUATION

The effects of the Reformation debates on faith are far less significant, however, than those which resulted from the discussions with the deists and rationalists of the post-Cartesian era. While the original Reformers left the basic notion of faith as something supernatural, the rationalist viewpoint demanded that reason take the place of faith — or at least that "faith" be explained in terms of reason and history. It is here that we must seek an explanation for the general misunderstanding of the Catholic concept of faith, for there are many outside the Church who feel that Catholicism has bowed down before the god of reason in this regard. Any number of non-Catholic theologians might serve as an example of this, but the strictures of Karl Barth against the Catholic position point up the fact well.

Barth should not actually oppose the Catholic theological teaching itself, but he has been most outspoken in his rejection of what he thinks it implies. His difficulty seems to stem more from a failure to grasp the authentic teaching than from a rejection of the position itself, as indicated in his discussions with Söhngen and Küng. In these instances, Barth shows that his primary fear is that the Catholic presentation of faith is really limited to the realm of the purely natural, and that the mystery or awe of faith has been destroyed by an unjustified appeal to reason and to history. As may appear from what follows, this is a common concern for many other Protestant theologians in their attempts to evaluate Catholic teaching.

Hans Küng contends, for example, that the teaching of Barth in regard to justification coincides, in its essential points, with the authentic teaching of the Church of Rome. Barth admits that this conclusion of Küng left him somewhat amazed.[5] Nevertheless, a return to the sources seems to indicate that these two theological positions are not nearly so opposed to one another as many had assumed for so long a time. Barth still has reservations concerning the fact that what Küng sets forth actually *is* the teaching of the Catholic Church.[6] This is understandable, of course, and Barth goes on to point out that if what Küng presents is the teaching of the Church as proclaimed at Trent, he might be pardoned for not recognizing it, since it is not quite so obvious in the text, and this doctrine has not been presented in so clear a fashion by most of the post-Tridentine theologians.[7]

What Barth does not see is that the fault lies less in the actual teaching of the Church than in the manner in which individual theologians have explained this teaching. In all honesty, the

Catholic must admit that the teaching on justification has not always been adequately presented by Catholic writers. There are reasons for this, however, and chief among them would be the fact that, with the advent of what we would term the "more recent" theories of faith in the seventeenth century, the entire supernaturality of justification and faith was somewhat slighted by many Catholic theologians. The Tridentine decree itself came to be read in the light of these theories rather than on its own merits alone. That this should have happened is not too surprising from one point of view. There was, first, the spirit of the age — mistaken though it was — which led to an attempt to meet the objections of the adversaries on their own terms. In this instance, this meant attempting to present Christian faith in a manner acceptable to the deists and rationalists of that period of history. The attempt was doomed to failure from the start, despite its comparatively widespread acceptance.

In addition, it was difficult for Catholic theologians to know the full mind of Trent because of an inability to make use of the historical sources of the Council. What Geiselmann states of the Tridentine decree on Scripture and tradition is also true of the decree on justification: that is, the various *acta,* the diaries, letters, and the like were hidden away in libraries and were not available for general use; as a result men could easily read something into the decree which the fathers at Trent had not intended to say.[8] Since the beginning of the publication of the *Acta* of Trent in 1911 (under the editorship of the Görresgesellschaft), the theologian has been able to come to a better grasp of the true mind of the Council in issuing its decrees. This historical method, which was developed to such a high point in the past century, has proved an invaluable aid to the Catholic theologian in his attempts to understand the official decrees of the Church.

Barth seems to have read the decree on justification, however, in an entirely different light, proceeding from a conviction that the Catholic's first appeal is to reason rather than to faith; this has, in turn, caused Barth so to emphasize faith that other theologians, following the lead of Emil Brunner, would accuse Barth of falling into a nominalism surpassing even that of Ockham (since he would imply that we speak of God as "Father, Son and Spirit" not because there is a certain resemblance here with that which we know naturally, but simply because God has said in Scripture that this is so).[9] Barth does not want to affirm such an extreme position; he is simply trying to stress the fact that faith is primary in the Christian life, and the Christian's knowledge of God is determined by revelation rather than reason.

ANALOGY OF BEING

A similar fear lurks behind the position adopted by Barth in regard to the analogy of being. He feels that this symbolizes the Catholic attempt to reduce faith to reason, and he considers it, therefore, as the chief source of evil in the Church of Rome: "I regard the *analogia entis* as the invention of Antichrist, and think that because of it one can *not* become Catholic. Whereupon I at the same time allow myself to regard all other possible reasons for not becoming Catholic, as shortsighted and lacking in seriousness."[10] He is convinced that any defense of "natural theology" will mean that reason ultimately becomes the foundation of Christian faith, so that it is no longer an acceptance of the Word of God, but merely a human statement in regard to the deity.[11]

In two detailed articles, Söhngen pointed out that there is also a vast difference in the Catholic tradition between the analogy of *being* and the analogy of *faith,* noting that the Catholic belief is rooted basically in the mystery of faith rather than reason. He contends that Barth, in his anxiety to defend the mystery element of faith, has so exaggerated the supposed role of the analogy of being in Catholic teaching that he has misrepresented its position entirely.[12] Barth admires the response of Söhngen, and remarks that "if this is the Roman Catholic doctrine of *analogia entis,* then naturally I must withdraw my earlier statement that I regard the *analogia entis* as the invention of Anti-Christ."[13] While he could accept the position outlined by Söhngen, Barth nevertheless holds on to his basic fear that the official Catholic teaching speaks of a participation of being on the natural level, something

knowable by reason and attainable by human effort, rather than
founding it upon the grace of God and faith.

Barth distinguishes, in a way, between the *Deus Creator* of
Vatican I and Yahweh who revealed Himself in Scripture. In
so doing he fails to appreciate the mind of Rome, but we might ask
if many Catholic presentations of the proofs for the existence
of God by reason might not have induced such confusion. Vatican
I assuredly teaches that man *can* know the existence of God by
reason, but at the same time it affirms that God can be known as
He truly is only through revelation. This is a knowledge which
rests upon a supernatural assent of faith, rather than any conclusion of reason; and it is this knowledge that the Christian
must have above all.

This same mentality appears in Barth's discussion of the traces
or indications of the Trinity in nature — the *vestigia Trinitatis.*
For some reason, confused perhaps by the presentation employed
by some Catholic writers, Barth seems to feel that the Catholic
would see in such traces a "proof" of some sort. Hence he insists:

> What are we to say to all this material, and what are we to do
> with it? The first task is to try to conceive it in the sense in
> which it was *originally* intended, as an interesting, edifying, in-
> structive and helpful *hint* towards understanding the Christian
> doctrine, not to be overvalued, not to be applied as a *founda-
> tion or proof* in the strict sense, because we must already know
> and believe in the Trinity, if we are really to apprehend its
> *vestigia* as such in the macrocosm and microcosm. . . .[14]

Certainly no Catholic would hold anything but this. Barth's
concern with "proof," however, calls to mind at once the more
recent theories of faith which do tend to "demonstrate" doctrines, as
it were, by structuring arguments which would supposedly satisfy
even the nonbeliever; it is for this reason that such theories go on
to affirm at least the possibility of a purely "natural" or "scientific
faith." It would seem that Barth's reading of Catholic teaching has
been done chiefly in the light of such theories, and it is this
which makes it difficult for him to appreciate the validity of such
presentations as those of Küng and Söhngen.

ECUMENICAL CONCERNS

While Barth serves as a good example of the confusion which does appear in evaluating Catholic thought, there are many other non-Catholics who, for various reasons, entertain similar views. Hence it is important that we analyze more precisely the Catholic tradition in this regard. Such a basic understanding is most important for the current ecumenical dialogue. It is often not the authentic teaching of the Church which causes difficulties for others, but rather the misrepresentation of the Catholic position. The essays in this volume attempt, therefore, to shed some light on this overall question; they center on one general topic: faith and reason. What we have attempted to do is single out the various lines of thought which have contributed to a certain amount of confusion, and then suggested positions which might be profitably pursued at the present time.

It has not been our aim to offer final conclusions as much as to stimulate discussion and analysis. The extended writings of the present decade, spurred on by Vatican II above all, bear witness to the "searching" quality of our current thinking. The scriptural studies, the return to theological sources, the interest in a more kerygmatic approach have all called forth a number of seemingly harsh criticisms of theology as it has been presented in our theological schools the past few hundred years. These criticisms are not entirely invalid, and we need not think of Catholic theology as so static that it cannot evaluate itself and its objectives in a frank and objective manner. There is much room for improvement; not everything has been perfect. However, it is essential that in our evaluation of theology, and in our suggestions for change we perceive the true problems and the real origins of these problems; it is solely in this light that the suggestions for change are seen as valid.

This is not always done, however; or at least we do not always take time and effort enough to search through history to uncover these real causes and discuss them in our theological writings. The result of this neglect can easily be a spirit of "change" for the sake of change; a harsh criticism of the "old," and an uncritical enthusiasm for the "new," simply because it appears as new. In point of fact, much of what passes today as "new" really represents something much older, and the "change" is more of a *return* to the authentic theological traditions of our faith.

We speak, for example, of the need to "revitalize" theology, to abandon the approach of "manual theology," and to present faith as something more than a lifeless acceptance of a list of doctrinal points. There is also a need to present the Church in a less legal-like guise, and to teach the sacraments as personal encounters with Christ. Apologetics especially needs to be discussed, and its proper role delineated. This is all true; but we must also set forth the true reasons for these demands. It is not our faith, nor the teaching of the Church which we are evaluating, but rather certain theological tendencies which have, in some instances, surrounded the presentation of that faith.[15] Apologetic theology, manual theology, school theology, or whatever else we might call it has resulted from faulty theories of faith and their corresponding theological methodologies rather than the authentic teaching of the Church; and such problems need to be investigated.

The living Church always needs to take stock in this manner, and it has nothing to fear from such self-criticism. If we come to think of this as a rejection of the "old," however, merely because it is old, we are in danger of confusing the true and unchanging with the secondary and mutable elements of religion. This confusion would seem to lie at the heart of many of the debates within theological circles these past few years, but the truth is that all Catholics want to retain the essentials; any suggestion of change will touch only upon the more secondary questions of precisely how the unchanging faith ought to be proposed.

EFFECT OF RATIONALISM

It is our conviction that the core of this problem lies in the age-old question of the relationship between faith and reason. There is one aspect now associated with it, however, that is proper to our age, namely, the grave concern for the role of the historical method in scholarship. This is intimately related to our scriptural studies, and to our investigation of theological sources; it cannot be ignored, but it must be properly evaluated. The essays of this volume would aid in showing how both reason and historical method can and must play a role in Catholic scholarship, while leaving faith itself founded on something more profound and supernatural than a well-annotated *Festschrift*. The fear that Catholic theology would subject faith to reason, and reduce this life-giving encounter with Christ to a mass of syllogisms has bothered Protestant critics both past and present. To be truthful, there have been some theological approaches within Catholic cricles which would tend to justify such fears, but, as mentioned above, these approaches are, in large measure, the result of attempts to answer particular difficulties in the past by making an appeal to the principles of the deists or rationalists. It is not surprising that many of these defenders of the faith ended up with the same difficulties they had sought to uproot. Having vitiated their principles, they could hardly hope to succeed in presenting the mystery of faith in the categories of rationalism alone.

Thus there has been a swinging of the pendulum from one extreme to another during these centuries, theologians at times becoming too rationalistic and at other times too unconcerned about the necessary role of reason and history in the Christian life. It was in the nineteenth century that much of this came to a head, leading to Vatican I's defense of human reason in its first dogmatic decree, *Dei Filius*.[16] The first chapter of this volume is intended to show that Vatican I did not define that every individual either can or must know the existence of God by reason — a not uncommon misunderstanding of the import of the decree. Quite the contrary, this Council held that most men would have to *believe* in God's existence; this is the usual approach of the Christian to God, rather than by means of philosophy. The Church does not "preach" metaphysics, but faith; and, associated with this, we ought not accept any theory of faith that ultimately roots the assent of the individual on a rational-historical proof of some sort. Faith is far more directly an encounter with God, and it must be presented as such.

It is in line with this fundamental thought that Chapter II discusses the approach of Kierkegaard to faith. He is an interesting and illuminating example of a thinker who exemplified the desire of a strong segment of nineteenth-century Protestantism to reject the utter rationalism of the period, and affirm faith as something truly supernatural, and something more than mere metaphysics. There is a striking similarity between his thought and the official teaching of Rome, although Kierkegaard fails to include in his view the possibility of any rational approach to faith. Catholic doctrine must insist on the *possibility* of such an approach, although we need not insist that each individual Christian either can or must approach faith by way of reason.

Closely allied to these questions would be the seemingly less practical matter of the various theories of faith proposed by Catholic theologians to explain the assent of faith and the type of certitude associated with it. While we have entitled Chapter III "Two Theories of Faith," this represents more correctly two general *tendencies* in regard to faith. Strangely, the one which has, until lately, enjoyed greater popularity in Catholic circles is really something of an innovation, introduced only in the seventeenth century. It has all the overtones of the rationalism of that period, and it ends up with an inadequate answer to the problem of the unswerving certitude of supernatural faith. We have outlined the two general tendencies, noting that the crux of the problem lies in determining whether the rational conclusion associated with the so-called judgment of credibility forms a part of the assent of faith itself. The sole logical answer would appear to be "no," quite in line with the older and acceptable theories of faith proposed by the Thomistic and Suarezian schools of thought.

MORE PRECISE PROBLEMS

Since Scripture has played a large role in the present discussions, it is necessary to consider the relationship of Scripture both to the Church and to tradition in our explanation of faith. Faith can only be appreciated when it is seen in the context of the living Church, since it is there that the authority of God is seen on the created level; and it would seem that the same thing is true both of Scripture and of tradition: their proper evaluation depends upon seeing them as essentially related to this living Church. This is the purpose of Chapter IV: a discussion of the meaning of "tradition" and its relationship to Scripture. The more recent theory of faith argued largely upon the hypothesis that the Bible was a strictly historical book, in the sense of eighteenth-century rationalism or nineteenth-century liberalism; it frequently identified "tradition" with the historical records of the early centuries of the Church.

All of this has now come to be questioned, and it is necessary to return to the Council of Trent to uncover its mind in this regard. As it happens, Trent did not oppose a theory that held all of revelation is somehow contained in Scripture; it insisted, however, that Scripture needs the living tradition in order to draw out, under the guidance of the Holy Spirit, this full revelation contained at least in seminal form in the inspired pages. This "living tradition" is the Church itself, the Christian community here upon earth; this does not mean the magisterium, since tradition is a larger concept than magisterium (the latter constituting but one function of that living Church).

Similarly, the difficulties of Protestant Liberalism and Catholic Modernism resulted not at all from scriptural scholarship itself, but from the insertion of the findings of scriptural scholars into the context of a philosophy of immanentism and evolution derived, above all, from Kant and Schleiermacher. Thus Chapter V is a return to the thought of Schleiermacher, delineating the close relationship between what he taught and what was condemned by the Church under Pius X. Modernism is a clearly definable theory, and to indicate what it was, it is necessary to delve into the historical roots of this particular kind of thought. Evolution of doctrine meant one thing for the Modernist and another thing for the Catholic today; it is the philosophic context which makes the difference. The Modernist was following the immanentist-evolutionary approach of post-Kantian thought, whereas the Catholic sees this unfolding process within the context of the living Church, ever guided by the Holy Spirit. While faith thus grows and develops, it does so only as God intends, but not at all in the sense defended by the Modernists and necessarily rejected by the Church.

Viewed from this angle, the absorbing work of the Catholic scriptural scholar today is not to be linked in any way with the approach of the Modernists at the beginning of this century. This can raise a difficulty, in that many fail to see the difference in philosophical subtleties involved; but it is essential that this be made clear. The same is true of the dogmatic theologian who would speak of the development of dogma. He must, in a sense, use the same words as the Modernist; human language imposes certain limitations upon the expression of similar thoughts. But it is the basic philosophical foundation that makes all the difference in the world. This needs to be appreciated more clearly by all concerned.

PARTICULAR APPLICATIONS

Chapters VI and VII are concerned with two particular studies which more or less sum up the theoretical questions of the earlier chapters, and show how they are applied to a particular question. Chapter VI deals with the question whether historical method can "prove" the divinity of Christ. The answer involves an appreciation of the influence of rationalism on current thought, of the impact of the so-called "post-Cartesian" theory of faith, of the historical concerns of the nineteenth-century scholar, as noted especially in such works as Schweitzer's *Quest for the Historical Jesus*. This chapter repeats many of the earlier thoughts — indeed, as with all collections, such "repetition" is inevitable; put perhaps in a context devoted to the solution of a particular question, the more theoretical discussions will be seen as having a real influence upon the problems immediately at hand.

The final chapter almost seems to be devoted to the dissection of a carcass; at least this is the impression of some. Bishop Butler, for all the influence he once exerted in Western thought, is very much "dead" intellectually. However, his teaching is presented as an example of the dangers which threaten those who would defend Christianity on the basis of rationalism, or any similar philosophy. Butler is a prime example of the failure of a Christian apologete who would attempt to treat Scripture as a "purely historical source," and on this basis defend Christianity by having recourse to "proofs" (especially miracles and prophecies) which are known to have existed because of historical evidence, and which are treated as "miracles" because of a definition of such events formulated by reason alone.

On the other hand, Butler is important for the Catholic theologian because of his influence upon Catholic thought, especially through Cardinal Newman (earlier one of his literary disciples). The phrase condemned in the *Lamentabili* of 1907 — "the assent of faith rests ultimately on an accumulation of probabilities"[17] — does not represent, as Loisy held, the mature teaching of Newman, but rather the position defended by Joseph Butler in the eighteenth century.

Basically, therefore, these various essays are closely interrelated; they represent different approaches to the same general problem. If they add anything at all to the discussions of the present hour, the writing of them will be justified. The chief purpose, however, has been to single out the supernaturality of faith in all its aspects, and to underline the spirit of mystery and awe which must attend any proclamation or acceptance of the Christian message. Faith is not reducible to syllogisms and proofs, but must remain — even for the theologian — a personal encounter with the divine, a humble response to the call of God, and a filial submission to the will of an all-loving Father.

Abbreviations

AAS — *Acta Apostolicae Sedis*

AER — *The American Ecclesiastical Review*

Analogy — Joseph Butler, *The Analogy of Religion*

CBQ — *The Catholic Biblical Quarterly*

CL — *Collectio Lacensis*

CTr — *Concilium Tridentinum:* Görresgesellschaft edition

Denz. — Denzinger-Bannwart, *Enchiridion symbolorum*

DS — Denzinger-Schönmetzer, *Enchiridion symbolorum*

DTC — *Dictionnaire de théologie catholique*

EB — *Enchiridion Biblicum*, 4th ed.

Journals (Dru) — *The Journals of Søren Kierkegaard*, edited and translated by Alexander Dru

LThK — *Lexikon für Theologie und Kirche*

On Religion — Friedrich Schleiermacher, *On Religion: Speeches to Its Cultured Despisers*

Proceedings: CTSA — *Annual Proceedings of The Catholic Theological Society of America*

RJ — Rouét de Journel, *Enchiridion patristicum*

The Christian Faith — Friedrich Schleiermacher, *The Christian Faith*

TS — *Theological Studies*

Yzermans — Vincent A. Yzermans (ed.), *All Things in Christ*

Contents

WITH THE EYES OF FAITH

Modern Man and God

Modern man in Western civilization has often been called a "godless man," and perhaps in the overall view this may not be an unjust description. If it were possible to balance off the number of those who believe in God against those who reject Him, the scale might tell a sad story. And yet this does not mean that modern man is not *concerned* with God. Quite the contrary: for centuries the history of Western thought has shown man denying God, running away from Him, fighting Him, even hating Him. But the modern world has by no means been ignoring God.

As we watch the progress of atheistic Communism throughout the entire world, we begin to appreciate even more the dimensions of this problem. We are forced by this situation to take an active part in the battle against the promoters of ungodliness. In a very real sense this constant searching for God which underlies so much of our current civilization is a reflection of this struggle. Men continue to seek God even while He is rejected more universally by others. This is reflected in our present-day literature, in our art and poetry, in our philosophies. Our stage plays, the movies, television programs all reflect this theme that is approaching ever closer to the man in the street, wandering far from God and becoming more bewildered with each step.

How is modern man to find God once again? This is the basic problem. Two roads open up before him: the way of reason and the way of faith. It may have been an unfortunate failing of the last centuries that men have attempted to defend God and religion more on the basis of reason than of faith. It is an understandable reaction, since those who have denied the existence of God most vehemently have done so in the name of reason. The defenders of faith have attempted to meet them on their own grounds, however; and in so doing, they may have neglected far too much the approach of faith in striving to defend the way of reason.

It has been above all in the post-Kantian era — the nineteenth and twentieth centuries — that philosophical atheism came into prominence. Kant had hoped in his own way to defend a belief in God, but his attempts to cast out forever the proofs for the existence of God by reason opened up paths which led later philosophers in two opposite directions. There were those who, like Schleiermacher, searched the subjective side of man's life, seeking to find there, within man himself, the traces of God, of religion and of revelation. They followed the path of a purely subjective faith and quite unwittingly perhaps led to the ultimate of subjective belief in the pantheism (or theopantism) of Hegel, for whom Reason became God, and God, as Absolute Reason, unfolded Himself in the history of mankind.

Others, however, chose the second road — the road of atheism or despair. Feuerbach and Nietzsche set the pattern for this; Marx and Engels, separating their thought from that of Hegel on this point, furthered the growth of militant atheism and incorporated it into the political system they devised.

There is perhaps no more somber phrase with which to describe the end result of both of these tendencies than "the speculative Good Friday." Christianity had preached for centuries that God died on the cross, for Christ of Nazareth was true God. But these modern philosophers understood the phrase in a far more universal sense. To the modern atheist, the phrase "God is dead" means that the very notion of God has been destroyed; it has been cast out forever from the mind of man.

THE SPIRIT OF OPTIMISM

It was in the writings of Nietzsche that this thought came to expression in its most literary and also its most shocking form. In 1886 Nietzsche wrote his famous description of the madman who came to proclaim the new truth, a truth which was in reality the gospel of Nietzsche himself:

On a brightly shining morning, the madman lights a lantern and sets out for the marketplace crying, "I am looking for God! I am looking for God!" Those who hear him, many of whom do not believe in God at all, laugh heartily: "Is He lost?" says one. "Has He lost His way like a child?" asks another. "Or is He hiding?" The madman springs into the midst of them and gazes upon them with piercing eyes:

> Where is God? I will tell you! We have killed Him — you and I! We are all His murderers! But how did we come to do this? How did we manage to drain out the sea? Who gave us the sponge to wipe out the entire horizon? What did we do when we unchained this earth from its suns? Where does it move now? Where are we moving? Far away from all suns? Are we not tossed about incessantly? And backwards, sidewards, forwards, in all directions? Is there still an above, a below? Are we not wandering as if through an endless nothingness? Is not the void breathing upon us? Has it not become colder? Does the night and more night not come on endlessly? Must not the lanterns be lit in the morning? Do we yet hear nothing of the noise of the grave-diggers who bury God? Do we yet perceive nothing of the odor of the divine decaying? — Gods also decay! God is dead. God remains dead! And we have killed Him![1]

His hearers understood him not, and the madman went away, giving them time to think over his words and realize what they had done: "And it is told still that on that same day the madman broke into different churches and there began to intone his *Requiem aeternam deo*. Led out and made to give an account, only this did he continually reply: 'What then are these churches now if not the tombs and monuments of God?' "[2]

We have here an astounding description of the godless man of the modern world: the man who has cast God aside and who must now make his way through the void, searching for a substitute for God, for someone or something that will give meaning to his life once more, that will be a new foundation upon which man may build and from which he may derive a sense of cosmic security.

The solutions offered to this problem have varied through the decades. For Nietzsche the solution was simple: man himself was to become a god:

> Now this God is dead! You higher men, this God was your greatest danger. It is only since he lay in the grave that you have risen again. Only now the great noontide comes; only now the higher man becomes lord! Do you understand this saying, O my brothers? You are frightened: do your hearts fail you? Does the abyss yawn at your feet? Does the hound of hell bay you? What of it? Forward! Higher men! Now at last the mountain of man's future is about to give birth. God is dead; now it is our will that the Superman shall live.[3]

The Supermen will replace God; they will be the foundation of human life. Nietzsche would not stand by in helpless despair, nor tremble in the void. He would set mankind to work in order that out of its nothingness there might be created something that will surpass it and rise above it. Moving ever forward, the Superman will triumph. This was, of course, the philosophy from which the ill-fated Nazism of Adolph Hitler sprang, and it is little wonder that the humbling defeat of this attempt brought with it the final collapse of Nietzschean optimism.

A similar type of optimism was expressed in the philosophy of Karl Marx. It is not, however, the Superman that replaces God in the aspirations of the Marxist man; it is the social community. Man lives not for himself nor for God; he lives solely for the ceaseless progress of mankind. As Pius XI emphasized: "In such a doctrine, as is evident, there is no room for the idea of God; there is no difference between matter and spirit, between soul and body; there is neither survival of the soul after death nor any hope in a future life."[4] The individual will live on after death only in that society of the future which he labored to create; it is for this that he lives.

The social atheism of Marx includes the famous axiom that "religion is the opium of the people," and Marxism insists that only when men have finally rid themselves entirely of the notion of God will they engage themselves properly in the pursuit of the economic and social progress envisioned. God and religion must first be cast aside, however. They are obstacles to this progressive movement, hence it is a necessary prerequisite: "The abolition of religion," Marx once wrote, "as the illusory happiness of men, is a demand for their real happiness."[5] Only in this way will men struggle for and finally achieve the Utopia of a truly classless society preached by the disciples of Marx.[6]

THE SPIRIT OF PESSIMISM

At the opposite extreme of these various sorts of philosophical optimism there is the despair and pessimism of the atheistic existentialist. Possibly Jean-Paul Sartre, the philosopher best known in this connection, gives the most precise statement of its views. For Sartre, man can be understood most basically as a desire to be God; this is the meaning of man. Not unlike Nietzsche, Sartre would hold this out as the answer to man's most fundamental desires, but contrary to Nietzsche, he paints it as an unattainable goal. Man desires to be God, but he cannot; hence he is doomed to endless frustration. His entire life is futility and frustration. He is born to suffer in vain, and death is simply the ultimate and unending frustration of a useless existence:

> Every human presence in the world is a passion, in that it is a project to lose itself in order to found being and in the same act constitute the *En-soi* which escapes contingency in being its own ground, the *Ens causa sui* which the religions call God. Thus man's passion is the inverse of Christ's, for man loses himself as man in order that God may be born. But the idea of God is contradictory and we lose ourselves in vain; man is a useless passion.[7]

After the horrors of World War II, following fast enough on the footsteps of World War I, there were many in Europe who turned to this type of thought. The optimism of the late nineteenth century was gone; things were *not* becoming better and better each day in every way. There were many, therefore, who had rejected God but who could no longer dream seriously of a man-made God and who were too bruised by the wounds of war to care much about the rise of a future utopian society; thus they gave expression to their innermost feelings, and turned to a darkened philosophy of despair.

OPPOSITE REACTIONS

This does not exhaust the general tendencies followed by various thinkers in the post-Kantian era. There was an important group, symbolized chiefly by Søren Kierkegaard, who, no less than Kant, rejected human reason as a means of coming to know God, but who also refused either to deify reason along with Hegel, or embrace despair with more recent trends of thought. They turned accordingly to "faith" as a means by which man could encounter God.

Kierkegaard lived out his life as the sworn opponent of Hegelian rationalism. He struggled with one of the most basic problems of human life: the relationship between faith and reason. His solution, however, failed to do full justice either to faith or to reason. For Kierkegaard, the entrance into the way of faith was a totally irrational act. It was a blind leap into the absurd. Once man had acquired the courage to make such a leap, Kierkegaard insisted that the shadows were lifted, but he refused to admit the possibility of any preparation whatsoever on the part of man or human reason for this act by which man plunged himself into faith. He failed, in short, to grasp the relationship between faith itself and the motives of credibility, by which the reasonableness of faith is established.[8] Kierkegaard was willing to admit no more than Kant himself in regard to the ability of the human reason to know the existence of God, but he also denied any possibility of a rational preparation for faith. In his system, faith came abruptly, violently, and it is presented as the only solution for man's dilemma; nothing else could save mankind from either the anti-Christian position of Nietzsche or the despairing pessimism of Sartre in the next century.

Among Catholic theologians there were also those who became engaged in the same debate; not all of their teachings were approved by the Church. There were, above all, those who accepted the Kantian position that God could not be known by the use of human reason alone. At the same time, these Catholic writers felt that prior to faith, there must be some manner in which man might come to the knowledge of God's existence as a preparation for faith. From this general line of thought there arose the condemnations of Traditionalism which occupy so great a part of the history of Catholic doctrine in the nineteenth century. Each in his own way, Bautain, de Lamennais, Bonald, and Bonnetty set forth the basic principle that man cannot know the existence of God by reason alone, and proceeded then to root his first approach to God in some form of either natural or supernatural "tradition," handed down from generation to generation in the human community.[9]

These various systems spoke of some sort of primitive revelation, reflected in the universal agreement of mankind; this was to be the explanation of man's acceptance of the existence of God. This "revelation" was not necessarily the Mosaic or Christian revelation; it was something more fundamental and more primitive, something preserved within human society itself. It was, moreover, only after the influence of this "tradition" or "primitive revelation" had been felt that human reason was able, of itself, to know the existence of God; without such a tradition, the Kantian position remained true.

FAITH AND REASON

It was with this post-Kantian problem above all that Vatican I was concerned in the Second Chapter of its Constitution, *Dei Filius*, on Catholic Faith.[10] Against the Kantian position, the Church asserted that "God, the origin and end of all things, can be known with certainty by the natural light of human reason from the things that He created."[11] At the same time, the Council dealt with the problem raised by the Traditionalists and Fideists concerning the necessity of revelation for man's knowledge of the existence of God.[12]

These statements of Vatican I touch on a number of important points and are couched in very precise terms. Perhaps this complexity has contributed somewhat to a misunderstanding of what the Church actually decreed at this Council. As a defender of the power of human reason to know God's existence, the Catholic Church has often been accused of overstating the work of reason and understating the role of faith. There are even some Catholic authors who tend to give the impression that Vatican I solemnly defined that every single human being is capable of knowing the existence of God, and that such a knowledge of God by reason alone is a necessary prerequisite to divine faith.

In his tract *De Deo uno et trino,* for example, Cardinal Billot tends to give this general impression, stating that "a certain knowledge of God can be had through the light of reason not only by the learned but also by the mass of mankind."[13] Unlike Vatican I, however, Billot limits the word "knowledge" to what he calls an "elementary knowledge" *(cognitio elementaris),* rather than the more complete knowledge excluding all doubts and error, spoken of by the Council.[14] Billot also adds a further condition, namely, that the ordinary individual receive the help of teachers who will unfold this truth of reason to him, since he is really incapable of discovering the knowledge of God's existence by his independent thought alone.

Even granting these various limitations, this is not an entirely satisfactory solution, since Billot asserts that what he holds is true only with a condition that is not always verified in fact, that is, that the "regular conditions of education" are preserved intact. Where this is not verified — as one might suspect would often be the case — his attitude in regard to the general knowledge of God by reason is considerably less optimistic.[15]

More important, however, it is Billot's contention that man must know the existence of God by reason *prior* to the act of faith; otherwise, he contends, faith will cease to be a "reasonable" act. As he points out, faith presupposes a judgment of credibility by which one judges that it is both necessary and obligatory to assent voluntarily to the truth of revelation on the authority of the One revealing. Chief among the truths included in the formation of such a judgment of credibility, however, Billot places the certain knowledge of the existence of God; this must be acquired by reason alone. The knowledge of God's existence cannot be included among those truths which are accepted on divine faith since, according to Billot, this would require — before the act of faith in Christian revelation — a prior act of faith in God's existence, which would in turn have also required a prior judgment of credibility, thus setting up an infinite series of such related acts.[16]

Billot's position on this question is intimately linked to his well-known teaching on the act of faith, itself, which affirms the possibility of a "scientific faith" or "natural faith," whose psychological motive would differ in no way from that of supernatural faith.[17] Such a natural faith would require a natural knowledge of the existence of God, since it is precisely "natural knowledge" and not "faith." The supernatural grace of faith would simply elevate this psychologically natural act to the supernatural level according to this theory; it would affect the act of faith only entitatively and not psychologically.

There are many theologians today, however, who teach that the effect of the grace of faith is also and above all psychological, holding with Trütsch that this position alone "does justice to the realism of grace."[18] In this approach, one is not faced with the same problem as that which concerned Billot. In the act of faith itself, psychologically different from all other acts because of the grace of faith, man is able to perceive not only the truths revealed by God but also the authority of God Himself revealing these truths. Thus there is no difficulty in explaining how God reveals the fact of His existence. There is no infinite series involved, since belief in the existence of God demands no prior judgment of credibility; the judgment of superhuman activity associated with the motives of credibility will also be the ground by which the reasonableness of one's belief in God's existence is established.

In general, it would appear that this second view would be more in accord with the teaching of Vatican I, and also with the doctrine of St. Thomas Aquinas which the Council adopted as its own in a large measure when dealing with this topic.

THE TEACHING OF ST. THOMAS

In the *Summa Theologiae* (I, q. 1, art. 1), St. Thomas points out why it is necessary to have another doctrine besides philosophy. This doctrine of which he is speaking is, of course, the teaching of revelation; this is another divinely inspired knowledge given to men by God and accepted in the act of faith.

St. Thomas insists that this added knowledge is necessary first of all in regard to *supernatural* truths which surpass entirely the natural power of human reason. Without revelation, mankind could in no way come to know them. Since God has *de facto* destined man for a supernatural goal, such a revelation is entirely necessary so that man might know that fact and the truths associated with it.

On the other hand, St. Thomas also insists that revelation is necessary in regard to those truths which, in themselves, do not surpass the powers of unaided reason if they are to be known by all men. He notes that such a knowledge of God when gained through the use of reason alone is acquired only "by few, and after a long time, and with a mixture of many errors. . . ."[19] Yet the salvation of man depends upon a knowledge of these truths, so that a revelation that includes them is also necessary; otherwise the salvation of man could not proceed properly and in due time.

In his answer to the second objection, St. Thomas also emphasizes that there is a generic difference between natural theology and the knowledge of faith with which theology deals. This, of course, touches upon a question treated in greater detail later on, that is, the possibility of believing something which could, of itself, be known by reason alone. In the *Summa* (II–II, q. 2, art. 4), St. Thomas asks "Whether it is necessary to believe those things which can be proven by natural reason?" His answer is that it *is* necessary to believe such matters, and he gives as a chief example the fact that "it is necessary to believe that God is one and incorporeal, which are proven through natural reason by philosophers."[20]

St. Thomas' entire discussion of this matter is existential in outlook; he is concerned with man as he exists in the present historic order, a child of Adam in need of God's redeeming grace. The *objections* he proposes argue that (1) revelation of these natural truths would be superfluous, and God does not do what is superfluous; (2) that knowledge (*scientia*) and faith (*fides*) are not concerned with the same things, so that what can be proven through reason cannot be held on faith at all; and (3) that if certain truths knowable by reason were proposed to be held on faith, all natural truths would have to be included in this revelation because they all pertain to the same category.[21]

The *answer* given by St. Thomas is that there are three reasons why man must accept on faith not only truths which are above reason but even those which can be known by reason alone:

1. That man might come to the knowledge of God *more quickly*. The knowledge of God by reason alone presupposes a great deal of information on other points of learning, so that the approach to God through reason alone requires a great length of time; these other fields of information must be conquered first. Thus faith removes the need for so long a delay in coming to know the existence of God and similar natural truths.

2. That the knowledge of God might be *more common* among men. There are many, St. Thomas insists, who cannot make great progress in learning. Native talents are not always equal to this; others, having the talent, are either so occupied with necessary work in the temporal order that they cannot undertake the lengthy study, while others simply lack the ambition to face up to this arduous task. Because of this, all these people would be kept from the knowledge of God's existence, unless it were revealed to them and could be accepted on faith.

3. That the knowledge of God's existence might be *more certain*. Human reason is deficient in many things. An indication of this is that even the philosophers who have carefully scrutinized human life by the means of reason alone have fallen into error on many points, and they openly contradict one another. Thus, in order that man's knowledge of God's existence might exclude any doubt and be rendered absolutely certain, it is necessary that

this and related facts of the natural order be revealed by God and accepted on supernatural faith.[22]

In analyzing the three objections posed at the beginning of the article, St. Thomas clarifies his own position. The first objection contended that God does not do what is superfluous and that therefore He would not reveal the fact of His existence, since this can be known by human reason. In answer, St. Thomas states simply that, while human reason can know certain things about God, it does not suffice *even in these matters* to give men the complete knowledge they need; hence revelation of these natural truths is not superfluous.

The second objection held that a man cannot *believe* what he can prove by *reason*. St. Thomas admits that this is true, but referring back to a previous article (II–II, q. 1, art. 5), which was mentioned in the objection itself, he repeats what was taught there, namely, that what can be known by one individual through the use of reason alone can nevertheless be accepted by another on faith.[23] The position of St. Thomas in this earlier article is simply that *if* a man has *de facto* acquired knowledge of God's existence through the use of reason, that individual cannot at the same time believe what he already knows of God's existence. For those, however, who have not or cannot acquire such demonstrative proof, it is both possible and necessary that they accept the existence of God and other natural truths on the authority of God revealing. Man must accept these truths on faith at least, since they are the foundation of other things accepted on faith and which pertain solely to the supernatural order.[24]

Finally, St. Thomas answers the third objection that, if one or two truths knowable by reason alone were included in supernatural revelation, *all* the truths of the natural order would have to be thus revealed since they all belong to the same category. St. Thomas simply states that this conclusion does not follow at all, since the reason for revealing certain truths and not revealing others is their intimate and essential relationship to eternal salvation. In this regard, there are many other truths of the natural order which are not so related to man's eternal happiness, and hence not all truths of the natural order are proposed in like manner as objects of faith.[25]

VATICAN I

It was this same teaching that was formulated by Vatican I in its solemn definition regarding the power of reason to know the existence of God. The mind of the Council appears first of all in the Schema and the Annotations distributed together with it to the bishops in attendance at the Council; these formulas had been worked out by the preparatory commission before the Council was convened.

Chapter Two of this Schema concerned the condemnation of rationalism first of all, and began with the words: "It must not be doubted that the true God can be known by the natural light of human reason itself through those things which are made. . . ."[26] This phrase differs little from the final form adopted by the Council.[27] The original Schema is presented with a special annotation (no. 6) which helped direct further discussion. It notes that this entire chapter was directed against the errors of nineteenth-century rationalism and its denial of supernatural revelation. This particular statement concerning the power of human reason was added more or less as a foreword to the defense of supernatural revelation; it was also directed against the teaching of those who denied this power of human reason. The authors of the Schema point out, however, that the opening words declaring that human reason alone can know the existence of God must be understood in the light of three points which would aid in understanding what they suggested to the bishops as important elements in any possible definition:[28]

1. They are speaking, obviously, only of those who had achieved the actual use of reason.

2. Moreover, what they are suggesting is "not a question of the *fact* whether individual men derive their first knowledge of God from this natural manifestation, and are not moved, rather, to seek God through a revelation proposed to them, and learn that God exists from this revealed doctrine itself proposed to them. . . ."[29]

It was the intention that this Chapter deal solely with the *native power* of human reason in itself, stating that the objective manifestation of God's existence through created beings is proportioned to these innate powers and that thus man, by using these powers alone, *is able* to know God's existence apart from faith. Hence, if other means of acquiring the knowledge of God's existence are not at hand, there nevertheless remains the obligation for man to come to know God's existence by the use of his unaided powers.[30]

3. Finally, the members of the preparatory commission indicated that their suggested decree was not intended to deal with the conditions necessary for a child coming to the use of reason (life, for example, within a social group, and similar questions which had been discussed by theologians of the nineteenth century). What was to be condemned was the teaching of those Traditionalists (referred to here and later as *Traditionalismus Crudior*)[31] who assert that the revelation of the existence of God is a necessary prerequisite to the proper development of human reason, and who taught accordingly that human reason could not come to the knowledge of God's existence through created beings unless this fact was *first* known through revelation. Then only, they contended, could human reason confirm and recognize this fact through a consideration of created things. The decree of Vatican I thus would be aimed against those who made revelation a prerequisite for rational knowledge. Hence it was suggested that the chapter might even add the phrase that the existence of God can be known by the light of human reason "even before (*citra*) the positive doctrine handed down by God."[32]

This suggested Schema and these Annotations became the basis of further discussion at Vatican I. The Schema originally proposed by the preparatory commission was changed in many ways, but merely to improve the form; the content remained essentially the same. The revised formula of the Schema is, with minor changes, the one used to state the doctrine of the Church regarding the natural knowledge of God (the first paragraph of Chapter Two with the corresponding canon).[33]

In the explanation concerning the first revised Schema, given by Archbishop Simor, it was emphasized that this section of the decree was aimed against both the Traditionalists and the phenomenological philosophy of Kant and his disciples who taught that human reason does not truly know things but only perceives sensations or phenomena.[34] Archbishop Simor, however, does not bother to repeat a detailed explanation of the manner in which this part of the Chapter and the corresponding canon are to be understood, since "these matters are clearly set forth in the annotations."[35]

After this first revision, there were a number of *emendationes* in regard to these passages, submitted to the *Deputatio fidei* by the bishops participating in the Council. Bishop Gasser, speaking for the *Deputatio fidei,* gave the reasons why these suggestions were either accepted or set aside. In his introductory remarks, he again emphasized the fact that the decree was concerned with the "active power" within man for knowing the existence of God.[36] In discussing the corresponding canon, he states the same thing: the teaching is directed against those who deny that man has such a natural power of knowing God.[37]

Bishop Gasser also spoke of a number of *emendationes* that touched on this particular point. One of them (no. 49) proposed that the words "ab homine" be set aside, "lest we appear to define as a dogma of the faith that there could never be any adult human beings who are invincibly ignorant of God." The suggestion was also made that the word "human" further modify the word "reason" in the canon.[38] This *emendatio* was accepted by the *Deputatio fidei* for the reasons given,[39] and later, officially, by the bishops participating in this session of the Council.[40] Thus the mind of the Council is clearly reflected in this particular change; it was not speaking of individual men and their personal ability to know the existence of God and other related truths of the natural order.

This twice revised formula was finally voted on by the bishops on April 12, 1870.[41] Following this, however, there were further *emendationes* attached by various bishops to their vote on April 12; hence Bishop Gasser, speaking for the *Deputatio fidei* in the general congregation of April 19, discussed these particular points.[42]

There were three suggested changes which add further light to the question of the natural knowledge of the existence of God and similar truths of the natural order. One of them (no. 51) objected chiefly to the use of the word *"certo"* and argued that not even the greatest of the philosophers, left to reason alone — neither Aristotle, nor Plato nor Cicero — "who exemplified almost all the power of reason, so much so that present-day philosophers might follow their footsteps, were able to know God with certitude as the beginning and end of all things. If none of the philosophers, therefore, were able to know this without a mixture of many errors, as is evident from their speculative theology, we should each see at once not the moral but the necessary truth of the impotency of human reason in coming to know God with certitude as the beginning and end of all things. . . ."[43]

Two other suggested changes (no. 52½ and 53) treated of the same problem — the term *"certo"* — hence they were treated simultaneously by Bishop Gasser.[44] He notes first of all that these bishops continue to be troubled by the word "certitude" despite the fact that it had already been explained that "in this chapter it is a question solely of man in general, no matter what the case may be with individuals . . . ," and that the decree speaks not only of a passive but of "an active power" which human nature possesses and by which man is able to know God's existence. In the light of this, they have still argued that, if this native power of man is not *de facto* activated in individuals, it ought not be called a power but rather "impotence, and indeed not only moral [impotence] but physical."[45] As evidence of this they set forth the inadequate learning of Aristotle and other great philosophers in regard to God.

Bishop Gasser passes over the question of whether a power that is not *de facto* activated is not truly a power, although he suggests further distinctions must be made; but it is not essential to his purpose to discuss this matter. In regard to the various philosophers, however, he insists that such men as Aristotle and Plato progressed further in the natural knowledge of God than these *emendationes* would imply. Hence he concludes that this objection need not upset these bishops, as though the Church were defining the existence of a power that had actually never been used by any individual men; there is evidence enough that the great philosophers did really activate this natural power, despite their shortcomings.[46]

Apart from this question of history, however, the decree is limited to a discussion of the power itself; it is not concerned with individuals. Thus Bishop Gasser considers another suggestion (no. 52) that the word "natural" (in the phrase "natural light of human reason") be removed, since man has never actually been placed in a state of pure nature. According to Bishop Gasser, the author of the *emendatio* has confused two things: "the principles of reason and the exercise of reason. We are speaking only of the principles of reason, that God can be known with certainty from the principles of reason; whatever may be the case concerning the exercise of reason."[47] In an earlier session, Bishop Gasser had pointed out in discussing a similar *emendatio*[48] that throughout the discussions, the Council has been concerned with the natural power of human reason alone, which would be the same whether in the state of pure nature or in the state of fallen nature.[49]

THE INABILITY OF INDIVIDUAL MEN

On the other hand, Vatican I also concerned itself with existential man and the individual in its discussion of the necessity of revelation. This section of the decree was also treated in a number of sessions, and the first reference to this side of the problem appears in the suggested Schema and Annotations drawn up by the preparatory commission.

Chapter Four speaks first of all of God's revelation of supernatural truths, that is, of mysteries in the strict sense, which can in no way be known by reason alone. In this regard, revelation is *absolutely* necessary; apart from the way of faith, there is no manner in which man might come to know these truths. It then goes on to note that the supernatural revelation of God must be acknowledged as the greatest help given mankind even in regard to knowing those *natural* truths which, in themselves, could be known by reason alone. In fact, considering the present historic state of mankind, that of fallen nature, such a revelation, accommodated to the minds of all men, is a great favor from God so that these natural truths might be known by all "in the proper time, with sufficient amplitude, firm certitude and with no admixture of error. . . ."[50]

The Annotation to this passage notes that *de facto* the revelation given to mankind by God contains within itself truths of two different types: supernatural truths (mysteries in the strict sense), and natural truths (truths which pertain to God and the natural law, and which could, absolutely speaking, be known by the power of reason alone). Hence, one cannot affirm an *absolute* necessity for a revelation of these natural truths, since they could be known by reason. Considering men as they actually exist, however, the "physical power is generally not activated without a special help," at least to the extent that men as individuals come to know these natural truths soon enough, with a certitude excluding all hesitancy, and without the admixture of other errors alongside of the truth perceived. The difficulties involved in this type of knowledge are simply too great for this to occur in the lives of most men.[51] Hence, while the Council ought to affirm, against the Traditionalists and the Kantians, that human reason of itself can know certain truths (that is, absolutely speaking, this human power is physically capable of doing this), yet it must also be stated that fallen man, because of the difficulties of the task, is faced with a *moral impotency* to which there corresponds a *moral necessity* of some special help if men are actually to know these natural truths properly.[52]

It has been the will of God to give men the special help needed by including natural truths in the supernatural revelation. Objectively speaking, God could have given this help in some other manner, but He did not choose to do so; thus the moral impotency of mankind is actually removed through divine, supernatural revelation. In this way, the moral impotency of mankind is removed through revelation, and the knowledge of these truths in their totality is again rendered *morally possible* for mankind through faith.[53] It is interesting to note also that this particular Annotation refers explicitly to the passages in the *Summa* of St. Thomas which were discussed above.[54]

In the revised form of the Schema this same doctrine was retained, although expressed in a far more summary form; with minor changes of two phrases, it is this revised form that the Council finally used in order to express its solemn definition.[55] The statement that man's certain and exact knowledge of these natural truths is due to divine revelation is followed by the phrase, directed again the Traditionalists, that one cannot on this account contend that revelation is "absolutely necessary." The Traditionalists, of course, taught that such a revelation was so necessary that unless God first reveals these natural truths, human reason could not come to know God's existence at all.

However, as Bishop Gasser explains in his discussion of the *emendationes* suggested for this revised form of the Schema, what the Council should intend to teach in this passage is a *moral necessity* that arises not from the object (since the truths can be known by reason alone), but from the *subject:* fallen man.[56] While God did not have to choose to elevate mankind to the supernatural order at all, He nevertheless did so "out of His infinite goodness."[57] Once God freely chose to do this, there arose a moral necessity of revealing to men these natural truths which are so important to their supernatural destiny and which must be known easily, quickly, and with no admixture of error if men are to enter into the way of faith and thus achieve their supernatural goal through cooperating with the grace of God. God's love and mercy, therefore, are the ultimate reason why the divine revelation included not only the supernatural mysteries proper to Christianity, but also those of the natural order.

In saying all of this, Bishop Gasser emphasizes the concern of the Council for existential man and for the individual. Unlike the first paragraph of Chapter Two, the Council here is concerned, he says, *"not* with the *power,* even active, of divine knowledge, but with *actual knowledge* of God, and indeed that God might be known by all men easily, not after a long delay of time and investigation, with a firm certitude even by those who are scarcely capable of grasping the arguments derived from reason; finally that God be known also with no admixture of error. If we are concerned, therefore, with *actual natural knowledge* in these circumstances, so many and such great difficulties hinder man as he now is, that supernatural revelation can be said to be *morally necessary.*"[58]

It is also interesting to note the truths included in one of the suggested changes, an almost entirely new formula praised by Bishop Gasser, but set aside since it would mean a completely new discussion in the conciliar chambers. The author states that it is due to revelation that men know with certainty and with no mixture of error not only supernatural mysteries, but also natural truths, such as ". . . the existence of God and His attributes, the spirituality and immortality of our soul and the primary principles of morality upon which human society is founded. . . ."[59] This is entirely in keeping with the mind of Vatican I and the meaning of the solemn definition eventually issued by it.

There were no changes in this part of the decree from this time on. There were two other *emendationes* following the vote of April 12 concerning the absolute necessity of revelation,[60] but they were both rejected.[61] Hence this section as it then stood was incorporated into the solemn decree of April 24, 1870.

THE QUESTION OF PREACHING

Viewing the teaching of Vatican I in this light, we can return to a consideration of what is the proper approach to be used in attempting to draw modern man to God and in helping to make faith more real and vital for the believer. Judging according to the mind of the Council, we can appreciate the importance of the questions raised by Etienne Gilson from another point of view. In his *Christianity and Philosophy,* Gilson discusses this same topic and asks a very pointed question that deserves more consideration in present circumstances:

Is it not possible that our pulpits might preach a little less technical philosophy and a little more of the Gospel? I refer here especially to that sort of philosophic inflation which authorizes the dialectical proving of the existence of God, by the first mover, or by the contingent and the necessary, to the faithful assembled for the eleven o'clock Mass. However cultivated and intelligent we may suppose them to be, they are not an audience of metaphysicians. I admit that there has been a general progress in knowledge, but what progress would have had to be made in order that we should reach that stage, when we recall that in the golden age of theology Saint Thomas found only the *paucissimi* to have the leisure, the desire, the intelligence and the knowledge required by anyone who wished to rise to the level of metaphysics! Having himself to speak one day before the masters and students of the University of Paris on the Apostles' Creed, the Angelic Doctor did not judge it expedient to preach to them technical and complicated proofs of the existence of God. If this select audience did not inspire him with more confidence, would it not be wise to use the same prudence with common men, and tell them: "The first thing that we have to believe is that there is One God only; the second is that this God is the Creator of heaven and earth. . . ."[62]

It is not difficult to see how, as a result of our continual debates with the rationalists and semi-rationalists during the last few centuries, an overemphasis upon purely philosophic concepts might arise. Our attempt to "meet them on their own grounds" may have led us to neglect inadvertently our strongest ground: the ground of faith. Perhaps our current tendency to emphasize the "intellectual Catholic" may be having much the same effect, as necessary as it is to stress the need of Catholics entering into the various fields of true scholarship. Yet this will always remain the task of a comparatively small elite, and it must not be confused with faith. There is a tremendous amount of truth in Gilson's statement that we may have allowed ourselves "to be carried away on the sea of intellectual democracy" so that "we accept the challenge flung down by the world, to demonstrate anything at all to anyone at all."[63] There is, as he hints, a confusion between the "scholarly approach" and "faith." We do not believe God's revelation because He has passed our rigorous tests and shown that His word is *wissenschaftlich* enough to be accepted; nor do we believe the truth of revelation because "all first rate scholars" have concluded that this is what God intended to say. We simply submit ourselves to God's divine authority, linked intimately, as it is, to the divinely-guided magisterium of His Church, the extension of Christ in time and space, through which the words of our Savior are made present to our ears and the pages of Scripture are interpreted for us.

Possibly there are indications of this same attitude in our tendency to confuse the motives of credibility with faith itself. The motives of credibility are essentially those rational judgments which declare that if one does proceed to faith, he will not be doing violence to human nature; he will be acting in accordance with the dictates of sane reason. Thus it is in these judgments that the reasonableness of the act of faith is rooted.

The act of faith itself, however, is distinct from these judgments concerning the reasonableness of the act of faith. Faith itself rests not on any rational judgment of our own, but on the authority of God revealing, which is, as Vatican I pointed out, the fundamental motive of faith.[64] It is not a result of philosophic proof, historical study, or exegetical research. As the suggested schema of Vatican I pointed out, this insistence on the unique quality of faith was occasioned by those in the nineteenth century who affirmed "that faith itself, by which the revealed truths must be believed, is a natural conviction of reason induced by necessary arguments according to the laws of human science. . . ."[65] This was a dominant concern throughout the entire discussion of this problem at the Council, and it is a clue to the true meaning of this part of the constitution *Dei Filius*.

If we emphasize properly the teaching of Vatican I we can see the primary importance it would attribute to supernatural faith in the life of the Catholic. We may accordingly hesitate somewhat more for fear of reducing our preaching to something which breathes less of the spirit of faith than it ought. Proofs from the pulpit might often be better replaced with a clear presentation of God's revealed truth in a spirit of humble acceptance. There is also something of a danger in preaching metaphysics. To quote

Gilson again, "let us remember, then, that for the ordinary man there is no difference between a proof which is not conclusive and a proof which he is unable to see is conclusive."[66] It may be that in our appeal to "reason," we sometimes tend to forget this, and may leave the faithful struggling with the question of whether God really exists, whether man truly has a soul and a free will, or if the soul is immortal, since they could not follow or accept the "proofs from reason" we have preached. It is not the goal of the Church by any means to "reason" men into faith; this simply cannot be done. Moreover, as Gilson adds:

> No man can be made responsible for not understanding what God simply asks him to believe, if he is unable or unwilling to make the effort necessary for achieving its understanding. When, therefore, the objection is put to us that *today* everybody wants proofs, the reply can only be that *today* technical proofs are accessible to everybody. Today as in the 13th century, technical proofs are good for those who can understand them; to those who cannot do so, it is good simply to recall the old saying of Hesiod, cited by Aristotle and commented on by Saint Thomas: "The excellent pupil is one who can learn all alone; the good pupil is one who can learn from others; as for him who can learn neither alone nor from others, he is not made for science."[67]

It is above all by following the directives and the spirit of Vatican I that we can give due importance to the role of faith in the lives of individual Catholics. Certainly human reason in itself has the power of coming to know the existence of God and such related truths, but relatively few human beings are able to activate that power, whether from want of time, talent, or interest. Faith, however, pertains to a different order; this we need to keep in mind: "To engage in natural theology for all those who wish it and yet lack the necessary preparations is to replace faith by science for all in those matters in which the voice of God makes itself heard simply because science is then reserved to some."[68] Faith is rooted in the authority of God revealing, and thus the certitude of faith remains untouched by the vagaries of history or exegesis or the waverings of philosophical thought:

There is reason, therefore, first of all for reminding those who demand metaphysical instruction from the Church, that intellectual modesty is a great virtue and that the first condition, for anyone wishing to approach God by the intelligence, is never to forget that if the intelligence fails us, our faith at least should never do so. Perhaps we might even recall that those only who are qualified for the task ought to attack problems of this kind and that we have no more right to require our first curate to prove to us in five minutes the existence of God by demonstrative reason than to require Einstein to prove his system to anyone at all in twenty-four hours. That is not, I am afraid, what we do.[69]

THE SEARCH FOR GOD

In the light of all of this, we may evaluate the basic problem of modern man and God. It may be justly asked, how is modern man to find God if not above all through that primary means intended by God Himself in His goodness, that is through faith itself. When a man has wandered far from God, when his soul expresses an anguish, even a despair, he is not looking for metaphysics or history; he is seeking a Person. God has actually revealed Himself to mankind, and He continues through His Church to do so today, even in the midst of all the hatred that marks the modern world, even in the face of so many denials. God speaks now within the restless, turbulent heart of today's man; He calls to him, asking only that he look to the proper source, and discover there the true meaning of the sorrow and despair, the evil and the fear, the frustration of life itself that continues to crush him with its weight.

St. Augustine is, in many ways, the earlier counterpart of today's man. All of the anguish and frustration he knew in his early life was, as it is for men today, nothing more than the cry of man toward his God. For years Augustine tried to satisfy his inner need with other things — with study, with success, with the pleasures of sex. But he knew no lasting peace. He finally cast them all aside, even his Manichaean teachers and their philosophy, refusing "to commit the cure of my soul's sickness to them."[70] It was only then when he had gone down "into the depth of the sea, and . . . lost confidence, and . . . despaired of finding the truth,"[71] that he finally found the truth through faith in God. Augustine knew then what he had been seeking all his life. As he expressed it later in his *Confessions:* "You have made us for yourself, O Lord, and our heart is restless until it rests in you."[72] This is not the man of reason but existential man: the man destined for the beatific vision alone. To describe man as a rational animal will tell us *what* he is, but faith alone informs us of the reason *why* he is.

The restless heart of which Augustine spoke was above all his own, but it was not simply the heart — the symbol — that he meant, but the entire man. Something deep within him had continued to cry out through all those years; nothing else would satisfy that need, that longing; nothing else could silence that voice. It was this that brought on the anguish of Augustine, the saddened, dejected, and broken man who fell headlong into the blackened pit, and there beheld the face of God.

Men may well pretend that God is dead, but this will not silence and has not silenced this inner voice, this insatiable desire. In the midst of all the pleasures of this world, there presses forth this "homesickness for heaven," and the road which leads there is the road of faith alone. In the words of the Psalmist:

> I stretch out my hands to you;
>   my soul thirsts for you like parched land.
> Hasten to answer me, O Lord, for my spirit fails me.
> Hide not your face from me, lest I become like those
>   who go down into the pit.[73]

It is the call of God toward modern man, leading him back through sorrow and despair to the fountain of eternal life which will quench this thirst for the divine.

CHAPTER II

Faith and Reason in the Teaching of Kierkegaard

In the current discussions concerning the true meaning of faith, there is no point more central than the nature of religious assent. Moreover, using the distinction between faith understood as the truths we accept — *fides quae creditur* — and faith as an act of believing — *fides qua creditur* — it is most apparent that the principal concern today is with the act of believing itself. Among Catholic theologians an ever increasing number of men have reaffirmed and established more solidly the general Thomistic position that the grace of faith also exercises a psychological and not merely an entitative influence on the believer.[1] At the same time, they have also emphasized the role of reason in the approach of faith, even though they contend that the motives of credibility do not enter into the act of faith itself; yet faith remains reasonable — an act doing no violence to human nature — because of this preliminary judgment of reason which continues to exercise its influence throughout the entire life of faith.

Non-Catholic theologians have also been concerned with this question, urged on chiefly by the existentialist approach of the day, coupled with a marked sense of disillusionment with the attempt to use the certitude of reason alone or of historical proof as a basis for faith. And as H. F. Lovell Cocks remarks: "Sooner or later, the serious student of modern theology is driven back on Kierkegaard. Behind Barth, Brunner, and Heim; behind Buber, Heidegger, Jaspers, Marcel, and the existentialist philosophers, stands the strange figure of this universal genius."[2]

It is not so much that Kierkegaard (1813–1855) solved the question of faith, nor that he introduced an entirely new notion into the discussion. It is rather that his position continues to serve as a good point of reference for the various solutions offered to this perplexing question. Kierkegaard's doctrine is neither that of the pure rationalist or historicist, nor that of those who admit a close relationship between faith and a visible church; he attempts to settle on something in between these two approaches. In this regard, his teaching reflects the middle-of-the-road attitude adopted in his personal life. Kierkegaard rebelled against the rationalistic Protestantism of the nineteenth century no less than he did against the ecclesiastical pretensions of the Established Church in Denmark. He was Lutheran in his inspiration, and yet far from Luther in many of his most basic positions.[3] He extolled faith over the claims of reason, and yet he committed himself to certain other positions which have led some of his critics to refer to him as "a Hegelian in spite of himself, the victim of a reason which was madly ambitious, an impenitent rationalist even in his defence of the 'moment of the absurd'" which he calls faith.[4]

Kierkegaard must be viewed above all in that historical context which formed and fashioned him. It is particularly important for Catholics to realize this, since it has become increasingly fashionable to read his diatribes against rational systems of philosophy as though they were primarily directed against Scholastic philosophy, and that Kierkegaard therefore "has a message for us" in understanding the true meaning of the act of faith.

In point of fact, nothing could be further from the truth. The Thomist himself can be nothing less than astounded when a non-Catholic theologian describes the philosophy of Aquinas and that of Hegel as two species of a single approach associated with the general principle that faith is coordinate with reason. Thus it is contended by H. V. Martin that, despite radical differences, Aquinas and Hegel both held that religious faith is ultimately rooted in human reason:

> Historically, there are two main forms of this theory, which, though differing radically the one from the other, show their

root affinity in their common tendency to relate religion intimately with philosophy, and thus ultimately to be rationalistic.[5]

As we shall note in detail later on,[6] possibly one of the best examples of the reduction of the assent of faith to a rational conclusion is the teaching proposed by the Anglican Bishop Joseph
Butler (1692–1752). Butler attempted to meet the deists of the
eighteenth century on their own grounds, and "prove" the truth
of Christianity on a purely rational and historical basis. The
teaching of Butler was thus very much concerned with the problem
of the relationship between faith and reason, but the difficulty was
solved by reducing faith to reason. Kierkegaard, on the other
hand, attempted to solve the problem by eliminating the role of
reason entirely. The position of this Danish theologian began to
formulate itself in his strong rebellion against the rationalistic
absolutism of Hegel which had become so deeply rooted in the
theological mind of his day. Hegel had identified everything with
reason; in his system of pantheism — or better, theopantism —
Absolute Reason unfolded itself in the world and found its earthly
expression in the reasoned faith of man.

Reacting against this deification of reason and the consequent
reduction of faith to rational assent, Kierkegaard came to speak
of faith as a far more personal and subjective act, entirely distinct
from (and for Kierkegaard, even contrary to) human reason. It
was this which ultimately led the Danish philosopher-theologian
to his doctrine of the "leap" into faith — a leap into the absurd. As
Martin describes this central position of Kierkegaard's thesis:
". . . faith does not arise through intellectual understanding, but
only through a decision of the will in the face of objective un-
certainty."[7]

VATICAN I

In evaluating this basic idea of Kierkegaard it is important to
examine the thought *behind* this teaching, the ultimate reason why
he came to this conclusion. Basically, the doctrine of the Catholic
Church teaches in a more profound and correlated fashion this

same truth that Kierkegaard strove to defend. Vatican I describes the act of faith as the act of the intellect supernaturalized by an infused virtue by which "with the inspiration and help of God's grace, we believe that what He has revealed is true — not because its intrinsic truth is seen with the natural light of reason — but because of the authority of God who reveals it, of God who can neither deceive nor be deceived."[8]

At the same time, the Council was careful to point out that the act of faith involves the entire individual, and is centered upon the personal action of the human will as an entirely free act, cooperating with grace and involving a personal decision and a personal commitment to God the Revealer. There is no way that the act of faith can be socialized or necessitated by anything outside the individual; not by reason or historical proof, not even by divine grace. Faith must be essentially a personal and free act on the part of every single individual, responding to the internal grace offered by God.

It is important to emphasize that this free act, and this commitment, is not a purely human act. To speak of faith in this sense as the "response" of man, acting solely according to his natural powers, to the revelation of God would be pure Pelagianism; this is in no sense the teaching of the Catholic Church. In the realm of faith and salvation, God must always take the initiative; in the words of Trent, ". . . by his own free will, without God's grace, [man] could not take one step towards justice in God's sight."[9] Man can only respond to a grace freely offered by God.

The very act of faith, then, precisely as an act of a human being, transcends the unaided powers of man's nature. At the same time, this response of man is also a free act, since God's grace never necessitates the will of man. Hence Vatican I describes the act of faith as a "gift of God," since it results from the grace of faith, while still being an act by which ". . . man offers to God Himself a free obedience inasmuch as he concurs and co-operates with God's grace, when he could resist it."[10] For this reason, the Council solemnly condemned those who would teach that ". . . the assent of Christian faith is not free, but necessarily results from arguments of human reason."[11]

Christian faith cannot be explained as an act that results necessarily from a series of arguments proportioned to human reason; it cannot be simply "taught" and "proved," but only proposed by the Christian teacher. The individual must enter into this process and, through his acceptance of God's grace, freely commit himself to the God who has revealed Himself, His truth, and His redemptive activity on behalf of mankind. This perception of the authority of God revealing will necessarily include two elements which, in our opinion, must both be supernaturally perceived through the action of grace. These two are the authority of God Himself, and the authority of the divinely guided magisterium of God's Church upon earth which proposes the message revealed by God; these two elements constitute what Vignon refers to as the *Uncreated* and *created* testimony of God revealing, one visible and the other invisible. But together they form the supernatural testimony of the supernatural authority by which we assent to the truths revealed and thus commit ourselves entirely to God and, at present, to the Christian way of life.[12]

In 1870, Vatican I was concerned with questions not unlike those which had disturbed Kierkegaard only a short time before. The Council was dealing primarily with the confusion introduced by Hermes and others who desired to relate Catholic faith to the pure rationalism of the post-Kantian philosophers. The end result of their attempts was the teaching that reason became absolute and necessitating, even in the realm of faith. As Gregory XVI indicated in his earlier condemnation of Hermes, the basic principle was defended that ". . . reason is the principal norm and the only means by which man is able to attain a knowledge of supernatural truths. . . ."[13] Ultimately, what Gregory XVI was complaining of in 1835 was not appreciably different from the complaints of Søren Kierkegaard a few years later. Hermes was following the line of thought that would make reason the sole criterion of truth, even in regard to faith — a line of thought which appeared in its most exaggerated form in the philosophical "system" of Hegel, in which God and Absolute Reason and faith all become identified.

KIERKEGAARD AND CATHOLICISM

Kierkegaard reacted against the very same tendencies which were being condemned so vigorously in the Catholic Church, but this failed to align him more closely with Rome. There is possibly a good deal of truth in the opinion of Haecker and others that, judging by the direction in which he was tending, Kierkegaard, had he lived, might logically have gone over to Catholicism.[14] Walter Lowrie agrees that this is a more plausible guess than the suggestion made by Georg Brandes that Kierkegaard would eventually have turned to the position of Liberal Protestantism or free thought. He indicates, moreover, that even Karl Barth admitted that the logic of Kierkegaard's thought should lead one to Rome, as it actually did in the case of some of those who read his writings.[15]

Be that as it may, it would have been in the Catholic tradition that Kierkegaard could have been able to solve the perplexing questions which continued to trouble him to his dying day. On this one central point in regard to faith, Kierkegaard was already at one with the Church of Rome, although he remained a convinced and faithful Lutheran on many other points; but he would not permit faith to rest on the conclusions of reason. Yet his complaints against the rationalism of Hegel coupled with his criticism of the Established Lutheran Church in Denmark show that he was far from Luther on many points, and would seem to indicate that he belonged elsewhere, even though he showed no clear indication of searching further, or perhaps of even knowing precisely in what direction to search.

As Collins notes, Kierkegaard possessed no more than a "sketchy acquaintance" with Catholic teaching[16] Toward the end of his life, he did consider, from a speculative point of view, the system of Catholicism and contrasted it with Protestantism; it was, however, only medieval Catholicism that he studied. He saw it as an historical state in the history of Christendom which had given us some valuable historical lessons that would be of use in determining the future course of Christianity.[17] Even then, "Catholicism was not treated by him as one of the serious alternatives in our time."[18]

Unfortunately, Kierkegaard was very much like a man who stands outside the gates of a walled city, complaining of his lot in life and relating that which he seeks, not realizing that only a few steps beyond, all that he seeks can readily be found. Before the time of Kierkegaard and after, the Church of Rome has presented the act of faith as something far closer to that which he was seeking, but he failed to perceive this. In his opposition to the unrelenting rationalism of Hegel, Kierkegaard mistakenly felt that he was returning to the forthright position of the Reformation, yet as history will record, he also compromised the position of traditional Lutheranism. Eventually he assumed a position halfway between that of sixteenth-century Lutheranism and the teaching of the Church of Rome.

Objectively speaking, there is a great similarity between both the complaints and the solutions of Kierkegaard and the Catholic Church in regard to faith. Kierkegaard has been hailed as the great defender of faith as a personal commitment and as a human act that does not result from a purely rationalistic or historical mode of argumentation. This is the basic position of Rome, although it may certainly be admitted that Kierkegaard's literary style enabled him to express this thought in a more attractive manner.

The supposed opposition between Kierkegaard's notion of faith and that proposed by Aquinas (and the Catholic Church) — in the manner suggested by H. V. Martin — can only be explained as a failure either on the part of Martin to understand the precise teaching of the Catholic Church, or (a strong possibility) the failure of Catholic writers to represent properly the official Catholic view. Hermes was not the only Catholic philosopher or theologian who bent over backwards to accommodate his belief to the position of the avant-garde thinkers of his day, thus vitiating the true Catholic position. The entire history of the Church in recent centuries seems to indicate a series of such attempts, so that Catholic thinkers in one decade must expend great effort in showing that the avant-garde view of the preceding decade was never the true view of the Church, but rather an unfortunate accommodation (on the part of certain individuals who achieved great notoriety) to the more recent and "popular" views of their time.[19]

Thus in regard to the act of faith, it would seem that the current emphasis on faith as an act of reason, or the end result of an historical or philosophical proof, which has crept even into Catholic literature, is actually the unhappy result of Catholic attempts in the past two centuries to answer the objections of the deists and rationalists. This concern may well have caused the Catholic populace to give less attention in the past century to the teaching of the Church as set forth by Vatican I and the Popes of the nineteenth century. We now have the popular fad among Catholic educationists of reading Kierkegaard's notion of faith as though it were a new revelation with a message for Catholicism, little suspecting, it appears, that Gregory XVI was concerned about this problem as early as was Kierkegaard, and that he gave the answer of the Church, one that was later crystallized in Vatican I. Unfortunately, Gregory XVI seems to be remembered more for his personal idiosyncrasies, not included in that area proper to papal infallibility — such as his refusal to admit the use of steam engines in the Vatican territories. In doctrinal matters, however, where the Holy Spirit is ever active, Gregory XVI may have been more of a "voice crying in the wilderness. . . ." For that matter, however, Kierkegaard was such an unheard voice as well.

KIERKEGAARD'S BASIC APPROACH

In view of this, it may be worthwhile to examine what lay behind the position adopted by Kierkegaard — the presuppositions which led him to this particular concept of faith. Of chief import is the relationship he perceived between the then current defense of Christianity and the true notion of faith itself. Kierkegaard is supposedly one of the greatest opponents of "traditional" or "classical" apologetics in the Christian Church,[20] but the truth is that he never clearly distinguished between faith itself and those preliminary judgments which pertain to the science of apologetics, properly speaking, by which the reasonableness of the leap into faith is justified.[21]

For Kierkegaard, the predominant view of his generation was that faith resulted from historical and rational investigation. This was the "Christianity" he attacked, a Christianity that found visible expression in the Established Church of Denmark in his day, and a Christianity that was largely Hegelian in spirit. Thus it was that Kierkegaard saw the most extreme form of this error in the doctrine of Hegel who became his *bête noire;* for him, Hegel reduced everything, including faith, to some form of participation in Absolute Reason (in which Hegel felt that he had uncovered the *Ding-an-sich* that was to remain eternally hidden from Kantian eyes). This meant for Kierkegaard that faith was no longer a mystery, an encounter with God; it was simply an unfolding of reason, associated with all the pedantry so essential to the historical and scientific approach of late nineteenth-century German scholarship. *Wissenschaft* ruled supreme, and attempted to subject even God's revelation to its carefully annotated laws.

Kierkegaard thus writes: "I simply cannot help laughing when I think of Hegel's conception of Christianity, it is so utterly unconceivable."[22] It had become quite common for theologians in Denmark to attempt an integration of some sort of Hegelianism and Lutheran belief. The result was a speculative interpretation of Christianity which sidestepped the reality of Christian history and spoke only in terms of the unity of Absolute Spirit and the Christian revelation, conceived simply as one stage in the unfolding of Spirit or Mind in history.

In the viewpoint adopted by Kierkegaard, all of these theologians had reduced faith to reason and no more; it was to this that he objected above all. Hegel had led the way and the others had followed blindly. "How often," he exclaims, "have I shown that fundamentally Hegel makes men into heathens, *into a race of animals gifted with reason.*"[23] The Hegelian approach to religion reduced everything to this level, and in so doing eliminated all but the universal. The "individual" was cast aside in this process. Faith no longer remained a personal commitment; it was simply a rational exercise associated with the necessary unfolding of the Absolute Mind. Moreover, in Denmark this mental-

ity had become associated with the Established Church, according
to Kierkegaard, and the individual no longer believed in a personal
way at all. He simply became a Christian because this was the
rational way of doing things under the Established Church.

In all of this, Kierkegaard saw a betrayal of true Christianity,
and quite rightly. His solution, however, verged to the opposite
extreme, and excluded entirely the use of reason and philosophic
concepts in the discussion of faith. This antirationalism of Kierkegaard is actually as extreme as the rationalism of Hegel, but in the
opposite direction. Faith became in the Kierkegaardian sense a
" 'leap into the absurd,' that is, a choice contrary to reason, lacking
any credible motive, an act of absolute confidence in Christ's
grace, without any reason whatever for hope."[24] Kierkegaard does
not mean that an individual believes precisely *because* the content
of faith is supposedly absurd. He simply means to indicate by such
a line of thought that what appears to reason alone as something
absurd is perceived by the man of faith as something perfectly
acceptable, even though the believer cannot, in turn, give a rational motive for believing, nor justify his mode of acting in any
philosophical fashion.

Thus Kierkegaard explains that the believer cannot quite understand the argument of reason, which is that of the unbeliever,
who contends that what the man of faith believes is absurd: ". . . it
is a matter of course that for him who believes, it is not the
absurd."[25] Kierkegaard is not concerned here with the notion of
mysteries in Christianity; his problem lies at a more basic level
and centers around the notion of religious assent. In the entire
argument of that period of history, of course, if the assent of faith
is a purely rational assent, it must eventually follow that the "mysteries" of Christian faith are somehow contained within the area
of natural reason. It was this precise line of thought that led
Hermes and like-minded theologians within the Catholic Church
into similar errors, and which had earlier ensnared Bishop Butler,
although in a different manner.

FAITH AND REASON

Kierkegaard, however, went to the opposite extreme, and admitted *no* rational preparation for faith. His chief complaint is against those who would attempt to remove this "tension of the life of faith," in which the believer must continue to believe even though he recognizes that the nonbeliever looks upon his faith as absurd since it is not provable by reason. Kierkegaard insists that this tension is essential to faith and must remain; it would be a total error to attempt to "explain" faith, or "interpret faith as direct apprehension." The man of faith must simply accept the fact that "what for him is the most certain of all, an eternal happiness, is and must be absurd to others."[26]

In *Sickness Unto Death*, Kierkegaard criticizes the clergy who would strive to achieve this impossible task. They are trying to rob faith of its unique character and reduce belief to a logical, reasoned process:

> But this is just the way Christianity is talked about . . . by believing priests. They either "defend" Christianity, or they translate it into "reasons" — if they are not at the same time dabbling in "comprehending" it speculatively. This is what is called preaching, and it is regarded in Christendom as already a big thing that such preaching is done and that some hear it.[27]

Kierkegaard strives to defend Christianity as a "God-fearing ignorance, which by ignorance defends faith against speculation, keeping watch to see that the deep gulf of qualitative distinction between God/and man may be firmly fixed. . . ."[28] This infinite qualitative difference can be preserved only in the paradox of faith; if this is set aside, the horrors of Hegelian religion will return so that "God/and man, still more dreadfully than ever it occurred in paganism, might in a way, *philosophice, poetice,* etc., coalesce into one . . . in the System," that is, the System of Hegel.[29]

In all of this, Kierkegaard reflects in large measure the basic teaching of the Catholic Church, which holds that the mysteries of faith cannot be proven, demonstrated, or comprehended. He is even more closely aligned to those Catholic theologians who hold that the grace of faith has a psychological, and not merely an entitative effect upon the individual believer — who say, in other words, that it is the grace of faith that makes *possible* the assent itself, as a psychological act. Man simply accepts — with the humility of faith — those truths revealed by God; and he does this solely by the grace of God, with whom the initiative in the supernatural order always rests.

In this entire discussion, however, it is important to note that Kierkegaard fails to make use of the distinction so important in present-day theological thought within the Catholic Church, that is, the distinction between faith itself and the motives of credibility by which the reasonableness of the act of faith is affirmed.[30] As a result, there is in the position defended by Kierkegaard something of the same confusion that can be noted in the writings of Bishop Butler, although approached from the opposite pole. In both instances, there is a question of whether faith is the end result of a syllogistic type of reasoning, based on rational and historical (or exegetical) arguments. Butler approved of this, and thus reduced faith to reason; Kierkegaard rejected this notion, but in so doing rejected also any rational preparation for the "leap" into faith. Neither Kierkegaard nor Butler made a proper distinction between faith itself and those preliminary conclusions which indicate to the individual that when he *does* proceed to believe on the authority of God revealing, he will not be acting contrary to reason, nor doing violence to his human, intellectual nature.

As will be noted later, for Butler a theological "proof," based on Scripture and history and aided by human reasoning, was to be identified with "faith." Actually, such a procedure ought never lead a man to conclude *Credo*. To say "I believe" does not mean that I have "rational proof" for what I am doing; the best approaches to the explanation of the act of faith within Catholic circles have rejected such a notion entirely. Reason and syllogistic conclusions based on historical evidence cannot become the ultimate foundation of the assent of faith. If they do, then faith rests ultimately on man and the powers of human reason rather than the authority of God revealing. The acceptance of God's authority in revealing becomes conditioned by prior "proof," deduced from reason alone, in which man finds the authority of God.

Nevertheless, there has been, both within and without the field of Catholic thought, a clear confusion of these two elements in the approach to faith, that is, the *preliminary* judgment that, from a purely human standpoint, there are indications enough to show the divine handiwork in revelation so that "to believe" would be in accordance with human reason; and the *second* element, the actual belief, rooted on the authority of God revealing and on this alone. This confusion is only now being clarified more and more, in part due to our current interest in the doctrines of such men as Butler and Kierkegaard.

SCIENTIFIC FAITH

Thus restoring to special prominence Tertullian's *Credo quia absurdum,* Kierkegaard gave to it his own interpretation and rejected all attempts to defend Christianity on any rational basis whatsoever, even one which would posit a qualitative difference between preliminary conclusions and the act of faith itself. For Kierkegaard, "he who defends it [Christianity] has never believed in it. If he believes, then the enthusiasm of faith . . . is not defense, no, it is attack and victory."[31]

There are other passages which indicate that what Kierkegaard actually has in mind in this discussion is the attempt to reduce faith to philosophy; but he went too far, from the Catholic point of view. When he continually speaks of the absurdity or irrationality of faith, he very clearly intends to say that it cannot be looked upon as the end result of a process of human logicizing or of historical, exegetic study of the Scriptures. But he leaves no room for a preliminary judgment concerning the fact that in so believing on God's authority alone, man knows — from rational and historical proofs leading at least to moral certitude — that he is not doing violence to his human, intellectual nature.

Thus, in his *Training in Christianity,* Kierkegaard strikes out against those who have "dethroned" Christianity, as it were, and set aside its claim to absolute, unswerving obedience to the revealed message: "Hence 'reasons' (believing on three grounds [that is, by a syllogism]) replaced obedience, for people were annoyed at obeying."[32] These religious debaters "defended Christianity; there was no talk of authority, nor was it employed, the 'Thou shalt' was never heard, for fear of arousing laughter. . . ."[33]

Unfortunately Kierkegaard lacked in his religious vision that absolute divine authority become incarnate in a living, hierarchical magisterium — the "created testimony" which is joined to the "Uncreated Testimony" of God revealing. Without such a living magisterium, Christian faith, as it has been given, could not help but lapse into the manifold vagaries which have arisen throughout the history of Protestantism. Since Christian revelation has not been given by means of a purely subjective illumination of some sort, there must be a divinely guided community which can preserve, interpret, and unfold the content of revelation. Exegesis cannot do this, nor can the historical study of patristic and theological writings throughout the centuries. There must be a divinely guided body which can authentically impose this message in the name of God, and not simply present it as the opinion current within the Church or as the conclusion of theological research.

Schleiermacher attempted to bridge this gap by rooting religious certitude in the personal experience of the individual's contact with Christ and Christianity, but this led inevitably to pure subjectivism and a theory of philosophical or theological relativism in regard to Christian truth.[34] Hegel and his disciples had tried to find religious certitude in the deified reason of the System; Harnack and others later in the nineteenth century attempted to find such certitude in historical research. Kierkegaard would have none of this.

On the other hand, Kierkegaard was also far enough removed from sixteenth-century Lutheranism to reject the principle of *scriptura sola* as the root of religious certitude. He did grasp to some extent the importance of the principle of tradition; in addition, the beginnings of the work of higher criticism were having

their effect in Protestant circles, so that the Written Word in
itself could not be identified with divine revelation, as it had been
in sixteenth-century Protestantism.

Unfortunately the only institution that might conceivably have
served as an authentic teacher of God's revelation in the life of
Kierkegaard was the Established Church of Denmark — which was
the precise religious body he has attacking. He seemed to be
hemmed in on all sides, and it was this which eventually drove
him to his peculiar doctrine of "Instant" in which the believer
became contemporaneous with Christ.

Logically, much of what Kierkegaard was seeking is proposed by
the Church of Rome; this is especially true of that authority which
Kierkegaard deemed so necessary for faith. As Jolivet asks: "If
the faith is to be 'proclaimed,' that is, announced, preserved and
transmitted, taught and made certain, how is this possible save
through an authority which has received from Christ Himself both
its visible titles and a promise of infallibility?"[35] Kierkegaard remained a Lutheran, however, despite his partial rejection of the
Established Church; and he remained far from the Catholic tradition on this one point in particular. His doctrine thus went about
looking for some firm basis of authority on which he might defend
his concept of faith against either the terrors of pure subjectivism
or a "faith" confined to the realm of natural reason.

SCRIPTURE AND HISTORY

In a way, Kierkegaard fell back on the authority of the Apostles;
this was at least the attempt he made. However, the historical gulf
between the believer of the nineteenth century and the apostolic
college of the first century raised grave difficulties. The fundamentalist sects could continue to look to the authority of Scripture as
the Word of God itself, and an expression of apostolic authority,
but the scriptural critics of that age had set about undermining
scriptural authority — as understood by sixteenth-century Protestantism — in a way that kept Kierkegaard from adopting the
fundamentalist position as well. At the same time, the biblical critics
did not please him either; they were far too scientific, scholarly, and

rational to fit into Kierkegaard's notion of faith. He felt, as
Jolivet expresses it, that the Church of his time had in general
produced "a scholar's religiosity which is a mere diversion, and
propagated a professorial Christianity."[36] He goes so far in his
Journals as to declare that "Christendom has long been in need
of a hero who, in fear and trembling before God, had the courage
to forbid people to read the Bible."[37] He was entirely opposed to
the direction which scriptural studies were taking in his day. For
Kierkegaard the Bible could be approached only as the Word of
God, even though he could no longer approach it as did the sixteenth-century Protestant.[38] But to approach Scripture solely as a
critic or savant was to risk substituting the wrong motive for believing. Kierkegaard would insist that the Christian accept revealed
truths not because all first-rate scholars agree that this is the meaning of scriptural texts, but because God authoritatively asserts that
it is so.

On the other hand, Kierkegaard also rejected the other argument for divine authority that so attracted the minds of men in
the Classical era: the appeal of antiquity.[39] To claim that something is true since it has been held as such for eighteen hundred
years (much less, the first five or seven hundred years) is no
argument at all for Kierkegaard:

> And verily the eighteen centuries, which have not contributed
> an iota to prove the truth of Christianity, have on the contrary
> contributed with steadily increasing power to do away with
> Christianity. It is by no means true, as one might consistently
> suppose when one acclaims the proof of the eighteen centuries,
> that now in the nineteenth century people are far more thor-
> oughly convinced of the truth of Christianity than they were in
> the first and second generations — it is rather true (though it
> certainly sounds rather like a satire on the worshippers and
> adorers of this proof) that just in proportion as the proof sup-
> posedly has increased in cogency . . . fewer and fewer persons
> are convinced.[40]

At his cynical best, Kierkegaard goes on to proclaim that "now
that Christianity has been *proved,* and on a prodigious scale, there

is nobody, or next to nobody willing to make any sacrifice for it."[41] What has brought this about has been the attempt to do the impossible — the attempt to prove Christianity by appeals to reason and to history.

Kierkegaard attacks this especially in his *Training in Christianity*, striking out heavily against any and all such attempts:

> Let me first put another question: Is it possible to conceive of a more foolish contradiction than that of wanting to *prove* (no matter for the present purpose whether it be from history or from anything else in the wide world one wants to *prove* it) that a definite individual man is God? That an individual man is God, declares himself to be God, is indeed the "offence" κατ᾽ ἐξοχήν. But what is the offence, the offensive thing? What is at variance with (human) reason? And such a thing as that one would attempt to prove! But to "prove" is to demonstrate something to be the rational reality it is. . . . One can "prove" only that it is at variance with reason.[42]

In an even more precise fashion, Kierkegaard sets forth some of the "supposed proofs" of which he is speaking: "The proofs which Scripture presents for Christ's divinity — His miracles, His Resurrection from the dead, His Ascension into heaven. . . ."[43] These, he insists, "have no intention of proving that all this agrees perfectly with reason. . . ."[44]

In what he says, Kierkegaard is quite right; a conclusion based on a study of Scripture as an historical document, considering the claims of Christ and the miracles worked in testimony of His claims, does not end up in faith but in a rational conclusion achieved by syllogistic reasoning.[45] What he complains about is almost exactly the position defended so strongly (and wrongly) by Bishop Joseph Butler. At the same time, it must be admitted that Kierkegaard betrays a faulty appreciation of what theological writing and doctrinal system are properly doing in the first place, at least within the framework of the Church of Rome. To say that the miracles recorded in Scripture and known from history give an individual sufficient certitude concerning the divine handiwork in Christian revelation to go on to believe is one thing; this is the problem of the credibility of revelation — the fact that there is evidence enough to conclude that *if* one goes on to believe he will not be doing violence to his intellectual nature, nor be acting contrary to reason.[46]

To come to such a conclusion, however, does not really "prove" that the fact that Jesus of Nazareth is God is something knowable and provable by reason alone. This is a truth surpassing reason and rational proof; it is a mystery in the strict sense, believed solely on the authority of God revealing. It can be accepted as a supernatural mystery only in the act of faith — which presupposes the preliminary judgment concerning the motives of credibility (in logical if not temporal sequence).

So also in regard to the argument from history, extending over eighteen hundred years, Kierkegaard is perfectly correct in stating that this fact proves "nothing *pro* nor *contra*, inasmuch as the certitude of faith is something infinitely higher."[47] He rejects the very basis of this argument, that is, that certitude increases regularly with each century, so that presumably "in our time, the nineteenth century, it is greater than it had ever been before, a certitude in comparison with which the first centuries seem barely to have glimpsed His divinity."[48]

On the other hand, while holding that these proofs do not prove the truth of Christianity, Kierkegaard lapses into a certain amount of Nominalism latent in his thought, and claims, in accordance with his general position, that the proofs of Scripture "prove that it [Christianity] conflicts with reason and therefore is an object of faith."[49] A Catholic would prefer to distinguish between something that is above reason or beyond reason, and something that is obviously contrary to reason; these are not identical propositions. Kierkegaard's violent antirationalism will permit him to grant no role to human reason in this entire question, no matter how distinct from the essential act of faith itself. For him, faith cannot be faith unless the leap involves, from a human point of view, some sort of violence to reason — an act of believing that will appear quite in order only when the violence has been done and man has cast himself into the chasm; in the very act of believing the human being will perceive that he has acted properly, but not before,

Apart from this, Christ remains "the paradox, which history can never digest or convert into a common syllogism."[50] Therefore Kierkegaard gives this warning: "History may be a very reputable science, but it must not become so conceited as to undertake to do what the Father is to do, to array Christ in glory, costuming Him in the brilliant robes of the consequences [of the syllogism], as though that were the Second Advent."[51]

THE ROLE OF THEOLOGIANS

In an even more limited fashion, Kierkegaard speaks about miracles as proof of Christianity, not unlike the approach of Bishop Butler: "Here is a miracle, and a miracle is proof, and it is by miracles that they have wanted to *prove directly* the truth of Christianity!"[52] There can be no doubt that certain Christian thinkers, Butler certainly among them, have held this position. It is unfortunate that Kierkegaard failed to perceive that this faulty approach in individual Christian writers was not a necessary indication that this had been a common failing in Christianity for centuries, or that it was necessarily the avowed position of the churches. His attack on theological professors is accordingly quite universal:

> But behold how different is the custom in Christendom! There they have written these huge folios which develop the proofs of the truth of Christianity. Behind these proofs and folios they feel perfectly confident and secure from every attack; for the proofs and the folios regularly concluded with the assurance, *ergo* Christ was what He said He was; by the aid of the proofs this conclusion is just as sure as that 2 and 2 makes 4, and just as easy as thrusting the foot into the stocking; supported by this incontrovertible *ergo*, which makes the matter *directly* evident, the docents and the parsons strut, and the missionaries go forth to convert the heathen with the help of this *ergo*.[53]

It is admittedly unfortunate that theological manuals even among Catholics ever came to be looked upon in any sense as stepped-up philosophical manuals where the truth of Christianity is proven by a series of exegetical, historical, and philosophical arguments; the living Church of Christ, however, the Catholic Church, has never taught that. Unlike the philosopher *qua* philosopher, the theologian lives out his life in the atmosphere of what are, to a large extent, predetermined conclusions. As Pius XII pointed out in his now famous statement in *Humani generis:*

> . . . Hence Our Predecessor of immortal memory, Pius IX, teaching that the most noble office of theology is to show how a doctrine defined by the Church is contained in the sources of revelation, added these words, and with very good reason: "in that sense in which it has been defined by the Church."[54]

Looked at from one point of view, the theologian is not unlike an algebra student who begins with the answers and works backwards (an early mathematical approach which may have led the present writer to theology, where he hopes to be somewhat more successful)! From a more basic point of view, the theologian lives out his life in the aura of faith. He attempts to show the various evidences for the teaching and faith of the Church as it is contained in Scripture; he strives to delineate the manner in which, under the ever present guidance of the Holy Spirit, this teaching has been further clarified during the centuries.

Therefore, as Pius XII also pointed out, the starting point is always the solemn teaching of the magisterium, the created testimony of the authority of God revealing. Hence, "for this reason even positive theology cannot be on a par with merely historical science."[55] And the same is true of scriptural studies; while they are important for a proper understanding of how we ought to read and understand the Written Word of God, they cannot become the determinative norm of what God has revealed. It is for this reason that Pius XII objected to the tendency of some to make scriptural exegesis play that role:

> Thus they judge the doctrine of the Fathers and of the Teaching Church by the norm of Holy Scripture, interpreted by the purely human reason of exegetes, instead of explaining Holy Scripture according to the mind of the Church which Christ Our Lord has appointed guardian and interpreter of the whole deposit of divinely revealed truth.[56]

There is an important distinction that must always be kept in mind. It is one thing to misunderstand the meaning of a text in Scripture, and it is quite another to teach erroneous doctrine. It is possible that the members of the Church have failed in the first regard, and that even conciliar and papal documents have quoted scriptural passages in a sense later shown to be inaccurate; but the solemn magisterium can never fail in the second regard, since its infallibility rests not on its reasons, its scriptural quotations or quotations from the Fathers, but simply on the divine promise of infallibility accorded to the authentic teachers of the Church — the Roman Pontiff and the bishops in union with him.

MANUAL THEOLOGY

Thus the "thesis form" we find in theological manuals was never intended to be a philosophico-historical "proof," but simply a summary of the scriptural and historical evidences associated with the teaching of the Church. It is a convenient tool with which to sum up the past history of a precise doctrinal statement, but it is intended to be only that. It represents the bare minimum that must be possessed by any future theologian before beginning theological research or before entering the pulpit to preach or the classroom to teach. We do not look to manuals for research; as Karl Rahner has expressed it: "Schoolbooks are — Schoolbooks. Anyone who has ever tried it knows that it is by no means easy to write an orderly textbook or even only a part of one."[57] Yet they are necessary as a starting point.

Moreover, even in his speculative labors the theologian must make use of the solemn definitions issued by the Church in the past; he may not set aside even for a moment any of these teachings. Thus when he sets out now and then on a personal attempt to elucidate some other point not yet sufficiently clarified, he must be guided by that which is taught clearly in solemn fashion. Moreover, his speculation is a purely tentative work. Whatever his conclusions may be, they are not binding upon the Christian until they have been taken up by the magisterium and incorporated officially into her teaching as a valid clarification of revealed truth;

and when this is done, the reason for accepting them is by no means the authority of the theologian nor even the syllogistic argument or historical, scriptural conclusions he has drawn. At this point, the doctrine elaborated by the theologian leaves the realm of theological reasoning and enters into the realm of faith because of the authority of the magisterium now attached to it. It is this that makes it possible that, should the reasons originally offered by the theologian later be called into doubt, the doctrine as proposed by the magisterium remains secure; the teaching Church speaks on its own authority as the representative of God, and is not tied to "proofs" of this nature. Thus the theologian must always serve the magisterium in this secondary, but important role. He may never, however, attempt to take its place.[58]

In other words, throughout the work of the theologian, there is no attempt to *prove* the faith by means of scriptural, historical, and rational arguments. This faith he takes for granted from the start; it is something that exists, rooted on the authority of God alone. It serves the theologian as a starting place, and his guide along the way. He then attempts to arrange these truths in some systematic manner, showing the inner relationship between them and comparing them to truths known in the natural order. He is following in his presentation the *ordo doctrinae* rather than the *ordo inventionis,* that is, he strives to give a systematic presentation of revealed truth once it has been clarified by the Church throughout various periods of history.[59]

The theologian does not try to "prove" these matters either to Catholics or non-Catholics; neither does the teacher of doctrine nor the preacher. Those who are already Catholic have made this passage into the realm of faith and need no such "proofs," and those not yet Catholic can merely have the revelation of God proposed to them by the Church and by those who have received a mandate to teach in the name of the Church; the truths of faith and the Christian way of life will be accepted, if they are, only by cooperation with the inner working of God's divine grace.[60] Thus the Church fully recognizes the fact that those who are not Catholic will never be "argued," and much less "forced" into belief; they will accept faith only by a personal response to the grace of Christ that will lead them to the leap into faith in which they will accept the truths and the way of life proposed by God through His Church on earth.

We can also note that in the writings of Thomas Aquinas a similar problem presents itself. There have been those who interpret him as writing a "typical" apologetic defense of the faith (understood in the modern sense), complete with "proofs" and syllogistic arguments. Others, for far better reasons, see Thomas as simply proclaiming the faith which is his; the seemingly syllogistic structure of his theological works represents merely the external framework which he prefered for teaching purposes (the *ordo doctrinae*) but the core of his argument rests in his appeal to faith as set forth in Scripture and the teaching Church. For all its apparent formalism, the *Summa* of St. Thomas is anything but an apologetic "proof." His appeal, time and again, both in the *Sed contra* and in the body of his argument is to the official teaching of faith as reflected in the sources of belief as he knew them.

In his discussion of Christology, for example, St. Thomas repeatedly gives the teaching of the Church as *the* reason for defending his particular response. When he discusses the nature of the hypostatic union, his decisive argument will repeatedly be the Councils of Ephesus, Chalcedon, or the Councils of Constantinople.[61]

Similarly, when St. Thomas speaks of the possibility of supernatural mysteries and of revelation, his primary concern is to point out that the man of faith is acting as an intelligent being when he does not reject from an *a priori* point of view the possibility of truths which human reason can neither discover nor comprehend. It is this same thought which pervades his insistence on the fact that man acts rationally when he accepts revelation, since the various miraculous signs granted by God in conjunction with revelation indicate the divine origin of those supernatural truths.[62]

At the same time, Thomas is anxious to point out that while arguments can be raised against these supernatural truths, they merely raise apparent difficulties; they cannot demonstrate positively that the truths are, in themselves, contradictory.[63] Here he is speaking more of what Hermann Lais would describe with the German word, *Apologie,* that is, the answering of such objections raised against any doctrine of revelation. As such, this *Apologie* (as differentiated from Apologetics in the usual sense) pertains to the entire realm of theological concern: dogma, moral, exegesis, and the other related branches.[64] When Thomas discusses the relationship of reason to faith, however, his constant emphasis is upon the supernaturality of that act of faith, and the uniqueness of the assent of faith itself, resulting in a certitude surpassing all others whatsoever.[65]

In the seventeenth century, however, the basic approach was quite different. Throughout the Age of Reason (roughly from 1650 to 1800) the chief emphasis was placed upon *reason* rather than faith; this had serious consequences for future generations. Because of this shift in perspective, reason (which was already regarded by the deists and later rationalists as solely sufficient) tended to be looked upon as something more basic, and in a sense even more important, than faith itself. It was taken for granted by many that unless reason *actually* first exercises its proper role in each individual, establishing the rational foundations, there can be no supernatural faith. Instead of speaking of the "root power" of natural reason and its native abilities (as distinct from the actual use of this power in each individual), many theologians came to insist that every single human being both can and must prove certain truths by rational argument before proceeding to make an act of faith — a position quite contrary to that of St. Thomas and Vatican I, who insist on the moral necessity of God revealing even such natural truths as His existence; the present historic order brings on this need of fallen man.[66]

KIERKEGAARD'S UNSOLVED PROBLEM

Kierkegaard never approached this Catholic concept of faith and the relationship between reason and faith; as a result he never solved his enigma. He continued to reject the various movements that were taking form in his own day, leading to the more complete system of so-called Liberal Protestantism. He was totally unwilling to go along with that rationalistic school of thought which would look upon the "scriptural proof" worked out by exegesis as the basis for Christian faith. Not able to look at Scripture alone, and unwilling to admit an historical proof — not to mention a logical or metaphysical one — and having no infallible magisterium to which he might turn, Kierkegaard's position remains ambivalent. He insists upon a personal relationship with God, but he fears the excesses of the other approaches he sees about him. At the same time, as Jolivet points out, "he reacts toward authority and hierarchy, but without successfully ridding himself of the erroneous opinion which makes him see the Church as a screen and an obstacle between man and God."[67] The hierarchical Church he rejected primarily was the Established Church in Denmark, just as it was the "Christendom" of this milieu that he attacked. He never grasped the position of the Church of Rome as the living embodiment of the authority of God who has chosen to speak and act through men; this alone would have been a fully satisfactory solution to his problem, as those who contend that Kierkegaard should logically have ended up a Catholic readily admit.

The only possible solution that offered itself to Kierkegaard, therefore, is associated with his notion of the "leap into faith." Kierkegaard hopes by his explanation to make each believer "contemporaneous with Christ," so that the divine authority will present itself immediately to the believer in this personal and intimate meeting with God. The doctrine of "contemporaneity" is, as Collins expresses it, Kierkegaard's answer to Hegelian theologians and purely rationalistic biblical scholars, and as such it has great advantages "in helping to restore a sane attitude, in the wake of theological and historical rationalism."[68]

The weakness of this solution is the opposite extreme: Kierkegaard goes on to exclude any rational activity in the approach to faith; he fails to analyze adequately the role of reason in establishing the reasonableness of making the act of faith itself.[69] This is sometimes spoken of as the "reasonableness of faith," but the phrase, which might easily be misunderstood, is intended to state that it is "reasonable" or "in accordance with the dictates of human reason" to plunge oneself into the realm of faith by co-operating with divine grace and thus entering into an area of truth and a way of life which surpasses the rational and the natural, and which man accepts solely on the authority of God revealing.

Kierkegaard's extreme reaction against the role of the intellect is closely associated with his notion of becoming "contemporaneous" with Christ, since this involves in his approach a *direct apprehension* of revealed truth. Man presumably does not need a reasoning process leading him to faith, nor need he concern himself with a system of doctrines; he perceives these truths intellectually when he meets Christ through faith. As Martin expresses it, in the mind of Kierkegaard "only the present is real to a man, and can form the medium of a real relationship. The past stands only in memory; the future stands only in expectation, only the present really exists. Therefore, if Christian revelation is to be effective . . . the believer and Christ must become contemporaneous."[70] In this way, Christ speaks directly to the individual in all ages; there is no need of the authority of the Church nor the force of scriptural or historical "proofs" nor any systematic presentation of "doctrines."

This attempt would focus our attention on the immediate experience of faith: it is the meeting of God and man. Yet Kierkegaard is faced with that grave problem which continually haunted his teaching, the problem of pure subjectivism. Having avoided the appeal to history and the historical revelation, and rejecting as well a living and supernatural magisterium through which the individual comes into this immediate and personal, existential relationship with Christ, Kierkegaard is hard pressed on all sides. He has come forth with a notion of authority, but it is difficult to understand how secure that authority is, since it constantly tends to fall back into pietism or subjectivism of some sort. Against any immanentist approach to faith, such as that proposed by Schleiermacher, he wants to insist on an objective truth revealed by God; but he has a difficult time putting man in touch with that objective Christian truth in his approach.

THE INSTANT

In his doctrine, Kierkegaard speaks of this meeting with Christ as the *Moment* or the *Instant:* a sort of synthesis of time and eternity, in which the believer becomes contemporaneous with Christ. It is an "atom of eternity," which breaks in upon man decisively in each succeeding period of time. Thus, Kierkegaard holds to a revelation that is somehow rooted in history and that has a definite content. The individual, however, will not approach this either by historical or philosophical proofs or through the activity of a divinely guided magisterium. By entering into this Moment, the individual becomes contemporaneous with Christ Himself and His teaching; the revelation is accepted on the authority of Christ Himself, and would, in regard to content, be the same for all.[71]

The obvious difficulty still remains: what is to be done if there should be an actual doubt concerning the true meaning of this revelation? It is more of an *a priori* assumption on the part of Kierkegaard that the content of revealed truth would be the same for each individual. If this theory does not work out in practice, Kierkegaard has no real answer; the danger of pure subjectivism remains. Granted that a man may experience Christ by entering into the Moment, unless he is certain what must be accepted and unless his belief and Christian viewpoint is identical with that of all other Christians, pure subjectivism and indifferentism will remain as the sole alternative. As Jolivet points out:

> Kierkegaard is a man defending an untenable and desperate position. Contradiction besets him on all sides, because he lived as it were divided up between the religious man and the poet, between the rationalist and the Christian, between the believer and the unbeliever, between the dialectician and the ironical critic of Christendom; he was these all at once, lacking any

higher means whereby they might be reconciled and pacified.
. . . The whole problem for Kierkegaard was to find a way out
of subjectivity, which seemed to lead to the immanence of the
self within itself, and to a reason set afire with impossible
demands.[72]

Kierkegaard worked himself into this position by positing "a
radical opposition between the spheres of reason (immanence) and
of faith (transcendency)," and, as Jolivet goes on to conclude,
"far from leading us to erect this conflict into the law of Christian
life, it should rather induce us to avoid the paths which involve
one in such contradictions."[73]

THE LIVING CHRIST

An unfortunate misunderstanding at the start can lead a man
far from the security he is seeking. The religious philosophy of
Kierkegaard led him to this blind spot, but only because he was
trying to avoid what ought to be avoided: the notion that faith
is something that can be "proven" by historical and philosophical
arguments. There *is* an alternative to these two extremes —
that of pure rationalism and that of pure subjectivism — but the
Danish theologian could not perceive it; hence the contradictions
in his approach remained unsolved. The role of the living magisterium which, under the guidance of the indwelling Spirit, preserves intact the content of that faith which the believer accepts,
implies a combination of the immanent and the transcendent, of
the historical and the eternal, of the unchanging authority of God
and the present moment of the believer, of the individual and
the social. The believer does not accept faith from the Church
in the sense that a purely human organization, a group of religious-
minded men, sets forth a system or a doctrine to be accepted on
its authority alone. Faith is and must remain an individual contact with God, but it is a contact with Him in His living Church,
the Mystical Body of His Son, and in the revealed doctrine which
He committed to that living Church, guaranteeing that through
the action of the Holy Spirit, that doctrine would never be more
nor less, not other than what God Himself had revealed. In this

way he becomes "contemporaneous" with Christ as the Catholic Church understands such a phrase.

Ultimately the believer accepts the truths of faith solely on the authority of God revealing, but he does not do so independently of the Church; the testimony of God includes that of His Church since it is God speaking through His Church. The Uncreated Testimony of God Himself, and the created testimony of His Church on earth both pertain to that divine authority which is the one and only motive of faith. They cannot be separated. The believer does not accept faith for the "reasons" the theologians, or even the Church, may give — reasons, that is, similar to those found in theological manuals. Theology is simply a reflection upon that which is already believed in the existential and intimate relationship within the Church which we call faith. Acting through His Church, God *imposes* these beliefs upon mankind; this is the essence of faith, and it is this which differentiates theology as a dogmatic subject from any philosophical system. Even speculative theology differs greatly from philosophy, since its starting point is also defined dogma, and its attempts at further clarification of revealed truths are guided — and restrained — from start to finish by the unchangeable truths already defined by the Church of Christ.

Similarly, doctrinal development does not mean the addition of new beliefs arrived at by a philosophical type of reasoning carried on by the unaided human intellect. It is something entirely supernatural; it is something far more profound and far more complicated than a simple process of reasoning. It is wrapped up in the mystery of the Church and her divinely guided doctrinal life. As Vatican I was careful to point out:

> The doctrine of faith as revealed by God has not been presented to men as a philosophical system to be perfected by human ingenuity; it was presented as a divine trust given to the [Church] to be faithfully kept and infallibly interpreted. It also follows that any meaning of the sacred dogmas that has once been declared by holy Mother Church, must always be retained; and there must never be any deviation from that meaning on the specious grounds of a more profound understanding. "There-

fore, let there be growth . . . and all possible progress in understanding, knowledge, and wisdom whether in single individuals or in the whole body, in each man as well as in the entire Church, according to the stage of their development; but only within proper limits, that is, in the same doctrine, in the same meaning, and in the same purport."[74]

Thus, through the guidance of the indwelling Spirit, the Church perceives ever more clearly the inner coherence of the doctrine it believes on the authority of God and teaches in His name; it plumbs ever more deeply the content of that faith. The first attempts toward this further clarification are made by individual theologians; this is a secondary role, and the theologian merely offers his tentative solution. Only when the teaching Church itself accepts *as its own* such clarifications, and teaches them authoritatively, do they enter into the framework of what the believer accepts on the authority of God revealing.

The theologian has his role to play, but in no case does he strive to prove that the infallible Church is right; this would have no more meaning than to strive to prove that God is right. The believer accepts these truths on God's authority alone; they cannot be proven to either the believer or the nonbeliever. They are simply proposed, proclaimed by the Church. Thus faith is not identified with reason or rational, historical or exegetical "proofs." Faith is totally "other," in the Kierkegaardian sense, and those who believe come to do so only through a personal and total commitment of self to God under the inspiration of divine grace.

There is a leap into faith, but reason points out the way. While reason cannot prove, establish, comprehend, it can show the reasonableness of going on to the act of believing. There is also a moment of faith; just as the Mystical Body is the extension of Christ in time and space, so also, through entering by faith into this Body, the believer comes into immediate contact with Christ in His fullness: the Whole Christ, the Mystic Christ. In this manner, the believer escapes those phantoms that pursued the way of Kierkegaard. He knows no fear of a purely rationalistic faith on the one hand, and no fear of an unavoidable subjectivism on the other, brought about by the inability to preserve intact and interpret correctly the objective content of divine revelation.

Through His Mystical Body, Christ preserves unchanged through the ages the historical revelation, yet all the while increasing within the Church's teaching a fuller understanding of that revelation. The development of doctrine in the truly Catholic sense has been well compared to a man entering a dark room; at first he sees only the dark outline of the various objects, but as his eyes become accustomed to the light, he perceives things ever more clearly. So through the centuries, the teaching of the Church, the understanding of the Church, becomes more precise; but it is not the objective truths which change — as Modernism wrongly taught — but simply our perception of their full meaning.

At the same time, through His Mystical Body and through the internal grace proper to the individual, Christ brings each one of us into personal and intimate contact with Himself, opening our eyes ever more to the vision of faith that rests far beyond the realm of reason, but which at the same time unfolds for us the true meaning of life and the true meaning of man in the present historical order.

CHAPTER III

Two Theories of Faith

One of the chief concerns of the present theological world is the question of precisely what it means to "believe" in the Christian revelation. It is a matter that touches on many closely allied topics: the relationship between Scripture and tradition, the concept of theological method, the problems of teaching religion and of preaching, the question of how to make faith a more personal and vital reality in the life of the faithful. There is a great deal of talk of faith as a personal encounter, an existentialistic experience by which the total person is committed to God and the way of faith. All of this is well said; there is always room for a further clarification of the true meaning of faith. Yet the essential point of the discussion is the problem of the *assent* of faith. Eventually all of the problems are somehow reduced to this one point, and in view of that, it might be worthwhile to summarize here the general teaching of the Catholic Church in regard to faith, and note the two divergent explanations in regard to the assent of faith itself. These are topics treated in every theological manual, but often not well grasped, particularly in relationship to the other questions being discussed today.

There is no debate among Catholics in regard to the general definition of faith. A suitable definition would still be that formulated by Thomas Aquinas: "The act of faith is an act of the intellect assenting to divine truth under the command of the will moved by God through grace."[1] This notion of faith has been attacked before the time of Aquinas and since, but the Church has consistently defended all of the elements which have traditionally been a part of her official teaching and have thus come to be expressed in this fashion by St. Thomas. We can note four chief elements in this concept of faith, some of which have been emphasized again in more recent times because of the attacks leveled against them:

1. *Faith is an act of the intellect.* This is the essential note of faith in Catholic teaching. There have been those who have claimed that faith for the Catholic is *merely* intellectual: an adherence to a doctrinal formula of some sort, and nothing more. This objection arises not from the Catholic concept of faith, but from a failure on the part of some to understand exactly what the entire definition implies; they have mistakenly concluded that this essential element exhausts the teaching of the Church on faith, so that there is no room for a personal, vital encounter with God and a wholehearted commitment to the way of faith. Nothing could be further from the truth, as a history of this definition as it has been evolved in the life of the Church would indicate.[2]

On the other hand, there is no reason for passing over this essential note in the interests of these other elements; this has been the cause of error throughout the centuries. The role of the intellect was particularly attacked by the Lutherans of the sixteenth century, who wished to place the primary emphasis on what is now termed "fiduciary faith," that is, a trust in the saving merits of Christ. The intellectual element of the act of faith was still admitted by these Protestant believers, even though it may have appeared to be something secondary.

In the post-Kantian era, however, in Schleiermacher and similar-minded philosophers, the intellectuality of faith underwent an even more severe attack. By reducing all of religion to "feeling" or "religious experience," a form of philosophical or theological relativism was deduced in which what a person believes, or what he professes in credal form, is nonessential. Provided an individual creed responds to the personal religious experience of an individual or a community, it is perfectly acceptable. In this approach, faith is no longer an act of the intellect terminating in the acceptance of an objective truth handed down through revelation; all such questions are set aside, and it matters not at all whether, in one's religious experience, he knows Christ as God or simply as a noble human being. This entire discussion is related to the problem of religious indifferentism which troubled the Catholic Church in the nineteenth century, and which was finally condemned most solemnly by Vatican I. It also lay at the heart of the heresy of Modernism, condemned during the pontificate of St. Pius X.[3]

2. *Moved by the will.* This point involves the question of the freedom of the act of faith. The problem has always been discussed in connection with faith as a meritorious act. Since faith is the foundation of justification,[4] it contains within itself a salvific aspect. In order to merit, however, a man must act freely, and thus the Church has defended the freedom of the act of faith on that basis. In the nineteenth century, the freedom of the act of faith was attacked once more by Catholic theologians, particularly by Georg Hermes, who attempted to argue from Kantian principles. Hermes holds that the mind achieves certainty only when the evidence is irresistible. He extends this principle to faith as well, and concludes that since we must have certainty in regard to what we believe, such a conviction must also be the result of an irresistible force; thus faith is not free.

Hermes does attempt to avoid a full denial of this element of freedom by distinguishing between "faith of the mind" which touches on the element of knowledge and is not free; and "faith of the heart" which is free, consisting in that habitual state of soul by which man commits himself to God and chooses to live according to the truths believed. Basically this is a rationalistic approach, reducing faith to reason, since faith is essentially a question of knowledge (or what Hermes calls "faith of the mind"). Hence Vatican I declares: "If anyone says that the assent of Christian faith is not free, but necessarily results from arguments of human reason . . . let him be anathema."[5]

Since that time, the freedom of the act of faith has also been defended against those who in any way would tend to force individuals to become Catholic against their will; the Catholic Church has consistently rejected such a teaching, never more clearly than in the decree on religious liberty to be issued by Vatican II along the lines of its previously published summary of the statement:

1. There is today a growing consciousness of human dignity which demands that in his actions man should enjoy freedom and be moved not by coercion but by the realization of duty. This postulate of liberty is particularly applicable in matters of religion. . . .

2. The Council declares that the right to religious liberty is based on the very dignity of human nature as known by reason and especially by the revealed word of God. Such freedom requires that man must be free from coercion, either by individuals or by social groups or by any human power, in such wise that in religious matters no one should be forced to act or be prevented from acting according to his conscience, in private or in public, always within due limits. The Council further declares that this right must be recognized in the structure of civil society as a right which all men and all religious groups may legitimately claim. The safeguarding of this right is the responsibility of individual citizens and also of public authorities according to the mode proper to each.[6]

3. *Under the inspiration of grace.* It was against the Pelagians and the Semi-Pelagians of the fifth and sixth centuries above all that the Church defended the supernatural character of the act of faith. While Pelagius and his followers contended that man possessed of himself the power to believe as he ought in order to be saved, the Church insisted that faith is entirely a free gift from God. Even the attempt of the Semi-Pelagians to limit man's unaided activity to the beginning of faith was rejected; in the way toward justification the very first step must, in all instances, be taken by God and not by man. The initiative rests with God alone. This teaching was repeated by the Council of Trent in the sixteenth century in its defense of the Catholic notion of faith; once again it was emphasized that "by his own free will, without God's grace, man could not take one step towards justice in God's sight. . . ."[7]

4. *The authority of God revealing.* This is the basic and fundamental motive of faith. Vatican I above all insists on this truth against the teaching of the Rationalists of the modern era who

would reduce faith to an assent of reason alone. When the intellect assents to a truth that can be known by reason, it is motivated by the intrinsic truth that it perceives by its native and natural power; that is a purely rational assent to a truth. On the other hand, when the intellect assents to a truth of faith, it does so solely on the authority of God revealing. The assent of faith is not an assent of reason, but the acceptance of divine authority, implying man's personal encounter with God who reveals.[8] In other words, the assent to the truths of revelation is given only because of God's authoritative word, and this is associated with the virtue of faith — a supernatural gift offered to man by God and freely accepted by those who choose to cooperate with that grace. As such, it is an encounter, not with a vague "authority," but with a person who reveals.

THE GENESIS OF FAITH

While there is total agreement among Catholics in regard to these basic elements of faith, there is still room for free discussion as far as other more specific points are concerned. One of these is the complicated question of the genesis of faith; another is a problem closely associated with the first, that is, the question of the psychological effect of the grace of faith on the intellect. These, in turn, are parts of an even broader topic, the reasonableness of faith itself.

To speak of the reasonableness of faith does not imply that faith can in any way be reduced to a purely natural assent, apart from grace; the position of the Church is clear on that point. What the phrase does indicate is that the act of faith, when made, is *in accordance with human reason*. In other words, a man is not doing violence to his intellectual nature when he assents to a truth on the authority of God revealing; he is not going contrary to human reason when he gives intellectual assent to truths in this fashion. Briefly, then, it is reasonable — or in accordance with human reason — to believe on God's authority alone.

This problem must be faced. Man as an intellectual being cannot do violence to his own nature by believing; he must know that he is acting in a rational manner. At the same time, there is the danger which entrapped many of the rationalistic and semi-rationalistic theologians of the past, namely, that of so defending the activity of the human intellect in regard to faith, that the ultimate assent of faith becomes a purely natural and rational act in which the object known is proportioned to the native powers of the intellect, and is accepted on the basis of human knowledge alone. It is against this opposite extreme that Vatican I issued its solemn definition.

Apart from more detailed points, there is general agreement among Catholic theologians and apologetes regarding the genesis of faith; this has resulted from the various elements noted in Scripture and clarified especially by the papal and conciliar definitions of the past few centuries.

The term "genesis" indicates the ultimate aim of this discussion, that is, to determine the manner in which faith arises as a psychological act of man. Its chief concern is the relationship of reason to faith, and it asks one central question: "How far can human reason proceed toward the act of faith without the necessary help of divine grace?"

In many respects, this is a metaphysical analysis. The manner in which the genesis of faith is discussed often gives the erroneous impression that we are dealing with a temporal process, as though there is always a "before" and an "after" in the genesis of faith. In the actual life of the man of faith, such a step-by-step procedure is rarely if ever traversed; yet such a speculative analysis is necessary if we are to understand the act of faith properly. Even the act of the intellect by which faith is declared reasonable must continue throughout every moment of the life of faith; it is not an act formulated once and then forgotten entirely. At every point, faith must be a reasonable act. This analysis is simply an attempt to tear apart, as it were, these various elements of the entire process of a saving faith and set them side by side in the order of priority of nature rather than of time.

So also in regard to that point beyond which the human intellect cannot proceed without divine grace, we ought not have the impression that this is always (nor perhaps even frequently) the case. Ordinarily God's grace accompanies a man along the entire path toward the act of faith itself. This is simply an attempt to analyze what human reason *could* perform of itself, as indicated in the sources of revelation and taught, accordingly, by the Catholic Church.

We can outline the genesis of faith in a rather schematic fashion; the presentation varies with authors, although the essential elements are always the same:

1. PRELIMINARY IMPULSE TOWARD FAITH

Following such statements as that of St. Paul in his Epistle to the Romans, where he says that "faith then depends on hearing," and asks, "how are they to hear, if no one preaches,"[9] the authors emphasize the importance of such an external presentation as the first step toward faith. It is something extrinsic and does not enter into the ultimate act of faith itself; but it is necessary.

From this, as a purely human reaction, there can result a certain curiosity — a vague desire to know more about this matter. In the case of a man who, as we may now suppose in order not to complicate the question, already admits the existence of God and also the possibility both of supernatural mysteries and of divine intervention through revelation, a *hypothetical judgment* could be fashioned: "If God has revealed anything, I should know something about this and be prepared to accept it." The judgment could also involve the will: "If God has revealed something, I desire to know it and accept it."

All of this obviously could be accomplished apart from grace. Quite clearly, the chief obstacle at this point would be a deistic philosophy that would reject the very possibility of revelation. But considered in itself, this preliminary impulse of an individual toward faith could result from contact with some preaching or writing concerned with Christian revelation, entirely apart from actual graces granted by God to draw a man to faith. On the other hand, no one would deny that God could, and perhaps most often does, take the initiative even in this matter, so that this vague curiosity itself would be the result of actual graces. These would affect inwardly both the intellect and the will, acting in union with the external preaching of the message. Viewed objectively, however, such graces are not absolutely necessary, no matter how frequently they may actually be given in human life.

2. INVESTIGATION INTO THE FACT OF REVELATION

At this point, having heard of the Christian message, an individual could institute an investigation into the fact of revelation. His aim would be to assure himself, if possible, that there has, *de facto,* been a revelation from God. His investigation would naturally include a more thorough study of the doctrine itself, but it would center especially on a consideration of any proofs presented to show that there has been a divine intervention of this sort. The two chief signs of the fact of revelation singled out by the Catholic Church are miracles and prophecies.[10] Other signs are also pointed out as observable facts in which something of the suprahuman and divine can be perceived in man. One of these is the Church itself which, in its two-thousand-year history, has given evidence of something more than merely human foundations; it is, in the words of Vatican I, "a great and perpetual motive of credibility and an irrefutable proof of its own divine mission."[11] Since the Church is to preach this revelation of Christ, there is an intimate relationship between the Church and the message. Hence, even apart from membership in the Church, an individual could perceive the more than human strength of this ecclesiastical body, serving as a sign that its message (which is the Christian message) is a revelation from God.

There are also elements within the life and history of the Church that can be considered more specifically in this regard: its marvelous propagation in the early centuries and up to the present hour; its remarkable effect on the morals of those who embrace it; the sublimity and inner coherence of its profound doctrine; the heroic constancy of its martyrs throughout history.

From a purely historical point of view, one might also consider the evidence that Christ is the Messiah, and that the Church is the kingdom He came to establish; this is a strong argument, particularly when a consideration of His marvelous wisdom and personal heroic sanctity are included in this study.

All of these could constitute, for the individual, a strong indication that there is something of the divine associated with this message that claims to be the revelation of God in Christ. This is not as yet faith; one still does not believe in Christ nor the Church and her doctrine. But he may come to a conclusion that there is ample evidence of divine activity in what he perceives. It is even possible for an individual to perceive all of this apart from any special actual graces given to draw his intellect to that conclusion. Because of the difficulty of some of these other signs, however, the Church looks upon miracles and prophecies, in history or in the present, as the signs best suited for men of all times and places, and of varying intellectual capacities.

Once again, God could and, it would seem, generally does grant graces to those individuals who undertake such an investigation as this; but, speculatively speaking, these graces are not absolutely necessary at this point. The importance of these signs is their probative value to human reason, showing man that when he does believe by cooperating with the interior grace of faith, he is still, because of the conclusion drawn from these signs, acting in accordance with reason. As Vatican I again states: "In order that the submission of our faith might be consonant with reason, God has willed that external proofs of His revelation, namely divine acts and especially miracles and prophecies, should be added to the internal aids given by the Holy Spirit." It is the purpose, then, of these marvelous events to serve as "signs of divine revelation."[12]

3. CONCLUSION CONCERNING THE FACT OF REVELATION

It is at this point in the genesis of faith that the authors make an important distinction in regard to the conclusion reached. We may consider the conclusion formulated either as a *speculative* or a *practical* judgment. In the speculative judgment the individual is not as yet personally involved, whereas in the practical judgment there is the admission of a personal responsibility toward the revelation. It is generally agreed that, since this practical judgment involves the personal attitude of the individual toward his own salvation through faith, and his personal response to the divine revelation, it could not be made apart from actual graces granted by God for that purpose. Without such graces, the practical judgment would not come into being. Thus we must discuss these two possible judgments separately:

a) The Speculative Judgment of Credibility: It must be noted above all that this judgment is not to be confused with faith itself. The judgment is concerned with the credibility of revelation. As Vatican I expresses it, these external signs "render divine revelation credible"; they are "the surest signs of divine revelation."[13] Or again, the "divine origin of the Christian religion" can be "successfully proved" by these signs.[14] Or, in the words of the encyclical, *Humani generis,* of Pius XII: ". . . it falls to reason . . . to prove beyond doubt from divine signs the very foundations of the Christian faith."[15]

All of these statements are various ways of expressing the doctrine that apart from actual graces, human reason can (even though most often it may not) come to recognize the stamp of the divine associated with Christian revelation. At the conclusion of the investigation, the individual, arguing from reason alone, can state that there is sufficient evidence here to prove that this revelation is from God. Therefore, if he goes on to belief itself, he is assured that he will not be acting contrary to reason nor doing violence to his human nature. From a purely human and rational point of view, this revelation is credible; the individual can justify the reasonableness of his act of faith on this basis. This is still not faith; the assent of this judgment rests not on the authority of God revealing, but on the probative force of the signs associated with this revelation, perceived by the light of human reason and following upon a purely human investigation into what is outwardly perceptible.

Thus the speculative judgment of credibility could be formulated in such terms as these: "This doctrine and the proofs given to show it as a revealed doctrine appear credible, that is, I *could* believe it, and — by so doing — act in a rational manner." It is important to note that the authors all insist that the type of certitude involved in this judgment need be nothing more than *moral certitude;* it is that type of certitude generally associated with any historical conclusion. There is no requirement that an individual achieve either physical or metaphysical certitude in regard to the fact of revelation, or (which is the same) the credibility of Christian revelation. Moral certitude is entirely sufficient to remove all doubts, and to serve as a basis for acting in accord with the demands of human reason.[16]

This position in no way weakens the certainty of faith, since the assent of faith is not based upon this conclusion, nor limited to the moral certitude associated with it. The judgment of credibility touches on the *reasonableness* of faith, whereas faith itself is concerned with an assent to truth that is based *solely* on the authority of God. Thus, because faith is rooted on divine authority, we can speak of the infallible certitude of faith. This is something that far surpasses not only moral certitude in the natural order, but even physical and metaphysical certitude, since it pertains to a higher order of things entirely.[17]

b) The Practical Judgment of Credibility: In this judgment (also called by some the "judgment of credentity"), the individual perceives a certain personal obligation to proceed to faith itself; it might be formulated in these terms: "I personally have an obligation to believe the doctrine associated with these signs, since these signs have given sufficient proof that the revelation is from God and that I would be acting in accord with reason, were I to accept this doctrine on faith."

Again, this is still not faith; it is only a personal recognition of one's own *obligation* in the face of this external proof of the fact of revelation. However, since this involves a positive step toward faith, the authors will generally hold that this practical judgment of credibility cannot be formulated apart from the actual graces given by God for that purpose. With good reason, Alfaro describes this judgment as the necessary meeting point of grace and reason;

if God had *de facto* given no grace previously, it would be absolutely necessary at this point so that this practical judgment might
be made. Hence he also notes that psychologically, this is "the last
point in the total process of faith in which reason, and, through
it, the signs of credibility make their presence known. . . ."[18] The
conclusion reached by reason alone still exercises its influence in
this act (the conclusion expressed, that is, in the speculative judgment of credibility); beyond this point, however, the intellect is
moved supernaturally by the authority of God alone which it
perceives under the graces leading to faith and under the grace
of faith itself.

We must note that when we come to discuss the speculative
and practical judgment of credibility, we are slowly passing into
the field of freely disputed questions in Catholic theology. While
all agree that the distinction between the two must be made,
there are different opinions concerning above all the psychological
influence of the signs and of these conclusions in the act of faith
itself.[19] What we present here is the approach that seems best to
us; we will return shortly to a more detailed discussion of the
point.

4. THE LAST PRACTICAL JUDGMENT

Since the act of faith is an act of the intellect, but also a free
act, there must be a final judgment of the individual that we
can express in these terms: "I now choose to elicit an act of faith."
This judgment is obviously a result of the working of grace, with
which the individual has cooperated. This judgment is made only
with the help of divine grace. By a supernatural illumination the
intellect perceives the authority of God revealing, and if an individual freely cooperates with the grace being offered by God,
this final practical judgment is made. The will, acting under the
inspiration of grace, then puts this practical judgment into effect
by moving the intellect to assent to the truth of revelation. Then
only do we have the act of faith itself: "An act of the intellect
assenting to divine truth under the command of the will moved
by God through grace."

It is at this very point that man personally encounters God and commits himself to the way of life outlined in God's revelation. In his perception of the divine authority as the sole motive of faith, man — in a completely personal and individual act — accepts this new relationship to God which has been brought about through Christ and His redemptive activity. Thus he enters into a new way of life entirely, a supernaturalized existence. Faith has opened up to him a full understanding of himself, his destiny and the world in which he lives. It is for this reason that the Council of Trent states that faith is the "foundation and source of all justification."[20] It is the starting place for man's personal encounter with God; apart from it, there can be no permanent supernatural life whatsoever. Even when man has lost sanctifying grace (and charity), and even when he may have lost the infused virtue of hope, he still can retain this basic contact with the world of the supernatural through faith.

In this way, the act of faith, while it involves the action of grace and the free cooperation of the human will, nevertheless remains essentially an act of the intellect. It is entirely supernatural, and rests solely on the authority of God revealing and not upon any purely rational judgments. Thus we can see the manner in which the certitude of faith surpasses the moral certitude of the judgment of credibility. So also can we see how the certitude of faith is identical in each individual who believes supernaturally, despite the wide difference in intellectual capacity in men and their greater or lesser acquaintance with the signs of credibility and the rational process of investigation associated with them. In all cases, the assent of faith rests on the authority of God revealing, and it is from this that its infallible certitude is derived. This remains the same in the child of ten, the untutored grandmother, the professional theologian, and the Roman Pontiff himself.

THE ASSENT OF FAITH

In regard to the assent of faith, there are many matters which are freely disputed, despite the overall agreement on the points mentioned above. Today all necessarily teach that Christian faith, which is a saving faith, must be supernatural. This is a question long since defined by the Church in her disputes with the Pelagians and the Semi-Pelagians, and repeated both in the Council of Trent and Vatican I.[21] Faith can never be explained as a purely human and rational act, the result of a simple syllogistic type of reasoning, independent of grace.

Accordingly, the act of faith must be defended as at least *entitatively* supernatural, that is, supernatural *quoad substantiam;* various terms are used to describe this concept. What is meant is that the act of faith, precisely as a saving act, must be supernaturalized and thus exceed entirely the natural powers of the creature. Apart from the supernatural grace of God whereby the act of faith is elevated to this supernatural level, a saving act of faith could not exist at all; it is at least this entitative elevation that renders it a saving act.

There is a dispute among theologians, however, as to whether the supernaturalness of faith is explained sufficiently well on the basis of this entitative elevation, or whether the grace of faith has an added effect in the psychological order as well. The general answers can be reduced to two more or less basic schools of thought, although there are many minor variations in the different authors.

NO PSYCHOLOGICAL EFFECT

One school, strongly influenced of late by the teaching of Cardinal Billot, holds that there is no special psychological effect added to the entitative (or merely ontological) effects of the grace of faith.[22] Thus, psychologically speaking, the assent of faith — precisely as an assent rather than as a saving act — is merely a human and rational act. It becomes a saving act only because it has been supernaturalized through grace, and thus grace is the ultimate elicitive principle of this assent *in the supernatural order;* but this means simply that the act of assent has been raised up, elevated to a higher and supernatural level. What is, psychologically speaking, no different from a purely rational assent is now rendered a saving act by this supernatural elevation on the entitative (or ontological) level. In other words, these theologians contend that the supernaturality of the act of faith is sufficiently explained by saying that the act proceeds from a supernatural source in this manner; but they reject the need of any distinct psychological influence effected by the grace of faith. They do not necessarily deny that such an influence could be present, but simply hold that it is not necessary.[23]

Along with this, these theologians introduce the notion of a "natural faith" or "scientific faith," as they call it. This is described as this same psychological assent of faith when elicited *apart* from the supernatural grace of God; it is the act of faith when not entitatively supernaturalized. In both a saving faith and a scientific faith, the psychological motive for the assent is identical; in both instances, it is the authority of God revealing, perceived in a purely natural fashion. Thus an act of scientific faith is described by de Aldama as an act "whose motive is the authority of God revealing, but whose elicitive principle is the intellect alone, joined to the natural *concursus of God*."[24] A *saving* act of faith, on the other hand, has as an elicitive principle not only the intellect, but also the supernatural grace of faith, which is the ultimate elicitive principle in that order. These authors distinguish the saving act of faith from a scientific faith in this way only. They do not today demand any scientific faith as a *sine qua non* for supernatural faith, but simply urge the possibility of such a purely natural act, apart from grace. Precisely as an assent, it does not differ from a saving act in any manner.

Lercher-Schlagenhaufen also defend this position. They hold that the act of faith, considered "as a vital act and therefore as a rational act," can be logically resolved beyond the authority of God revealing, so that "the resolution of the act of faith can be made in syllogistic form in this manner: 'Whatever God reveals is true. But God has revealed that He is triune. Therefore (I believe) God is triune.' "[25]

Against those who hold that the grace of faith has a psychological effect, Lercher-Schlagenhaufen argue that the reasonableness of faith would be lost if the individual simply believed not only the doctrine revealed but also the authority of God revealing (as perceived, according to these others, in a supernatural manner through grace). They hold that the motives of credibility (the speculative and practical judgments of credibility) not only serve to assure the reasonableness of the act of faith itself, but that they enter into the very nature of the act of faith: "Thus the motives of credibility . . . are motives of the act of faith itself."[26]

Lennerz is another example of this line of thought; he defends basically the same position in these words: "The act of faith insofar as it is an intellectual assent, is resolved as in its internal motive in the sole authority of God revealing, known certainly but not by divine faith."[27] Even in supernatural faith man does not believe the authority of God; this is something known by reason alone. Lennerz introduces another concept by which he would show that this does not make the assent of faith rest on a purely human type of reasoning. He distinguishes between a syllogism that would lead to scientific faith and that with which he is immediately concerned; the distinction, however, is somewhat difficult to grasp. In supernatural faith, he claims, there is a special element that does not enter into scientific faith, namely the desire to do what God has commanded. There is, nevertheless, a reasoning process involved in supernatural faith; Lennerz explains it in this fashion:

> It is certain that I can believe (with just as much firmness as there is *authority* itself in the witness) that which a knowing and truthful witness testifies. But: it is certain that God is a witness of *supreme authority,* who can neither deceive nor be deceived, and that He has revealed that He is triune. Therefore: it is certain that I can believe with an assent firm beyond all others that God is triune because of the *supreme authority* of God revealing.[28]

According to Lennerz, the assent to this conclusion is still not the assent of supernatural faith; it represents merely the knowledge that the assent of faith is both possible and right. Moreover, this type of syllogism must be distinguished from the syllogism which leads to a purely scientific faith, which is expressed as follows: "That to which a knowing and truthful witness testifies is true;

but God is a knowing and truthful witness who testifies that He is triune; therefore, God is triune."[29] Actually, there seems to be no basic difference here at all. Lennerz insists, however, that in order to have supernatural faith, a totally distinct element must be present; the individual must know that the assent of faith has been *commanded* by God. Therefore, when describing supernatural faith, he emphasizes the concept of "supreme authority" (although this notion of supreme authority would necessarily seem to be present in his syllogism associated with "scientific faith"; anyone who knows who and what God is, perceives this supreme authority, even though it not be expressed in so many words in the syllogism).

Following this line of argumentation, however, Lennerz asserts that the *will* acts freely to command the assent of faith, motivated by the good perceived in the performance by the intellect of a possible and righteous act that has thus been commanded by God. The will commands an assent, in other words, that is proportioned to the authority of God as perceived by man, and the intellect accordingly elicits this act: it believes the truth proclaimed on the authority of God revealing.[30]

In Lennerz' theory, this assent of faith is supposedly not proportioned to the certitude by which the authority of God is known (that is, by reason); the firmness of the assent would be proportioned to the infinite value of the motive itself: God's supreme authority commanding the assent. Thus Lennerz looks upon the assent of supernatural faith as the strongest of all assents, one which differs from that of scientific faith because of this precise element of doing what God has commanded.[31]

It is difficult, however, to see just how the human assent in this theory really differs from that of purely scientific faith, and how the assent becomes so strong since it is, ultimately, a human judgment. According to Lennerz, man perceives God's supreme authority and His command to believe by the use of his human reason, which also declares that God's authority is of so high a value that when one obeys His command to believe, his faith is necessarily such as would possess the absolute certitude associated with faith. All of this, however, presupposes the metaphysical proofs for the existence of God, and (in regard to Christian revelation) the historical proofs concerning what God has revealed. Yet, if the knowledge of these truths is to be based only on historical and rational proof, the question remains as to precisely how the assent of supernatural faith acquires this absolute certitude beyond the level of even metaphysical certitude, not to mention moral certitude (of which historical certitude is generally admitted to be a species).[32]

De Aldama falls into this same difficulty in his defense of the more recent theory of faith, holding that the assent of saving faith, as distinguished from that of scientific faith, is not present until the *will commands* the intellect to assent. The motive for the act of the will is the "goodness (*bonitas*) which is had in the submission of the intellect and will to God, the Creator and our final end."[33]

This response, however, both places the distinguishing characteristic of supernatural faith in an act of the will, and still leaves the nature of the certitude of the assent unaltered: it is the certitude proper to some form of rational conclusion.

These authors are following the general position of Billot, who argues especially against the teaching of Suarez and de Lugo.[34] Billot contends that human reason can, of itself, attain the object of the supernatural virtues. He strongly defends the possibility of a "scientific" or "natural" faith:

> Nevertheless, if we presuppose the external grace of revelation as once being given, the aforesaid objects [of faith] can be grasped by a natural act, that is, by an act elicited by natural powers alone, if at least the physical power of the nature itself be considered. However [this is not done] in that manner which would be efficacious in leading one to the possession of that good towards which they are directed.[35]

For Billot, a truly "saving faith" involves something more, but this "something" is effective solely on the entitative or ontological level. Viewed in relationship to certitude, the certitude of a saving act of faith is identical, no more and no less, than that of a "natural" or "scientific" act of faith.[36] As in all the other theories, however, this approach leaves the certitude of faith in the rational and historical order — less even than metaphysical certitude, since the type of reasoning process involved includes a great deal of historical data, thus limiting the conclusions to the area of moral (historical) certitude.

The classic objection of the Thomist-Suarezian schools of thought against all of these more recent theories has been based on the axiom that "acts are specified by their formal object," so that an act which would assent to supernatural truths (the formal object) would have to be, even psychologically speaking, a specifically different act from that associated with any purely human or scientific faith. Quite apart from this, however, there is a further question of certitude and the manner in which Christian faith, as a saving act, achieves the absolute certainty required of faith. Today's great concern with historical studies and the nature of certitude have made of this an even more telling argument.

There is no claim that these post-Cartesian theories fail to answer the demands of II Orange and Trent that in order to believe "as is required" (*sicut oportet*), man needs the grace of God.[37] These theories all admit this; the discussion concerns solely the extent to which the grace of faith effects the individual believer. Is it purely entitative, or does it include as well a psychological effect which makes the act of faith itself possible?

A PSYCHOLOGICAL EFFECT

The second school of thought is that defended in general by the Thomists, by Suarez, Vasquez, and in our own times by an ever increasing number of theologians throughout the world.[38] Writing in the revised edition of the *Lexikon für Theologie und Kirche,* Josef Trütsch asks the question whether the act of faith is supernatural even in its intentional aspect and thus is to be distinguished from an act of natural or scientific faith. His response is that "the affirmative answer alone will do justice to the realism of grace; the grace of faith fulfills its function in the intellect as the light of faith, and in the will as 'inspiratio fidei.' "[39]

This opinion, which we prefer to the first, is really a line of thought more ancient in the history of Catholic theology. The first system outlined above is largely rationalistic in its approach, and has resulted from the ill-advised attempt to "meet the adversary on his own terms." With the rise of deism and rationalism in the post-Cartesian era, these explanations of faith began to appear as an attempt to present faith in a manner pleasing to the deists and rationalists.

This second, and older opinion, holds that the supernaturality of faith is not sufficiently explained by an entitative elevation of a psychologically natural act to the supernatural level; it demands *in addition* a psychological influence of the grace of faith which makes the act of faith not only supernatural entitatively, but simply makes such an intellectual assent psychologically *possible*. Without this grace, there can be no assent to the authority of God revealing; the notion of a so-called natural or scientific faith is rejected entirely.

Ultimately, in the act of faith itself, the motive for believing is the authority of God revealing. Since both the doctrine which God reveals and the fact that He is revealing are perceived supernaturally, the assent of faith is supernatural on both the entitative and the psychological level. Moreover, since the truth of revelation is always contained in some created and visible testimony, chiefly the Church with its two sources of revelation — Scripture and tradition — there are those theologians who rightly affirm that this authority of God revealing (which is perceived supernaturally, and which serves as the ultimate motive of faith) will include in itself the visible and created testimony through which God speaks. The "authority of God revealing," therefore, involves two intimately related elements: the eternal authority of God Himself, and the created testimony of His Church upon earth, through which He speaks to man. In this way, the created testimony does not enter into the act of faith as an unrelated element, nor as something known only by reason, nor much less as an obstacle of some sort, standing between God and the believer. This created testimony of God's speaking must be conceived as an integral part of the one and only motive of faith perceived by grace: the authority of God revealing. Hence this created testimony is also *believed* by the grace of faith as an essential element of the authority of God revealing, joined to this authority as an expression of the uncreated and eternal testimony of God Himself.[40]

In this way, the act of faith on the part of the individual believer is always an essentially personal encounter with God, and one accomplished entirely on the supernatural level. The Christian message — the *kerygma* — is essential to this note of faith, but it is something living and vital, rooted within the life of the Church and its divinely guided magisterium; it is not something of the far distant past, pertaining to the apostolic era alone and given expression in Scripture, so that the believer comes in contact with it solely by a process of exegetical and historical study. This Christian message is proclaimed at all times and in all places by the voice of God, speaking through the magisterium of His Church — the Mystical Body of Christ, by which both Christ and His saving message are extended in time and space.[41]

THE REASONABLENESS OF FAITH

The motives of credibility, according to this approach, are known by reason (or are at least knowable by reason)[42] and can thus establish the reasonableness of the act of faith; but these motives do not enter into the act of faith itself. The supernaturalness of faith touches not only upon the object of faith (the supernatural mysteries), and the virtue of faith as an elicitive principle which supernaturalizes a psychologically natural act, but it extends also to both the act and the motive of faith — the authority of God revealing, and the created testimony associated with this — which is thus believed no less than the object itself.

By enabling the intellect to perceive supernaturally the motive for believing these truths, the grace of faith opens up a motive specifically distinct from what could be known by reason alone. Even as a psychological act of assent, the *act* of faith is specifically distinct from any purely rational assent; there is no psychological possibility of what these other authors call a natural or scientific faith. Without this grace, an individual can know "what" the believer accepts, but he himself is totally incapable of assenting to it even on a purely natural or scientific level. It has no personal import or meaning for him, even though he understands clearly the doctrines of Christian faith and the ramifications of those truths.

At the same time, this act of faith is entirely in accord with human reason, since the *fact* of the reasonableness of faith continues to rest on the judgment of credibility which in itself is capable of being formed by human reason apart from grace. It is for this reason that above we noted the statement of Alfaro to the effect that, in the genesis of faith, man could, theoretically, proceed as far as the speculative judgment of credibility without grace, acting solely with the powers of human reason and the evidence available to it. The practical judgment of credibility would, however, be the necessary meeting place of reason and grace; without a special actual grace, this particular judgment could not be made. At the same time, this is "the last point in the total process of faith in which reason, and, through it, the signs of credibility make their presence known. . . ."[43] When man goes on to believe, he acts solely on the basis of this supernaturally perceived motive. He leaps beyond the realm of reason, of rational and historical proof, and roots his faith on the unfailing authority of God Himself as perceived, through the light of faith, in both God Himself and in His Church upon earth which continually proclaims this message for the acceptance of the believer.

It is this approach alone, we feel, that can adequately explain the Catholic concept of faith. In its further applications, it does much to clarify the topics mentioned at the beginning of this chapter: the relationship between Scripture and tradition, the concept of theological method, the problems of teaching religion and of preaching, the question of how to make faith a more personal and vital reality in the life of the individual. It does much to emphasize as well the manner in which the Catholic notion of faith differs essentially from that accepted by many present-day, nonfundamentalist Protestants for whom faith in the Christian revelation must be approached through a scholarly technique, and — as for Ebeling — through a use of the historical method alone, which is the logical development of the Reformation principle of *Scriptura sola,* and which becomes the sole means of coming in contact with the truth found in Scripture and of understanding properly the meaning of that text in terms of what God actually has revealed.[44]

For the Catholic, the phrase "I believe in the Church" implies his perception of the divine life of that Church and the ever present guidance of the Holy Spirit within that body, assuring a total identification between the faith and teaching of the present-day Church and that of the primitive era, despite any further clarifications throughout the centuries. It is in this total complex of divinely guided realities within the visible and hierarchical Church on earth that is achieved that often-quoted axiom of St. Vincent Lerins: "In ipsa item catholica ecclesia magnopere curandum est ut id teneamus, *quod ubique, quod semper, quod ab omnibus creditum est.*"[45] And it is in this total complex that these other words of this same sainted writer, which Vatican I made its own, bestowing upon them its conciliar authority, acquire their true and full meaning:

> Therefore, let the understanding, knowledge and wisdom grow and progress greatly and forcefully, both in single individuals and in all, in each man as well as in the whole Church, through the course of ages and centuries: but only within its own realm, that is, with the same doctrine, the same significance and the same teaching.[46]

CHAPTER IV

Unwritten Traditions at Trent

In the fourth session of the Council of Trent, it was decreed that the Gospel of the New Testament was originally promised by the prophets in the Old Testament Scriptures, and was first actually preached by Christ Himself who then ordered His Apostles — as the source both of all saving truth and all training in regard to disciplinary and liturgical practices (*mores*)[1] — to go forth and preach this Gospel truth to all mankind. Moreover, the Council pointed out that this "truth and discipline is contained in the written books and in the unwritten traditions which (having been received by the apostles from the lips of Christ Himself, or from the apostles themselves [acting] under the inspiration of the Holy Spirit), have come down to us, handed on, as it were, from hand to hand. . . ."[2]

These phrases indicate the general line of thought followed by the bishops at the fourth session of Trent. For them, not everything pertaining to the New Testament was necessarily preached verbally by Christ Himself; part of it was also given to mankind by the Apostles, acting under the guidance of the Holy Spirit. In this we see the importance of the primitive Church in regard to the New Testament revelation, as implied at Trent. It was in this era that the public revelation was completed. The giving of this revelation, therefore, pertained to the entire era of the primitive Church was not not limited merely to those years when Christ Himself dwelt upon this earth. It was continued even after the Ascension of Christ into heaven. This is a truth generally described in Catholic theology by the phrase that "revelation ended only with the death of the last Apostle."

Our present concern, however, is chiefly with the phrase "unwritten traditions." In the Latin we read: "hanc veritatem et disciplinam contineri in libris scriptis *et sine scripto traditionibus.*
. . ." Only too easily some may have assumed that the phrase indicates that there were certain things revealed to the primitive Church which were never written down at all. Unfortunately, this was not the meaning attached to the phrase by the Council of Trent itself. Trent was faced with the Protestant principle of *Scriptura sola,* and it answered by stating that there *are* other things which must be taken into account when discussing revelation besides the inspired books of the Bible. It is this that is indicated by the phrase *sine scripto traditionibus.* It refers to matters concerned with Christian revelation which were not contained explicitly *in the canonical books of the New Testament.* For this reason the phrase "unwritten traditions" means more precisely "traditions not written down *in the inspired scriptures,*" although they may well have been written down any number of times in noncanonical sources.

The distinction here lies merely between that which is clearly contained in the Scriptures — *in libris scriptis* — and that which also pertains to revelation, but is not to be found expressly in the inspired books: *nonscriptae traditiones.* At the same time, it is well to note that in the sixteenth century in general as well as at the Council of Trent, the word *traditiones* had a more comprehensive meaning than we might associate with it at present. It was not limited merely to "dogmatic truths" or "dogmatic traditions" but included as well a large number of purely ceremonial or liturgical practices which were accepted in the Church but which could not be found in Scripture; these were also considered to pertain to Christian revelation, even though they were not written down in Scripture.[3]

In regard to strictly dogmatic truths, however, we may well have to adopt a slightly different point of view to understand the theology of this period and the decree of Trent. We find in these writings a far more intimate union of Scripture and tradition than we frequently express today, and it is only by taking into consid-

eration *both* elements — the scriptural and the extrascriptural —
that the fullness of Christian revelation can be understood according to Trent. Thus there is a constant stress upon that which is
or is not *clearly* or *expressly* stated in Scripture, as well as the statements of some that *everything necessary for salvation* — all dogmatic truths — are "somehow" contained in Scripture, even though
by no express terms. Thus the phrase "sine scripto traditionibus"
would not be well translated as "nonscriptural traditions," since
it would tend to pass over this other facet of Tridentine thought.
The decree of the fourth session of Trent is intended as a direct
denial of the basic principle of sixteenth century Protestantism that
"Scripture alone" sufficed, and that "I and my Bible" would be
all that could possibly be required in order to know the full truth
revealed in the New Testament era.[4]

DISCUSSIONS AT TRENT

In February, 1546, the Council began to discuss the decree on
Scripture and tradition. Debate varied between the general congregations, including all the bishops, and the meetings of three
particular groups (called the *classes*), each one presided over by
one of the three cardinal Legates (Giovanni Maria del Monte,
Marcello Cervini, and Reginald Pole). In this way the discussions
were handled more easily in the smaller groups, limiting the work
of the general congregations to the most important matters and
the taking of votes.

On February 11, a statement was distributed to the bishops at
the various *classes*, indicating that they would now begin to draw
up a decree accepting the books of Sacred Scripture and that such
a decree should also make mention of the fact that "besides the
scriptures of the New Testament, we have the traditions of the
apostles. . . . "[5] This use of the plural —*traditiones* — rather than
the singular when referring to these matters represents the usual
manner of speech at Trent; in the minds of those who issued the
decree, the apostolic traditions were specific things which could be
enumerated, should one choose to do so.[6] They were considered
to pertain to divine revelation no less than the matters expressly

noted in Scripture. This approach is summed up in a letter of the cardinal legates written that same day to Cardinal Allessandro Farnese in Rome, informing the Pope of their intentions. By accepting both Scripture and these traditions, they wrote, the Council would oppose adequately the contention of those who held that if "such a thing is not found in Scripture, therefore it is not true."[7]

Once more, at the general congregation the following day (the 12th), Cardinal del Monte pointed out to the entire group that, as they knew, our faith comes from divine revelation, and that this revelation has been handed down to us by the Church "partly from the scriptures which are in the Old and the New Testament, partly also from a simple handing-down by hand [*ex simplici traditione per manus*]."[8] Perhaps this would be the first use at the Council of the *partim . . . partim* phrase which eventually found its way into the first version proposed for the decree. Considering the expressions used at this time, however, del Monte appears to indicate nothing more than what is stated elsewhere, that is, that contrary to the statements of the Reformers, Scripture alone does not suffice for the preservation and understanding of divine revelation.

In the discussions which took place in the *classes* on February 18, a number of the bishops repeated this same line of thought, pointing out that these various traditions were equal in importance to what is contained in Scripture. In the group meeting with Cardinal Cervini, Pietro Bertano, the Bishop of Fano, gave as the reason for this the fact that they "were dictated by the same Holy Spirit as were the Scriptures."[9] In his summary of their discussions, Cervini pointed out once again that these traditions do not differ from the books of Sacred Scripture except that Scripture is written and traditions are not, but they both come from the same Spirit.[10] In Cervini's discussion we may note a clear delineation of the various steps involved in the promulgation of the New Testament revelation; it is, in reality, the Tridentine equivalent of the "Gospel before the gospels" so emphasized by form critics at the present time. The accounts of his statements differ verbally between the

Acta and the *Diary III* of Massarelli,[11] but substantially they are the same. Massarelli was present at the *classis* presided over by Cervini, although he had not as yet been named secretary of the Council (this occurred on April 1). Because of this, the version given by Massarelli in the *Diary III* may possibly represent a more detailed account, shortened for inclusion in the *Acta.*[12]

Cervini singles out three bases or foundations for Catholic faith: *first,* the revelation itself (both in the Old and the New Testaments), which was perfected by Christ "who planted His gospel not in writing, but orally; not on paper, but in the heart . . ."[13] *Second,* there is a twofold principle — what we would call Scripture and tradition: "Of those things which proceeded from Christ, some were committed to scripture, some were left in the hearts of men. . . ."[14] *Third,* since the Son of Man was not to remain with us forever, the Holy Spirit was sent into the world; He would "declare the secrets of God and those things which were doubtful among men."[15]

In the account given in the *Acta,* Massarelli has simplified this thought somewhat, listing as the three principles the sacred books, the Gospel, and the Holy Spirit. In regard to the Gospel, he emphasizes even more clearly that this means "the gospel which Christ Our Lord did not write but which He taught verbally and which He implanted in the hearts [of His followers]; later the evangelists committed some of this gospel to writing, but many things were also left in the hearts of men."[16] Moreover, in the *Acta* the role of the Holy Spirit is also emphasized as an enduring task; the Pentecostal role of the Paraclete in "teaching" and "bringing to mind" all that Christ had said would not be accomplished in a day, but would continue until the end of time:

> *Third,* since the Son of God was not to remain with us bodily forever, He sent the Holy Spirit who would reveal the secrets of God in the hearts of men and daily until the end of the world would teach the Church all truth, and who would clarify [*declararet*] matters if something doubtful should occur to the minds of men.[17]

In this presentation we can see the overall concept of the Gospel as a vital reality, existing as such long before the actual writing of the canonical scriptures; this was a common enough position in sixteenth-century Catholic apologetes.[18] In the ever present guidance of the Holy Spirit — "daily until the end of the world" — we can also note the beginnings of that concept of a *living tradition* which would be evolved so much more completely in later centuries, especially during the era of Romanticism.[19] This, coupled with the Tridentine notion of the New Testament revelation being completed in its essentials during the life of the Apostles,[20] also gives some basis for the distinction emphasized in 1931 by Deneffe between "constitutive" and "continuative" tradition: *constitutive* tradition referring to the teaching and faith of the primitive Church (the Church until the death of the last Apostle), through which Christian revelation was completed and constituted, to be handed down to later generations; and *continuative* (or conservative) tradition referring to the preservation and clarification of this original deposit of revelation by the Church in postapostolic times, acting under the ever present guidance of the Holy Spirit.[21]

LIST OF AUTHORITIES

On February 20, the so-called "minor theologians" (that is, those professional theologians who attended the Council in order to give advice to the individual bishops — the "major theologians") met and discussed this general problem and on the 23rd, the three *classes* met once again under the three cardinal legates. The legates each related the opinions of the minor theologians at these gatherings, noting how they agreed that both the books of Scripture and the apostolic traditions ought to be included in the same decree. It was also announced that a committee of six bishops would be named to draw up the actual decree to be submitted to the General Congregation for its consideration; nominations were made during these meetings.

Following this, a list of "authorities" was read by which testimony both from Scripture and the early writers of the Church was adduced to show that there are these apostolic traditions in the Church, and that they should accordingly be accepted together with the canonical books of Scripture in the forthcoming decree.

As might be expected, the scriptural texts cited are those which indicate that there were other things the Apostles had taught apart from their writings, or that they promised to teach on a later visit; or those which stress that the truth of God is written primarily on the hearts of men rather than on parchment.[22] In these passages, one could see the emphasis on the need of something beyond Scripture in order to know the fullness of God's revelation.

Following these, there are brief quotations from Pseudo-Dionysius, St. Irenaeus, Serapion of Antioch, Origen, Epiphanius, Tertullian, St. Cyprian, St. Basil, St. Jerome, and St. Augustine,[23] as well as two sections of the Decree of Gratian[24] and the decree, *Cum Marthae,* of Pope Innocent III.[25] In general, we find here the various texts usually noted in any Catholic presentation of the existence of tradition as something necessary beyond Scripture.

In all of these citations, therefore, the same theme recurs over and again: the fact that the Protestant principle of *"Scriptura sola"* does not suffice, but that we must have recourse to that which was not included in the canonical books of the New Testament — the "unwritten" element of Christian revelation.

A rather free citation from *De ecclesiastica hierarchia* of Pseudo-Dionysius includes the phrase *partim . . . partim* in regard to the sources of revelation; it is the phrase later encountered in the first version suggested for the decree of the fourth session.[26] The quotations from St. Basil include the phrase *par . . . pietatis debetur affectus,* which almost certainly influenced the formulation of the decree which uses these very words.[27] Similarly, in the passages taken from Origen and Tertullian, we may note the inclusion among the apostolic traditions of those same liturgical and disciplinary practices which recur frequently in the official discussions of the bishops at Trent: prayer toward the East, genuflections while praying, the threefold immersion at baptism, and the like.[28] All of this undoubtedly helped influence the minds of the bishops and prepared, in a way, for their later discussions. At the same time, a list such as this undoubtedly represents the mentality apparent in the theological teaching of the sixteenth century such as the bishops had received and which appears in other writings of this period of history.

In the report in the *Acta* concerning the discussions held on February 23, this same line of thought is repeated. Claude Lejay, S.J., the procurator for the bishop of Augsburg, suggested a distinction between those traditions which refer to faith and those which concern such disciplinary questions as the abstention from blood and similar matters mentioned in the *Acts of the Apostles*.[29] Girolamo Seripando, the General of the Augustinians, approved of this distinction,[30] but apart from his statement, the distinction itself does not seem to have had too great an influence on later discussion, nor did it apparently exclude these disciplinary and liturgical practices from the final decree. In the suggested formula, proposed on March 22, 1546, there is mention (in line 24 of the Görresgesellschaft edition) of the fact that the Apostles were to go out to preach, and that they were the norm (*regulam*) of all saving truth and discipline in regard both to saving truth and such disciplinary or liturgical customs or practices: *regulam omnis et salutaris veritatis et morum disciplinae. . . .*[31] In the light of the entire discussions at Trent, this seems to be the only possible adequate understanding of this particular phrase which was incorporated into the final decree with but one change: the word *regulam* was replaced by *fontem*.

MEANING OF "MORES"

Frequently the phrase *morum disciplinae* is translated "moral teaching" or something similar, but considering the mentality revealed in the *Acta* this is most likely reading something into the Council of Trent that does not actually appear there. Throughout the discussions, both before Lejay's suggestion on February 23 and until the day of the final decree, there was a great deal of emphasis upon "traditions" which do not at all pertain to moral teaching, but which are better described as purely disciplinary or liturgical practices. It was these which, along with matters more directly related to dogmatic questions, were to be accepted together with the books of Scripture. The precise relationship of these other more dogmatic questions to Scripture may still be a point for discussion, but throughout the fourth session there was practically no mention of what we today would term simply "moral principles."

Thus when Cardinal Cervini summed up the positions assumed at his *classis* on February 23, he noted that it would seem best at the present time to discuss the traditions in general, without attempting to specify any of them, since there "are many things both in regard to the essentials of faith and in regard to ceremonial matters [*quoad ceremonialia*], which are not written down but which are only handed down to us, as in the ceremonies of Lent, which can scarcely be proven from Scripture."[32] Thus, while he praised the distinction made by Lejay,[33] Cervini also went on to cite from the Decree of Gratian a passage from St. Basil's *De Spiritu Sancto* which enumerates a number of traditions not found in Scripture but which are largely disciplinary or liturgical in character.[34]

This same mentality is evident in the position ascribed by Severoli to Cardinal Reginald Pole. When speaking of the abuses both in regard to Scripture and the traditions, Pole pointed out that the abuses of Scripture touch on the manner of preaching the Word of God and interpreting the Sacred Books, but that the abuses in regard to the traditions concern "practically the entire ecclesiastical discipline. Indeed, our creeds and all our ceremonies fall back on those traditions."[35] In his use of the word "discipline" (*disciplina*), we may note a valuable indication of the meaning of the same word in the final decree of Trent. This use of the word to represent not only beliefs but also disciplinary and liturgical practices reflects the mentality not only of Cardinal Pole, but of the other bishops present at the discussions.

Eventually, on March 29, a number of questions were proposed to the bishops concerning changes to be made in the final decree. One of them (No. 7) asked if the words *quibus par debetur pietatis affectus* ought to remain in the decree or if they should be replaced by another phrase.[36] Behind this question there seems to be the objection voiced by some that the reverence due the traditions was different from that due Scripture: the bishop of Fano, Pietro Bertano, in particular, opposed the phrase.[37] Earlier it had already been made clear to the assembled bishops that the decree would speak only of those traditions which pertained to the primitive revelation and came to us from the Apostles; those "ecclesiastical traditions" which had been introduced later purely by the authority of the Church were to be treated elsewhere by the Council.[38] Moreover, in answer to earlier demands, the six bishops delegated to draw up the suggested decree[39] purposely included the phrase *traditiones quae . . . ad nos usque pervenerunt,* in order to eliminate from the decree those apostolic traditions which were only intended to be temporary and were later set aside by the Church.[40]

In answer to this question (No. 7), it appeared that the majority of the bishops preferred to have the words *par pietatis affectus* remain,[41] so that the following question (No. 8) is of equal interest. It asked whether, if these words were to remain untouched in the decree, the manner of speaking should be changed to distinguish between those traditions (both in Scripture and "unwritten" which referred to doctrine (*dogmata*) and those which referred to disciplinary practices (*mores.*)[42] In this instance, the majority were not concerned with the question at all. Eleven voted in favor of the distinction; eleven voted against it; and the rest, representing the majority, evidently did not think that there was any real problem here, since they had nothing at all to say.[43] Thus the final decree was not altered so as to limit traditions to dogmatic questions (or moral principles), but also accepted those apostolic traditions of disciplinary and liturgical nature which have come down to us from the primitive Church. A phrase was added in the final versions of the decree to indicate that there *were* traditions which pertained to faith, and others which pertained to these various customs (*tum ad fidem tum ad mores pertinentes*), but *all* were to be accepted along with the Scriptures. No further distinction was made, and no attempt was made to enumerate them. Both these traditions and the Sacred Books were to be accepted with the same reverential spirit: *pari pietatis affectu ac reverentia*. For the same reason, to the word *veritatem* was added the phrase *et disciplinam*, indicating that the truth of revelation and these various disciplinary and liturgical practices were not contained in Scripture alone, but also in the apostolic traditions.[44]

FURTHER DISCUSSIONS

Thus throughout the entire discussion, there is a constant return to the fundamental point that the Protestant principle of Scripture alone cannot be accepted by the Catholic Church. God had never intended that His divine revelation be given and understood through the written word alone, but joined to it an extrascriptural source which was equally important. As the cardinal legates pointed out in a letter to Cardinal Farnese on March 9, 1546, the unwritten traditions were being attacked most vehemently by the Protestants. In fact, they were attacking them more than anything else at all in order to try to establish their own principle that everything necessary for salvation was written (*era scritto*) — that is, in the inspired books alone.[45] This was quite in keeping, of course, with the Reformers' desire to eliminate the living magisterium from the concept of the Church entirely. The legates felt, therefore, that the establishment of this twofold basis of revealed truth was one of the most important things to be determined by the Council, since it touched on one of the points most controverted at that time.[46]

In the various sessions from February 23 (when the "Auctoritates" were read) until the final decree was approved, one bishop after another spoke in terms that would reemphasize this basic distinction between that which is found in Scripture (*scripta*) and that which has come down to us in a nonscriptural fashion (*non-scripta*). Cardinal Pacheco, the bishop of Jaén, noted that beyond (*ultra*) the sacred books, there are certain things which are not written.[47] Cardinal Cervini also gave as an example of the "unwritten traditions" the ceremonies of Lent, "which can scarcely be proved from the Scriptures."[48]

When speaking of the "unwritten traditions," Thomas Caselli, the bishop of Bertinoro, indicates clearly enough that some of them have been written down in nonscriptural books; he cites Cyprian as having written that the mixing of water with wine at Mass was one of those traditions. The phrase *non-scripta* again is used merely in contradistinction to that written in the canonical books.[49] The bishop of Fano, Bertano, is particularly clear in this regard, noting that if the Council accepts these traditions in order to establish her teaching, it will directly oppose the Protestant dictum that nothing ought to be received by the Church which is not found written in the sacred books. Thus he suggests a slightly different formula which he feels would express their minds more clearly and remove all difficulties: "Since this holy synod knows how many other things there are in the Church, dictated by the Holy Spirit, which have not appeared in the sacred books [*in sacris litteris*], it therefore also accepts and venerates these things."[50]

Another suggested formula, submitted by della Rovere, the bishop of Sinigaglia, is equally clear: "Besides the doctrine which is contained expressly in these sacred books mentioned above, we firmly believe and confess that there are in the Church traditions of Christ and the apostles, concerning both faith and customs [*moribus*], which have come down to us by continual succession. . . ."[51] So also the formula suggested by Enrico Loffredo, the bishop of Capaccio: "Besides those things which have been handed down to us in writing in the aforementioned books, there are also other traditions not written in the books already spoken of, which were either accepted by the Apostles from the lips of Christ Himself or were handed down by the Apostles themselves under the direction of the Holy Spirit."[52]

THE TRACTS

This same general line of thought is also revealed in the various *Tracts* included in the Görresgesellschaft edition of the *Acta* of Trent. While they are not a part of the official discussions, they do help to shed some further light on the minds of those who participated in these debates.

Tract 68, for example, expresses the views of Girolamo Seripando concerning traditions; it was probably written in February, 1546.[53] His opening phrase notes that traditions have always existed in the Church, and he describes these traditions as "sacred and saving ordinances [*constitutiones*] of the apostles or the holy fathers."[54] Some of these traditions were "written in the holy apostolic books," and are enumerated by Seripando.[55] Others, however, were not written in the canonical Scriptures, and these constitute the unwritten traditions; yet these also came from the apostles, as Tertullian and above all St. Augustine indicated.[56] As in the official discussions at the Council, the traditions enumerated here include both liturgical and disciplinary practices as well as matter pertaining more directly to dogmatic questions. Seripando also quotes the frequently cited passage from Augustine's letter to Januarius, noting that the passage shows that apart from the "Canonical Scriptures," there are in the Church two kinds of unwritten traditions: those which are *universally* held and are thus permanent; and those which pertained only to *individual,* local churches and are therefore subject to change. He is concerned, of course, with the first type only.[57]

The rest of the tract is, for the most part, a series of quotations from St. Augustine above all, intended to bolster his position. His final paragraph is especially interesting in that Seripando cites with approval a passage attributed to St. Augustine which teaches that all of the truths necessary for salvation are somehow contained in Scripture:

Lest the true religion and the hope of salvation be based on external traditions, we must consider those about which Augustine speaks: "Divine Scripture does not pass over in silence all of those things which pertain to seeking and adhering to the true religion. Moreover, although the Lord Jesus did many things, not all of them have been written down, as John the Evangelist testifies that the Lord Christ both said and did many things which have not been written; those things were chosen to be written [in Scripture], however, which seemed to suffice for the salvation of those who believe."[58]

In a treatise which dwells at length on the existence of traditions not contained in Scripture, this position might at first glance seem to involve a contradiction. It represents, however, a line of thought that has been found in other sixteenth-century theologians; it was expressed most clearly by John Driedo.[59] In answer to the Protestant emphasis upon *Scriptura sola,* these theologians respond in a manner that would emphasize the exaggeration of that principle by the Reformers, who would make of Scripture a totally independent, self-contained source of revelation which would be so crystal-clear in itself that it would need no living magisterium as an interpreter, and which would be so absolutely complete as to justify the rejection of anything else — any "traditions" — not *expressly* contained in the inspired books.

On the other hand, as reflected here in the words of Seripando, these controversial theologians before and at the time of Trent entertained a high regard for Scripture. For them the Bible is *the* inspired basis for the Church's belief. Thus they insist that Scripture does contain all that is necessary for salvation, but they limit this in two ways:

First, it would apply only to doctrinal matters: questions of faith, properly speaking, which would "suffice for the salvation of those who believe." They would readily admit that there is no scriptural basis for some of the disciplinary and liturgical practices accepted by the Church.

Second, even granting this, these theologians would insist that it is absolutely necessary that Scripture be understood and unfolded in the life of the divinely guided Church. Here alone can the full content of what has been written in the inspired books come to light. This cannot be understood as a mere question of exegesis. These sixteenth-century theologians proposed a far more intimate intertwining of Scripture and the Church than would be possible in the light of later developments in theological thought which became overly dependent upon purely rationalistic or historical techniques.

The Church is absolutely necessary for the proper unfolding and clarification of Scripture itself, as well as for the preservation of those other disciplinary and liturgical customs not mentioned in Scripture but handed down from the time of the Apostles,[60]

IN SCRIPTURE "APERTE ET EXPRESSE"

The author of Tract 69 has tentatively been identified as Claude Lejay, although the editor of the tracts, Vinzenz Schweitzer, doubts this.[61] The line of thought, nevertheless, is very typical of the sixteenth-century theologians. The author begins by emphasizing that the Catholics do not by any means replace the authority of Scripture with the authority of the Church, as the Reformers occasionally charged. For the Catholic, there is a faith "written on the hearts of men" within the Church; this is, however, the work of the same God who is the principal Author of Scripture. He also speaks, in effect, of the Gospel before the gospels, that is, this truth rooted in the hearts of those who formed the Church even before the New Testament Scriptures were written.[62]

At the same time, the author notes that "the Church knows of many truths pertaining both to faith and morals which scripture does not contain *openly* and *expressly*."[63] Here again, in his enumeration of those matters which pertain to "faith and morals," he mentions both dogmatic truths and disciplinary or liturgical practices. In his editorial note, Schweitzer wrongly criticizes the author for listing these various practices.[64] In point of fact, the author was simply giving expression to the overall point of view among theologians of a Tridentine era for whom "apostolic traditions" meant things of both a doctrinal as well as a more disciplinary nature. Moreover, the author does actually distinguish between dogmatic truths and disciplinary practices; he does not confuse them, as Schweitzer implies. Yet for him, as for the decree of Trent itself, those disciplinary practices "which have come down to us" and have not been changed must be considered as representative of the true apostolic tradition.

Another point may be noted about the original passage from this tract cited above, that is, the emphasis on what is or is not contained "openly and expressly" (*aperte et expresse*) in Scripture. This same viewpoint is repeated when the author speaks of the General Councils within the Church: "Indeed," he states, "in the general councils, the Holy Spirit revealed to the Church, according to the need of the times, many truths which are not contained openly [*aperte*] in the canonical books."[65] Such an approach, so common to those speaking and writing on this matter at the time of Trent, would not necessarily exclude the further notion that some such matters were contained implicitly, or at least insinuated, in Holy Scripture (in the manner proposed by Driedo in 1533).[66]

The use of the word "revealed" in this passage of Tract 69 must be understood in the light of the author's entire presentation. He is not speaking here of a "new revelation" in postapostolic times. Quite the contrary, he is concerned with the work of a divinely guided magisterium which gradually comes to understand more perfectly the original deposit of revelation. It is the belief in this supernatural quality of the magisterium which he would urge against the Protestant insistence on *Scriptura sola*. Thus he points out that, while Scripture does not use such words as "person, essence, trinity," when speaking of God, these terms are nevertheless legitimate, since they express in more precise terms the ultimate meaning of revelation as uncovered or revealed to the Church through the guidance of the Holy Spirit.[67]

This divinely guided authority of the magisterium is particularly stressed when the author speaks of disputes concerning the basic truths recorded in the Scriptures; the authority of both St. Augustine and St. Jerome is invoked in formulating this position:

> Moreover, since heresies have arisen from no other cause than from a false understanding of the scriptures, or — to use the words of St. Augustine — when the good scriptures are not well understood — what authority, I ask, in opposing the opinions concerning the same document can settle the dispute except the Church which, taught by the power of the Holy Spirit [*Spiritus sancti magisterio edocta*], comprehends that very truth which the context of the document signifies.
>
> Nor is it to be thought that the gospel is present among all those who accept the four books of the gospels, as Jerome taught most forcefully in his preface to the Epistles to the Galatians. "Marcion and Basilides," he said, "and the other plagues of heretics do not possess the gospel of God because they do not have the Holy Spirit, without Whom the gospel which is taught becomes human. We do not consider that the gospel rests in

the words of the scriptures, but in the sense; not on the surface
but in the marrow of the bones; not in the pages of discourses,
but in the root of the discourse."[68]

In this passage we can detect the deep respect for the living
magisterium of the Church which underlies the thought of this
author. He defends four elements above all: (1) Scripture, properly understood; (2) the traditions of the Apostles; (3) the definitions of the apostolic see and the sacred councils; and (4) the
concordant teaching of the holy fathers and doctors of the Church.[69]
He merely mentions this last element, but explains it no further.
Considering the time in which this was written, however, it would
not seem to indicate the more precise distinction between "fathers"
and "doctors" of the Church which first appeared only in a later
century.[70] Throughout the tract, however, the author is most insistent on pointing out that the decrees of the Popes and the General Councils are legitimate clarifications of the message of revelation. In a rather remarkable passage, he points out that the divinely guided magisterium is very much a truth of faith and a
supernatural mystery, so that the believer is able to see beyond
the human frailty of those who constitute the teaching authority
of the Church in order to perceive the divine power which sustains
their official decrees:

> The assistance of the Holy Spirit in legitimately convoked
> councils does not depend on the judgment, the holiness or the
> large number of bishops congregated there, but on the part of
> Christ and on His promise; just as neither the power of the
> sacraments comes from the sanctity of the minister, nor does
> the power of the Church come from the holiness of those who
> preside.
> One would insult the Holy Spirit and the Church which is
> ruled by His power [*magisterio*] were he to place in doubt those
> things once defined by the legitimately celebrated councils. Nor,
> as Innocent II stated, should it be considered reprehensible if,
> according to the diversity of times, human statutes are also
> changed, especially when urgent necessity and evident utility
> demand it, which we must understand in regard to those statutes
> concerning customs [*mores*]. In the matter of faith, however,
> and in defining dogmas there can be no change in the legitimate

councils, since all things are governed by the same Spirit of Truth. Indeed, it happens not rarely that one is given the graces of faith, wisdom and prophecy and thus teaches correctly, although he by no means possesses the Holy Spirit by Whom he is justified or the grace which renders him pleasing to God.[71]

ADDITIONAL CONSIDERATIONS

Tracts 70 and 71 merely repeat this same line of thought in slightly different words. The first of these, attributed to Angelus Paschalis, the bishop of Motula, emphasizes the fact that the Holy Spirit can guide the living magisterium just as well as He moved the human authors of Scripture to write the inspired books. Thus he who accepts the canonical books ought easily perceive, just as well, the voice of God when He speaks through the decrees of the Church.[72] Paschalis' principal argument for accepting the entire teaching of the Chuch as an expression of the Word of God is the fact that the Church must point out for us those books which are truly inspired. Apart from this, he insists, we would have nothing more than endless and insoluble doubts as to whether these were truly the canonical books or not. Thus he argues that if one is willing to accept this most basic teaching of the Church, why should he not go on to accept the entire doctrine of that same Church, even in regard to those matters for which there are no explicit passages in the Bible.[73]

Again, in contrasting the inspired books with these other traditions, Paschalis reflects the later decree of Trent by noting that there are many such matters "not written down in the canonical books" (. . . *scriptis minime fuerunt mandata*).[74] They may well have been written down elsewhere, but not in Scripture.

This same manner of speaking is evident in Tract 71, the author of which remains undetermined. He states, however, that there are many things which are not "contained *expressly* in sacred scripture," but which have come down to us from a continuous tradition, stemming from the Apostles and continued through their successors.[75] The author also speaks of the "unwritten traditions," such as mentioned by Trent, by quoting the words of Pseudo-

Dionysius. The divine revelation, he notes, is contained in two sources: one would be the "holy theological books" — that is, the Scriptures; the other would be a nonscriptural source — *sine litteris transfusa* — which has come down to us through the supernatural, living voice of the Church: *"alia, praeterea, quod ex animo in animum medio intercurrante verbo corporali quidem sed quod carnis sensus penitus excedat. . . ."*[76] This version of the citation from Pseudo-Dionysius also contains the phrase *partim . . . partim* which may have had some influence on the formulation of the originally suggested decree.[77] Yet the entire approach of the author is well summed up in these words; it is another statement concerning the Gospel before the gospels:

> And just as before the written gospels and the epistles of St. Paul there was the Church without any New Testament scripture, so it is of no consequence that many things have come down to us, not in writing [*non scripto*] but by the handing down of the fathers [*patrum traditione*]; nor does it follow, therefore, that sacred scripture would be imperfect, since it was by no means necessary that everything be handed down to us in the scriptures, since Our Saviour commanded His disciples: "Going therefore teach ye all nations: baptizing them in the name of the Father and of the Son and of the Holy Spirit," rather than write."[78]

TWO-SOURCE THEORY OF REVELATION

From all of this, we may justly conclude that at Trent very little more was stated except the basic principle that the position implied in the Protestant principle of *Scriptura sola* is unacceptable to Catholic teaching. The decree does not adequately portray the total manner in which God willed that His revelation should be communicated to men and interpreted for them throughout the centuries. In stating this, therefore, Trent still left the door open for further clarification concerning the precise nature of this extrascriptural source of revelation and its more intimate relationship to Scripture.

On the other hand, while the Tridentine decree in itself simply negates the sixteenth-century scriptural principle of Protestantism,

without going into further detail, it does not in any way contradict the approach to this question which has been discussed with
such avid interest throughout the present century. More and more
theologians have taken a second look at the two-source theory of
revelation, supposedly based on the teaching of Trent, and have
been led to ask whether this doctrine actually reflects the true
mind of Trent at all.

If we are to think of revelation as coming down to us from
two entirely distinct and unrelated sources of revelation — Scripture and tradition — we may be reading into the Tridentine decree
a good deal that actually pertains to a later age in which a theological method was cultivated which attempted to "prove" things
by scriptural texts and historical arguments drawn from the patristic writings and the arguments of the theologians. This was
done in large measure in an attempt to meet the modern deist and
rationalist on his own grounds, and it was an attempt to do the
impossible. Christian faith cannot be "proven" by such purely
human methods alone. To attempt to do so is actually to attempt
to reduce Christianity to the level of the purely natural, rooting
the assent of Christian faith on rational and historical grounds
rather than on the authority of God perceived in a truly supernatural manner.

Actually, there is a long and recognizable teaching within Catholic theological circles which affirms that the believer can perceive the intimate union of Scripture and tradition solely in
the total life of the Church; it is a perception made possible by
the eyes of faith alone, and it is an approach to Scripture as far
removed from mere exegesis as the merely human is removed from
the supernatural. According to this view, Scripture and tradition
were never meant to be separated into two totally distinct entities,
but find their real meaning in the total supernatural reality which
embraces simultaneously the inspired books, the traditions handed
down apart from Scripture, and the divinely guided magisterium
in the postapostolic era. Here alone, while remaining distinct
from one another in one sense, these three elements acquire their
true import. They are mutually related one to another, and can

be adequately and correctly viewed only within this total complex of supernatural realities intended by God from the beginning.

It is interesting to note, for example, the lengthy list of Catholic authors who have embraced this more organic view, as enumerated by Lengsfeld in his study of the notion of tradition in modern Protestant theologians in Germany.[79] This is a field that must still be studied in greater detail, but it is already certain that the list could be expanded to even greater length. Such a study is all the more important in view of the fact that some voices have been raised, suggesting that this present concern is a result of a misguided enthusiasm motivated by the ecumenical concerns of the present hour. It is, therefore, most necessary to ferret out and present the authentic Catholic tradition, formulated long before our current interest in ecumenism, and established entirely independently of it. It is this authentic doctrinal position which lies behind present-day Catholic thought on this question, and as such it needs to be pointed out more clearly. Obviously, Catholic theology cannot depart from its own principles and the doctrinal directives of the Church of Rome in formulating its position on such delicate matters. But the position indicated here has its roots in a deeper Catholic line of thought; it can be found there, and should be set forth chiefly in these categories.

THE CLARIFICATION OF SCRIPTURAL TRUTH

One of the principal points stressed in speaking of the intimate union of Scripture and tradition is that Scripture remains ever the starting point for the teaching of the Church, but that the complete unfolding of the meaning and content of these scriptural texts can take place only within the living tradition of the true Church, ever guided by the Holy Spirit. It is within this context rather than in a purely exegetical approach that the message of Scripture will be unfolded. In itself, this position is not in any way opposed to the basic position defined by Trent, that is, that something is necessary apart from Scripture. While Trent stated this fact, and the bishops present were concerned more about isolated practices which resulted from the apostolic teaching, this other approach can well be understood as a further clarification of the Tridentine definition.[80]

This position has also been expressed in the statement that "all the truths necessary for salvation are somehow contained in Scripture." This has perturbed some Catholic theologians, but the difficulty seems to be rooted in a misunderstanding of this position rather than in the statement itself. Many automatically understand this as a reaffirmation of the Protestant principle of *Scriptura sola* and a denial of Trent's insistence on the need of an extrascriptural element in revelation. This is not the meaning attached to the phrase, however, by those Catholics who accept it and who accordingly reject the so-called "two-source" theory. They are thinking actually of a *unified source* theory of revelation (a term which seems better than "one-source theory," since Scripture and tradition *are* distinct elements). In this sense Scripture and tradition complement one another and need to be kept together.

There is admittedly a possibility of equivocation in the use of these words. Much depends upon the theory of faith followed by an individual theologian, as well as his position on the question of the development of doctrine as understood in the Catholic sense. The criticism of Geiselmann's position offered by the late Heinrich Lennerz rather gives the impression of two missiles passing one another in different orbits.[81] Certainly Geiselmann does not deny the existence of tradition as a distinct, extrascriptural element;[82] his chief concern is the *relationship* between these two, and it is closely linked to a theory of faith quite distinct from that adopted by Lennerz.[83]

Thus, while to state that everything is "in" Scripture might mean for Lennerz that these truths are stated explicitly, or can be deduced by some form of logic, the phrase means the Geiselmann and others nothing more than that we can find in Scripture a *starting point* of some sort, from which, under the guidance of the Holy Spirit, the full doctrine revealed by Christ will eventually emerge. This cannot be done by any simple process of exegesis, nor by the use of simple logic; it takes place solely in the entire supernatural context of the Church's life, under the guidance of the Holy Spirit and the living magisterium which He directs. In other words, to be "in" Scripture according to these theologians does not mean that Scripture alone suffices, nor that there are clear or express statements in Scripture by which every doctrine can be "proved" or "deduced." Behind this statement there lies for these Catholic writers a theological concept of the inner unity, the reciprocal relationship, between Scripture, tradition, and the magisterium. Apart from this total reality, the fullness of revelation as contained in Scripture could never be grasped properly by mankind.

PARTIM . . . PARTIM

Because of these particular questions, there has been a recurrent discussion about the change in the Tridentine decree concerning Scripture and tradition. In the form originally suggested, it was stated that the truth of revelation was contained *partly* in the written books, *partly* in the traditions outside of Scripture: "hanc veritatem *partim* contineri in libris scriptis, *partim* sine scripto traditionibus."[84] In the final decree, however, the *partim* . . . *partim* was dropped, and it was simply stated that this truth was contained in the written books *and* in the traditions: "in libris scriptis *et* sine scripto traditionibus."

It has been almost impossible to determine from the *Acta* precisely why this change was made; the records are far from what we might wish on this particular point. As is well known, there were only two objections raised to the *partim* . . . *partim* terminology — or at least only two that have been recorded for us in the *Acta*. One of the objectors was Giacomo Nacchianti, the bishop of Chioggia; the other was Agostino Bonucci, the General of the Servites. Apart from this, there is no other record of an objection and no further information concerning the reason for the change.

It is not at all impossible that the *partim* . . . *partim* was dropped and the *et* substituted simply because it said more precisely what the Council wanted to say, without going on to commit itself on the question of whether revelation was "divided up," as it were, between Scripture and tradition. At least, with the small amount of historical evidence available to us, it would involve an apriorism of sorts automatically to identify totally the phrase *partim . . . partim* with the *et* later adopted.

At the Council, and in the tracts as well, there had been objections to the position holding that all the truths necessary for salvation were somehow contained in Scripture, in the sense that absolutely nothing but Scripture was required by the devout Christian. There was also the repeated emphasis upon that which is contained openly and expressly *(aperte et expresse)* in Scripture, which could very well reflect the mentality found in Driedo and others which affirms that certain other things are "insinuated" in Scripture, or find there that scriptural starting point from which the full doctrine will be realized in the divinely guided life of the Church. Hence, it may have been concluded that it would not be necessary for the decree to state further that there was any such dividing up as the *partim . . . partim* phrase implied. To say simply that Scripture alone is not sufficient would satisfy the chief intention of the Council and express its rejection of the Protestant principle of *Scriptura sola*. As we noted above, this was consistently set forth as the principal goal of all of those concerned with formulating the decree of the fourth session at Trent.

Moreover, there was a strong position assumed by the sixteenth-century Catholic controversial theologians which affirmed, as we have noted, the opinion that there *is* a sense in which a Catholic may admit that all of the truths necessary for salvation are somehow contained in Scripture. Chief among these was John Driedo, mentioned above. He was a Louvain theologian who died in 1535 and who has been shown to have had a definite influence on the formulation of the decree of the fourth session of Trent, insofar as it was concerned with scriptural questions.[85] Perhaps more clearly than all others, Driedo also affirmed the fact that all of the truths necessary for salvation are somehow contained in Scripture — a position which approximates in rather startling fashion the viewpoint defended by an increasing number of Catholic theologians today.[86] Before him and his sixteenth-century colleagues, however, there was a similar line of thought in the medieval writings of St. Anselm, St. Bonaventure, St. Thomas Aquinas, Duns Scotus, and others.[87] Francis de Vitoria, who died in 1546, also seems to have embraced a position similar to that of Driedo;[88] there are in addition early patristic writings which defended this same approach.[89]

In view of this, it is quite possible that those bishops partaking in the discussions of Trent may have wished to give expression to this rather well-established and valid Catholic position, and may have wished the *partim . . . partim* phrase to be eliminated for that very reason. There was, of course, the ever present possibility that others might misunderstand this line of thought, and consider those who defended it to be doing nothing more than repeating the teaching of the Reformers. The ill-starred bishop of Chioggia, Nacchianti, may have run into this obstacle; despite the possible validity of his arguments, he also appears clearly to have been a man who was constantly saying the wrong thing at the wrong time, and who tended to upset others more by the manner in which he spoke than by the teaching he proposed.

Speaking at the General Congregation on February 26, Nacchianti contended that the reception of the apostolic traditions ought to be dropped entirely, since it was, in his opinion, quite unnecessary: "No one is ignorant of the fact that all those things which pertain to salvation are contained in the sacred books. . . ."[90] Unfortunately, he at once went on to speak of the Council of Florence, and got involved in a debate concerning its final decrees, so that the discussion is somewhat confused even in the truncated versions which have come down to us.

The reactions to his performance were not too flattering in some quarters. Relating the incident in *Diary III,* Massarelli describes Nacchianti as a man who is "overfond of new things," and who repeatedly brings something new into the midst of the conciliar discussions.[91] Cardinal Cervini, writing to Cardinal Farnese, also notes that, in his opinion, many of the bishops were scandalized by the statements of Nacchianti.[92] However, the Cardinal does note that the bishop of Chioggia finally admitted that there were many things not contained in Scripture, above all those matters pertaining to the sacraments, and thus he finally admitted that there was a certain unwritten tradition in the Church.[93]

Precisely what Nacchianti intended to say is somewhat difficult to determine. In a later session, he again angered others by stating that he thought it was "impious" to equate such a practice as praying toward the east with the Gospel of St. John; thus, he stated, he could not approve of the phrase *pari pietatis*, etc.[94] In the back of his mind, however, there may have been the position that the inspired word of God was on a different level than such a changeable liturgical practice which was then considered by the Council to pertain to the apostolic traditions. Whatever he actually meant he was once again understood to claim either that the decree or that the bishops who drew it up were impious. The whole debate would seem to indicate something of a failure on the part of those concerned to reach a true meeting of minds; Nacchianti eventually had to apologize to the entire group for whatever offense he had committed.[95]

At any rate, Nacchianti *did* introduce this line of thought into the discussions, despite the many side issues. The other individual who proposed this position was Bonucci, the General of the Servites. He was a very learned man, and, so far as we know from the records, his statement caused no comment; but it could hardly have gone unnoticed after Nacchianti's earlier remarks. In stating his opinion on the proposed decree, Bonucci said that he did not like the *partim . . . partim* phrase: "I judge that all evangelical truth is written, therefore not *partim*."[96] Such a clear statement in regard to similar changes in any other Tridentine decree would usually be described as something of great import and influence; it would not be too wise to exclude this evidence as insignificant in the present discussion.

CONCLUSION

Possibly this entire question will never be adequately settled on a purely historical basis with our present sources; they are simply not sufficiently detailed to admit of a definite conclusion. The solution must come from a wider area in which the further development of this line of thought in the past four hundred years will be considered. It must be admitted, however, that there was *some* reason for the change. It is an obvious change, and one made after at least one sharp and obvious dispute concerning this particular phrase. To say that the truth of revelation is contained in the written books *and* in the unwritten traditions does not include in itself the notion of a separation into two distinct and somewhat unrelated sources such as the *partim . . . partim* phrase would imply. Moreover, in view of the upset attending Nacchianti's statement of his position, whatever the reaction was to the words of Bonucci, it would hardly seem that the bishops would have made such a change thoughtlessly, or for stylistic reasons alone. Apart from the fact that the *et* seems to say something different from the first phrase, it would also not seem very probable that those in charge of completing the decree would make a change which would seem to favor a position like Nacchianti's and Bonucci's unless they saw some good reason for it.

For a definitive answer to this doctrinal problem, however, we must look to the future rather than the past. For the present, it can hardly be claimed that the position assumed by many Catholics today that all of the truths necessary for salvation are somehow contained in Scripture would really oppose the teaching of Trent. Indeed, if understood correctly in the manner intended by these present-day theologians and by their earlier counterparts, such a position appears to be in total harmony with what Trent defined, since the proposition accepted by the Tridentine bishops does not, of itself, exclude the further clarification that this tradition — or extrascriptural element — is necessary in order that the full and accurate meaning of these scriptural starting places might be unfolded in the life of the living magisterium, acting under the ever present guidance of the Holy Spirit.

The case of Scripture itself does not of necessity preclude this point of view. It is true that there is no clear statement in the Scriptures indicating that these books alone are inspired and canonical. We are dealing, however, with something so fundamental at this point, that the canon of Scripture ought to be considered as a case apart. We are really touching upon something so basic here that it precludes further proof founded on some prior scriptural reality. The situation in regard to the life of the Church is similar to the first principles in philosophy which the Scholastics contend are self-evident; they are too basic to be proved by any form of syllogistic reasoning.

In the same way, the inspired Scriptures are so fundamentally linked to the Church and her divinely guided life, both in the apostolic and the postapostolic era, that their inspiration and canonicity can be clarified only within the life of that Church itself. The scriptural starting point is the fact that the Scriptures *exist* and that they are recognized, under the guidance of the Holy Spirit, as the inspired word of God. In this instance, it is not so much what the Scriptures say that is important, but what they are; and only in the total complex of supernatural realities, involving Scripture, tradition, and the magisterium, can this come to full light. Similarly, the nonscriptural element — the "unwritten traditions" — affirmed at Trent, will also find its more complete explanation in the doctrinal life of the Church, so that the Tridentine decree would not only not be opposed to the present-day suggestions, but would find in them its more complete explanation.

CHAPTER V

Modernism and the Teaching of
Schleiermacher

1907 brought to a head the difficulty that had been growing within
the Catholic Church for a number of decades, a theological approach that came to be described as Modernism. On July 3 of that
year, the Holy Office issued the decree *Lamentabili,* condemning
these errors; this was followed by the encyclical of Pius X,
Pascendi dominici gregis, of September 8, 1907. The encyclical
was a far more detailed statement of the basis upon which
Modernism was built. In its many facets, this theological approach
involved not only philosophical and theological principles opposed
to Catholic Faith, but also faulty historical and scriptural theories,
and a dangerous application of this entire system to the liturgical
and parochial life of the Church. So far-reaching was it in its
implications that Pius X was moved to describe Modernism as the
"synthesis of all heresies."[1]

The chief foundation for all of these errors, however, was the
philosophical position adopted. This became the norm for interpreting all the other matters which came under consideration. It
cannot be denied, of course, that many important findings had been
made in the field of historical and scriptural studies during the
past century, many of them now accepted by the highest authority
of the Church today.

In 1943 Pius XII pointed out the value of the historical method
in regard to scriptural study, thus giving great encouragement to
the growth of scriptural scholarship within the Catholic Church.
Scripture, like dogma, had suffered at the hands of the Modernists,

and the Catholic theological world needed some such statements as those made by Pius XII to reaffirm the legitimacy of the historical method in these fields of endeavor. Since the condemnation of Modernism, almost any use of more critical methods in dogma or scriptural studies was looked upon as suspect in many circles; if ever there was an example of some wanting to throw out the baby with the bath water, it was the attitude of those who identified Modernism with the various facets of historical research.

In his encyclical, *Divino afflante Spiritu,* Pius XII indicated the legitimacy of textual criticism, noting that even this had been grossly misused only several decades before.[2] But, more importantly, he also approved the proper use of the tenets of higher criticism; encouraging the scholar "with all care, and without neglecting any light derived from recent research," to "endeavor to determine the peculiar character and circumstances of the sacred writer, the age in which he lived and the sources, written or oral, to which he had recourse and the forms of expression he employed."[3]

What he encouraged the Scripture scholar to do, however, is not something peculiar only to this field of theological endeavor. The dogmatic theologian must also make use of a similar type of historical criticism, not merely when investigating the texts of Scripture, but when analyzing the texts of *any* period of the Church's life. Whether he be studying the decrees of Nicea or Trent, the statements of Leo the Great or Boniface VIII, the theologian must also — *mutatis mutandis* — do what Pius XII directed the scriptural scholar to do: "The interpreter must, as it were, *go back wholly in spirit to those remote centuries* of the East, and, with the aid of history, archaeology, ethnology and other sciences, accurately determine what modes of writing, so to speak, the authors of that ancient period would be likely to use, and in fact did use."[4]

The theologian does not have to travel back as far at times, nor will he encounter all of the complexities of the scriptural studies. Nevertheless, he must also go back in spirit to the times of Nicea or Trent, Leo the Great or Boniface VIII in order to grasp the real meaning of the Church's decrees. It is not only in a study of the Bible that one needs to put on another mentality, as it were. The Hebraic and Hellenistic minds of Scripture are different from ours, but the twentieth-century American or German theologian is vastly different from the Byzantine bishops of the early centuries or the feudal bishops of the Middle Ages. Even the Latin and Greek they used had unique and changing meanings. What they and their theologians wrote in those centuries must, accordingly, be understood in the light of their historical circumstances.

This implies a rejection of that concept of theology, held by many, which would compare it to a philosophical system of some sort. At times theology is variously described as being "atemporal" or "metaphysical," as contrasted with the biblical concern for the temporal and historical. Actually, there can be no such thing as an "atemporal and purely metaphysical" theological system for the Catholic believer. In analyzing any decree of the Church, we must admit the presence of historical situations which brought forth the official terminology of the Church. Certain phrases (such as "nature," "person," or "hypostatic union") were frozen, so to speak, and designated as official terms with precise meanings for Catholic theology. What Aristotle may have meant by "nature" or "person" is an interesting and valid historical question, but the "precise meaning" of these words for a Catholic can be understood only when we have recourse to the historical situation in which the decrees were formulated. It is the Church herself, a living reality, which made these decisions. Hence there is a need, perhaps, to use some such phrase as *Sitz-in-Kirche* in regard to every dogmatic decree we view in Denzinger. If we fail to realize this, we fall at once into the trap of *eisegesis,* and read into the decrees of the Church something which is in our own mind, but which was never envisioned by the Church at the time the decree in question was drawn up, in a precise historic milieu which contributed to the import of the decree.

The theologian not only can but must realize that his theological vocabulary is not derived from Plato or Aristotle, and that the concepts of faith as expressed during the centuries involve a rather flexible type of vocabulary that he must endeavor to understand.[5]

The doctrine certainly remains the same; but the manner of expression has obviously changed.

With the advent of the post-Cartesian theories of faith and their particular theological methodologies, the theologians of the Catholic Church, no less than the Scripture scholars, were at times hard-pressed to meet the problems thrust upon them by the concerns of Liberal Protestantism and Modernism. In the light of these theories, the Bible was reduced to a strictly historical book; it was supposedly something which pertained to a literary form more closely allied to journalistic reports — a day-to-day account, so to speak, of God's dealings with men in the Old Testament, and through Christ and His Apostles in the New.

Theology, for its part, was reduced to a rigid, highly rationalistic system, in which words presumably took on "universal" meaning; it was taken for granted by many, it would seem, that a theologian of the twentieth century could sit down with theologians from the fourth, twelfth, and sixteenth centuries and encounter no difficulties whatsoever in discussing Catholic doctrine. The Modernist suggestions that this was not necessarily true threatened to destroy the entire edifice, no less than it threatened to ruin the basic "proofs," if it should turn out that the Bible was not a strictly historical book in the sense then envisioned.

Today, in a much calmer period of history, the Catholic scriptural scholar is free to consider the various types of literary forms in the Bible. The clearest statement of all is the Instruction of the Pontifical Commission for Biblical Studies, *On Bible Research,* issued April 21, 1964. In many areas it settled past discussions, and placed a final stamp of approval on the use of form criticism in both Old and New Testament study.[6]

Applying these principles to the New Testament, the Instruction points out the "three stages" or *strata* which mark the teaching of Christ, and which can be discerned in the final Gospel form in which it has come down to us:

First, there was the life of Christ itself, and the manner in which

He verbally preached the message of the Christian era. We do not encounter this strata directly in our Scriptures, but only in that framework in which the primitive Church placed them. The Gospels are not a day-by-day account of what Christ said and did. What Christ actually said and did historically can be perceived at the basis of our Gospel message, but we do not possess anything like a tape recording of the message as He first preached it.

Second, there was the preaching of the Apostles in the primitive Church. The early Church took the words and events of the life of Christ as they now understood them in the light of the Resurrection and the outpouring of the Spirit on Pentecost, and proclaimed the Christian message to the world. In so doing, however, the primitive Church took into account the "needs of the various persons who listened" to the preaching; it "explained the facts and the words according to the needs of their listeners." Thus there arose a divinely guided *interpretation* of the message of Christ, in which the words and thoughts of the primitive Church — still in the era of the so-called Constitutine Tradition, in which revelation was being given — were joined to the original words of Christ. At times the message was incorporated in different forms; we can note, among them, "catechesis, narration, testimonies, hymns, doxologies and prayers."

Third, a final step was taken by the writers of the New Testament, who used as their starting point — their source — the preaching of the primitive Church. Once again, each individual author of the Gospels formed and adapted this oral teaching in accord with the purpose he envisioned in his own writing: "Some elements they chose, others they expressed in synthesis, they developed some elements, bearing in mind the situation of the various churches . . . [choosing] that in particular which was suitable to the various conditions of the faithful and the aims they had set themselves, narrating it in such a way as to meet those conditions and that aim."

As a result, it happens that in one Gospel a particular saying or event from the life of Christ appears in a context that is different from that found in another Gospel. This was in accord with the purpose they had in mind: "When the evangelists present different contexts in reporting the sayings and the deeds of the Saviour, it is to be thought that they did this for the convenience of the readers."

Since they were not giving a day-by-day account of what Jesus said and did, they did not hesitate to paraphrase what Christ said, or to move one or another statement to another context (combining statements Christ may have made at many different times in one sermon, for example, such as the Sermon on the Mount). The Bible, therefore, does not necessarily present the very words of Christ when and as spoken by Him historically — *ipsissima Christi verba* (as had been presumed in the more recent theories of faith and their insistence that the Bible is a strictly historical book in the sense of nineteenth century historical writing, or the "pure history" of seventeenth or eighteenth century deism and rationalism).

NOT MODERNISM

This does not mean that the Gospels are "unhistorical" or that Christ and His teaching are so altered that He appears as a "mythical person" or that His teaching is in any way "distorted." We are concerned with a question of understanding properly what the New Testament authors intended to do when, under the inspiration of the Holy Spirit, they set in writing the preaching of the primitive Church: "It does not go counter to the truth of the account that the evangelists report the sayings and the deeds of the Lord in a different order, and express His sayings not literally but with some diversity, yet preserving their sense." Some, overly attached to a faulty theory of faith and its equally faulty assumption that the New Testament is a "purely historical" book in the manner explained by them, expressed needless fears concerning this manner of understanding the New Testament.

This is worlds apart from Modernism, as the Instruction also emphasizes. As we shall note in great detail in this chapter, the error of Modernism lay in the philosophical and theological context in which it placed the findings of more recent scriptural study. Thus, while the Commission states that "when convenient it will be permissible for the exegete to examine possible positive elements offered by the 'method of the history of forms' [*Formgeschichte*] and make due use of them for a more extensive understanding of the Gospels," it still points to the errors of Modernism as an evil to be avoided: "He will do it with caution because the said method is often connected with inadmissible philosophical and theological principles which often vitiate the method itself as well as conclusions on the literary matter."[7]

All of this demands today a more careful delineation of the use of Scripture in theological study. What the theologian seeks from Scripture, as a result, are not "proof texts" that might be incorporated into the syllogisms of his "atemporal, metaphysical theology." On the contrary, he finds in the Bible that scriptural evidence, the "starting point" of this divinely guided development of doctrine which he must study. Even the theological note *ex clara scriptura* becomes questionable in this present approach. Apart from the fact that it seems to reflect far too much of the more Protestant notion of "My Bible and I," even when elevated to the level of the critical method, it still seems too rationalistic and subjective. At best it leaves open the question as to whom this meaning of Scripture is clear, and on what basis, and for how long. It indicates basically a purely historical assent, and it carries with it the difficulties of the "more recent" theories of faith to be discussed later.

This does not imply Modernism, as we said, for one important reason which was indicated clearly enough by Pius X, but which has only been more widely understood within the immediate past. It is not these approaches to the Bible and to the development of dogma which constituted Modernism; it was the *philosophic context* into which the Modernists placed their findings. The precise error of the Modernist view of history, Scripture, and theology stemmed from the philosophical suppositions which became the norm for all such interpretation. Scientific data in the field of history, archaeology, biblical criticism, and the like remain nothing but inert data until an interpretation is given to these facts, and there are many different, even diametrically opposed, ways of interpreting the evidence on hand. For the Modernist the sole backdrop against which all data could be set was nothing but the philosophical system endorsed at the very start.

Failure to realize this fact still raises confusion in the minds of some who view Modernism as a condemned system, and yet see certain historical or scriptural data used by the Modernists now being accepted by Catholics; they immediately conclude that the Catholic Church is making concessions to Modernism. Nothing of this sort happens at all. The use of the findings of historical and scriptural study by Catholic theologians today does not imply at all the prior acceptance of this all-pervading philosophical approach which was the foundation and guiding norm of all Modernist interpretations. This makes all the difference in the world. The data in themselves are rather neutral; it was the Modernist interpretation of them that made the conclusions wrong and brought about the strong condemnation of the Modernist system under Pius X. At the time the philosophical assumptions and the data were so closely joined together in the Modernist interpretation that the condemnation of the entire system might seem to imply the condemnation of the data themselves or of the valid work of scholarship. Nothing could be farther from the truth. The Modernist interpretation of the data is what was condemned, along with the false philosophical system that determined that interpretation; the Church was not condemning the scientifically and historically proved data themselves.

As Pius X points out, everything in Modernism was guided by its philosophical norms; it was an *a priori* system from start to finish. Thus when the Modernists came to deal with history this soon became apparent:

> Some Modernists, devoted to historical studies, seem to be deeply anxious not to be taken for philosophers. About philosophy they profess to know nothing whatever, and in this they display remarkable astuteness, for they are particularly desirous not to be suspected of any prepossession in favor of philosophical theories which would lay them open to the charge of not being, as they call it, *objective*. And yet the truth is that their history

and their criticism are saturated with their philosophy, and that their historic-critical conclusions are the natural outcome of their philosophical principles.[8]

The same thing was true of the Modernist approach to Scripture: "As history takes its conclusions from philosophy, so too [biblical] criticism takes its conclusions from history."[9] Accordingly, the biblical critic would presuppose a distinction between "real history" and the "history of faith," and the resulting distinction between the "Christ of history" and the "Christ of faith." Thus "the critic, on the data furnished him by the historian, makes two parts of all his documents."[10]

Even here, however, philosophy would have a more direct influence on the biblical critic, for "the dominion of philosophy over history does not end here. Given that division, of which We have spoken, of the documents into two parts, the philosopher steps in again with his dogma of *vital immanence,* and shows how everything in the history of the Church is to be explained by *vital emanation.*"[11] There is a constant harking back to the basic philosophical positions that serve as the guide of all Modernist thought. The end result is described by Pius X in these words:

This done, he finishes his work by drawing up a history of the development in its broad lines. The critic follows and fits in the rest of the documents. He sets himself to write. The history is finished. Now We ask here: Who is the author of this history? The historian? The critic? Assuredly neither of these but the philosopher. From beginning to end everything in it is *a priori* and an apriorism that reeks of heresy.[12]

To complete the picture, we must note that "the Modernist apologist depends in two ways on the philosopher."[13] He begins by working with history as "dictated . . . by the philosopher," and he adopts as his own the immanentist and purely psychological methods of the philosopher.[14] The entire scheme of apologetics is to be built on these principles which are, in fact, nothing more than "an *a priori* assumption of agnostic and evolutionist philosophy. . . ."[15]

WHAT IS THIS PHILOSOPHY?

In the opening paragraphs of *Pascendi* the type of philosophy of which Pius X is speaking is sketched in clear and definable lines. The starting point is the Kantian philosophy which so dominated the philosophical thought of Europe in the nineteenth century; it is designated by the name of *Agnosticism* in the encyclical:

> We begin, then, with the philosopher. Modernists place the foundation of religious philosophy in that doctrine which is commonly called *Agnosticism*. According to this teaching human reason is confined entirely within the field of *phenomena,* that is to say, to things that appear, and in the manner in which they appear: it has neither the right nor the power to overstep these limits. Hence it is incapable of lifting itself up to God, and of recognizing His existence, even by means of visible things.[16]

This is the basic position of Kantian philosophy; it served as the negative aspect of the philosophy of Modernism. Added to this, however, was a positive element, introduced more by his disciples than by Kant himself, although he certainly laid the seed for such a further development: namely, the concept of "vital immanence." As Pius X explains, once the negative aspects of this system have been admitted, the explanation of religion, whether natural or supernatural, "will be sought in vain outside of man himself. It must, therefore, be looked for *in* man; and since religion is a form of life, the explanation must certainly be found in the life of man. In this way is formulated the principle of *religious immanence.*"[17] Religion is portrayed as an "inner sense," originating in a deeply rooted "need of the divine" in man.

It is in this inner sense that the Modernist formed revelation; all creeds and religious formulas are, accordingly, nothing but further reflections on this inner experience of the individual (or community), and the expression of these reflections in various formulas. The purpose of these creeds and formulas is "to furnish the believer with a means of giving to himself an account of his faith."[18] As a result of this, these creeds have only a relative value; "it is quite impossible to maintain that they absolutely contain the truth."[19] Since the religious experience of individuals and communities can change, it is obvious that creeds and "the formulas which we call dogma must be subject to these vicissitudes, and are, therefore, liable to change. Thus the way is open to the intrinsic *evolution* of dogma."[20] The formulas "in order to be living, should be, and should remain, adapted to the faith and to him who believes. Wherefore, if for any reason this adaptation should cease to exist, [these formulas] lose their first meaning and accordingly need to be changed."[21]

All of this was equally true of the work of the Modernist as a theologian, for in this realm "the Modernist theologian takes exactly the same principles which we have seen employed by the Modernist philosopher — the principles of *immanence* and *symbolism* — and applies them to the believer."[22] The Catholic Modernist was interested in applying this philosophical system to Catholic doctrine, so that his efforts involved something more than a mere repetition of a philosophical position; but the philosophy remained his fundamental norm and guide throughout. It is in the light of these principles that the Modernist went on to evaluate the Church, the sacraments, Scripture, and tradition. Modernism within the Catholic Church was not identical with Liberal Protestantism of the late nineteenth century, since it included this added attempt to combine in some fashion both the principles of Liberal Protestantism and the traditional notions of Catholic faith. Modernism, however, very obviously derived its inspiration from the teaching of Liberal Protestantism, in which its own position was deeply rooted.

What the Modernist attempted to do was doomed to failure from the start; it was an attempt to do the impossible. The ultimate reason for this was the philosophy upon which the entire movement was based and which served as a guide throughout. It is a philosophy opposed on almost every point to the undying principles associated with Catholic faith. It replaces objectivity with subjectivity and unchanging truth with temporary verities. Once this philosophical position was accepted as the norm for discussing Catholic faith, everything was to be uprooted, and even the data resulting from valid historical and scriptural research was to be falsely interpreted. Thus it was not against scientific research as such that *Pascendi* spoke out, but rather this faulty interpretation of it brought about by the ruinous philosophy which pervaded the entire Modernist system.

SOURCE OF THIS PHILOSOPHY

The sources of Modernism are so varied that it is difficult to single out one isolated example as the basis of everything, but in regard to the philosophical starting point, there can be little doubt that it ought to be traced back in large measure to Friedrich Schleiermacher (1768–1834). It has been said, and with good reason, that "Schleiermacher and Darwin were probably the two persons most directly responsible for the shaping of modern Protestant religious thought."[23] Schleiermacher contributed above all the notion of *vital immanence* in religion, and Darwin added the concept of *evolution* which spread far beyond the limits of natural science into history, philosophy, and religion as well. Insofar as Modernism in the Catholic Church was related to Liberal Protestantism, this same thing may be said, proportionately, of its philosophical sources.

Modern Liberal Protestantism is a post-Kantian form of Protestant life, vastly different from that of the sixteenth-century Reformers, and Schleiermacher is one of the dominant links between this present-day development and the philosophy of Immanuel Kant.[24] It is for this reason that Schleiermacher has come to be called the father of modern liberal theology.[25] What Schleiermacher did was to extend the immanentist qualities of Kant's thought to the entire field of religion. If man was to find God within himself after Kant, it was also in himself that Schleiermacher would have him find the essence of *all* religion — or at least in the communal conscience that he came to attribute to the Christian community.

The Fathers at Vatican I were already concerned over the immanentist philosophy of Schleiermacher and its emphasis upon a religious sense and the need of the divine. The *Adnotationes* to the first *Schema* on Catholic doctrine proposed to the Council contain a direct reference to Schleiermacher's works.[26] Little did they realize the even greater impact these teachings would have on the life and history of the Church in the thirty years following Vatican I by their influence on the principles of Modernism.

There is an acknowledged difficulty in determining whether Schleiermacher was properly more of a philosopher or a theologian, or a curious mixture of the two. Felix Flückiger begins his study of Schleiermacher with a discussion of this precise point.[27] There is no question that a very close relationship exists between Schleiermacher's philosophical and theological views; the center of discussion concerns chiefly the *degree* to which his theology has been influenced by his philosophy, and the extent that the two can be separated. Involved in this question is the more basic problem of whether Schleiermacher actually reduced religious experience to the philosophical and purely natural level, or whether his starting point was a truly Christian experience as he conceived it, springing from man's confrontation with the self-manifestation of God.

Flückiger divides the various opinions into three groups: (1) Some hold that Schleiermacher's theology is nothing more than an extension or deepening of his philosophical views. This would, in effect, reduce his theology — and his grasp of Christian faith — to a purely natural, philosophical experience. (2) Others say that not everything of Christianity was abandoned in his system, but only that which could not be brought into accord with his philosophy. (3) Still others contend that there is nothing more than a similarity between his philosophical and his theological views, so that the "religious feeling" of which Schleiermacher speaks is formally distinct in the Christian context from that which might be attributed to any mere philosophical notion of religion in general. In its deepest roots this may, indeed, be the same "feeling," but in the Christian it is something proper and distinct, a response to the unique Christian revelation; it could not occur under any other circumstance.[28]

This last view may well add greater insights into current appraisal of Schleiermacher's position. He was above all a theologian and a preacher. As a Protestant clergyman, he was attempting to save Protestant Christianity from the evils he saw associated with it in his day. He was particularly concerned over the apparent conflict between the claims of traditional religion and the results of scientific and philosophic study such as it was portrayed in his time. As Brandt notes:

> There are many assertions which Christians have become accustomed to make, [Schleiermacher] says, which it is important for them to get on without — such as the statements about creation, miracles, the Mosaic chronology, and so on. For these statements conflict with reliable scientific knowledge, and, he says, it would be scandalous if religion were to ally itself only with a crude and unsound science, while reliable scientists were forced by the unnecessary claims of religion to ally themselves with the irreligious elements of society. Schleiermacher seems particularly to have felt the sting of the results of the (at that time) new internal criticism of the Bible. All these facts, he thinks, have the effect of putting the religious man in a dilemma and of forcing him to find a way of reconciling his two legitimate interests.[29]

Schleiermacher's solution to this problem facing the Christian grew out of his general theory on the essence of religion; that may be granted. It may not be a correct estimate of his views, however, to say that he reduced all religion to a common denominator, making all of them nothing more than rather arbitrary expressions of the same, identical "experience." Many of his statements appear to contradict such an analysis. He considers Christianity as the most perfect expression of religious experience, and he does so in a way as to indicate some objective norms proper to Christianity itself, distinct from the individual. Moreover, he claims that no one would admit "that Christian piety could anywhere arise, as it were of itself, quite apart from any historical connexion with the impulse which proceeded from Christ."[30] Christ definitely enters into the formation of Christianity. Schleiermacher views Mohammedan and Jewish piety in much the same fashion as Christianity, it is true, but he always insists that the highest development of religious piety is to be found in Christianity "and thus in the most perfect form (which we may say in advance is Christianity) the inward peculiarity [of a particular faith] must be most intimately bound up with that which forms the historical basis of the outward unity."[31]

The overtones of this approach may well reflect the spirit that came to more complete expression in later existentialistic theology among Protestants, with its emphasis upon the personal reaction (of the individual or the community) to the historic fact of Christ. In one of his letters, Schleiermacher explains the root of religious experience as he understands it, foreshadowing this later approach: ". . . what I understand by pious feeling does not at all come from representations, but is the original expression of an immediate existential relation."[32] The "feeling" which results from this experience is basic, primary, fundamental; whatever thought content or religious formula may be associated with it would result only from a reflection on that experience.

LIFE AND TIMES

In order to understand the position of Schleiermacher, it is most important to view him in the historical situation in which his approach developed. It has been pointed out by those who have studied him in detail that, while such an historical view is necessary for evaluating any philosopher, it is doubly necessary in regard to Schleiermacher. Any attempt to study merely his "ideas," apart from the spirit of the time which helped formulate them, will lead only to serious misunderstandings.[33]

Friedrich Daniel Ernst Schleiermacher was born in Breslau on November 21, 1768; he died on February 12, 1834. He was the child of Moravian parents, and was raised in the strict moral atmosphere of this pietistic group. He eventually entered the seminary at Barby, at that time the University of the Moravian Brethren; he was seventeen at the time. Schleiermacher continued to receive here the type of training approved by the Brethren, but he also set about a private study of current philosophical questions. This brought him into contact with the first dominant influence in his academic development: the philosophy of Immanuel Kant.

Schleiermacher was at this time won over almost entirely by the new critical philosophy of Kant, and he soon found that it was in serious conflict with the religious beliefs and attitudes of the Moravian seminary. Finally, in 1787, after overcoming the bitter opposition of his father, he entered the University of Halle — at that time enjoying the height of its fame, and almost entirely dominated by the spirit of the Enlightenment. He remained there until 1789, studying philosophy. He became more and more acquainted with the discussions of that day concerning Kant, as well as those which debated the merits of the Leibniz-Wolff school of thought. He also did some work in translating parts of Aristotle, indicative of a lasting interest in Greek philosophy that later brought forth other translations from the works of Plato.

After a year of study and writing at Drossen, he passed the church examination in theology, and in October of 1790 accepted a position as tutor in the household of Count Dohna of Schlobitten; he remained there until 1793. These seem to have been years of great skepticism in the life of Schleiermacher; the acceptance of the Kantian position had all but destroyed his belief. The contact with this cultured family also deeply influenced his appreciation of a more liberal and free manner of life, considerably different from that which he had known as a child of Moravian parents.

In 1793, Schleiermacher set out for other labors. He taught for a time in a boys' school, and then served at a church in Landsberg for two years. But in 1796 he moved to Berlin as a chaplain of the Reformed Church, where he remained for six years. This assignment was to bring about the second great influence in his philosophical career: namely, his contact with the leaders of the Romantic Movement, especially with Friedrich Schlegel (with whom he shared rooms for a time) and Henriette Herz.

Due to a number of problems in which he became involved (both through his writings and because of an unfortunate affair with a married woman), Schleiermacher was more or less forced to accept a position in Stolpe in Pommerania; this was in 1802. After two unhappy years there, however, he returned to Halle as extraordinary professor in theology and university preacher. His work there was interrupted by the Napoleonic war in the winter of 1806–1807. In the summer of 1807 he was back in Berlin, giving lectures on the history of Greek philosophy; in autumn of that year, he moved to Berlin permanently, where he remained until his death in 1834. In 1808 he was appointed preacher at the Trinity Church in Berlin, where he became famous as a noteworthy preacher; in 1810 he was appointed professor on the theological faculty, being then forty-two years of age. He lived out his life in Berlin, interested not only in philosophy and theology, but also taking an active part in political questions and in the organization of ecclesiastical affairs.

HIS PHILOSOPHY OF RELIGION

The first important work produced by Schleiermacher on the philosophy of religion appeared in 1799, during his first stay at Berlin. It was published anonymously, but the name of its author was soon widely known: *On Religion: Discourses Addressed to its Cultured Despisers*. It was one of his most notable works.

The "cultured despisers," in this instance, were his new friends of the Romantic Movement in Berlin. Schleiermacher was beginning to formulate his own position in the debates of the era, and it was to be a unique position, differing greatly both from that of the eighteenth-century rationalists and deists and from that of the romanticists.

The deists and their natural, purely rationalistic religion had sought to work out the conflict between faith and reason — between rationalism and Christianity — by reducing religion to certain essential elements that could be defended by reason alone. These essentials were chiefly moral principles and a few very general statements concerning God. Kant had entered the picture and endeavored to preserve Christianity from this attack while still accepting the basic tenets of deism. Kant attempted to overcome this spirit of the Enlightenment, but he was, at the same time, trying to overcome himself. His deistic religious views could not preserve what was then considered "traditional" Christian belief among German

Protestants; the deists, no less than the rationalists, had in effect rejected all such orthodox belief.

Kant attempted to found religion on a moral or ethical basis (much as the other deists before him had done). This approach was never entirely acceptable to Schleiermacher, even though he was won over in general to the Kantian spirit. As time went on, he grew more and more dissatisfied with this mentality; he did not wish to join forces with the deists. Thus his original acceptance of Kant's position came to be modified by a new approach toward the preservation of Christianity. It is important to note that he did not actually reject the teaching of Kant in regard to such matters as proofs for the existence of God by reason. He had little regard, it would seem, for the cosmological and teleological proofs as outlined by Kant; he rejected them for much the same reason. On the other hand, Schleiermacher did make some efforts at formulating certain arguments for God's existence that may have been closer to the ontological proof. At any rate, he frequently came close to pantheism in his system, and these arguments generally ran along this line.[34]

What Schleiermacher did reject in Kant was above all his attempt to place the essence of religion in the *ethical* order. He chose to follow Kant's position in the *Critique of Pure Reason* (rather than the *Critique of Practical Reason*), and therefore posited, in effect, some sort of *a priori* category proper to religion; in this would its essence lie. As Dillenberger-Welch note: "For Schleiermacher, religion itself was a unique realm of experience, related to but not determined by knowledge or ethics. Only in this way could Protestant theology begin again."[35]

Following this general line of thought, Schleiermacher felt that he could criticize *both* sides of this discussion, and for much the same reason. Both the leaders of the Enlightenment and those of the Romantic Movement were making the same mistake. They all looked upon religion as a way of thinking or as a set of beliefs and a moral code. The romanticists had reacted against both the cold intellectualism of the Enlightenment and the vigorous moralism of Kant and Fichte. In place of these approaches they proposed an idealized concept of the free man, a notion that came close to a rather pantheistic doctrine involved in their praise of the "divinity" of human nature. Yet their position still remained tied in some way to beliefs or codes of action.

As a result, Schleiermacher begins his discourses to these "culture despisers" by asking first of all the most general question:

> Let us then, I pray you, examine whence exactly religion has its rise. Is it from some clear intuition, or from some vague thought? Is it from the different kinds and sects of religion found in history, or from some general idea which you have perhaps conceived arbitrarily?[36]

Schleiermacher rejects the view that religion is derived from different sects, insisting that the concept of religion is far more profound than that. He notes that the romanticists still view religion from this aspect; they consider the general religious teaching of the various churches, and then reject two doctrines, above all, that they find in all religions and to which they object: providence and immortality. These they consider the hinges of all the traditional religions, but the romanticists themselves feel that these doctrines must be cast aside, and a more personal, subjective basis for religion established.

By acting in this manner, Schleiermacher insists, the romanticists are also wrong. Like the philosophers of the Enlightenment, they have mistakenly identified religion with a set of beliefs, with doctrines, or with a certain ethical code. Actually, something more is needed than an emphasis upon the subjective and personal as opposed to the objective and intellectual elements of religion. In its very essence, according to Schleiermacher, religion is neither metaphysics nor ethics nor a combination of the two; in this lies the common error of the romanticists and the leaders of the Enlightenment. For Schleiermacher, religion is something far deeper, something unique in man's experience. Instead of approaching the heart or the essence of religion, the romanticists, like the philosophers of the Enlightenment, have started with a consideration of what is most apparent, i.e., the beliefs of the various sects:

You start with the outside, with the opinions, dogmas and usages, in which every religion is presented. They always return to providence and immortality. For these externals you have sought an inward and original source in vain. Wherefore religion generally can be nothing but an empty pretense which, like a murky and oppresive atmosphere, has enshrouded part of the truth. Doubtless this is your genuine opinion.[37]

Before going on to "despise" religion, therefore, Schleiermacher suggests that his friends of the Romantic Movement ought first of all ask if they themselves have ever properly grasped what religion actually is. He grants, from his own point of view, that there have been many different sects, many religions "from the senseless fables of wanton peoples to the most refined Deism, from the rude superstition of human sacrifice to the ill-put together fragments of metaphysics and ethics now called purified Christianity. . . ."[38] And he agrees with the romanticists when they say that all of these are "without rhyme or reason."[39] On this point, he claims, there is no argument between them. All of these various sects and doctrines, however, must be looked upon only as the external manifestations of religion; *in its very essence,* religion is something far different. None of these systems, theories, analyses represent the true character of religion. Since the romanticists — like the leaders of the Enlightenment — have considered *only* these elements, they also "do not yet know religion itself."[40] Hence what they "despise" is not religion at all, but only these external elements which they have mistakenly identified with religion itself.

BASIS OF SCHLEIERMACHER'S SYSTEM

In this we find the kernel of Schleiermacher's religious thought, such as it was to develop in later years, above all in two works: *Kurze Darstellung des Theologischen Studiums* (1811, 1830) and *Der christliche Glaube nach den Grundsätzen der evangelischen Kirche* (1821, 1830) — translated as *The Christian Faith.* Schleiermacher thus asks his readers to turn "from everything usually reckoned religion, and fix your regard on the inward emotions and dispositions. . . . You must transport yourselves into the interior of a pious soul and seek to understand its inspiration."[41] He will not attempt to defend religion by the argument that it maintains justice and order in the world, nor will he emphasize doctrines or the weakness of man and his need of God's directing strength. Others follow this line of argument, but he will not; to do so would mean making the same mistake they have made.

In his Second Speech, Schleiermacher concerns himself directly with the *true* nature of religion as he sees it. If religion is neither "a way of *thinking*, a faith, a peculiar way of contemplating the world," nor "a way of *acting*, a peculiar desire and love, a special kind of conduct and character," what precisely is it?[42] "Piety cannot," he insists, "be an instinct craving for a mess of metaphysical and ethical crumbs."[43] All of these outward appearances and formulas are merely *secondary* elements of religion itself:

> Religion never appears quite pure. Its outward form is ever determined by something else. Our task first is to exhibit its true nature, and not to assume off-hand, as you seem to do, that the outward form and the true nature are the same.[44]

True religion is something that rests deep within the heart of man; it is this contemplation of the Infinite, which is neither knowledge nor science, but an *experience* in which God is perceived:

> It is true that religion is essentially contemplative. . . . But this contemplation is not turned, as your knowledge of nature is, to the existence of a finite thing, combined with and opposed to another finite thing. . . . The contemplation of the pious is the immediate consciousness of the universal existence of all finite things, in and through the Infinite, and of all temporal things in and through the Eternal. Religion is to seek this and find it in all that lives and moves, in all growth and change, in all doing and suffering. It is to have life and to know life in immediate feeling, only as such an existence in the Infinite and Eternal.[45]

As he goes on to explain, this religion is not knowledge and science, either of the world or of God. Without being knowledge, true religion recognizes knowledge and science, but *in itself*, it is essentially an affection — a revelation of the Infinite in the finite,

God being seen in it and it in God. The same thing is true of ethics. The pious man contemplates God's activity among men and sees the meaning of ethics, but he does not formulate any ethical system.

It is important to note that at this time of his philosophical development, Schleiermacher continued to include two elements in his complete notion of true religion: Intuition and Feeling. Later on, in those works which most represent his influence upon modern thought, he dropped the notion of Intuition (which had overtones of an intellectual grasp of faith and an objective belief), and emphasized only feeling. This Intuition of which he is now speaking, however, is not perception. As Schleiermacher understands it, Intuition involves a more personal, immediate *influence* of one thing upon another:

> All intuition proceeds from the influence of the thing perceived on the person perceiving. . . . What is perceived is not the nature of things, but their action upon us, and what is known or believed of this nature is beyond the range of intuition. . . . Religion neither seeks like metaphysics to determine and explain the nature of the Universe, nor like morals to advance and perfect the Universe by the power of freedom and the divine will of man. It is neither thinking nor acting, but intuition and feeling.[46]

The basic principles of Kantian phenomenology can be recognized in this statement, joined to Schleiermacher's notion of religion as something entirely beyond the outwardly perceptible. In his later works, and in the second edition of the discourses *On Religion,* Schleiermacher, for various reasons, set aside this element of Intuition in his concept of religion. He had reworked his concept of science, and Intuition was now also rather important there. At the same time, he may have wished by that time to avoid confusion with the "intellectual intuition" proposed by Schelling, with whom he now disagreed.[47]

This is one of the reasons why it is so difficult to analyze the position of Schleiermacher; he was constantly progressing toward a newer, more explicit formulation of what he was thinking in general, although he never set forth a fully worked-out system such as we might desire. By a peculiar trick of fate, this may be the reason for his profound influence on modern religious thought in Protestantism and in Catholic Modernism. Had he perfected a system, any acceptance of his concepts would have been conditioned by an acceptance of his system. At it was, the concepts he proposed were able to be assimilated in various ways by rather diverse schools of thought, and thus Schleiermacher gave the impulse to equally diverse systems. As Brandt expresses it: "Being vague, his idea was elastic and adaptable. Had he carried through a rigorous analysis of his concepts of 'feeling' and religious experience, it is quite possible that the idea would have proved less powerful."[48]

DAS GEFÜHL

Schleiermacher did attempt to explain what he meant by "feeling" (*das Gefühl*), however inadequate were his efforts. In his earlier concern with intuition and feeling, he held that each intuition is, from its very nature, linked to a feeling. Once he had transferred this notion of intuition to the realm of science or knowledge in general, making it a part of his epistemological system, he *redefined* religion in terms of feeling alone; this was from about 1806 on. This meant, in effect, that his religious views, and his concept of religious belief, became increasingly *subjective,* since this concept of intuition — vague as it was — had implied some contact with an objective religious truth. As Oman notes:

> In 1806 he stood opposed to an entirely different state of matters. . . . Schleiermacher solved the difficulty by saying that one part of the mind can take the other for its object. Thus the mind can make its feelings the object of its thought, and doctrines arise. Religious *ideas* are reflections on religious *feeling*. This is the conception he works out in the *Glaubenslehre* [*The Christian Faith*].[49]

It is this notion of religion, dating from his later period, that has come to be associated with the name of Schleiermacher, and has become the starting point for so many modern systems of religious thought, including the Modernism condemned by Pius X. It sets aside intuition and is identified with "feeling" alone, not an emotional or psychological feeling, but "an *immediate conscious state,* the result of an interaction between the individual and his environment, a mirroring of the effect of that interaction on the individual, its enhancing or depressing his life in a specific way; and feeling is either pleasant or unpleasant in tone."[50]

There can be, of course, feelings of this nature that are not religious; for Schleiermacher, religion is simply one species of a genus.[51] On a purely philosophical basis, all mankind finds God on the basis of this feeling of *absolute dependency.* In this, Schleiermacher remains an intuitivist. When man perceives himself as a dependent being, as a part of the Whole, he at once achieves certitude; he needs no further reasoning process, no further proof.[52] In this idea of the Whole, the individual perceives God, the Cause of all things.

In the Christian, however, there is question of a further, unique experience. The dogmatic statements which pertain to that belief are a result of the reflection on the *Christian* consciousness, rather than merely this primal feeling of absolute dependency on God, common to all mankind. The Christian consciousness is that associated with the experience of redemption in Christ; it could not be experienced in any other situation. It might be called the *highest* and *most profound* experience with the feeling of absolute dependence on God; while this feeling might be somewhat vague and misty apart from Christian revelation, it is clear and domineering in this experience, strong enough to exclude all hint of shadow and hesitancy.[53]

All of this is the work of the Spirit, and this working finds expression simultaneously in "revelation" and in the devout, Christian "consciousness." Schleiermacher understands this term "consciousness" more in a metaphysical than in a psychological sense.[54] It is that which places man in contact with God; hence it is, in the Christian, that which places man in contact with God through Christian revelation. The same Spirit that was active in Christ is also active now in the devout Christian, and the heightened activity of this Spirit that is apparent in the Christian church and which unites all Christians in a common feeling of holiness actually *constitutes,* for us, the Christian revelation. "Just as the self-consciousness of Christ was a revelation of God in him," writes Flückiger in his interpretation of Schleiermacher, "so is the Christian, devout, self-consciousness a revelation of God in us."[55] The Spirit is the same in all instances, but in the Christian, this heightened activity of the Spirit progresses *only* under the impulse of the preaching of Christ; apart from this preaching, there might be religious activity of the Spirit, but never that activity proper to the Christian. The work of the Spirit in the Christian is necessarily linked to the preaching of Christ. Thus there is a necessary *identity* between the self-consciousness of Christ and that of the Church. It is necessarily a question only of *one* revelation, being manifested in both Christ and His Church. The Christian message, therefore, is really the preaching of the self-consciousness of Christ, which is, necessarily, that of the Christian community as well.

Because of this, there is, in Schleiermacher's view, an essential link between Christ and Christianity. His theology is not a purely rational, philosophical outgrowth; it is something associated *only* with Christ, and it is the working of the one Holy Spirit. Thus Schleiermacher can write:

> No true Christian can wish to retain anything in his inner life, and at work there, in which he does not recognize Christ; so, too, no one can wish, in his self-communication within the Christian fellowship, to commend and disseminate himself and his own things, but rather Christ alone and whatever of Christ lives in him. Similarly, no one can wish to take up anything into his life for self-advancement, save as he takes it from Christ.[56]

If one accepts the philosophical and theological principles adopted by Schleiermacher, all of this does make sense, and his "Christian faith" might be called truly "Christian." But only if one accepts his philosophical position. As he views it, Christianity is something that could never occur apart from the impulse given by Christ, but every statement of this nature must be understood in the philosophic categories in which he himself labored. Otherwise, we miss the meaning of Schleiermacher entirely.

Modern-day Protestantism has rejected much of Schleiermacher's approach, but one basic element has continued to exercise its influence. As Dillenberger-Welch point out:

> Even his sharpest critics are one with Schleiermacher in the recognition that God and faith belong together. We cannot speak significantly about God from a neutral corner. We know him only as we meet him in a venture of trust and obedience, i.e., as we respond in faith to his forgiving and liberating work in Christ.[57]

It is important to note that it is the philosophic basis of this approach to Christian revelation that makes all the difference in the meaning of these same words. A Catholic might say this same thing about man's relationship to God, but he would necessarily mean something greatly different from what Schleiermacher meant to say, or from what a large number of present-day Protestant theologians intend. Again, a Pelagian might also describe Christianity as a "response in faith" to the activity of God, but mean nothing more than man's totally independent and natural activity in the way of salvation. Man's response to revelation is still a response under grace. God retains the initiative, or else we again lapse at once into Pelagianism.

THE CHRISTIAN FAITH

In his later writings, Schleiermacher built upon these philosophical positions. Their application to Christianity appears with greater clarity in his chief dogmatic work, *The Christian Faith (Der christliche Glaube)*. It is a *Dogmatik*, covering the entire field of doctrine to which Protestant theology can point. It has something of the appearance of a theological manual, being frequently a commentary on sections of the Augsburg Confession and other such doctrinal statements.

The entire work is pervaded by Schleiermacher's own approach to religion and thus almost everything receives a somewhat new interpretation. There is a special emphasis upon the *community*, on the social concept of the Christian Church (as understood, of course, by Schleiermacher). Hence, Schleiermacher notes at the start that "a Church is nothing but a communion or association relating to religion or piety."[58] The piety of such a communion may seek expression in various manners, but there is always a basic and common element present, i.e., the self-identical *essence* of piety which is "the consciousness of being absolutely dependent, or, which is the same thing, of being in relation with God."[59]

This Christian feeling, which represents the highest activity of the Holy Spirit in man is, for Schleiermacher, the source of the Christian religion. As such, it also represents for him the highest grade of human self-consciousness.[60] It is this common Christian consciousness that leads necessarily to living fellowship or communion: to a Church.[61]

We can note in this the fact that it is the piety or religious feeling which forms the Church, and not the opposite. In Schleiermacher's system, the Church is not accepted as a teacher, speaking on the authority of God. Religion knows one basic contact with God, and that is within the depths of the individual being. This experience or feeling (*das Gefühl*) is the essence of all religion, even of Christianity. In assuming this position, Schleiermacher separates himself not only from Catholic doctrine but from the theological position of sixteenth and seventeenth-century Protestantism as well. Though his words may sound the same, everything in this theological system takes on a new meaning since everything is colored by this completely different approach.

Borrowing from those propositions formulated earlier in his general philosophy of religion, Schleiermacher goes on to discuss the diversities of religious communions in general. His solution to this problem is unique. He does not consider the division of religions an indication of break with authority or failure to perceive God's objective revelation; he rejects *no* religion and is careful to point out that all religious communions — from idol worship and polytheism, on the lower plane, to monotheism on the higher — reflect this basic feeling of *absolute dependence*. For this reason they are all perfectly acceptable. He does grant, however, that there is a hierarchy among these various beliefs, since some represent a more profound and intimate experience of the divine; monotheism is the highest plane of all, and history exhibits only three great monotheistic communions: the Jewish, the Christian, and the Mohammedan.[62]

In this we can note Schleiermacher's evolutionary concerns. The religious experience of mankind has undergone a purifying process through the centuries. Thus in his opinion both the Jewish and the Mohammedan form of monotheistic belief involve obvious imperfections:

> Judaism, by its limitation of the love of Jehovah to the race of Abraham, betrays a lingering affinity with Fetishism; and the numerous vacillations towards idol-worship prove that during the political heyday of the nation the monotheistic faith had not yet taken fast root, and was not fully and purely developed until after the Babylonian Exile. Islam, on the other hand, with its passionate character, and the strongly sensuous content of its ideas, betrays, in spite of its strict Monotheism, a large measure of that influence of the sensible upon the character of the religious emotions which elsewhere keeps men on the level of Polytheism.[63]

Christianity alone among the Monotheistic communions "remains free from both these weaknesses," and therefore it "stands higher than either of those other two forms, and takes its place as the purest form of Monotheism which has appeared in history."[64] On the basis of this comparison of Christianity with other similar religions, Schleiermacher concludes that "Christianity is, in fact, the most perfect of the mostly highly developed forms of religion."[65]

This line of argumentation brings out more clearly than any others the close relationship between the philosophy and the theology of Schleiermacher. While he does not reduce Christianity to a purely natural instinct or to mere philosophy, there is nevertheless an element within it that is common to all religious experience and to all forms of religion. Christianity is distinguished from all other faiths simply "by the fact that in it everything is related to the redemption accomplished by Jesus of Nazareth."[66]

The root of this corporate union is faith in Christ the Redeemer; apart from that, Schleiermacher insists, there can be no participation in the *Christian* communion.[67]

In Schleiermacher's approach to Christianity, we can also perceive the element of religious indifferentism. As his basic principle, he holds that "the only pertinent way of discovering the peculiar *essence* of any particular faith and reducing it as far as possible to a formula is by showing the element which remains *constant* throughout the most diverse religious affections within this same communion, while it is absent from analogous affections within other communions."[68] Religious differences within the sects must, in other words, be boiled down to a common denominator. This search for the essential of a particular form of religious belief encounters unique problems in regard to Christianity, according to Schleiermacher:

> Christianity presents special difficulties, even in this fact alone, that it takes a greater variety of form than other faiths and is split up into a multiplicity of smaller communions or churches; and thus there arises a twofold task, first, to find the peculiar essence, common to all these communions, of Christianity as such, and secondly, to find the peculiar essence of the particular communion whose right is to be authenticated or whose system of doctrine is to be established.[69]

For Schleiermacher, the secondary elements of belief contained within the Creeds of the various Christian sects must be looked upon as nonessential; the *core* remains the common and all pervading notion of *redemption through Christ*. Any Christian religion, therefore, which adheres to this essential concept is to be accepted as truly Christian, despite further differences on other matters of doctrine. Such a religious experience is truly Christian, and thus distinct from all other forms of Monotheistic belief, provided it is rooted in this notion of Christ the Redeemer.

Apart from this essential core, when Schleiermacher comes to discuss the essence of Christian dogma, he follows this same general pattern: the essence of religion is that inner, personal experience. Creeds and dogmas can be nothing but an outward expression of this personal experience; churches are formed by the association of those who have shared a similar experience.

RADICAL DEPARTURE

It is in these further applications of his basic position that we can perceive even more clearly the far-flung effects of Schleiermacher's theorizing, and the result of his philosophical starting points. It is in these applications, moreover, that the Catholic theologian recognizes the philosophico-theological relativism imbedded in his overall approach.

"Christian *doctrines*," according to Schleiermacher, "are accounts of the Christian *religious affections* set forth in speech."[70] The root of doctrinal statement in credal or dogmatic form is, always was, and always must be, nothing more than these "religious affections." These lead the way and determine the belief of the Christian community at any given time.

As Flückiger notes, it is rather astounding that Schleiermacher failed to realize the vast difference between his approach and the position of the sixteenth-century Reformers. In this, Schleiermacher was undoubtedly a product of his own age and philosophical development, and presupposed that his dogmatic views were a significant and logical outgrowth of the Reformation principles. His grasp of the historical truth must have been deficient, for in actual fact Schleiermacher transferred the center of religious experience to a completely different point, as Flückiger indicates:

> The Church, as he presents it, does not live by the Word of God, as subject to its sovereignty, but entirely and without reservation from its own revealing power. Its own Christian, devout self-consciousness is itself the divine "Word" which it proclaims, and at any given time it possesses, in that present state of development of this consciousness, the highest expression of Christian truth then available.[71]

In adopting this approach, Schleiermacher necessarily abandoned the Reformation attempt to formulate Creeds or Confessions as *norms* of belief. For him this was equivalent to stopping the wheels of historical progression within religion, and latching on to former stages of doctrinal development, freezing them for future use, as it were, when actually they ought to retain their fluid state and give way to new expressions of faith and new Creeds more fittingly adapted to the religious experience of the present moment.

Since Schleiermacher was writing a *Dogmatik,* this view of religious Creeds naturally raised a further question: What is the role of the dogmatic theologian within the Church? He himself was writing a theological work, and had to justify that task somehow. His answer is that to dogmatic theologians must be assigned the task of "describing" more than anything else: "Dogmatic Theology is the science which systematizes the doctrine prevalent in a Christian Church at a given time."[72] Thus the task of theology is never ended. As new religious experiences replace old ones, new doctrines will replace old ones in similar fashion; and the dogmatic theologian must look upon it as his essential task to set forth the doctrines prevalent during his lifetime rather than those taught a century ago, a thousand years ago, or in the era of primitive and apostolic Christianity. All of these former beliefs pertain to history rather than a living belief, and the theologian betrays his particular vocation if he attempts to present these records of the past as norms for current belief.

This approach has many ramifications. It means ultimately that any such *Dogmatik,* just as the confessions and the doctrines which it describes, can be valid only for a time; it cannot be looked upon as a universal and unchanging statement of Christian belief. Schleiermacher recognizes that such a position is not to be found in the writings of most theologians, but this fails to perplex him; he feels that others have simply taken it for granted:

> That each [dogmatic] presentation confines itself to the doctrine existing at a certain time, is indeed seldom expressly avowed, but it nevertheless seems to be a matter of course; and this seems, for the most part, to be the only possible explanation of the large number of dogmatic presentations which follow upon each other. It is obvious that the text-books of the seventeenth century can no longer serve the same purpose as they did then, but now in large measure belong merely to the realm of historical presentation; and that in the present day

it is only a different set of dogmatic presentations that can have the ecclesiastical value which these had then; and the same fate will one day befall the present ones too.[73]

Schleiermacher admits the vast difference between Protestant and Catholic creeds; for him, each of these represents the religious experience of the individual communities so that "a presentation suitable for Protestantism cannot possibly be suitable for Catholics, there being no systematic connexion between the doctrines of the one and those of the other."[74] Because of this, Schleiermacher could not be accused of wishing to fuse various beliefs in the interests of ecumenism; his system left no place for such effort and he notes accordingly that "a dogmatic presentation which aimed at avoiding contradiction from either of these two parties would lack ecclesiastical value for both in almost every proposition."[75]

From Schleiermacher's point of view, the inner religious *life* of each separate community is its sole guide, and this guide must be followed. Apart from this there can be no personal conviction; the individual must enter into a convinced presentation of his own particular belief. Thus "a dogmatic presentation which takes no sides but is purely historical will always be sufficiently distinct from a presentation which is also apologetic — the only kind now in view."[76]

This reworking of dogmatic presentations is not to be understood as something which touches merely the manner of presentation — a work of revision in regard to style, as it were, or a new ordering of dogmatic textbooks in line with further insights into the meaning of the old doctrine. In the teaching of Schleiermacher, the changes are far more radical; they involve changes in *doctrine itself,* based upon the changes in the manner in which Christians grasp and understand revelation. At any given time, the Church will understand revelation only partially and imperfectly, he insists; hence there is ever present a necessary work of perfecting and correcting. This does not imply, for Schleiermacher, a homogeneous development of doctrine, to use Marin-Sola's phrase. On the other hand, it is not a doctrine of pure subjectivism; he is most careful to insist on some kind of objective reality, the result of the work-

ing of the Holy Spirit. The various churches do not *create* doctrine
and creeds by dint of their own reasoning powers; they are always
"receiving" this from the Spirit in this profound Christian experience. Only then can they formulate this experience in confessions
and creeds, and describe it in dogmatic presentations. But it may
always be an essentially different doctrine that is so received.

ROLE OF THE COMMUNITY

The influence of the Spirit is generally observed more clearly
in the whole Christian community than in only one individual.
Schleiermacher stresses quite strongly the social element in belief
and the role of the Christian community in recognizing a true
religious experience. Without some stamp of approval given by the
Church, we have only personal opinions:

> In the first place, everyone will admit that a system, however
> coherent, of purely and entirely individual opinions and views,
> which, even if really Christian, did not link themselves at all to
> the expressions used in the Church for the communication of
> religion, would always be regarded as simply a private con-
> fession and not as dogmatic presentation, until there came to
> be attached to it a likeminded society, and there thus arose a
> public preaching and communication of religion which found its
> norm in that doctrine.[77]

Thus the concept of religious belief as it appears in *The Christian
Faith* must be understood in relationship to Schleiermacher's notion
of what the Christian Church itself really is. Obviously, he does not
require any definite and essential organizational aspect for a
"Church." He points out that "according to Christ's original intention there was not to be any such visible Church. . . ."[78] It is
only the invisible Church that is the true, perfect, undivided and
infallible Church. The *visible* Church is but a faint reflection of
this; it is, accordingly, something divided, imperfect, subject to
error and ever changing. The outward expression of belief on the
part of the visible Church implies these very imperfections. The
doctrinal expression of the prevailing "Christian feeling" represents

truth for the moment, but it is never the total and accurate account of the faith of the invisible Church:

> When this innermost consciousness comes to be particularized in definite ideas, it no longer has the same full truth. . . . Hence the outward expression of the inner truth becomes more or less distorted, and of its organized form the Spirit takes possession only gradually.[79]

Out of this basic approach there necessarily arises a universal truth that lies in the center of Schleiermacher's thought: namely, the relativity of all externalized formulas of belief. This relativity is extended not only to the earlier confessions of sixteenth-century Protestantism, but to all the ancient creeds as well. The Nicene Creed is essentially no different, in this system, from the Augsburg Confession: they both represent valid, but temporary and imperfect formulations of faith corresponding to the particular religious feeling of the Christian communities in each era. All creeds known to history represent the "prevalent doctrine" of the Christian community at the time and in the circumstances in which they were composed, but they must not be looked upon as irreformable statements of belief for all time. They are only partial and imperfect expressions of Christian truth:

> No definition of doctrine, then, even when arrived at with the most perfect community of feeling, can be regarded as irreformable and valid for all time. This is pre-eminently true of definitions which arose after controversy as presentations put forth by a larger or smaller majority, for controversy more than anything else rouses all those impulses that lead to error. Hence no one can be bound to acknowledge the contents of such presentations as Christian truth except in so far as they are the expressions of his own religious consciousness, or commend themselves to him by their scriptural character.[80]

There is, accordingly, a never ending task of revision of the Church's public doctrine to which everyone, according to his own ability, must contribute. In this lies the second task proper to the theologian. Like all others he may — through his speculations — contribute to the progressive understanding of revealed truth.

His own individuality may "have an influence upon the form and manner of treatment, and even assert itself at particular points by intentional correction of the usual position."[81] The ultimate norm for the prevalent doctrine, however, remains the Christian community which either accepts or rejects any insights proposed. Schleiermacher insists that there is room for controversy, debates, analyses within the Church, but generally such "improvements and new developments of Christian doctrine . . . hardly ever proceed directly from the dogmatic discussions themselves, but are for the most part occasioned, in one way or another, by the proceedings of public worship or by popular literature for the dissemination of religion."[82] In this entire process, as he notes elsewhere, there runs a natural agreement concerning the basic principles by which error is to be counteracted, but even in regard to these, "this agreement is a thing of gradual formation in each Church, and can only arise when the Church has come to self-consciousness."[83]

Following this basic approach, Schleiermacher proceeds to praise the sixteenth-century Reformers for their refusal to submit to the decisions of a General Council; only the Christian community could solve the controversies of that era. At the same time, he criticizes these Reformers for accepting the creeds of the ancient Church. In doing this, they were most inconsistent "for these Creeds are but the product of similar Councils, which besides were due to divisions within the Church, and hence were not pre-eminently fitted for the ascertainment of truth."[84]

In this fashion, Schleiermacher rejects not only all creeds, but all Councils; there is no room for an authoritative teaching body in this notion of the Church. For this reason he finds another inconsistency in the actions of sixteenth- and seventeenth-century Protestants. They eventually came to formulate various Protestant creeds (such as the Augsburg Confession or the Westminster Confession) and made the acceptance of these a requisite for membership in Protestant churches. Schleiermacher grants that under the historical circumstances in which the Reformers found themselves it was only natural and good that they should have set forth the "prevalent doctrine" (that is, the convictions they then held) by means of these confessions. He considers it a grave mistake, however, and a matter of deep regret, that these same confessions were later imposed in authoritarian fashion as the *norm* of Protestant belief "as if they had been irreformable."[85]

In Schleiermacher's system, all such practices were an attempt to freeze the expression of religious experience at one stage of its development. He feels that neither the ancient Councils (such as Nicea or Chalcedon) nor the Protestant confessions had the right to do that. None of them have anything more than temporary value. Each generation has the right to express in its own formulas the religious experience that is proper to it, but any attempt to make particular confessions permanently valid will simply "hinder the performance of the very task to which [these Creeds] owed their birth."[86]

IMPORTANCE OF SCRIPTURE

Not even Scripture is exempt from this universal approach of Schleiermacher. It must also take its position in the long line of temporarily valid expressions of religious experience; it ranks first in the line, but apart from that it is in no way different. Schleiermacher is careful to point out, therefore, that one ought not give the impression "that a doctrine must belong to Christianity because it is contained in Scripture, whereas in point of fact it is only contained in Scripture because it belongs to Christianity."[87] The New Testament is the product of the Christian conscience of the primitive Church, and as an expression of some primitive element in the Christian experience it may influence present-day faith, "but in no sense conditionally on the acceptance of a special doctrine about these writings, as having had their origin in special divine revelation or inspiration."[88]

In Schleiermacher's system, the Holy Scriptures are "the first member in the series, ever since continued, of presentations of the Christian faith."[89] They may be considered a "norm" for all succeeding generations, but only in a very limited sense. Insofar as the early Church was a unity, a Christian community of the apostolic period, whose faith is reflected in Scripture, it possessed a valid expression of the Christian revelation. It could not, however, set forth its perception of that truth as a norm, pure and simple, to be used to determine the faith of later ages. There was much imperfection, much that was conditioned and temporal in the primitive Church's understanding of the truth of revelation, and it was this imperfect grasp that is set forth in the Scriptures. The very idea of revelation "signifies the *originality* of the fact which lies at the foundation of a religious communion, in the sense that this fact, as conditioning the individual content of the religious emotions which are found in the communion, cannot itself in turn be explained by the historical chain which precedes it."[90] Revelation happens at every moment, in each century, in every new community; it is not something of the past.

As a result, the various churches must, with the passing of time, restate the essential and true message and only that element of Scripture which corresponds to the present experience can be said to persist. There is an historic link to this first expression of faith in Scripture, since we can note that *de facto* "all that has approved itself in the way of oral presentation of Christian piety in later ages of the Church has kept within the lines of these original forms, or is attached to them as an explanatory accompaniment."[91] But the ultimate norm remains the present community alone. Even in regard to Scripture, "the general rule is first of all to be applied that in every kind of fellowship the individual element approves itself only in so far as it gives expression to the common spirit. Here too, accordingly, everything of the kind which persists in influence alongside of Holy Scripture we must regard as homogeneous with Scripture; while nothing that does not persist can be given a place in the series."[92]

In this fashion the churches of later centuries will restate that which has persisted through time because it is present now as an element of their personal religious experience, but they will also set aside those less perfect, confused, or erroneous statements which the Apostolic Church had at the same time incorporated into its profession of faith in the Scriptures of the New Testament. These later churches, however, differ from the Apostolic Church in one respect. The canonical Scriptures could be fashioned only in that primitive Christian community; it alone was able to set forth a *relatively pure* expression of Christianity. The Church in later centuries could not reproduce these canonical Scriptures "for the living intuition of Christ was never again able to ward off all debasing influences in the same direct fashion, but only derivatively through the Scriptures and hence in dependence on them."[93]

This still does not mean that Scripture becomes an ultimate norm; Schleiermacher places great limits on the authority of Scripture. Whatever authority he grants, he does "not ascribe uniformly to every part of our Holy Scriptures . . . so that casual expressions and what are merely side-thoughts do not possess the same degree of normativeness as belongs to whatever may at each point be the main subject."[94] Moreover, the content of Christianity is not limited to the apostolic period, much less to Scripture:

> Nor is it meant that every later presentation must be uniformly derived from the Canon or be germinally contained in it from the first. For since the Spirit was poured out on all flesh, no age can be without its own originality in Christian thinking.[95]

In the final analysis, it must be the Church of the present hour which determines what is in harmony with the scriptural message: this Church alone can serve as the final norm for determining religious truth. The present consciousness of the Christian community is all-important, and, as Flückiger notes, Schleiermacher consistently assigns to Scripture only a secondary role:

> Here Scripture no longer has the last word. In the course of the ecclesiastical development of doctrine, certain immanent principles evolve of themselves, which make it possible for the Church to distinguish between truth and error. . . . It is obvious that here the Scriptural Principle is replaced by an evolutionary Principle of Tradition. The principles which, as guiding principles, crystallize through time in the development of a dogmatic comprehension, the more the Church "learns to know itself," are also determinative for the ecclesiastical conviction concerning the truth of her dogma. And what are decisive for their further development are the immanent evolutionary tendencies of the ecclesiastical tradition itself.[96]

PROTESTANT LIBERALISM

In all of this we see the starting point of what has come to be known as Protestant Liberalism, and it is this which justifies calling Schleiermacher the father of modern liberal theology. This liberal movement reached its climax in the last decade of the nineteenth century; the final stage of development is frequently associated with the famous work of Adolph Harnack, *The Essence of Christianity (Das Wesen des Christentums)*, which is a transcript of extemporaneous lectures delivered at the University of Berlin in the winter of 1899–1900. By that time a good deal of liberal water had flowed under the bridge and what appeared in 1900 was not entirely identical with what Schleiermacher produced eighty or ninety years earlier. The philosophical basis, however, remained basically the same.

The later liberal theology placed great importance on Schleiermacher's insistence on the authority of Christian experience. As Dillenberger-Welch note in their work, *Protestant Christianity*, there were three principal movements in the nineteenth century which contributed to the eventual formation of liberal theology, and the *first* of these was the notion of religious experience as worked out by Schleiermacher:

> Enough has now been said to enable us to see the crucial place of Schleiermacher in the development of Protestant thought. Though Kant had anticipated the turn to a realm of subjective experience as the beginning-point for theology, Schleiermacher first made explicit the understanding that the teachings of the church are really explanations or explications of Christian experience. . . . The affirmations of faith are not dependent upon the constructions of natural theology or ethics, nor are they simply deduced from an infallible scripture or creed. The Bible and the creeds are important, but as records and interpretations of the experience of Christ.[97]

In addition to the teaching of Schleiermacher mention might also be made of the influence of Albrecht Ritschl (1822–1889), whose theology of moral values was also incorporated into much of liberalism. Ritschl accepted the position of Schleiermacher, as well as the teachings of the higher critics, but went on to lay special emphasis upon the *ethical* goals of Christianity. He looked upon God as love alone and, in rejecting the notion of original sin, presented an optimistic view of the kingdom of God on earth as an organization of humanity through action inspired by love. For a Protestantism fast stripping itself of dogmatic truths, this ethical notion was ripe for acceptance as the true meaning of Christianity. Ritschl greatly influenced the formation of the "social gospel" in modern Protestantism.

BIBLICAL STUDIES

To the immanentist and subjectivist teaching of Schleiermacher and the moralism of Ritschl, there was then added a *second* element, namely, the approach of biblical (or historical) criticism which was being developed at about the same time. It is important to remember that in nineteenth-century Protestantism, the religious philosophy of Schleiermacher and the findings of biblical criticism were actually two elements of one reality; the conclusions of the biblical critics were evaluated and interpreted against the backdrop of Schleiermacher's philosophy. It was a concern not for textual criticism, which was quite old by the nineteenth century, but for "higher criticism." Treated in union with Schleiermacher's position (shared, of course, by many another and expressed in slightly different language), biblical criticism in the developing liberal theology of the past century meant treating the Scriptures as purely human creations, as expressions of the religious experience of the primitive Christian Church alone. The Bible was not considered either as an inspired book or as the Word of God in the sense of sixteenth-century Protestantism (or of Roman Catholicism). As a result, the legitimate findings of scriptural study all took on a new meaning through this philosophic system with which they were associated.

As the debates of the past few years have shown, there are still many individuals who fail to understand the approach of the Catholic Church to modern scriptural studies. Many Catholics still seem to fear the entire scriptural movement, but what they fail to realize is that their fears really center upon this immanentist philosophy (and its faulty concept of the evolution of dogma), or on their own more rationalistic theory of faith (which demands that the Bible be considered a purely historical book in the modern sense). Catholic theologians and Scripture scholars today, however, are not working along these lines at all. They accept the legitimate findings of scriptural research, but they refuse to interpret it in the light of any immanentist philosophy. And as the recent Instruction of the Biblical Commission indicates, this work is carried on with full approval of the teaching Church.

This does not mean, of course, that there is any supposed opposition between the decrees issued in 1907 under Pius X and those of the present day. Dillenberger-Welch, for example, seem to have misunderstood the Catholic position on this point. They state that "Pius X specifically forbade Roman Catholic scholars to use the methods of 'secular' historical analysis on the Bible," but conclude that "the effect of the proscription against the use of such critical methods has been moderated in recent years. . . ."[98] This is not quite the situation. Leo XIII and Pius XII were necessarily as much opposed to what Pius X condemned as this sainted Pontiff was himself. It was the philosophical basis coloring all of the interpretations offered both by the Protestant Liberals and the Modernists within the Catholic Church which made the difference. In the days of Pius X it was well nigh impossible to disentangle the complicated web of Schleiermacherian thought and the biblical criticism then offered. What was condemned was the common acceptance by Catholics of both systems — the philosophical and the critical — as evidenced in the teachings of the Modernists. A problem such as that can only be faced in the total complex of human activity in which it appears. The objective data concerning authorship of the Bible, literary forms, the relationship between the various books, and so forth, were then receiving an interpretation in accord with such philosophy as that of Schleiermacher. What was condemned by Rome then is condemned today.

On the other hand, it is considerably easier for the scriptural scholar to advance his findings today quite independent of the philosophical matrix into which similar findings were inserted by Liberals and Modernists at the turn of the century. Thus the Roman Pontiffs have given frequent encouragement to such scriptural studies, related, as they are, to the philosophical and theological principles proper to Catholicism.

THIRD ELEMENT

In addition to the philosophy of Schleiermacher and other immanentists, and the concerns of biblical criticism, a *third* cause contributed to the rise of liberal theology; this was the emphasis on science and the scientific method in the nineteenth century. Darwin's general notion of evolution extended far beyond the realm of natural science and pervaded the thinking of all men; and the scientific method of the nineteenth-century historian came to be looked upon as the answer to all doubt and insecurity. Science would now establish the belief of Christianity, and it would appear — in conjunction with these other two elements — as a progressively evolving and changing expression of the religious experience of Christians in successive centuries. History in this sense appeared as that "historicism" so opposed by Pius XII as irreconcilable with Catholicism insofar as it designates a philosophical system limited to the temporal, to change and evolution, and which accordingly rejects the spiritual, the permanent, and eternal.[99]

It was the most famous Protestant historian of the past century, Adolph Harnack, who finally brought all these varied tendencies together and set forth a purely natural explanation of the essence of Christianity in these terms. It was a Christianity approached from the point of view of science and the scientific method, accompanied by a good deal of skepticism and an emphasis upon inner religious experience. It absorbed the spirit of evolution and constant improvement, and gave expression to its unbounded confidence in man and his future. This general spirit flowed over into all of Christian doctrine, and brought forth new "liberal interpretations" of every doctrine known to Christianity.[100]

Within the Catholic Church there were those who were not untouched by these trends within Protestantism. Throughout the eighteenth century there had been repeated efforts on the part of Catholic theologians to incorporate Kantian philosophy into an explanation of Catholic doctrine. Many of the Traditionalists and Fideists used the Kantian doctrine as the starting point for their own efforts to find God by some other natural means (since Kant had presumably destroyed the proofs from reason for God's existence). There were also those who had become acquainted with the philosophy of Schleiermacher and others of similar mentality; some had turned to the problems of biblical criticism, and encountered the philosophic basis associated with it in Protestant Liberalism. It might only be expected that there would be those who would conclude to something very much like the synthesis of Protestant liberal theology.

All of these tendencies came to light in the *Pascendi* of Pope Pius X. The Church had recognized the errors that were developing on some sides, and moved to stamp them out. The *Pascendi*, far more than the *Lamentabili*, points out the interrelationship between the various trends of thought being pursued at that time. The *Lamentabili* makes no attempt to analyze; it is simply a series of sixty-five statements to be condemned since they pertain to this entire mentality. Included among them are such typical positions as these: the scientific method is supreme, and even the Church must submit to the judgment of exegetes;[101] God is not the author of Scripture, and inspiration is very limited;[102] the Bible must be interpreted as a merely human document;[103] revelation is nothing except the consciousness that man has of his relationship to God;[104] revelation did not end with the death of the last Apostle;[105] the divinity of Christ is something derived from the gradual evolution of the Christian conscience;[106] dogmas are only interpretations and evolutions of the Christian intelligence;[107] the chief articles of the Apostles' Creed did not have the same sense for the early Church as they have today;[108] modern Catholicism can be reconciled with true science only "if it is transformed into a non-dogmatic Christianity; that is to say, into a broad and liberal Protestantism."[109]

The roots of these statements lie in the field of Liberal Protestantism. This is the key to a proper understanding of Modernism within the Catholic Church. These isolated statements which were condemned, however, were set forth in the far more synthetic outline of Modernist thought presented by Pius X two months later in the *Pascendi,* in which the Pontiff explained the general Modernist teaching, its causes and its remedies.[110] The opening paragraphs of this encyclical read in large measure like a summary of the teaching of Schleiermacher. It is, in its own way, no less than amazing that the Catholic theologians involved in this debate were able, in the heat of controversy, to go to the very root of the problem. They saw at that time what appears so clear to us today, that is, that anyone wishing to understand the origins and development of Modernism within the Catholic Church must assuredly turn to a study of the writings of Schleiermacher and the manner in which they were interpreted by nineteenth-century Liberal Protestantism.

There is an important difference between Modernism and Liberal Protestantism, of course. The Modernist attempted to bring into harmony both the traditional Catholic faith and these principles of Liberalism; this would naturally result in a rather distinct system. Obviously, because of the opposite directions taken by the underlying philosophical principles of both systems, this attempt could not possibly have succeeded. It was in reality an attempt to reconcile the irreconcilable, and it could only have ended by the abandonment of one or the other element: either accept the condemnation of Pius X or forsake the Catholic Church. This last was the choice of some. Alfred Loisy, for example, rose to defend the Church against Harnack's *The Essence of Christianity,* but his *L'évangile et l'Église* showed that he too had absorbed a good deal of the liberal position, even though he now aligned himself with those in the eschatological school of thought who reacted against much of Harnack's teaching. The same is true of the Tyrrell and the other leaders of the Modernist movement within the Church.

Their defense of Catholicism indicated time and again that they had made more concessions to Protestant Liberalism than orthodox Catholic doctrine could endure.

At the present time, the Liberalism of the past century is generally looked upon with disfavor among Protestant theologians. In a comparatively short time, a reaction set in against the extremes of liberal thought. Perhaps the best known rejection of this position is Karl Barth's commentary on St. Paul's Epistle to the Romans. In the first edition in 1919, Barth was still very much a liberal, but the second edition (1921) marked a violent rejection of liberal theology and a desire to return to more orthodox Protestant belief. Involved in this was the concern of the present century in the philosophy of existentialism; this is perhaps the most noteworthy element in present-day Protestant developments. Apart from the fundamentalist churches, Protestant theology today is largely dominated by this type of thought, although the influence of Schleiermacher is far from dead. Any attempt to understand present-day Protestant thought, however, must necessarily involve an approach by way of Kantian principles, of Schleiermacher's application of these, and of the existentialist restatement of the concept of religious experience. Kierkegaard spoke out against the absolute deification of human reason in the philosophy of Hegel; he desired a more personalist approach to God. This is reflected in much of Protestant thought today which is concerned not so much with man's discovery of God, but with God's self-manifestation to man by which the personal confrontation of faith is accomplished:

So far, the emphasis of recent thought is not unlike that of the liberal stress on religious experience. . . . But the connotation of this view is quite different from that of liberalism. . . . *God* reveals himself to faith. His Word to man stands in judgment on all human words and conceptions. The final court of appeal is not rational norms, or conscience or experience, but the self-revelation of God, and there is a "given-ness" in revelation which makes it always "over-against" man.[111]

In line with this new concern for existentialistic philosophy, however, there has arisen a question as to whether the nineteenth-century liberals actually grasped the real import of what Schleier-macher was trying to say. There is an undeniable existentialist and personalist facet to his complicated thought, and for this reason Schleiermacher continues to exert an influence on modern religious thought. This explains in part the interest of such an existentially motivated theologian as Karl Barth in the thought of Schleier-macher; it is not purely historical. Schleiermacher would probably have rejected the extremes of liberal thought in the era following his. Despite his immanentist concerns, he did not want to reduce Christianity to a purely natural and historical level. It is, therefore, the opinion of Flückiger that Barth has perceived the key to Schlei-ermacher's true thought, and "for the first time" has brought to light the originality and the exact meaning of Schleiermacher's scientific method.[112] As Barth views Schleiermacher, he is not to be studied either from a philosophical or a dogmatic point of view alone, but from combination of the two. All of these elements must be used so that, through contrast and synthesis, the com-plete picture may be drawn. For Barth, therefore, religious truth in the teaching of Schleiermacher is "life." This is the key to his thought. It is, however, a life couched in existentialist terms — a life which is realized only in the endless breach between being and existence.[113]

Kierkegaard (1813–1855) was only twenty-one when Schleier-macher died, but the intellectual climate that produced Kierkegaard may already have influenced Schleiermacher. In many respects Kierkegaard was not any more antirational than Schleiermacher; neither of them would agree to any attempt to reduce religion to reason, and both refused to grant reason any special power in the realm of natural theology. While Schleiermacher admits that Chris-tian dogmas can be presented rationally, in logical and intelligible phrases, he insists that they can be known or perceived only by a unique experience on the part of the Christian and not by reason:

> In one respect all Christian dogmas are supra-rational, in another they are all rational. They are supra-rational in the respect in which everything experiential is supra-rational. For

there is an inner experience to which they may all be traced: they rest upon a *given;* and apart from this they could not have arisen, by deduction or synthesis, from universally recognized and communicable propositions. If the reverse were true, it would mean that you could instruct and demonstrate any man into being a Christian, without his happening to have had any experience.[114]

No less than Kierkegaard, Schleiermacher would oppose any attempt to freeze this vital experience into a closed, complete, static, dead system. He insists that the presentation of Christian dogmas in any rational form is only temporary; it describes the "prevalent doctrine," but nothing more. Life does not stand still in this system, and it is for this reason that Barth would single out the concept of "life" in Schleiermacher's thought. Kierkegaard, on the other hand, while stressing life and personal encounter, made explicit the notion of the "Moment" in which all Christians encounter Christ, something not noted in Schleiermacher.

It may possibly be that this more existentialistic outlook would account for the sharp division between the thought of Hegel and Schleiermacher which eventually even reached the point of personal antipathy. Hegel felt that an approach such as Schleiermacher's would in the end frustrate religion by disparaging the rational side of life.[115] On the other hand, it was largely by way of opposition to the totalitarian claims of Hegelian reason that Kierkegaard set forth his position, which would also suggest the possibility of further investigation into the relationship of Schleiermacher's thought to present-day existentialism.

Be that as it may, the fact remains that the religious philosophy of Friedrich Schleiermacher did exercise a great influence on the development of Protestant liberal theology. Despite the influence of Barth and other existentialist theologians, it is illuminating to note a continued interest in basic liberal viewpoints. Even with tags of Neo-Orthodoxy and Neo-Liberalism, there has been for a long time a feeling that present-day Protestant theology has not really approached too closely to orthodoxy nor bid too final a farewell to Liberalism. As Gustave Weigel has remarked, "Seemingly, there-

fore, the Neo-Orthodox are a Center theology, but a closer examination of their thought has led many critics to believe that they
are basically liberals in a strange guise."[116] Neo-Liberalism is even
more obviously attached to its nineteenth-century predecessors.[117]

This has been brought out most strikingly, however, by the remarks of H. Richard Niebuhr in 1960. He himself was originally
a product of the liberal theology of Protestantism in the past century. From this he passed over into the concerns of Karl Barth,
generally referred to as Neo-Orthodoxy. But eventually he tended
to reject Barth in turn, and return to a theological position more
in line with that which he had adopted originally — a liberal point
of view. Speaking of the postliberal theologians in Protestantism
he has this to say:

> So many of them seem to me to have gone back to othodoxy
> as right teaching, right doctrine, and to faith as *fides*, an assent;
> they tend, it seems to me, toward the definition of Christian life
> in terms of right believing, of Christianity as the true religion,
> and otherwise toward the assertion of the primacy of ideas over
> personal relations. When I think about this I have to say to
> myself that important as theological formulations are for me,
> they are not the basis of faith but only one of its expressions,
> and that not the primary one. I discover further a greater kin-
> ship with all theologians of Christian experience than with the
> theologians of Christian doctrine. So I find myself, though with
> many hesitations, closer to Edwards and Schleiermacher, to
> Coleridge, Bushnell and Maurice than to Barth and the dogmatic
> biblical theology current today in wide circles. . . .To state my
> understanding of our theological situation briefly. I believe that
> the Barthian correction of the line of march begun in Schleier-
> macher's day was absolutely essential, but that it has become
> an overcorrection and that Protestant theology can minister to
> the church's life more effectively if it resumes the general line
> of march represented by the evangelical, empirical and critical
> movement.[118]

In this we see striking evidence that the spirit of liberalism is far
from dead; this approach to Christianity is not yet ready for the
historical junk pile. Obvious traces of liberal thought have continued to influence present-day Protestant thought and scriptural

study, despite such newly hewn names as Neo-Orthodoxy, Neo-Liberalism, or Existentialistic Theology. While Bultmann and Tillich have reacted against the liberal tradition, there may yet remain some question as to whether they have not simply out-liberalized the liberals in their wave of antisupernaturalism.[119]

In any event, the movement influenced so forcefully by the teaching of Schleiermacher is still very much with us, and Catholic theologians have a great need of understanding this historical background. Without such a knowledge we can only too easily misinterpret the past and misunderstand the present.

CHAPTER VI

Can Historical Method Prove Christ's Divinity?

This question is peculiarly a product of the era of modern thought, and by this we would indicate that period of history reaching roughly from the seventeenth century down to the present time. The very question would have made little sense to a medieval Christian or to a member of the primitive Church, not because they lacked interest in history but because theirs was not the peculiar concern which we share in regard to the historical method. There has always been within the history of Christianity a regard for history and historical problems, but when the question is phrased in this particular fashion, we lay emphasis upon a particular and highly developed technique which grew out of the philosophical, theological, and scriptural concerns of modern thought and which has brought to an unprecedented peak our appreciation of history and our ability to evaluate it properly.

Garraghan defines historical method as "a systematic body of principles and rules designed to aid effectively in *gathering* the source-materials of history, *appraising* them critically, and present-ing a *synthesis* (generally in written form) of the results achieved."[1] All three of these elements are important, although the second is clearly the most subtle and for that reason the most difficult. The gathering of the source materials is a *sine qua non* of historical scholarship; if the past has left no traces, or if we are unable to locate such evidence, we cannot even begin our historical study. Yet the historian is no mere collector of relics from the past; his most essential task lies in the proper and objective evaluation of

157

the source material. For this task he must, as far as possible, divest himself of his own subjective presuppositions or prejudices, and attempt to immerse himself in the spirit and the mentality of the era which he is investigating.[2] Should he fail to do this, he will scarcely be able to avoid reading into the evidence on hand something which is not there and which does not represent the spirit of the past but simply the preformed conclusions of his own mind.

Only when such an evaluation has been adequately completed is the historian able to present the results of his studies in either an oral or written fashion. This will involve, of course, a synthesis of some sort rather than a mere enumeration of data — a synthesis which represents the prior synthetic activity of his mind in appraising and evaluating the evidence. Much of this is surely an art as well as a technique, and while the "historical sense" and the "historical mind" can be cultivated in some fashion, the truly successful historian must also be blessed by nature with that perceptiveness and imagination which will enable him to grasp a valid insight into the situation he is investigating; he cannot be a mere reporter.[3]

In accomplishing his task, therefore, the historian strives to achieve a personal encounter with the past as it reveals itself to him in the documents or evidence before him. This cannot be done without putting off, as it were, the closed circle of his own personality, his own concerns, his own world, and opening himself up to the world and concerns of others. The inability to do this, as Marrou points out, can be productive only of bad historians and purely statistical history.[4] Central in this process is the ability to isolate those individuals and events, the particular mental attitudes or philosophical positions, which dominated the course of human life in each successive era. In this way the real past, the past as lived, unfolds for the historian, and he himself comes in contact with others who may have lived in a world not his own, but which was once living and vital and which had profound influences both upon the men of that time and those in later generations as well.

Research must thus be joined to imagination and originality on the part of the historian; he cannot deal simply with documents and hope that they of themselves will tell him all he needs to know. His entire background, the wealth of his information, his current interests, his appreciation of related fields will all enable him to ask the right questions and to recognize the pertinent answers when he encounters them in his documents. He does so, not with any pre-suppositions nor with any desire to superimpose upon the texts an import other than that which they have to relate, but simply to be able to act as an historian and to approach the problem both with an open and an inquisitive mind that will not overlook those matters which, from an *a priori* point of view, the historian himself may never have expected to discover.[5] In this way alone can he come to a fruitful knowledge of what actually took place in the past, and why it happened, and what the total meaning of it might be. A technique is necessary so that the truth will unfold clearly, but a proper historical mentality is equally as important for the same reason; it is not the subjective mind of the historian which we seek to know, but the objective truth of the past.

Thus ultimately the question of the historical method reduces itself to the question of historical *truth*. For this reason, Garraghan defines historical method more briefly (citing Clarke) as "a system of right procedure for the attainment of [historical] truth."[6] There is a very close relationship between the method and the general epistemological problem of man's ability to attain truth. It is here that we can note the intimate connection between historical method and the concerns of modern philosophy, since the great problem ever since the time of Descartes (1596–1650) and his methodical doubt has been man's relationship to extramental reality and his ability to come into valid contact with it.[7]

THE RISE OF RATIONALISM

Even before the seventeenth century the spirit of humanism (which had so great an influence upon the debates of the Reformation era) indicated the beginnings of this general trend which centered attention on man and his native powers; eventually this attention was to be more or less limited to the human intellect alone. In the sixteenth century, however faith remained primary, and the full spirit of rationalism never came to the fore and had no real influence upon the basic attitude of Christians in either the Protestant or the Catholic camp. On both sides of the Reformation debates, there remained a living faith in at least the basic truths of revelation, and an acceptance of Scripture as the inspired word of God. While the Protestant reformers limited their attention to Scripture alone, they nevertheless insisted that the Bible was a divinely inspired book and represented a further entrance of God into the life of mankind after creation. The Catholic position remained the same, despite the Tridentine insistence that Scripture alone does not suffice and that something else — what they referred to as the "unwritten traditions" — also had to be accepted in order to possess the fullness of Christian truth.

On both sides, however, the notion of a special, even a supernatural, intervention of God in history was consistently defended by the leaders of the two groups and accepted by the faithful. Indeed, as McNeill remarks, "one source of the effectiveness of Zwingli's arguments lay in the fact that nobody really questioned the authority of Scripture."[8] This was quite generally true of all the Reformation leaders; the difficulties arose more over the question of the interpretation of Scripture. In practice, the interpretation accepted in the distinct circles was that proposed by the respective leaders — by Luther, Zwingli, Calvin, and the others. A modern Protestant, viewing this historical situation, does not hesitate to say, with McNeill, that the entire matter involved a certain naïvete on the part of these leading spirits. They felt certain that *their* interpretation of the Bible was the only true and acceptable understanding. Thus he says of Zwingli:

> The Bible presents for Zwingli a unified body of teaching, comprehensible to all who hearken to the voice of the Spirit, and supplies not only the true doctrine but also the basis of brotherly agreement and unity. He was willing to believe that if the Bible were given free course the faithful would, under its unitive impulse, abandon their contentions and dwell together as brethren. Even the Anabaptist commotion did not entirely disabuse him of this rather naïve supposition.[9]

A similar complaint might be levied against Calvin who "rejected the requirement of the Athanasian Creed on grounds of liberty of conscience . . . [but] saw no inconsistency in requiring the acceptance of his own confession. This he regarded as transparently and undeniably scriptural. Almost naïvely he thought its rejection a violation of the resolution of the people to live in accordance with Scripture."[10] And while Luther stressed nothing more than the authority of the Bible alone, his attitude toward the scriptural interpretations of Carlstadt and Müntzer, of Zwingli, and of the Anabaptists would indicate clearly enough that he regarded any other Protestant understanding of Scripture contrary to his own as nothing less than heretical.[11] As Bainton points out, despite his defense of the written word, in his debates with the sectaries and his rejection of their use of the New Testament, Luther "employed the very slogans of the radicals and became himself the champion of the spirit against the letter."[12]

Thus throughout the early history of Protestantism and even more so in the period of Protestant Orthodoxy (or the so-called Protestant Scholasticism),[13] there was a constant appeal on all sides to the Bible as a "proof" of a particular doctrinal position, and the Catholic apologetes reacted by citing other scriptural "proofs," along with their interpretation of those texts, as a demonstration of the validity of the Catholic belief. In addition, because of the growing interest in patristic literature which eventually resulted from the humanistic concerns of the Renaissance scholars for ancient Greek and Latin literature, a further appeal was soon made to the writings of such men as St. Irenaeus, St. Augustine, or St. Jerome in an effort to "prove" the correctness of a specific Protestant or Catholic belief because of its supposed agreement with that discovered in the writings of these respected ecclesiastical writers. No less a personage than Adrian VI is said to have encouraged Erasmus to extend his interest in ancient writings to both Scripture and the works of these ancient authors.[14] Such an interest soon became a part of the spirit of that age.

In these developments we can note the first origins of the thesis method into which the basic approach of the Scholastics eventually evolved so as to take a prominent place in our theological manuals today. Yet we may ask if in all of this there has not arisen a serious misunderstanding in regard to the purpose of the thesis, and — more basically — in regard to the nature of theological method itself. This is not to attack the theological manuals as such; they have their role to play, but it must be properly understood.[15] Unfortunately, these early developments underwent the later influence both of deistic thought in the Baroque era and the emphasis on antiquity associated with the classic spirit in the last half of the eighteenth century and the opening decades of the nineteenth century, so that the so-called "proof from Scripture" and "proof from tradition" gradually took on new meanings. There were those who felt that the new critical approach to the Bible would finally establish the true meaning of Christian revelation, while others chose to look upon the consensus of the fathers or churches of the first 300 or 500 years of the Christian era as an absolute proof of true doctrine.[16] This early belief was set forth as the norm or criterion of faith for successive generations, so that the belief of the Church at the present time would be acceptable and apostolic only if it were identified with this belief of the first 500 years or so.[17]

Under the aegis of Romanticism in the nineteenth century, however, greater importance was attributed to the concept of life and vitality, and as transferred to the realm of faith, this notion brought out the importance of the living Church (the faith of the community as well as the teaching authority of the magisterium); thus the proof from tradition would necessarily extend up to the present century, giving special place to the solemn definitions of the authentic teaching authority throughout history.[18] The Church of the fifth or sixth century would thus be on an equal plane with the Church of the present century; the Holy Spirit abides always with the living community, so that the sole valid distinction would be that between the apostolic Church and the Church from the second century on.

Along with these other developments, the nineteenth century also brought a new emphasis on the historical approach to the

Bible; it made use of a more precise and highly developed technique for investigating the documents of the past, and this applied to Scripture as well. Thus so-called "proof from Scripture" took on an historical dimension since it was recognized that the New Testament was not an impersonal statement of doctrinal truths but a reflection of the faith and teaching of primitive Christianity. In the present century the Form critics added to this realization by their emphasis upon the oral tradition before the books of the New Testament were composed. As a result, Scripture and the prescriptural tradition came to be drawn into an ever closer relationship both in Catholic and Protestant theology, thus opening up for Protestant consideration the possible need of tradition after the writing of these books as well.

This entire shift of emphasis represents the outgrowth of the Christian's encounter with (and rejection of) the unbalanced rationalism and excessive historicism which threatened to invade the field of theological scholarship (with its consequent repercussions upon faith), and thus destroy the concept of the supernatural and reduce to a purely human level any attempts to analyze the sources of revelation and the teaching of the Church. In this way, the very rejection of these excesses emphasized the supernaturality of faith for the Catholic and the unique role of theological method; each encounter with a new overemphasis resulted in a more positive statement of the Catholic position, serving as a starting point for further clarification.

THE INFLUENCE OF DESCARTES AND DEISM

In Descartes's dictum, *cogito ergo sum,* there is an extreme insistence upon only one constituent aspect of personality, the intellect. Feeling and will are not denied in his system, but they tend to be more or less ignored. Following this line of thought, modern philosophy has in large measure tended to gravitate toward rationalism. At the same time, it also absorbed another facet of Cartesian thought, that is, the spirit of doubt which tended to replace the role of certitude. Thus both the unbridled rationalism and the excessive skepticism of later centuries can be viewed, at least in part, as logical outgrowths of the basic positions defended by Descartes.

In the realm of faith (and the field of theology associated with it), this same approach exercised a strong and almost ruinous influence. On the rationalistic side, there was first of all the theology — or philosophy — of *deism*. For the deist, religion was to be brought into accord with human reason entirely; not even Christianity was excluded from this process. It is a strange paradox that in the history of modern Western thought, there has been no period in which the chief concern of the philosopher was more theological than the era now known as the Age of Reason (roughly from 1650 to 1800). This very attempt of the men of that period to reduce everything, including religion, to the realm of the purely reasonable tended to rivet philosophical attention even more strongly on questions of faith and religion. This is something true of the entire period of modern history, for that matter, due to the influence of the deists at the very start. In a certain way, the deistic thought reached a climax, often unrecognized, in the absolute philosophers of the nineteenth century whom Przywara speaks of as "de-theologized theologians."[19] Their terminology and interests were largely theological, but their philosophy gave it all a completely different twist. Thus, as Maritain has pointed out:

> Modern philosophy itself from Descartes to Hegel remains enigmatic without . . . [a serious theological background], for in actual fact philosophy has burdened itself through modern times with problems and anxieties taken over from theology.[20]

When Descartes died in 1650 the philosophical world was ripe for the development of new lines of thought. This deistic movement, first evidenced in the sixteenth century,[21] entered into that world and came into its own in the following century. As Gilson remarks, Toland's *Christianity Not Mysterious* (1696) contained "the whole of Deism in a nutshell."[22] Yet, while deism was largely rationalistic in tone and aimed not actually at destroying religion but at removing it from the realm of anything that could be called supernatural or mysterious, it nevertheless tended to retain what we might call the Christian vocabulary. It sounded Christian enough, but closer analysis showed it to be something far removed from what Christianity has always claimed to be. This deistic Christianity was nothing but natural religion itself, couched in the terms of Christian revelation. In content it remained a set of religious truths arrived at by reason alone, or (if any revelation be admitted) a set of truths contained by their very nature within the boundaries of human reason and thus at least humanly provable. The very titles of Locke's *The Reasonableness of Christianity* (1695) and Tindal's *Christianity as Old as Creation: Or, the Gospel, a Republication of the Religion of Nature* (1730) express this pervading view.[23] Not significantly different from English deism was the rationalistic spirit of the German *Aufklärung* or the French philosophy of Voltaire and his disciples in the eighteenth century; even Kant's late theological work reflects this basic mentality: *Religion Within the Limits of Reason Alone* (1793).

Thus throughout the Age of Reason this rationalism ruled supreme, even among many who claimed to be Christian. Reason was the sole and absolute norm, and Christian faith itself had to be reduced to the level of the purely human and rational. At the same time, there was another element that was delicately woven into this fabric of deistic rationalism; it touched upon the nature of religious assent. As Theodore Greene expresses it, for the deist "faith was now sought exclusively by the path of argument: logical demonstration, like that found in Euclid, was considered the sole adequate basis for conviction; reason claimed to be autonomous and set itself up as the unique court of appeal."[24]

BISHOP BUTLER

The response of many Christian theologians, both Catholic and Protestant, was not what one might expect at first blush; their reactions, however, give us an insight into the widespread influence of this emphasis on logical demonstration in Christian theology. As an example of this group, we may consider one of the most influential (indeed a great influence in the intellectual formation of Cardinal Newman): Bishop Joseph Butler (1692–1752), whose major work, *The Analogy of Religion, Natural and Revealed, to the*

Constitution and Course of Nature (1736) was intended as an answer to the attacks of the deists upon traditional Christianity.[25] Butler chose to meet the deists on their own ground, however, and while he strove to defend the existence of true supernatural mysteries within Christianity, he attempted to do so by an appeal to reason and a concept of faith that would root the assent in just such a logical type of demonstration as the deists sought; ultimately this tactic proved to be his theological undoing. An Anglican bishop, Butler was anxious to defend the traditional notion of Christianity; it was simply in his doctrine of religious assent that he turned to deistic principles. But the end result could only be a faith that rested upon reason and historical certitude alone.

As with many other Christian apologists of the eighteenth century, the cool intellectual religion of Butler was limited almost entirely to the power of human reason; the interior workings of grace are scarcely mentioned. But the rationalism of it stands out the most. For Butler, religion — even the Christian religion — "is not intuitively true, but a matter of deduction and inference."[26] As such, the truth of Christianity "is not forced upon every one, but left to be, by some, collected with heedful attention to premises."[27]

Butler also serves as a good example of the difficulties which arose in regard to the question of moral certitude and historical knowledge. The problem centered around the argument from probability, as worked out in the seventeenth century, as well as in the approach to the Bible as a purely historical book; these are interrelated questions.[28] For the deist, if no mysterious or supernatural elements are to be admitted in Christianity, the problem immediately arises concerning what is to be said of the mysterious elements recorded in Scripture. The answer, of course, was frequently that they resulted from overactive imaginations, if not from downright fraudulent practices; the Bible would have to be understood apart from them.

As did many others, Butler rejected this conclusion and defended the reality of the supernatural and the miracles and prophecies recorded in Scripture. At the same time, he pointed to these miracles and prophecies (viewed merely as historically observable *facts*) as *proof* of the truth of Christianity. In doing this, he accepted the challenge of treating the Bible as a purely historical book, and thus soon involved himself in the difficult problem that has troubled men to this day, that is, the nature of historical assent.

Butler recognized the chief objection to his line of argument. If the proofs (miracles and prophecies) are historical facts, how could the argument exceed the rational and historical order? On the other hand, if the argument remains in this historical order, how could we conclude to anything more than a high degree of probability as regards the truth of Christianity?

Butler's answer was very simple. He admitted the weakness of his arguments, but he chose to take his stand on the notion of probable evidence, using the argument from probability. Far from denying it, Butler admitted that this was the best type of certitude that the Christian might hope for; it was all that the evidence could offer, and he would have to be satisfied with it.

In doing this, Butler was following the general lead of John Locke, who had earlier distinguished between demonstration and probability.[29] "Probability," Butler insists, "is the very guide of life."[30] We have to act on probable evidence all day long, in all the varied concerns of our life; we cannot escape it. Hence why should we demand more even in regard to our Christian faith? We must learn to accept the evidence it offers, and live with it.

The application of this principle to Christianity, however, was the fatal mistake in Butler's defense of Christian belief; it was the source of his unwitting encouragement to agnostic and frankly atheistic thinking in later generations.[31] Butler simply could not bring his historicorational conclusions concerning the truth of Christianity to support the unswerving stability that Christian faith demands. He left the believer hesitant and insecure.

In discussing Butler's position in relationship to certitude (metaphysical, physical, or moral), we must say that his assent of faith pertains, in the last analysis, to the category of moral certitude — that category in which both philosophers and historians now place historical certitude.[32] There are some, of course, who claim that there may be certain instances where the evidence is so strong that the conclusion might be said to approach metaphysical certitude, but this position is well challenged. In practice we must admit at least an outside chance that some evidence has escaped our grasp, or that we may have evaluated wrongly the evidence on hand. It is perhaps with this thought in mind that even those who defend a reduction of historical certitude to the metaphysical will add that the entire question "whether anything in history can be metaphysically certain is only of speculative interest."[33] Apart from all debates, history does its actual work in the realm of moral certitude alone.

The entire history of modern thought regarding the assent of faith, however, shows a constant fluctuation between extremes. There are those who would root faith on a rational and historical assent alone, but they are inevitably challenged by others who claim that this will lead only to doubt and insecurity and the ultimate destruction of Christianity. Others attempt, therefore, to bypass history and establish faith on the authority of God alone; some of these tend, like Schleiermacher, to lapse into a vague and futile form of mysticism or a type of absolute subjectivism, while others, as does Bultmann, ignore history to such a great extent that little resembling traditional Christian truths can long continue to be accepted. Nevertheless, there are also those who distinguish carefully between the role of reason in the preparation for faith and the totally supernatural character of the assent of faith itself; those who find the Christian message in history but who do so without admitting historical certitude as the ultimate basis of their religious assent. To this question we shall return presently.

SCRIPTURE AS HISTORY

Having rejected the mysterious and the supernatural for *a priori* reasons, the deists also ran headlong into another serious problem which was destined to increase in gravity in later centuries. This was the problem of the historicity of Scripture. Granted their position, the deists had no alternative but to claim that the

Bible contained unhistorical additions; later deists felt compelled to show that the writers of the New Testament (upon which the debates centered) were either stupid knaves blindly misled by their enthusiasm, or scheming masters of deception who knowingly related as history what they knew to be untrue. Lurking beneath this response, however, there was the very real fact that the Bible presents certain problems to the historically oriented reader, and these questions could not be put off forever.

Unfortunately many of the Christian believers who faced the first attacks of the deists and their rationalistic evaluation of the Bible had no better answer than that of Bishop Butler. It amounted to a repetitious emphasis upon the strict historical nature of the inspired books and the integrity and reliability of the sacred writers. This response was something of a trap since these defenders unwittingly chose to accept the unreal demands of their opponents. By arbitrarily reducing Christianity to the rational level they had chosen, the deists gave clear evidence of their lack of true historical insight; but the ready answers of many Catholics and Protestants to these deistic claims reflected an equally dangerous, though subtle, lack of historical perspective. Because the deists had claimed loudly that the Bible was to be viewed from a purely historical and rational point of view, rejecting all that is supernatural, these defenders of Christianity felt that they had to prove the strict historicity of the inspired books. What men like Butler and many others failed to realize is that the deists were wrong in superimposing a more modern concept of historical method on the writings of the primitive Church; this led ultimately to nothing more than further confusion.

In the seventeenth century the Oratorian priest Richard Simon (1638–1712) felt that he had an answer to the attacks raised against the Bible at that time, namely, a critical approach to Scripture. His suggestions, however, were rejected by his superiors, and he was expelled from his congregation; his efforts knew no success within the Catholic Church. Engaged in a losing battle with Bossuet, Simon was looked upon as an opponent of Catholic truth and an enemy of the Sacred Books. Perhaps at that time in history there would have been difficulty in achieving complete success; Simon and his age were not equipped to bring to its best development this critical approach to Scripture. Yet it was at least a beginning, and basically it constituted a better response to the attacks than those then being given. The rejection of Simon's views cut the movement short within Catholic circles, although the ultimate verdict concerning the worth of Simon and his work was to be in his favor in later centuries.[34]

As a result of this, the critical approach to Scripture passed on to other hands outside the Catholic Church, indeed, even outside of Christianity. Despite his break with the Jewish faith and community, Baruch Spinoza (1632–1677) retained his familiarity with the Old Testament above all, and in his *Tractatus theologico-politicus* (1670), he defended the proposition that one ought to read the Bible as one reads any historical document.[35] As these writings became better known, his new approach to Scripture was more widely appreciated.

Two Calvinist leaders, however, were destined to play a more influential role than either Simon or Spinoza in popularizing these views. Hugo Grotius (1583–1645) had advanced the critical and historical approach greatly in his *Annotationes in libros evangeliorum* (1641) and his *Annotata ad vetus testamentum* (1644). He also had a great deal of influence upon the development of apologetics in the seventeenth century. On the Catholic side, Michael de Elizalde appears to have issued the first systematic response to the deistic attacks: *Forma verae religionis quaerendae et inveniendae,* published at Naples in 1662. Bossuet, de Huet, and Pascal also developed facets of this line of thought, and thus influenced seventeenth-century developments greatly. Grotius, however, composed an almost similar response from the Protestant view; the extent to which all sides were affected by the deistic attacks is evidenced by the similar type of rationalistic responses they gave:

> In the field of *Apologetics* Grotius achieved a great and enduring success by the publication of his treatise *De veritate religionis Christianae* (1627). . . . In this work Grotius may be said to have erected apologetics into a science, and thus rendered

immense service, even though his treatment of the subject does not meet all the wants of the present age. It is divided into six books, of which the first treats of the existence of God; the second, of the excellence of the doctrine and ethics of Christianity; the third, of the authenticity of the books of the New Testament; the last three, of objections supposed to be made on the part of pagans, Mohammedans, and Jews.[36]

This is a treatment very close to that offered by the Catholics as well. More on the scriptural level, however, another even greater, but destructive, influence was exercised by Pierre Bayle (1647–1706), who was most effective on the popular level. His *Dictionnaire historique et critique* (1695) brought the critical approach to Scripture to the attention of many far and wide. Unfortunately, Bayle's activity did not lead to an adequate solution to the problem but merely added fuel to the fire, since he surrounded his scriptural views with a virulent form of rationalism and skepticism, derived from his basic principle of an absolute antithesis between faith and reason. As Cragg points out:

> With his marvelous flair for popularization, Bayle not only expounded Simon's theories, he expanded them. His *Dictionary* proved a mine from which Deists and sceptics could quarry material for their attacks on the Bible and on the faith which it sustained. Bayle insisted, of course, that his purpose was not destructive. He had an insatiable intellectual curiosity and an irrepressible itch to write. He was not an original thinker, but in one area after another he suggested avenues of investigation which others (Voltaire or Diderot) would subsequently pursue. But whatever his purpose may have been, the spirit which he fostered was critical, and it was not subservient to any constructive ends. To a greater extent, perhaps, than any other man, Bayle created the sceptical spirit which was to prevail throughout so much of the eighteenth century.[37]

This generally rationalistic use of the critical approach to the Bible continued to enjoy favor through the following decades, but reached a certain climax under the influence of the historicocritical school of the nineteenth century. Such men as Barthold G. Niebuhr (1776–1831), Leopold von Ranke (1795–1886), and Theodor Mommsen (1817–1903) strove to establish an historical method which would permit the historian to treat his subject with the same type of objectivity as the chemist or physicist uses when dealing with his experiments. In this ideal the historian was to be a detached, almost depersonalized individual who was left unswayed by any other considerations except the cold and lifeless facts set before him in his investigation. The effect of this mentality in the approach to Scripture was to be most damaging.

HISTORICAL SKEPTICISM

It is recognized far more generally today that this ideal of the nineteenth-century positivists was an error, since the historical task cannot be accomplished by the supposedly totally detached, critical personality — if for no other reason than the basic fact that no such depersonalized human beings can exist. Man cannot divest himself of his own emotions and preconceptions; he must constantly check himself to be sure that they are not exerting a faulty influence on his conclusions.[38] The human being cannot turn himself into a type of scholar who undertakes his work with no more of the human, the subjective or the personal than an IBM machine; he must remain human.

The attempt to achieve such pure objectivity was a futile one, and the conclusions of the nineteenth-century critical scholars are undoubtedly the best proof of this. While imagining themselves to be purely objective and detached, they still remained human beings, with all the prejudices and failings of human nature. Yet this very conviction that they need not correct any such human tendencies within their own critical personalities left them open either to a subjectivity without constraint (since its existence was not even admitted), or to a form of skepticism that leads ultimately to the total abandonment of all hope of achieving the truth. Thus there were those among them who introduced into their supposedly "objective" conclusions a large number of subjective presuppositions of the very worst kind, vitiating in this way their entire research; while others, in their effort to remain purely objective, challenged every document so sharply for fear of not being detached enough that they saw nothing on all sides but the possibility of false witnesses and frauds, thus forcing themselves to abandon all hope of real success in their search.[39]

Nevertheless, despite our recognition today of its failings, this positivist spirit reigned supreme in the past century, extending the realm of historical certitude and its stability to all forms of human life. As Marrou states, this nineteenth-century historical spirit little by little invaded all domains of thought:

> The *historical sense* became one of the specific characteristics of the Western mentality. Indeed, the historian was king, all culture depended upon his judgments: it was for him to say how one must read the *Iliad*, what constituted a nation (historic frontiers, hereditary enemy, traditional mission) — it was he who would know if Jesus was God. . . . With one stroke, the historian succeeded the philosopher as guide and counselor.[40]

Present-day historians are far less enthusiastic in their claims, and in more modest fashion admit that historical research does not give the answer to all problems. Since historical certitude is accepted as a form of moral certitude at best (indeed, there are some points where, for lack of proper sources the scholar cannot even acquire moral certitude, but must settle for opinions and hypotheses), we must admit that there is always something relative in the findings of historical research. There is always the possibility of some change in the face of new evidence, or of a more adequate interpretation of the facts we now possess.

This is true even in regard to our approach to Scripture from an historical point of view.[41] Without passing over into unbridled skepticism, the thought of Paul Tillich in regard to Jesus reflects the historian's current concern for the nature of historical assent:

> But it is necessary systematically to raise once more a question which is continuously being asked with considerable religious anxiety. Does not the acceptance of the historical method for dealing with the source documents of the Christian faith introduce a dangerous insecurity into the thought and life of the Church and of every individual Christian? Could not historical research lead to a complete skepticism about the biblical records? Is it not imaginable that historical criticism could come to the judgment that the man Jesus of Nazareth never lived? Did not some scholars, though only a few and not very important ones,

make just this statement? And even if such a statement can never be made with certainty, is it not destructive for the Christian faith if the non-existence of Jesus can somehow be made probable, no matter how low the degree of probability? In reply, let us first reject some insufficient and misleading answers. It is inadequate to point out that historical research has not yet given any evidence to support such skepticism. Certainly, it has not yet! But the anxious question remains of whether it could not do so sometime in the future! Faith cannot rest on such unsure ground. . . .[42]

This may seem to be an extreme position to some, but once one approaches the Scriptures from a critical point of view, applying to it the tenets of the historical method, the question is almost bound to arise. This does not necessarily imply that one must also embrace the extreme rationalism associated with the critico-historical approach in the context of Liberal Protestantism or Catholic Modernism; but it does mean that the assent of faith cannot rest ultimately upon historical certitude, despite the importance of history for the Christian. The critical method as used in the past century failed because of the context in which it was applied; as Pius X was careful to point out in regard to Modernism, what vitiated these conclusions was not necessarily the use of the historical method nor the acceptance of critical findings in regard to Scripture, but rather the *philosophical context* in which all of this was interpreted.[43] From start to finish, everything in Modernism (as in the nineteenth-century Protestant liberalism) was guided by the post-Kantian type of philosophy which reduces faith to a subjective contact with the divine and explains its growth according to purely natural principles:

> As history takes its conclusions from philosophy, so too criticism takes its conclusions from history. . . . This done [the historian] finishes his work by drawing up a history of the development in its broad lines. The critic follows and fits in the rest of the documents. He sets himself to write. The history is finished. Now We ask here: Who is the author of this history? The historian? The critic? Assuredly neither of these but the philosopher. From beginning to end everything in it is *a priori*, and an apriorism that reeks of heresy.[44]

Apart from this philosophical context, a Catholic may analyze the *same* data by means of the historical method and recognize the *same* critical findings, but he views them in the light of the Church as the living Body of Christ, directed in its clarification of the original deposit of revelation by the divinely guided magisterium. Thus whatsoever may have been incorporated into the life of the primitive Church under the guidance of the Holy Spirit, and later found expression in the writings of the New Testament under the direction of that same Spirit, is not the result of any immanentist need of the divine nor any naturally explainable process of evolution of thought, but a part of the eternal plan by which God chose to bestow Christian revelation upon mankind in the era of the primitive Church, and to prepare for its further clarification in the life of the postapostolic community up to the present moment. It is in this total context of Scripture, tradition, and the living Church that the Catholic historian-theologian approaches both the Bible and the ecclesiastical documents of the past and present; and it is this difference in approach that separates him entirely from those more rationalistic scholars of the past and present who defend a purely natural and immanentist *creative* function of the Church in regard to the development of Christian truth.[45]

In line with this, Pius XII distinguished between "history" and "historicism," noting that the Church does not fear history, but urges the use of it; even in proposing new definitions in solemn form, the Church must be in intimate contact with the past. The Church must, and does, reject, however, this "historicism," which reflects the spirit of the historicocritical school and the past century and which really indicates a "philosophical system which perceives in all spiritual reality, in the knowledge of the true, in religion, morality and law, nothing but change and evolution, and which consequently rejects everything that is permanent, eternally valid, and absolute. Such a system is assuredly irreconcilable with the Catholic conception of the world, and, in general, with every religion which recognizes a personal God."[46]

THE PROBLEM OF HISTORICAL ASSENT

If John Locke (1632–1704) was a prophet pointing out the direction toward the skepticism born of extreme rationalism, it was David Hume (1711–1776) who pressed this line of thought to its logical conclusion and embraced a system of pan-phenomenalism and consequent skepticism. Man became more and more limited to the perceptions of sense, and hence was driven on to despair of ever grasping the ultimate reality of things. By his disagreement with the deistic emphasis upon the powers of reason, Hume directed the man in search of God to an analysis of his own *personal experience;* in doing this he prepared the way for the stress on the emotional or volitional bases of religion as indicated first by Kant (1724–1804) and brought to fuller expression by Schleiermacher (1768–1834) and likeminded thinkers during the early part of the past century. In this way, rationalism was first attacked by skepticism only to see both of them replaced by a new immanentist approach to religion and to faith.

As he ventured out on this new journey to save the world from both rationalism and skepticism, Kant hoped to find once again some secure and unchallengeable foundation for the acceptance of Christianity. As a deist, Kant faced personal difficulties in this attempt, since he had not actually extricated himself from some of the lines of thought he was striving to replace. Nevertheless, he did realize that certain of the deistic principles could no longer be defended. The *rationalistic* explanation of belief, and the acceptance of *history as the foundation* for the assent of faith both had to be set aside; in place of this Kant would structure a far more immanent type of religion, rooted in the innermost consciousness of man himself.

In his *Religion Within the Limits of Reason Alone,* Kant aims at setting forth a religion — even a Christian religion — which is reducible to the standards of pure reason alone; in this he proves to be a true deist. Kant was not at all attuned to the established Lutheran Church of his time and the strict demands laid upon the faithful by the Protestant Othodoxy of the theologians and clerics;

nor had he been able to absorb too much of the spirit of Pietism in which he was reared. Hence he rebelled openly against certain practices, and eventually refused to attend church services; indeed, even when elected rector of the University of Königsberg, Kant followed the custom and duly led the academic procession to the cathedral, but deserted it at the church.[47]

It is not surprising, then, that his work on religion is in large measure an attack upon the Established Church. But of greater interest for our purpose is one of the basic reasons he gives for assuming his position; it touches closely on the nature of religious assent. Kant is greatly concerned with the role of the scholar, the biblical theologian, and the philosophical theologian especially (as he speaks of them); in certain instances he sounds much like Kierkegaard in a later century, railing against the religion of the scholars and pedants. Kant's ultimate solution, of course, is quite different from that of the Danish theologian, but the problem which troubled them both is similar.[48]

Basically Kant defends a position of religious indifferentism. He holds that "there is only *one* (true) *religion;* but there can be *faiths* of several kinds."[49] He admits, however, that "the constitution of every Church originates always in some historical (revealed) faith which we can call ecclesiastical faith; and this is best founded on a Holy Scripture."[50] The visible Church necessarily demands an historical revelation of some kind, and since this is true, the Church also demands the right to serve as an *interpreter* of that religious truth. It is to this especially that Kant objects. In so doing, he takes a stand against those who would defend Christianity against the deistic attacks by recourse to the argument from miracles (as proof or evidence of the truth of the doctrine preached) or by formulating an argument based upon the words of Scripture; this only encourages ecclesiastical rule.

Kant insists that if man seeks *proof* of the truth of religion by asking for miracles, "he confesses to his own moral *unbelief,* that is, to his lack of faith in virtue. This is a lack which no belief that rests upon miracles (and is merely historical) can repair."[51] It is the type of argument offered by Butler and many others that

Kant is here rejecting; for him the religion of pure reason is rooted in virtue alone and demands no such historical proof.

Even more, Kant rejects such proof because its acceptance would at once involve the believer in a prior acceptance of the scholar who stands behind the claims of Scripture and its accounts of miraculous proofs: "Hence, in a holy book miracles and mysteries find a place; the manner of making these known, in turn, is also miraculous, and demands a faith in history; which, finally, can be authenticated, and assured as to meaning and import, only by scholarship."[52] The Kantian faith of pure reason, however, stands in need of no such documentary authentication; it proves itself and stands in need of no other miraculous evidence. It would therefore be a free faith (*fides elicita*), deduced from insight into adequate theoretical proofs, rather than a *fides imperata,* which demands blind obedience and in which a "small body of textual scholars (the clerics) . . . would drag along behind itself the long train of the unlearned (the laity). . . ."[53] Ultimately, he insists, since "there is no norm of ecclesiastical faith other than Scripture, and no expositor thereof other than pure *religion of reason* and *Scriptural scholarship* (which deals with the historical aspect of that religion)," such a system of faith under the clergy "must finally become mere faith in Scripture scholars and their insight."[54]

It is on this basis above all that Kant rejects the faith of the Established Church he knew. Seeing no such a thing as a divinely guided magisterium (a claim certainly not made by the Lutheran Church), Kant perceives nothing but the human and scholarly, and in this he sees enough possibility of error to warrant a certain historical skepticism:

> Since assurance on this score rests on no grounds of proof other than the historical, and since there ever will remain in the judgment of the people (if it subjects itself to the slightest test) the absolute possibility of an error which has crept in through their interpretation or through previous classical exegesis, the clergyman would be requiring the people at least inwardly to confess something to be true as is their belief in God, i.e. to confess, as though in the presence of God, something which they do not know with certainty.[55]

Kant expresses better than anyone else the philosophical principles which were to guide the religious debates of the next century. Some scholars would continue to develop a purely scholarly type of faith, only to be rebuked all the more by such men as Kierkegaard; others would emphasize the immanentist approach to faith and, following the lead of such men as Schleiermacher, would relegate the whole of Scripture, along with all other formulas and creeds, to a temporary and historically conditioned expression of belief, valid for that time but not destined to become a definitive and absolute norm of belief. The two approaches were eventually joined in modern liberal theology which strove simultaneously to be both scholarly and immanentist. It was in the spirit of this theology that the various historical studies of Jesus were generally made in the nineteenth century.

THE QUEST FOR THE HISTORICAL JESUS

As a result of this entire development, the historical method became the chosen instrument for studying the life of Jesus and the problem of His divinity in the past century. In 1906 Albert Schweitzer published his famous work, *Von Reimarus zu Wrede,* known in English as *The Quest of the Historical Jesus: A Critical Study of its Progress From Reimarus to Wrede.* It is an historical summary of the attempts to write a critical life of Jesus during the past hundred years. The study begins with a discussion of the writings of Hermann Samuel Reimarus (1694–1768), which were first published by Gotthold Lessing (in 1774 ff.) as the *Wolfenbüttel Fragments.* In this work, Reimarus assumes as his starting point an essential distinction between what Christ had preached and what His Apostles had later expressed in their writings; this signified a start at the critical approach to this problem at least.

From Reimarus, Schweitzer passes on to the various lives of Jesus produced in the era of early rationalism (less radical than later forms); the earliest *fictitious* lives of Jesus — attempts to explain the relationship between the history of Jesus and the miraculous events described in Scripture — led to the conclusion that they were due to the intrigue of a secret society of which Jesus was the tool. He then discusses the later rationalistic approaches of Heinrich Paulus, Karl Hase, and Schleiermacher. All of these writers followed a more or less familiar pattern of rationalism in evaluating the life of Jesus, laying special stress on their *a priori* exclusion of miracles (as impossible) and an overall rejection of the supernatural. Everything is explained in a purely human fashion, with Schleiermacher in search not so much of the Jesus of history as the Jesus Christ of his own system of theology according to Schweitzer's evaluation.

It was only with the advent of David Friedrich Strauss (1808–1874) that a new solution was found for the problem of *miracles* and the supernatural. As Schweitzer notes, Strauss concluded that "these events have no rightful place in the history [of the life of Jesus], but are simply mythical elements in the sources."[56] Schweitzer accordingly divides all the lives of Jesus as pertaining either to the pre-Straussian or post-Straussian period; but Strauss remains the chief landmark in this entire development, and though he met with both praise and opposition, his profound influence could not be denied.

Following close upon the conclusions of Strauss were other developments which pushed different facets of the problem to the fore, especially the Marcan Hypothesis, defended primarily by Christian Hermann Weisse (1801–1866). Choosing the Gospel of St. John as his starting point, and following a literary rather than an historical method, Bruno Bauer (1809–1882) set about writing what became the first skeptical life of Jesus. Other more imaginative lives of Jesus followed, doing little credit to their authors, even though the saccharine life written by Ernest Renan (1823–1892) was to achieve the greatest popularity of any at the beginning of the second half of the nineteenth century (and can be found today in a paperback edition at many corner drugstores)![57]

At this point, another reaction set in and the pendulum having swung from rationalism to historical criticism, it was time for the liberal theology to exercise its influence on the lives of Christ. These authors eventually found themselves in debate with those who (like Schweitzer) were insistent upon building a life of Jesus on the theme of eschatology above all; it is here that Schweitzer lets his case rest, closing with a comparison between his own *Sketch of the Life of Jesus* (1901) and *The Messianic Secret in the Gospels* (1901) written by William Wrede (1859–1907). Wrede followed the point of view of literary criticism, while Schweitzer was committed to the historical recognition of eschatology; the end result, in Schweitzer's opinion, was that men were now faced with a choice: *either* thoroughgoing skepticism *or* thoroughgoing eschatology. In the light of his own and Wrede's conclusions, he could see no other alternative.

History since 1906, however, indicates that there was not quite the dilemma that Schweitzer envisioned. The data of the New Testament have been repeatedly subjected to further analysis, each group guided by a slightly different philosophical or methodological approach, but tending in general to avoid either extreme outlined by Schweitzer. At least they did not produce the precise type of skepticism or eschatological thought that Schweitzer had in mind. Of all the contributions, that of the Form Critics was the most influential. With time, Wrede's work was accepted as having indicated the need of a new approach, as McCool points out, and the concept of the Bible as a strictly historical book had to be set aside:

> It was because of this double presupposition, i.e. that the combination of the philosophy of the Enlightenment with the historical skills of the nineteenth century had *de facto* recovered the true Jesus of Nazareth, that the Liberal school was shaken to its foundations in 1901 by Wrede's demonstration that dogmatic ideas had shared in the shaping of the Marcan Gospel. Wrede's book forced them to admit that, far from being the "authentic record" they had imagined it to be, the Gospel of Mark, as its title had always proclaimed, was in its way quite as theological as the fourth Gospel. What made the work of Wrede appear so negative to the Liberals that it caused them to despair was not that he had proved, as he and they thought, that the second Gospel was unhistorical. What Wrede had proved was rather that the concept of the "pure" historical source which the historico-critical school had canonized fitted Mark no better than the other Gospels.[58]

Today we are faced with an approach to the entire question which is unique in its own fashion, another example of the constant process of action and reaction in all such matters. Throughout the first half of the present century Form Criticism gained in popularity and was eventually quite dominated by the negativistic approach of Rudolf Bultmann (b. 1884) who so despaired of the quest of the historical Jesus that he centered his attention almost entirely on the remains of a demythologized Gospel, passing over almost completely the concern for the historical Jesus. As Bultmann wrote in 1926:

> I do indeed think that we can now know almost nothing concerning the life and personality of Jesus, since the early Christian sources show no interest in either, are moreover fragmentary and often legendary; and other sources about Jesus do not exist. Except for the purely critical research, what has been written in the last hundred and fifty years on the life of Jesus . . . is fantastic and romantic. . . . However good the reasons for being interested in the personalities of significant historical figures, Plato or Jesus, Dante or Luther, Napoleon or Goethe, it still remains true that this interest does not touch that which men had at heart; for *their* interest was not in their personality but in their *work*.[59]

As a result, Bultmann concerned himself with what Christ *intended* to do, the message he wished to communicate. Christ wished only to teach, so that we ought to study the scriptural accounts with a view to uncovering the message; to concern ourselves with the personality of Jesus, or to attempt to discover a biography of Jesus is a waste of time. It is only the *message* that Bultmann would seek, a message which has come down to us overladen with myths; hence he makes use of the hermeneutical technique of demythologizing to pierce through to the essential message itself: the *kerygma*. Ultimately, for Bultmann Jesus' message is important; Jesus is not.

By way of reaction to this extreme, the post-Bultmannians (such as Ernst Fuchs, Günther Bornkamm, Ernst Käsemann) believe that beneath the Gospel presentation there is still a basic historical nucleus corresponding to the actual words and deeds of Jesus.

They have thus set out upon a new search which hopes to avoid both the rationalistic and historicist extremes of the past century and the negativism of Bultmann in the present, convinced that the historical Jesus may still be encountered in the Gospels.[60]

VARIED CONCLUSIONS

A more detailed examination of these varied lives of Jesus, or, for that matter, even a cursory reading of Schweitzer's *Quest*, reveals the extremely complex and subtle nature of the data on hand. Men, both in the past and at present, have worked with very much the same data, but have come to different and even contradictory conclusions concerning the life of Jesus. What has brought about the varied conclusions has not been so much the discovery of new evidence in regard to the life and personality of Jesus, as it was the *philosophical* and *historical presuppositions* brought by each investigator to the study of this complicated problem. Even in 1835 we find that Strauss was greatly concerned with questions which are very much to the fore today and which had, in fact, been the center of serious debates in the past. Strauss opens his treatment of the life of Jesus with an analysis of the three types of *myths* (historical, philosophical, and poetical) which the biblical critics of that time recognized in Scripture.[61] Strauss sums up the position of Eichhorn as holding that "we have *neither* miracles to wonder at, on the one hand, *nor* deceptions to unmask on the other; but simply the *language* of a former age to translate into that of our own day."[62] But while Eichhorn and others applied this mythological explanation to the coming of Jesus into the world and His departure from it, Strauss proposes to apply it more consistently to the *entire life* of Jesus. He felt that the acceptance of the mythological explanation was too frequently limited to the Old Testament (as in the account of creation in Genesis); this application now needed to be made on a wider scale.

Gabler had also noted the value of the mythical interpretation at an earlier date, emphasizing that while the greater part of a narrative frequently belongs to the mythical representation, one can still perceive a "nucleus of fact" once the miraculous envelopments have been cast off.[63] This again is reminiscent of our present positions, minus the antisupernaturalism so strong in the past. So also, once it had been admitted that the first three Gospels originated from oral tradition, Eichhorn could write in the first quarter of the nineteenth century that there was a "slender thread of that primitive Gospel" running through the synoptic accounts, although he discarded many narratives from the history of Jesus as being unhistorical legends, "for example, besides the Gospel of the Infancy, the details of the temptation; several of the miracles of Jesus; the rising of the saints from their graves at his crucifixion; the guard at the sepulchre."[64]

The similarity of data is also reflected in a further application of this mythical principle by Strauss to the influence of midrashic literature in the formation of the canonical Gospels: "Hence the rabbinical principle: as the first redeemer (*Goel*), so shall be the second; which principle was carried out into many particulars to be expected in the Messiah after his prototype Moses."[65] Thus Strauss concludes:

> Many of the legends respecting him had not to be newly invented; they already existed in the popular hope of the Messiah, having been mostly derived with various modifications from the Old Testament, and had merely to be transferred to Jesus, and accommodated to his character and doctrines.[66]

Indeed, much of this is material which has appeared again and again, in different garb, throughout the past century. The data have been relatively static; such finds as the Dead Sea Scrolls do not come upon us every year. But the interpretations of these data have varied greatly and perhaps necessarily. Granting the constantly changing philosophical and historical approaches influencing these various investigators, the data could not help but take on a slightly different color in each instance. Strauss himself recognized the difficulty of working with the data in hopes of discovering that which is truly historical: "The boundary line," he writes "between the historical and the unhistorical, in records, in which as in our Gospels this later element is incorporated, will ever remain fluctuating and unsusceptible of precise attainment."[67]

THE ESSENCE OF CHRISTIANITY

What is to be said, in the light of these various problems, concerning the relationship of the historical method to Christianity, and more specifically to the Catholic faith? Up to this point, we have been dealing in large measure with non-Catholic scholars, and a mere mention of the names of some of them will remind the Catholic reader that their use of the historical method led them far from what he would consider essential to Christianity. Many, by using this method, came to read the Gospel accounts in a manner which disclosed Christ as a mere man rather than the true Son of God; others, as Schleiermacher, passed over the historic elements of the life of Christ to the "Christ of faith,"[68] or, in agreement with Bultmann, to the message of Jesus.

Admittedly the false interpretation of objective data by certain individuals has led to error, yet this does not indicate that the data in themselves are erroneous or that the Catholic ought to refrain from considering them. In some instances there is a great deal of equivocation present in the use of certain material or the acceptance of particular phrases. The very word "myth," for example, can be understood in a variety of ways and actually has been so understood throughout history.[69] Despite his lack of concern for the distinction, Strauss himself notes the suggestion of Ullmann that because of its non-Christian overtones, it might be better to avoid the word "myth" and speak only of Gospel legend (*Sage*) or the legendary element.[70] Some scholars today might advise the same thing.

For the Catholic, however, there is another equally important matter that must be considered in regard to this question. He can never work with the data alone once he leaves the area of philology. Even the simplest exegesis or the work of translation will involve further interpretation so that many have asked if the Catholic scholar can make use of the historical method at all. The answer is that he not only can but that he must; at the same time, he must also realize that such historical work is always of a secondary nature since something not subject to the historical method must be considered at every step, namely, his belief in a divinely-guided

Church whose faith and teaching reflect the present work of the Holy Spirit.

One of the basic errors of Modernism was the common aspiration to be purely objective scholars on the part of those who embraced the historicocritical method as the final court of appeal in regard to the meaning of Christian truth. Not wishing to confuse "scholarship" and "faith," they attempted to separate the two roles of historian and believer as they exist within the individual; but by neglecting the magisterium and its role in the unfolding and clarification of Christian revelation within the living Body of Christ, they ended up by proclaiming a religion based on history but which was no longer Catholic. It was an attempt, again, to do what the opponents were demanding; in this case, it meant an attempt to prove Catholicism by means of the historical method alone. This could not help but lapse into failure for there are many elements in the Catholic faith about which history can report, but for which it has no convincing proof. The Catholic Church must continue to proclaim her message as the message of Christ — the kerygma which was not simply proposed in the past nor encountered outside the confines of history, but which continues to be announced daily by Christ living in His Mystical Body even to the end of time. Anything less than this total view will result in a vitiation of the Church's message which, understood properly, is nothing but the message of Christ.

As a climax to the Liberal Protestant movement, however, Adolf Harnack wrote his *Das Wesen des Christentums* (1900) in which it became apparent that his historicoevolutionary thought had led him to a complete rejection of all that is properly Christian; the combination of historicism and philosophical naturalism could not lead in any other direction. Thus for Harnack, the essence of Christianity was reduced to three principles: (1) the kingdom of God and its coming; (2) God the Father and the infinite value of the human soul; (3) the higher righteousness and the commandment of love.[71] This is, however, a religion far from Christian, as later Protestant theologians admitted. With the appearance of Karl Barth's *Der Römerbrief* in 1919 there appeared an ever growing movement away from the extreme liberalism of the nineteenth century, and while some have left Barth to follow Bultmann, even these have agreed on rejecting the extremes of Harnack's position.

As Harnack himself indicates, his work grew out of a total commitment to the historical approach: "What is Christianity? it is solely in its historical sense that we shall try to answer this question here; that is to say, we shall employ the methods of historical science, and the experience of life gained by studying the actual course of history."[72] He rejected any other approach, both that of the apologist and that of the religious philosopher, but above all that of the Church-oriented theologian; there is no room in Harnack's system for a Church conceived as a living extension of Christ in time and space. His purely historical method, by which he had also studied the history of dogma, led him to reject as later additions the entire body of uniquely Christian truths: Christ the God-Man, the redemption, the visible Church, the sacraments. Nothing but his three, very general principles remained.

As a reaction against Harnack's work, Loisy set out to write a Catholic answer in his *L'évangile et l'église* (1903). His basic error in this defense, however, was not unlike the methodological error of Butler and many others: he attempted to meet the opposition on its own terms. Already committed personally to the historical method alone, Loisy made use of this same Harnackian tool as a defense of the Catholic faith. He tells us that he rejects Harnack's de-Christianized Christianity; he admits that one may well ask whether Harnack is really an historian or merely a theologian who takes from history as much as suits his theology (thus presenting a history that has been interpreted in the light of a preconceived theory).[73] In fact Loisy admits that it has been a common failing of theologians that they tend to bring to their historical studies a system to which they are fully committed and by which, consciously or unconsciously, they "bend the texts and the facts to the needs of their doctrine, though often honestly believing they avoid the danger."[74]

In formulating his own answer, however, Loisy still feels committed to the historical method; the difference is that he will strive to remove any prejudices that might alter the objective understanding of the evidence. Since he will frequently deal with Scripture, he is especially anxious to deemphasize, as it were, the dogma of biblical inspiration which, he says, has *de facto* hindered many from reading the Bible as *true history*, seeing there only the Word of God. At the same time, he fully rejects that mentality which is guided by the "conviction, arrived at before examination of the facts, or from motives other than historical, that a certain religious system, that is believed to be true, must have been the gospel of Christ."[75]

For the Catholic, to read Scripture in the manner suggested by Harnack and Loisy is equivalent to setting aside his belief, his faith; it is an application of the Cartesian methodical doubt to the realm of Christian truth, joined to the insistence that "historical motives" can be the sole valid ones for again accepting that truth. In this way, Loisy subjects the Church and its teaching to the judgment of the historical method and the historian; with this premise stated, he sets about determining "historically the essence of the gospel."[76] The first step is a critical analysis of the teachings of Scripture; then this same technique is applied to the records of primitive Christianity and, one by one, to the successive epochs in the history of Christianity, down through the Middle Ages to the sixteenth century and up to the present moment. For Loisy, this is the only way we can determine "if Christianity has remained faithful to the law of its origin."[77] Only those features which have remained until today, or which can be recognized as valid developments of the original Gospel, can be accepted as constituting the essence of Christianity. The believer, trusting in the historical approach, is justified in accepting these things alone; other things must be looked upon as nonessential accretions.[78]

This very approach set the stage for the ultimate conclusions drawn by Loisy. He does admit growth, development in Christianity; he is not ready to admit the conclusion that the essence of Christianity excludes any developments beyond those matters clearly perceived in the primitive Church. Nevertheless, when he comes to distinguish between the valid and invalid developments, it also becomes the task of the historical method to say which are which.[79] Thus even with a constant return to the primitive source, it is the historian who must formulate judgments in the end; on this score, Loisy's eschatological conclusions are indicative enough of where this methodology led him and what distinctions he felt forced to make between the essential and nonessential elements of Christianity.

ROLE OF THE MAGISTERIUM

In contrast to this, the position of the Catholic Church has become increasingly clear, due in large measure to the historical and theological concerns of recent decades, leading to more precise statements by the magisterium on the nature of the Church and the role of the authentic teaching authority within that community. Following closely upon his description of the Church as the living Body of Christ and the further application of the doctrine of the Mystical Body to the communal worship of the Church,[80] Pius XII sketched the role of the magisterium in his encyclical, *Humani generis,* issued in 1950. Far from being a purely negative document, this encyclical incorporates in its positive statements a precise explanation of the relationship of the Catholic scholar (and believer) to the magisterium. In all of this, it is the authentic teaching authority which must lead the way officially, although the scholars within the Church must, through their prior activity, prepare the way for such action. The biblical scholar and theologian act as handmaids, as it were, of the magisterium. They not only can but must formulate hypotheses; they must speculate and synthesize according to the best methods of their respective disciplines. Their labor is always of a tentative, secondary nature, but this does not mean such labor is not important; it is essential to the full growth and development of the Church's life. Because of this tentative nature of their work, however, they do not compromise the authentic teaching of the Church should they make mistakes by following a wrong line of thought. This possibility is envisioned by the Church, and what is required is simply obedient acceptance of the decision of the ecclesiastical authorities. If the theologian must attempt to solve such problems, with no personal guarantee of infallibility, it is only to be expected that he may at times come to a false conclusion; the test between orthodoxy and heresy at such a point is simply the fullness of faith on the part of the loyal theologian who places the authority of the Church above his own scholarship, something the heretic refuses to do. The danger is not so much false conclusions as a defective faith which no longer perceives the Church as the Body of Christ, preserved from doctrinal error through a divinely guided magisterium, and which therefore refuses to accept, as from Christ Himself, the decision of the Church.

On the other hand, if a particular theologian has said something especially well, the magisterium may accept it and incorporate that statement into its own official teaching; the bishops or the pope do this, however, not precisely because this scholar *said* it, but because he said it *well.*[81] The infallibility associated with this solemn teaching rests with the magisterium and not with the scholar, nor with the proofs and arguments offered by him in defense of his conclusions.

In this way, Pius XII indicates that the "deposit of faith our Divine Redeemer has given for authentic interpretation not to each of the faithful, not even to theologians, but only to the Teaching Authority of the Church."[82] Thus, quoting Pius IX, he reaffirms that "the most noble office of theology is to show how a doctrine defined by the Church is contained in the sources of revelation . . . 'in that sense in which it has been defined by the Church.' "[83]

To an outsider this may seem like an undue limit placed upon the Catholic scholar, or as an instruction to approach the evidence on hand armed with prejudices and preconceived conclusions. For one who does not perceive the Church as the living Body of Christ, and who admits only the historical method as the norm by which Christian truth may be uncovered, this is not an illogical conclusion. For the Catholic, however, this statement means simply that, since he *does* believe in the supernaturality of the entire reality in which God has willed to give His revelation to mankind and continually clarify it down to the end of time, he must accordingly work within the framework of this supernatural reality to which he as a believer is committed. And this involves an acceptance of a divinely guided magisterium. The theologian or biblical scholar is not commissioned with the task of "proving," through his study of the sources, that the infallible Church is correct; this would involve a contradiction in his own position as a believer and could mean nothing more than that he was to attempt to prove that God is correct. His first task, therefore, is to indicate the line of development in those matters now clearly stated by the magisterium, the manner in which these particular truths are contained in Scripture and how they have, under the guidance of the Holy Spirit, gradually been unfolded and clarified through the life of the Church.

Insofar as the Catholic scholar goes on to speculate concerning matters as yet unsolved (and there will always be such matters associated with revelation), he has every freedom, being guided here more in a negative sense by his realization of the boundaries set for his speculative attempts by the solemn definitions already issued in the past and thus necessarily forming a part of the unchanging faith and teaching of the Church here and now. However, even in his attempt to set forth the line of development in regard to the Church's solemn definitions, the theologian may bring added light to a proper interpretation of one or another decree; the historical method has this value, in that it can assist the Church of today to understand more exactly what the magisterium of another century really said, thus enabling the living teaching authority to go on to reaffirm that doctrinal statement in even clearer and more all-embracing terms.[84]

THE USE OF SCRIPTURE

All of these varied points have come to be incorporated into the present-day discussions concerning the relationship between Scripture and tradition. There are many who see here a more intimate blending, a more essential unity, between these two elements; they speak of a unified source theory wherein Scripture and tradition complement one another, and together find their more express clarification in time through the ever living magisterium.[85] This again presupposes a belief in the entire supernaturality of the Church's life. Only on this basis can one understand Pius XII's insistence that "even positive theology cannot be on a par with merely historical science,"[86] and that the Church rejects the position of those who would "judge the doctrine of the Fathers and of the Teaching Church by the norm of Holy Scripture, interpreted by the purely human reason of exegetes. . . ."[87] This pontiff points out an exactly opposite path, one which takes into consideration the *entire* life of the Church of Christ so that the statements of Scripture and tradition might find their full and clear meaning within that framework. Moreover, should these sources of themselves fail to lead to a definite conclusion, God has willed that His Church be so guided by the Spirit that the final teachings of the magisterium can, in a real sense, accomplish that which scholarship cannot; it speaks on the authority of God and does not base its own authority ultimately on the conclusions of rational or historical science. It is in this way that the Church lives on in the certitude of faith, free from the hesitations of historical certitude; as the Body of Christ she solves in the present the difficulties which at times cannot be clarified by the most exacting historical analysis of the documents of the past.

How widely this approach differs from that adopted by Loisy and others tied to the purely historical method is quite obvious, and it is not really surprising that the two approaches should lead to such opposite conclusions. Yves Congar has expressed this same thought in a somewhat different fashion, indicating not a form of anti-intellectualism but a spirit of total Christian faith as the Catholic professes it:

> When someone says to us, for example, that the *kecharitomene* of Luke 1:28 means "favored one" and not "full of grace," and that therefore it cannot serve as a foundation for the Catholic theology concerning the Virgin Mary, I answer in

turn: philology is an excellent thing, an exegetical science based on philology, archaeology and history is necessary and good; but these things do not establish the limits of revelation, of that which has been confided to the Church and of which the Bible bears testimony. The sole force of that fidelity and intelligence commensurate with the gift of God is not the spirit of the exegetes, it is the *sensus ecclesiae* stirred up in her by the Holy Spirit. I respect and I interrogate unceasingly the science of the exegetes, but I reject their magisterium. . . .[88]

Congar speaks therefore of the "fundamental error" of those who hope to determine what Christians ought to believe by means of an "exegetico-historical study." That which the Christian must accept is *id quod traditum est, id quod traditur,* "that is, the Christian reality itself."[89] The teaching of this living Church goes beyond that which was written in the inspired books and which can be drawn out by the historical method — by exegesis — alone; yet it is not for that reason an unscriptural teaching. Certainly the Church of today must continue to oppose the Protestant principle of *Scriptura sola* if it be understood in the sense originally meant by the sixteenth-century Reformers, or in a more modern garb after the manner of Gerhard Ebeling, who sees in the purely critical and historical approach to the Bible the logical outgrowth of this sixteenth-century principle.[90] In both cases the need for something besides Scripture is denied. On the other hand, those Catholics today who contend that all the truths necessary for salvation are somehow contained in Scripture mean simply that there are *scriptural starting points* for those truths, but the fullness of the revelation becomes apparent only in the living tradition of the Mystical Body of Christ.[91]

Once one begins to grasp the fuller significance of this "total" view of the Catholic approach to the dogmatic teaching of the Church (an evolutionary process, under the guidance of the Holy Spirit, including both Scripture and the living tradition with its unfolding *consensus ecclesiae*), he finds that he is much more ready to speak of "scriptural themes," and is not as concerned with a supposed need to find precise scriptural texts which will serve as "proofs" or pegs" upon which to hinge our entire belief. The theologian is not looking for these anymore, nor does he look upon the Bible as a source book for "proofs."

There is, in reality, no reason for expecting that the scriptural presentation of a particular dogmatic teaching will agree — point by point, phrase by phrase — with the more precise and more developed presentation of a later period of the Church's history. If, for example, Scripture were so precise in its statement on the divinity of the Logos, Nicea and Chalcedon and their more exacting (though nonscriptural) definitions would never have been necessary. This is not to say, of course, that the doctrine of the divinity of Christ is not contained in or taught by Scripture; it is, but not with the precision that God willed for it in later stages of the life of the Christian community. The same is true of the dogma of the Assumption, which does have a scriptural basis of some sort.[91]

It does become a somewhat futile attempt to begin with a dogmatic statement of Nicea, IV Lateran, or Trent and then attempt to find phrases or texts in Scripture which will equate these statements entirely. The mentalities are very distinct, although the doctrine remains essentially the same. There has been growth, for it is in this ever unfolding manner that the fullness of what was revealed to the primitive Church is even now coming to us, as it has, indeed, down through the last 2000 years. This is the mystery of Christian revelation, that while it had been first given, and given totally, in the revelation of the primitive Church, and while it is set forth in its essentials in Scripture ("all truths necessary for salvation are somehow contained therein"), yet the more complete explication of what God revealed is always being drawn out. This message is ever more precisely expressed, or at least expressed in terms which better meet the needs of the present moment. This more complete explication, however, is also a work of God, accomplished through His divine power, now at work within the Christian community here upon earth.

TWO THEORIES OF FAITH

Considering this development through rationalism and historicism up to the present time, it would only be expected that traces of these movements would have brought forth a similar reaction and concern among Catholics; they have never lived entirely in the intellectual ghetto so often allotted to them. Thus it is that we can note that precisely during this same period — from the time of Descartes on — there arose a Catholic approach to faith which many today look upon as committed entirely too much to the rational and historical arguments of those centuries. The center of this question rests, for our purposes, on two distinct theories of faith and, more precisely, upon a debated point which lies at the center of these two theories: that is, whether the grace of faith has only an entitative (or ontological) effect upon the believer, or whether its influence extends to the psychological level as well.

What is commonly thought to be a more "traditional" opinion is actually of more recent origin. As Vignon notes, this Thomistic opinion was generally accepted by all theologians up to the time of de Lugo (1583–1660);[92] it was only then that this more recent theory came to be put forth and was gradually defended by more and more theologians from the seventeenth century to the present time, so that many look upon it as a theory with deep roots in the past. As Charles Davis remarks:

> The vogue and influence of this view in modern theology makes it a surprise to learn its comparative novelty. . . . The more recent analysis of faith was introduced under the influence of Cartesian philosophy. Put forward in the seventeenth century, it was at first opposed as a daring innovation, but it later gained that ascendancy that is only gradually being thrown off. Its straightforwardness is only deceptive, and it leads to insuperable difficulties when we try to save the essential characteristics of faith.
>
> What are its implications? Faith ceases to be an encounter with God in which He Himself becomes the motive of my belief and the light of my thought; it is reduced to a natural knowledge in which my assent rests ultimately on my own reasoning and on the light native to my mind. What I accept may be

supernatural truths, but the reason why I accept them is evidence assessed by the mind using its own power and resources.[93]

This more recent theory is surprisingly like the approach adopted by Bishop Butler, and would seem to reflect many of the same influences. Hervé, for example, begins his discussion of this question with a rather puzzling paragraph. He states that all Catholic theologians admit that, if the authority of God and the fact of revelation are admitted in the act of faith because of *philosophical and historical reasons,* the act of faith itself is ultimately reduced to a merely human act. As reasons for this he gives: (1) the sources of revelation, the documents of faith, and theologians all agree that the one and only motive of faith is the authority of God revealing; (2) a faith resting solely on human reasons would no longer be a theological virtue; (3) the assent of faith would not possess the highest certitude (*super omnia firmus*), but would be limited to that certitude associated with purely natural arguments; (4) faith would not be specifically one, but diverse among the faithful since each one would possess his own motives of credibility. Therefore, he states, the sole problem to be solved is how the authority of God revealing can be explained as the one and only motive of faith.[94]

FURTHER ANALYSIS

All of this is well said, although there may be here some confusion. The first point apparently recalls the condemnation of those in the past century who would attempt to reduce supernatural truths to the rational level, thus dispensing with the need of accepting them on divine authority; the assent of reason would suffice.[95] The second point would also be a rephrasing of the Tridentine canon that no one can believe *sicut oportet* unless he be given the grace to do so;[96] and the fourth point seems to allude to the rejection by the Church of a purely subjective faith, differing as to object with each individual, as it appeared in the teaching of Modernism.[97]

It is the third point, however, that might be questioned. Would "all theologians" be able to agree on this point? While it is perfectly true that a faith resting on human arguments alone would not have the certitude proper to faith, we may ask whether this more recent theory actually escapes this difficulty. It does root the assent of faith on the authority of God; by its defense of an entitative elevation of this act to the supernatural level, it adequately explains the supernaturality of the act insofar as it is a virtue; and it does not in any way propose a purely subjective type of faith. Yet the central question, one to which the problem is ultimately reduced, concerns the *certitude* of faith. In this more recent theory, the believer comes to know *that* God has revealed something, and *what* He has revealed, by a purely rational and historical process. If this is not granted, the very possibility of a so-called "natural faith" or "scientific faith" would have to be denied, and one would have to say with the Thomists that the nonbeliever has no certitude (and thus no "scientific faith") in regard to supernatural truths. The most that can be said is that he knows *what* Christians believe (just as a Christian may know what Mohammedans believe without thereby accepting that system himself, nor entertaining any certitude in regards to the truth of that belief).

In other words, if the grace of faith has no psychological effect, it cannot have an effect upon the certitude of the assent; it cannot render a purely natural or scientific assent any more firm by effecting what is nothing more than an entitative (ontological) elevation of that act to the supernatural level. The *certitude* or firmness of that assent necessarily remains as strong or as weak, as invincible or as beset by difficulties as it was before the advent of grace. For this reason, we feel compelled to conclude that the defenders of this more recent theory do not sufficiently explain how the act of faith is *super omnia firmus*. As a saving act, the certitude of such an act of faith must be that of the "natural, scientific faith"; and that is something essentially joined to rational and historical arguments, and consequently involved in the lack of absolute certitude associated with such a line of argumentation. There are two reasons for making this statement:

1. The nature of historical assent is tied to the realm of moral

certitude. The fact of revelation as well as the truths revealed by God do come to us in the guise of human documents (Scripture as well as the documents of the Church); but the question remains as to how an individual believer (or the entire Church) is to know the precise meaning of that message so that, even apart from grace, he could assent to its truth in an act of scientific faith. Recourse cannot be had to the direct inspiration of the Holy Spirit given to each reader of the Bible (as the sixteenth-century Reformers claimed); nor to the role of the magisterium (as we feel the Catholic must claim). In either instance, one would have recourse to something outside the purely natural in order to acquire certitude concerning the truths of revelation; but that very recourse would render impossible any such "natural, scientific faith" as the more recent theory defends. If the assent of faith (both natural and supernatural) is to be explained on the basis of historical certitude (as it must in this theory), there seems to be no real difference between this explanation of the act of faith and that given by Bishop Butler and those who thought like him. Butler merely failed to lay emphasis upon the need of grace for an entitative elevation to the supernatural order. But since faith is essentially an act of the intellect, through which the individual personally encounters God and thereby commits his entire being to God, that basic intellectual act can be no more firm than the arguments upon which it is based.

2. There is a second reason for calling into question the explanation offered by this more recent theory of faith, and that is the present-day approach to Scripture. As the theory was originally formulated, it leaned heavily upon the concept of the Bible as a strictly historical book (as Butler also envisioned it), setting forth the very words of Christ (*ipsissima verba*) from which logical arguments — rational "proofs," based on historical evidence — could be formulated to demonstrate the fact that Christ actually revealed these truths Himself (or through the Apostles acting under the inspiration of the Holy Spirit), as well as the obligation of the individual to assent to those truths.

However, once we grant that the Bible (with emphasis here

on the New Testament) is a book written from the viewpoint of faith rather than objective history in the nineteenth-century meaning of the term, this more recent theory is faced with grave problems. The historian *qua* historian may not allow the supernatural faith of the Christian community to affect his conclusions; the historical method is a technique intimately linked with the powers of nature and purely human events. When, therefore, the Catholic admits that the Bible, as an inspired document of faith, consists of writings composed by believers for believers, he places the book in the entirely supernatural context of the Church, the Mystical Body of Christ. The Bible teaches what God has willed it to teach, and it is a solid, divinely fashioned basis for the development, both in understanding and in presentation, of the fullness of Christian revelation. As many readily admit today, Scripture scholars can perceive an historical nucleus beneath the Gospel presentation, but to recognize this fact and to separate that which represents a purely historical statement or action of Christ from that which represents the further statements of the primitive Church, issued under the guidance of the Holy Spirit, are two different tasks. The Gospels as we now see them are not a verbal transcript of events in the life of Christ, but accounts written to present to the Christian those things which he must believe in order to be saved; to look upon them as purely reportorial documents is akin to reading a didactic poem as though it was strict history. This is not falsification, nor the answer of a purely natural type of evolutionary faith; it is simply another way of professing the Catholic belief in the continued guidance of the living Church as it was exercised in the primitive community. Granting this, however, it would be extremely naïve, as Marrou notes, "to imagine that we could decompose that witness and, separating the good grain from the weeds, isolate a pure nucleus of authentic 'facts'. . . ."[98]

The Gospels include the historical evidence for the life and teaching of Christ, but we do not encounter this directly in them, but rather as this history is embedded in the context of the primitive Church's catechetical and liturgical uses. For this reason, the attempt to formulate a syllogistic argument which would lead to a "natural faith" becomes totally impossible; the historian cannot deal with such sources, for they are the documents of the believer. Using them alone, the historian could conclude to the belief of the primitive community, to *what* they believe as revealed; and he can detect within the entire account some historical nucleus; but he would be beset by difficulties on all sides by trying to isolate that nucleus, to prove the *objective truth* of what this community teaches. The faithful, on the other hand, as members of the Church herself, take as the starting point the canonical Gospels and the Epistles, and under the guidance of the Holy Spirit go on to accept and understand ever more clearly the Christian message they accept on *faith*. In line with Trent, the Catholic admits that the Christian revelation was not completed before the death or the ascension of Christ, but that it continued to be made up to the death of the last Apostle; thus from the viewpoint of Catholic faith, nothing in this approach raises a serious difficulty at all.[99]

The same thing would be true of an argument based on the documents of tradition; they also might be understood in various ways, and used as a foundation for diverse statements of faith (as the early Reformers used the writing of Augustine and others to defend their positions). The sole judge of the acceptability of the statements of earlier writers is the living Church to whom revelation has been confided, above all to the authentic teaching authority within that Church.

THE LIVING CHURCH

All of this is another way of saying that historical certitude cannot be viewed as sufficiently stable to serve as a foundation for the absolute certainty of faith; even if the arguments were universally convincing, the ultimate conclusion could not go beyond moral certitude, should it achieve the highest degree of that type of certitude. Faith must rest on a certitude beyond moral or even metaphysical certitude (since faith is not reducible to human reason); and in order to do that, it needs to be entirely supernaturalized, both in its entitative *and* in its psychological aspect.

We feel compelled, accordingly, to set aside the theological note *ex clara scriptura* to imply the objective basis of faith, since it involves the very same difficulties; at best such rational argumentation can achieve only moral certitude. Moreover the very phrase leaves open a series of questions: to whom is it clear, and on what basis, and with what certitude? If such a theological note is to signify anything except a purely subjective conclusion, a personal interpretation of Scripture, or one common to a particular group, it would have to signify something more than it possibly can by the very nature of historical study. As long as the possibility remains open (as it must in historical research) that there is more evidence not yet uncovered that might change the final conclusion, or a better evaluation of the evidence on hand, no infallible certitude can result. This pertains to a totally supernatural act of faith alone.

Because of these difficulties, we also feel that we must emphasize two things necessary for the act of faith: (*a*) the inward grace by which the believer supernaturally perceives the authority of God revealing and the truth of what He has revealed; (*b*) and in addition, an external, authoritative proclamation by a living, divinely guided magisterium of the truths to be believed.[100] There seems to be no escape from the need of somehow including the Church in the motive of faith — not as a second "something," standing between the believer and God, but as a divinely sustained body, serving as an ever present instrument of God in the proclaiming of His revelation. This is but an application of the mystical unity of the Church with Christ, applied here to the teaching role of that Mystical Body. Thus the "bringing to mind" and the "teaching" of the Paraclete is something to be accomplished not merely on the day of Pentecost, but throughout the entire life of the Church. Through this constant guidance of the Spirit, the Church will make progress continually in understanding the Christian message, and therefore in proclaiming it ever more clearly, but without ever departing from that basic axiom so well phrased by St. Vincent Lerins: "In ipsa item catholica ecclesia magnopere curandum est ut id teneamus, quod ubique, quod semper, quod ab omnibus creditum est."[101]

The faithful are not left, therefore, to their own personal understanding of Scripture or the documents of tradition; nor are they handed over to a prior belief in the conclusion of historical scholars. Much less are they to expect a personal illumination which, though possible, is not in accord with God's general plan of public revelation in the New Testament era. The magisterium, therefore, reflects upon Scripture and tradition, and proclaims the message of Christ it perceives there. It has an essential role to play, one which may be described as representing the authority of God in its created aspect, for it is not a purely human Church who speaks, but God who speaks in and through her. God Himself is the one and only motive of faith, the uncreated testimony in His eternal being and infinite authority, but the created testimony insofar as He speaks to us now through His Church.[102] Not two motives, but one, for as the Church is not distinct from Christ, so also is its teaching not distinct from that of Christ and the Father and the Holy Spirit.

This would also appear to hold true in regard to those outside the Church who, through invincible ignorance, fail to become full members of the Mystical Body but who nevertheless believe the revealed truths because of the grace of faith. Just as their entire possession of grace must somehow be explained in terms of their relationship to the visible Church (in line with the Catholic dogma of "No salvation outside the Church"), so also must their faith be somehow linked to the public proclamation by the magisterium of that Christian truth. *De facto,* what other churches believe and proclaim correctly has been proclaimed ultimately by that Church (as, for example, their acceptance of the scriptural message or the early Councils); the solution to this problem is in effect no greater than that associated with the more general question of the relationship of non-Catholics to the Church of Rome.

THE DIVINITY OF CHRIST

In the light of this lengthy discussion, we are now able to give an answer to the problem proposed in this study. Following as we do the Thomistic-Suarezian approach to the assent of faith (affirming a psychological effect resulting from the grace of faith), we would answer the question in the negative: The historical method *cannot* prove the divinity of Christ. This must be understood properly, however; the very phrasing of the question involves some equivocation and already presupposes in the asking one's own position in regard to the two basic theories of faith now discussed by Catholic theologians. To "prove" would indicate a demonstration of some sort, and in this case a demonstration achieved by means of the criticohistorical method.

Because of the nature of the Gospel accounts and the difficulty concerning the nature of historical assent, we can see no reason for affirming the result of such a demonstration as something possessed of sufficient certitude to serve as a foundation for the stability and infallibility of Christian faith. We reject, accordingly, the very possibility of any "natural, scientific faith." Rather than involve Christian faith in the limited certitude of historical conclusions, we prefer to reject this entire theory and defend the far more ancient theory associated with the Thomistic-Suarezian approaches.

On the other hand, there is such a thing as "human faith," which, as distinguished from "divine faith" rests on the authority of another human being (or the evidence of human documents); but these are not univocal concepts. They both enjoy entirely distinct types of certitude. My faith in the word of another human being does not extend beyond the realm of moral certitude (and as such, it may at times prove to be a misplaced faith). Such a human faith does have a role to play, however, in *apologetics,* and within the realm of apologetics, it is possible to formulate some valid argument concerning the mission or possibly even the divinity of Christ.

One of the chief reasons for the misunderstanding we perceive

204 *With the Eyes of Faith*

on these questions is the rise of apologetics as an autonomous branch of theology in the seventeenth century (precisely as a re-action against the deists, the rationalists, and the indifferentists of the modern era). Some have tended to confuse faith with apologetics. Indeed, the word "apologetics" is at times used with such abandon as to imply it has no real meaning at all. We might well limit the notion of apologetics, therefore, to the relationship between reason and faith, as Hermann Lais suggests.[103] It is in this sense that the science of apologetics (as opposed to the art of apologetics, or pastoral or popular apologetics) has an important role to play in the rational preparation for faith; the clearest directives for an understanding of apologetics in this sense have been given us by Vatican I.[104]

At the same time, Lais sugests that we distinguish apologetics from what he calls *Apologie;* the Latin word would be *apologia,* but English still needs an acceptable word. By this he means the answers which must be given to objections raised in regard to Catholic doctrines. As such, *Apologie* pertains to moral, dogma, exegesis — in fact, to the entire scope of Catholic scholarship. This task, however, ought not be envisioned as a proof or a demonstra-tion of some point; it is more of an attempt to show that there is no obvious contradiction between Catholic teaching and the objection raised. At times the ultimate conclusion may be some-thing of an impasse; we may show there is no obvious contradic-tion, but we may not be able to draw a firm conclusion as to the actions of Pope Honorius I, the teaching of Cyprian in regard to the primacy of the Roman Pontiff, or the formula of baptism used by the primitive Church. These are, of course, valid questions, and the Catholic scholar must attend to them; but Catholic faith does not and cannot wait upon the success or failure or impasse of his attempts.

Related to this is the problem of the genesis of faith, actually a theoretical analysis of the relationship of grace and the natural powers of man in the realm of faith. All Catholics must agree that there is a preparation on the part of reason for the act of faith; the sole disputes concern the relationship of the motives of credibility in which this reasonableness of faith is expressed and the act of faith itself. The Thomistic approach, once again, distinguishes carefully between the rational judgment which declares that, examined from a purely rational and historical point of view, I can perceive the action of God, and that therefore I would not be going contrary to reason or doing violence to my intellectual nature were I to go on to the act of faith itself. Such a judgment, however, based upon rational and historical conclusions, does not extend beyond the limits of moral certitude; this is the type of certitude by which man must guide the practical conduct of his life, and it suffices for this judgment.

This does not mean, of course, that moral certitude is not true certitude. In human life, man not only can but must act upon physical and moral certitude in vast areas of his life. Even though he is often working in the realm of probable knowledge where certitude is based upon his judgment of a number of observable events, he recognizes that he has no other choice; the problems and decisions of daily life leap beyond metaphysical questions and the absolute certitude they engender. Nevertheless, probability and certitude are not mutually exclusive; certitude is verified essentially in firmness of adhesion.

It must be remembered that when we speak of metaphysical, physical, and moral certitude we are not dealing with univocal concepts. In the realm of reason, unswerving certitude is found only in those matters related to metaphysical principles. Physical and moral certitude, as Phillips notes, must be considered "imperfect forms of certitude, the name being applied to them analogically inasmuch as they proportionally share in the essence of formal certitude, the exclusion of fear of error." But as he adds, "though certitude implies firmness of adhesion, it does not entail the absolute necessitating of the mind; in other words, probable arguments can generate certitude."[105]

This type of certitude — firm, but not necessitating — suffices for the judgment of credibility; faith, however, demands something more than this. For the Thomist, therefore, the judgment of credibility does not enter into the essence of the act of faith itself;

it is a prerequisite, a condition, but it is not to be identified with the act of faith, nor does it form an essential part of that act of faith. For this reason, while the judgment of credibility does not extend beyond moral certitude, the assent of faith, rooted in the authority of God alone, possesses that unswerving and infallible characteristic proper to faith alone. It is in the act of faith itself that the grace of faith finally brings about that psychological effect which makes it possible for the individual to believe not only so as to be saved (a merely entitative elevation to the supernatural order), but simply to be *able* to believe with absolute certitude (and thus be saved). It is a totally supernatural act of faith, both in its entitative and in its psychological aspects.

LEO XIII

It is in relationship to this type of apologetic argument that we must also understand the statement of Leo XIII, at times quoted as a defense of the more recent theory of faith. The text is usually translated as follows:

> But since the divine and infallible *magisterium* of the church rests also on Holy Scripture, the first thing to be done is to vindicate the trustworthiness of sacred records, at least as human documents, from which can be clearly *proved,* as from primitive and authentic testimony, the *divinity* and the mission *of Christ our Lord,* the institution of a hierarchical Church and the primacy of Peter and his successors.[106]

In regard to this passage, two things must be said. First, the translation seems to say more than the Latin text. Where we read "prove," the Latin has "quibus ex libris . . . Christi Domini divinitas et legatio . . . *in tuto apertoque collocentur."* A better translation would be that from these books, the divinity of Christ, as well as these other matters, "are set forth in a full and clear (distinct) manner." Thus the text of Leo XIII does not actually state the problem as formulated in the title of this study. Basically, what Leo XIII was concerned about in 1893 was the historicity of the sacred books which was then being attacked so strongly by the various schools of thought discussed earlier in this paper. The entire context in *Providentissimus Deus* indicates this concern, insisting that the New Testament is not to be looked upon as mere fiction or myth unrelated to any history, or merely the expression of the subjective experiences of an individual or community. Accordingly he at once enumerates the steps to be taken to meet these attacks: the study of both Oriental languages and the art of criticism; a refusal to exclude *a priori* the possibility of all prophecy and miracles (as so many were then doing); a study of natural sciences in order to grasp better the relationship between biblical statements and the findings of modern science; and a study of history and the historical method.[107]

Over and above this, we find a further indication of the meaning of Leo XIII's statement by comparing the reference to Christ's *divinity* to the other topics mentioned: the mission of Christ, the institution of the Church, and the primacy of Peter and his successors. These are all matters treated in the apologetic section of the usual *Tractatus de ecclesia*. Reference is implied, therefore, to rational and historical arguments which would lead an individual to a conclusion which, though limited to moral certitude, would yet be valid. The question of whether such conclusions could also serve as the foundation for the act of faith itself would depend, once again, upon the particular theory of faith being followed. Many feel today that the theologians of an earlier period extended this apologetic argument too far, but if they did so, it was only under the impetus of this more recent theory of faith which was then coming to enjoy such favor and may have led to a confusion between the respective roles of faith and apologetics.[108]

Today it would seem preferable to emphasize a consideration of these same facts, not so much from an apologetic point of view, but as truths of faith, closely associated with the continuation, here on earth, of the redemptive work of Christ. We do not deny in any way the validity of these apologetic arguments, so far as they go; but we do insist that such an approach may encounter more grave difficulties in regard to the nature of historical assent and the literary form of the Gospels than may have been recognized in an earlier century. In any event, it is important to realize that such an apologetic treatment of these topics will not by any means exhaust the full meaning of these truths. The divinity of Christ, His mission, the Church, and the visible headship of Peter and his successors all have a more profound meaning as truths of faith accepted on the authority of God revealing.

We have a similar instance in the resurrection of Christ. We may consider it from an apologetic point of view, and by an investigation based on historical evidence, we may conclude that Christ rose from the dead; it is a conclusion based on the testimony of those who saw Him dead and who later saw Him alive. The certitude proper to this, however, is moral certitude; it is an historical conclusion. On the other hand, we may also consider the resurrection as a truth of faith, accepted like the Trinity and the Real Presence, not because of any historical demonstration, but on the authority of God revealing. In this instance, it is a mystery intimately linked to the redemptive activity of Christ, through whose death and resurrection we have been freed from the power of Satan and been made members of Christ. Viewed in this way, the resurrection is something in which we *believe* rather than prove; the same is also true of the divinity of Christ, His mission, the Church and the visible headship of Peter and his successors. They all pertain to the fullness of the Christian mystery, and as such are deep dogmatic truths and objects of our faith.

Leo XIII wrote, of course, in the milieu of the nineteenth century, and it must be remembered that popes no less than other members of the Church are, to a very real extent, children of that era in which they live. Much of this is reflected in some of the statements of *Providentissimus Deus*. Like any other papal or conciliar document in the history of the Church, it must be read in the context proper to it — in this case, the debates of the nineteenth century. Not only Scripture needs to be approached in this manner, but every decree of the Church, for although Christian truth is not proved *by* history, the statements concerning it are formulated *in* history and we would only fail to understand their proper meaning were we to ignore this fact in our use of them.

CONCLUSION

In emphasizing the importance of supernatural faith on the psychological level, the Catholic is able to escape a good many of the difficulties which disturb his non-Catholic brethren at the present time. We have already mentioned Tillich's recognition of the problem of historical skepticism and the thought of Reinhold Niebuhr,[109] but they are only two of many who realize the need for a faith rooted on something more secure than the certitude of history. Bultmann's extreme negativism in regard to our knowledge of the life of Jesus, as well as his distinction between *Historie* and *Geschichte*, are both closely associated with his desire to escape the limitations of history and root his faith on something more abiding.[110] Although he agrees with Harnack in saying that traditional church Christology committed the decisive error of developing Christianity as a doctrine, Bultmann does not want to abandon the Christian message for a vague form of Harnackian ethics. Thus he criticizes the position of Harnack in this fashion:

> Harnack's failure to formulate this distinction [between faith and a "world view"] more lucidly rests on the fact that he did not clearly see the difference between the *kerygmatic* ("proclamatory") character of the Gospel and an "Enlightenment" doctrine or an ethical appeal. . . . Only Christ can give the kerygmatic character to everything which is "taught" as Christian. It is only Christ who transfigures the doctrine into kerygma. Therefore, Christ is correctly preached not where something is said *about* him, but only where he himself becomes the proclaimer. Harnack should have, at least, made an effort to conceive of Christ from this standpoint.[111]

Bultmann's view of Christianity does not include Christ living in His Church and speaking through its doctrine, so that he feels compelled to seek Jesus outside of history in a totally personal encounter. He does not wish to hear about Jesus, but to know him. Yet his search leads him to abandon the historical and the earthly, so that it becomes little more than a phantomlike search for the message of Christ apart from His Person.

For the Catholic, an entirely different point of view prevails. He looks for and finds Christ in history, but without identifying either theological scholarship or historical research with "faith." For him, Jesus of Nazareth, the eternal Word, also lives very much in the present and gives visible, sacramental expression to that presence in the Church and her entire life. While faith remains for the Catholic a personal supernatural act by which and in which the individual believer encounters God, the *kerygma* of Christ is neither something to be sought outside of history nor a message to be dug up out of the past by historical research alone. For him the Church *is* Christ, His extension in time and space, and as such has no need to uncover the message of the past by leaping through the centuries to a New Testament text which will "prove" to all the world the validity of its teaching. The authority of the Church is the authority of Christ, living on in His Mystical Body. What that Church teaches is not simply a doctrine *about* Christ; nor is it the repetition by someone else of what Christ once taught. Quite the opposite, the Church *is* Christ endlessly proclaiming Christ and the Christian message to the end of time. The *kerygma* is not something of the past to be recaptured, but a proclamation repeated for us daily, here and now; it is the voice of Christ ringing in our ears through the ministry of His living Church.

If we now believe in the divinity of Christ and in His message, and perceive Him only "through a mirror in an obscure manner," we yet look forward to that day when "face to face" we shall gaze upon Him together with the Father and the Spirit. But in either event, the encounter, here or hereafter, in faith or in vision, is always and ever more a personal, vital, and living contact by which man comes to know himself and the meaning of the world in which he lives as well as that world for which he is destined, made known to him through the loving mercy of that eternal Father who "at sundry times and in divers manners spoke in times past to the fathers by the prophets," but who has now "last of all in these days spoken to us by his Son, whom he appointed heir of all things, by whom also he made the world. . . ."[112]

CHAPTER VII

Bishop Butler and Agnosticism

The possibility of defending the truth of Christianity by an appeal to "proofs" of a rational and historical nature has been discussed in earlier chapters, but we find in Bishop Butler an example of one individual who attempted to do this in a lengthy and systematic fashion. A study of Butler's writings and of the varied reactions to what he said can be more enlightening. At one time his reputation as a defender of the Christian faith could hardly have been more exalted, and yet his attempts have been so consistently downgraded that he is current spoken of, with good reason, as a "rationalist apologist for Christianity."[1] From almost universal praise at the start, the judgment of history has passed into one of generally accepted condemnation, coupled, of course, with a feeling of pity for a Christian apologist who could have missed the target so widely. Even as a warning, his views can be most helpful for those interested in the perplexing question concerning the relationship between faith and reason.

Joseph Butler was the youngest of eight children; he was born on May 18, 1692, at Wantage, Berkshire.[2] The family was Presbyterian, and Butler's early training was along these lines, first at the Latin school of his home town and later at a dissenting academy conducted by Samuel Jones (first at Gloucester and afterward at Tewkesbury). Overcoming the objections of his father, Butler conformed to the Established Church and then entered Oriel College at Oxford in 1714. In time he accepted Anglican orders, thus entering upon an ecclesiastical career in the Establishment rather than in the Presbyterian body (as his father had at one time hoped).

Butler's rise within the Established Church began with his appointment as preacher at the Rolls Chapel in London in 1719. In 1725 he received the parish at Stanhope which afforded him a better income and also the leisure to do further writing; it was at this time that he did the greatest amount of work on his *Analogy of Religion.* In 1738 Butler accepted the bishopric of Bristol — then one of the poorest in England. He was offered the primacy of England in 1747, but refused it, reportedly because he thought "it was too late for him to try to support a falling Church." In 1750, however, he did accept the offer of the see of Durham where he continued the same type of administrative work and interest in social problems that had preoccupied him at Bristol. He died in 1752, at the age of sixty, a victim of stomach and intestinal disorders.

Throughout his career, Butler was greatly concerned with the inroads of deism in the Established Church; it was largely this which caused him to refuse the primacy of England. In his view this rationalistic approach had only resulted in an increase of unbelievers, who not only rejected Christianity but even went so far as to dismiss it as unworthy of inquiry and as something totally fictitious.[3] In writing his *Analogy,* therefore, Butler wrote as a truly religious-minded man who worked to overcome the irreligious attitudes associated with the deistic movement in England. While his earlier interest as preacher at the Rolls Chapel had been directed toward moral, ethical, and social questions (as were his years as bishop in Bristol and Durham),[4] the *Analogy* was largely speculative.

Others before him, especially Samuel Clark, had attempted to meet the deistic position by an *a priori* type of argument, attacking the system on the basis of traditional Christian principles by which the approach of the deists would supposedly be proved inadequate. This was not an entire success, however, so that Butler, influenced more by the methodology of Shaftesbury, preferred to adopt an *a posteriori* type of defense, free from all personal, *a priori* convictions. He hoped to institute a purely objective observation of man and the universe, and then proceed to consider the evidence in favor of Christianity; in this way, he felt his readers would conclude to the truth of Christianity in a scientific and objective manner.

It was this attempt on Butler's part to meet his adversaries on their own grounds that gave to the *Analogy* its unique character and whatever appeal it possessed; but it was also the reason for the faulty understanding of his defense of Christianity by later generations.[5] His attempt to be objective in this instance led to the ultimate downfall of his project. His attempt, however, serves as an excellent example of the futility of hoping to found the certitude of faith upon historical evidence and the argument from probability alone. Once hailed as one of the greatest Christian apologists of modern times, Butler eventually fell into such disrepute that some came to consider him almost an enemy of Christianity. To understand how this happened, we need to have some grasp of *The Analogy of Religion, Natural and Revealed, to the Constitution and Course of Nature* (1736), Butler's great work.[6]

GENERAL ARGUMENT

The core of the discussion is the nature of religious assent as proposed by Butler. It is, from start to finish, a purely rational assent, based upon historical evidence (chiefly miracles and prophecies), and set forth with the frank admission that an argument along these lines moves entirely in the realm of probability. Butler's often repeated axiom that "probability is the very guide of life"[7] sets the tone for his whole approach to faith. He attempts to answer the objection (that probability does not give much in the way of certitude) by doing nothing more than defending two very unsatisfactory propositions regarding the problem at hand. *First,* he grants that the certitude of which he speaks is not overwhelming, but he also insists that we must be realistic enough to see that we have no more than such probable evidence in regard to Christian faith, so that we must learn to live with it.[8] *Second,* he tries to indicate that, although the certitude involved is not all that might be desired, it is still not as insignificant as some would make it, since "probable proofs, by being added, not only increase the evidence, but multiply it."[9]

In this Butler reveals much about the nature of religious assent as he understands it. Since he freely grants that there are mysteries in Christianity, and since he must somehow defend the logic of accepting truths which cannot be proven by reason, he falls back upon historical and rational arguments, emphasizing above all the miracles and prophecies worked by God in testimony of the truth of Christianity and contained in the Bible (regarded here as a strictly historical book). These arguments — the evidence or proof — become the ultimate basis for belief in this system.

Fundamentally, Butler's position would be that readily accepted today which contends that historical certitude is a form of moral certitude. History, like the physical sciences, must "suspend judgment" at a certain point. Just as there is always the possibility of some new scientific fact being discovered and thus forcing the scientist to alter his conclusions, so also must the historian recognize that at some future date new evidence might be uncovered, further documents or historical records might come to light, thus demanding a reevaluation of all the evidence and perhaps some alteration of the final conclusions. This is a very real problem for many Christians today who have come to question whether the historical method, when used as the sole basis of Christian faith, would not necessarily lead to complete religious skepticism.[10]

Following this approach, however, Butler sums up his entire historically orientated argument in the *Analogy* by noting that the proof of Christianity rests chiefly on the appeal to miracles and prophecies. Other seemingly insignificant elements must be considered as well, and they help to form his total argument; indeed, Butler's complete defense of Christianity consists of a "long series of things, reaching, as it seems, from the beginning of the world to the present time, of great variety and compass, taking in both the direct, and also the collateral, proofs; and making up, all of them together, one argument. . . ."[11] This extended argument unfolds for us that revelation which "may be considered as wholly historical."[12]

Thus Butler centers his proof on the concept of "scripture-history,"[13] reaching from the time of creation, through the period of the Old Testament, down to the Christian era. It is for this reason that he stresses so emphatically "the historical evidence of miracles wrought in attentation of Christianity. . . ."[14] Since his proof is so strongly historical, and since these miracles are so central to the proof, it is most important to defend the historicity of the miracles recorded in the Old Testament, in the Gospels and Acts, the Pauline Epistles as well as the writings of the early centuries of the Christian era.[15] The objection that these scriptural miracles are purely imaginative and due to the enthusiasm of the faithful must be rejected; these miracles are truly historical.[16] The same thing is true of the argument from prophecy.[17]

It is not the historicity of the miracles as such that is of importance here, but rather the use and significance of them in Butler's argument; a Catholic would defend the historicity of the miracles no less than Butler. It is, however, the fact that this historical certitude concerning the "proof" becomes the basis for the assent of faith itself that causes grave difficulties, some of which even Butler perceived. The eighteenth-century philosophers, because of their concern with probability, were already beginning to be troubled by the question of "historical certitude"; since his was basically an historical proof, Butler could not allow this difficulty raised by others to go unanswered.

THE ASSENT OF FAITH

Because of its central position in the system of Butler, the assent to revealed religion, as he understands it, has been the point most frequently challenged by his critics through the centuries. In itself, his explanation is inadequate simply as a theory of faith. If one perceives the authority of God by means of an argument which moves entirely within the confines of reason and history, there is no way in which the absolute and unswerving certitude of faith may be defended; it must be limited not even to metaphysical certitude, but to moral certitude (because of the dimension of history involved).

While it is true that Butler affirmed the existence of supernatural mysteries in the traditional sense (truths, that is, which
reason could never discover nor comprehend, once revealed),[18] the
motive for accepting those truths remains something purely rational.
Thus Butler insists that while one might debate the "reasonableness of the system of religion," that is, whether it can or cannot be
understood by reason alone, such objections still do not touch at
all on the "credibility or truth of it. . . ."[19] What Butler means by
this is that one can believe in these incomprehensible mysteries of
revelation precisely because of the proof offered as testimony
of the truth of these mysteries; but this proof is perceived by
reason alone in its study of the historical evidence. It is, in other
words this objective and historical evidence which motivates one
to accept these supernatural truths (truths which are not "reasonable," as Butler puts it). He is not attempting in any way to reduce
the *content* of Christianity to the purely rational, but the *assent*
is another question. For Butler, while the truths cannot be
"reasonable" (that is, proportioned to the power of unaided
reason), the assent is that and nothing more. To say that Christianity or the Christian revelation is "reasonable" would mean
for Butler that there were no supernatural mysteries at all; this
he emphatically denies. But man's acceptance of those truths is, in
Butler's explanation, an acceptance based upon a purely rational
type of argumentation.[20]

It is in this element that the question of the motive of faith in
Butler's system deserves our attention. The motive is, for him, the
"authority of God revealing," so that the believer is not to question the mysteries; they are "to be believed upon the mere authority
of its Author."[21] The difficulty arises, however, in Butler's notion
of the *manner* in which the Christian is to perceive this divine
authority. His entire approach indicates that God's authority is
to be perceived psychologically in the external proofs alone — those
proofs which God has given for the truth of Christianity, chiefly in
the "evidence of miracles wrought in proof of Christianity."[22]
This is, however, a purely human and rational act from the psychological point of view, based on nothing more than historical

evidence. It is not enough to say that we believe these truths "on the authority of God revealing"; the central point rests in the question of precisely *how* man perceives that authority. If it is a purely rational-historical path that the individual follows, terminating indiscriminately in either a "natural" or a "supernatural" act of faith (dependent solely upon an entitative elevation of the act to the supernatural order), the essential note of faith still remains locked up within the purely human and rational.

SUPERNATURAL FAITH

To avoid any misunderstanding, it is good to emphasize that Butler does not even make this attempt to supernaturalize the act of faith by insisting upon an entitative elevation; he appears much too rationalistic for this. Throughout the *Analogy* and in his *Sermons,* the virtue of believing in Christianity appears as nothing more than a purely human act in every sense; man is guided by the intellect in its evaluation of the objective evidence, draws his conclusions, and there the case rests. There is scarcely any consideration of supernatural virtues in which God would take the initiative and man's role would be to cooperate freely with divine grace, as there is in this more recent theory of faith among Catholic theologians. For Butler, supernatural activity seems to be limited to informing us of truths beyond reason, so that we might guide our lives accordingly; but the decision to accept these truths and to live in accord with this pattern is a purely human act in every sense. Upon occasion he does speak of the Holy Spirit as our Sanctifier, and of the inward principle involved in religion, but these are always explained in terms of accepting the Christian revelation which came from the Spirit, as an external message, of adapting the moral virtue of religion to include this Christian scheme. When Butler speaks of the "inward principle" of Christianity, "to be exerted in such and such inward acts of the mind and heart,"[23] there is very little indication that such phrases mean for him any type of inner renewal through grace. Nowhere does Butler present a notion of Christian virtue that would involve an elevation of the believer to a new and supernatural mode of existence, even on the entitative level; in fact, rarely does he even speak in a manner that would be vaguely reminiscent of the Catholic teaching on grace and the infused virtues. Butler remains very much a man of his own age, and traces of both deism and rationalism can be perceived in all he writes.

For this reason, Butler also failed to sympathize with the religious aspirations of other non-Catholics of his era; his approach to Christianity was quite diverse. As Mossner suggests in regard to the teaching of John Wesley:

> There was little likelihood that the author of the *Analogy of Religion* could understand such doctrine, for Butler voiced the dominant religion of the intellect, and Wesley the revival of the religion of the heart. The two might speak alike of religious faith, but to Butler *faith* meant intellectual conviction, while to Wesley it meant an inward sentiment of instinctive feeling.[24]

The cool, intellectual faith of Butler was quite thoroughly out of tune with the emphasis upon the inner workings of the Spirit as preached by Wesley. The two men met in 1739 and the carefully reasoned faith of Butler clashed with Wesley's doctrine of a more personal encounter with God. Butler's words of advice, spoken as the Bishop of Bristol, were short and to the point: "Well, sir, since you ask my advice, I will give it to you very freely. You have no business here; you are not commissioned to preach in this diocese. Therefore I advise you to go home."[25]

While the Catholic will feel that Wesley overemphasized the activity of the Spirit in the individual (by way of personal inspiration), he will readily agree with his emphasis upon faith as something distinct from mere reason, despite the obvious relationship between the two in the genesis of faith. In a sermon delivered at St. Mary's, Oxford, in 1738, Wesley pointed out that the required faith "is not barely a speculative, rational thing, a cold lifeless assent, a train of ideas in the head; but also a disposition of the heart. . . ."[26] The faith that Wesley sought was more than a conclusion to a syllogism, based on a study of the historical evidence of the truth of Christianity. Butler, however, could hardly have understood his dissatisfaction with such a concept of belief.

In his entire treatment, Butler repeats but one answer time and again: everything depends on the "historical evidence for the truth of Christianity."[27] The Incarnation of Christ is referred to as an "invisible miracle," which, being secret or hidden, must in turn "be proved by visible miracles."[28] Butler looks upon any objections against Christianity as a system as frivolous; what must be considered are solely the objections "against the evidence of Christianity."[29]

What he seeks to give in all instances are "reasons" for believing. In place of the calm acceptance of the Word of God, received in all humility, Butler would set the Christian out on a reasoned road. Stripped of all its verbiage, the answer of Butler to the question of faith is simply that the assent of faith rests ultimately on a purely human investigation. It is an intellectual assent to a rational proof based on the evidence of history in regard to miracles, prophecies, and similar signs associated with the Christian Gospel. At times Butler has been compared with Pascal, but considering their different views of faith, Mossner rightly objects to the comparison. "Pascal," he notes, "had at once greater doubts and greater faith than Butler, and his faith [that of Pascal] was not derived from reason."[30] In the last analysis, Butler would have the Christian accept supernatural truths simply because he has been intellectually *convinced* that this is the thing to do. Butler would never have been able to understand even the basic problem Kierkegaard was trying to solve when he spoke of the necessary "leap" into faith.

FAITH AND REASON

It may be noted that there is a great difference between Butler's defense of reason (together with his insistence upon the probative force of miracles and prophecies) and the teaching of Vatican I. The official doctrine of the Catholic Church stresses the role of reason in laying a substratum, as it were, for the act of faith. As an intellectual being, man has the power of knowing that *if* he does go on to believe, he will be acting in accordance with reason; he will not be doing violence to his intellectual nature by taking what must appear as something of a "leap" into faith. In rejecting the immanentism and subjectivism of the nineteenth century, Vatican I defends the power of reason to know God and to recognize in miracles and prophecies, as well as in the entire life of the living Church, valid motives of credibility.[31] The speculative judgment of credibility based upon those motives can be a judgment reached by reason without the help of grace; it states that there is evidence enough at hand to indicate that God *has* spoken, that He has intervened in the history of mankind, that there is a divine revelation; the handiwork of God is evident, so that an individual would be acting as a rational being were he to go on to accept, on the authority of God revealing, the truths and the way of life associated with this revelation.[32]

In Butler, however, there is a total confusion between the judgment of credibility and the act of faith. In the nineteenth century, Kierkegaard reacted against a similar rationalistic type of faith, but he passed over what we would call the judgment of credibility entirely, in favor of a totally blind leap into faith. Butler, however, had made faith precisely that which Kierkegaard wanted to reject, namely, a purely rational judgment of man, inbedded in carefully worked-out syllogisms.[33]

The question constantly placed before those Catholic theologians today who defend the possibility of a "natural" or "scientific" faith, therefore, is not whether they adequately defend the supernaturality of faith, but whether the *certitude* they affirm is actually any different from that defended by Butler. They present a faith that is supernatural, but can their limitation of the supernatural effect to the entitative level save them from the pit of purely rational assent into which Butler fell — an assent that cannot rise above the level of moral certitude associated with historical conclusions? In affirming the possibility of a "natural" faith in supernatural truths, have they gone beyond Butler, for whom the judgment on the basis of external evidence (miracles and prophecies) terminates in the assent to supernatural truths itself? It *is* a belief based on authority of God revealing, but on that divine authority only insofar as it is uncovered and perceived by the means of a purely rational and historical study.[34] For this reason the certitude involved in the conclusion: "I believe" is mediated by rational arguments alone, and must be limited to the rational and historical order. For his part, Butler would not deny this in any way. He even placed the possible question of the deist: "How can we accept the entire scheme of Christianity, with all its mysteries, if we have nothing but this flimsy evidence to support our decision?" His answer was to admit almost all the difficulties proposed in the objection, and insist once again that this is the best we can do.[35] This viewpoint appears with equal clarity in Butler's *Charge to the Clergy of Durham*,[36] but it is especially emphasized in his sermon delivered before the House of Lords in 1747 on the anniversary of the King's accession to the throne. In this sermon he contrasts the Church of England and the Church of Rome, complaining that in the Roman Catholic countries the Church will "substitute force instead of argument; and external profession made by force instead of reasonable conviction."[37] Butler seems somewhat oblivious of the fact that the English penal laws were still in effect at this time, but the point to be stressed here is that for him "reasonable conviction" and "argument" are *the* means by which people are to be truly converted to Christianity. It is not a question here of a personal and free acceptance of Christianity such as the Catholic Church insists upon so strongly, but of a rational assent in which the essence of faith lies. Thus Butler glories in the approach he attributes to the Church of England since, he says, "our religious establishment disclaims all principles of this kind, and desires not to keep persons in its communion, or gain proselytes to it, by any other methods than the Christian ones of argument and conviction."[38]

There are various ways in which such a statement could be understood, of course; any true faith must be a personal conviction. For Butler, however, it is precisely by argument and conviction that one comes to formulate that rational assent which *is*, for him, the act of faith itself — a conviction achieved by syllogistic reasoning based on the evidence of history.

CONCLUSION

In view of this, it is not surprising that the judgment of history on Bishop Butler is one designating him as a "rationalist defender of Christianity." Essentially Butler is no different from those nine-teenth-century Hegelian theologians against whom Kierkegaard complained, noting that "they have written their folios which de-velop the proofs of Christianity," so that "the docents and parsons strut, and the missionaries go forth to convert the heathen with the help of this *ergo*."[39]

These words of Butler from the *Analogy of Religion* sum up his entire position: ". . . religion is not intuitively true, but a matter of deduction and inference."[40] This is the core of Butler's doctrine and the source of all the difficulties associated with it. Although Christian faith has its close and necessary relations with reason, it lies on a higher level, where the divine power becomes evident to the believer within the confines of the living, divinely guided Church. The specter of Bishop Butler lifts a warning hand to those who would ignore this approach, indicating that should faith become confused with historical certitude and rational argumenta-tion, one or the other will suffer; faith lapsing into rationalism or reason giving way to skepticism or agnosticism.

OTHER INTERPRETATIONS

Upon reflection, it is easy to see how this same approach as outlined by Butler can also be reversed, and become the cause of the greatest doubts or lead even to the total rejection of Christian truth. If one must remain in the realm of probability in regard to faith, he might just as easily claim that Christian faith has no real basis for an absolute and unswerving assent; one might just as well embrace agnosticism or even atheism. It is just as easy to argue that Christianity is probably *not* true, as to argue — with Butler — that it probably *is*. This is not the type of Christianity that Butler really wanted to portray, but it is involved in what he says. If Christian faith does not stand apart from all else, in a class of its own, the uniqueness of Christianity vanishes from sight.

And this is the interpretation given to the *Analogy* in later centuries, due largely to the change in philosophical approaches with the passing of time, thus causing men to read Butler's works from a different point of view, and leading them to draw quite opposite conclusions. In this way, the *Analogy of Religion* was eventually recognized as a subtle danger to Christian faith when later readers came to perceive the basic rationalism and potential skepticism which it contains. The weakness is inherent in the principles upon which Butler built his defense of Christianity, so that it was inevitable that in time this other aspect of the work would come to light.

In view of this, it is somewhat surprising that during the first century after the appearance of the *Analogy* the work was generally highly praised; all things considered, attacks upon it were surprisingly few in number. Within Butler's lifetime, he was able to see the *Analogy* and the *Sermons* go through four editions each in England, as well as a Dublin reprint of the *Analogy*. As Mossner relates: "In 1752 Butler's authority in theology was unrivalled except by that of Tillotson, S. Clarke, Sherlock, and perhaps Edmund Law and Warburton. But of all those eminent reputations, that of Butler alone was not on the wane."[41] Indeed, the influence of Butler continued to increase, even on the Continent (thanks to a German translation of the *Analogy* in 1756). His works were soon highly recommended in the universities of England, and about 1833 the *Analogy* was added to the list of standard authors for the final examination at Oxford. Thus, in Mossner's judgment, Butler only reached the peak of his popularity a hundred years after the Analogy first appeared — roughly from 1837 to 1860.[42]

This triumph, however, was short-lived. Once the influence of Kantian philosophy began to exercise its force, there were certain voices gradually raised against Butler and his rationalistic approach to faith. Those who read the *Analogy* from vastly different philosophical backgrounds became highly critical, so that his popularity began to decline in some circles; yet, precisely because of this criticism, his writings gained favor in others, so that Butler met with both favor and disfavor in the debates of the early part of the nineteenth century. He was particularly praised by those involved in the Oxford Movement, especially by John Henry Newman. On the other hand, the *Analogy* drew the attention of those who shared in no way the aspirations of the Oxford Movement, but who perceived the skepticism latent in Butler's approach and who wished to make use of his authority or his now recognized failure in order to argue their case for rationalism, skepticism, and agnosticism.

In this fashion, Butler was credited by various groups as defending opposite movements, neither of which he himself had ever favored. Some thought he was a pro-Romanist leader in the Anglican Church, while others looked upon him as an unwitting promoter of the unencumbered skepticism or even atheism of the nineteenth-century liberals. Among those who embraced neither extreme, however, the influence of Butler simply declined with the rise of newer philosophical interests. For those who had accepted the immanentist approach to faith in the post-Kantian era, and for whom religion became ever more subjective, there simply was no longer any place left for Butler and the *Analogy*. Although in 1852 Newman felt he could describe Butler as "the greatest name in the Anglican Church," his success was actually near its end; as Mossner expresses it: "Modern knowledge discloses his many dialectical and theological errors, and it is only sentiment that attempts to keep him in the position of honor as an apologist."[43]

STARTING POINT: JOHN LOCKE

Basically, Butler's concept of the argument from probability, which is so essential to his system, is derived from John Locke, who in his *Essay on Human Understanding* distinguishes between demonstration and probability. For Locke, a demonstration means that one has shown the argeement or disagreement of two ideas by means of one or more proofs indicating a constant, immutable, and visible connection between the two ideas. Probability, on the other hand, results when such a constant connection is not present (or at least is not perceived by us); yet the agreement we note between the two ideas in this instance arises because whatever we do perceive is sufficient to induce the mind to draw a firm enough conclusion to make the individual feel justified in going on to act.

As an example of this, Locke refers to the various theorems of geometry which speak of the equality between the angles of a triangle. One man, he claims, may study the proof of these statements and grasp them entirely; this man perceives a demonstration. Another, however, may hear a respected mathematician state these theorems, and though he fails to understand the full argument, this individual nevertheless concludes that the statements are true. He does this on two counts. *First,* what the mathematician says sounds "probable"; it is this perception of probability that becomes the basis of the assent. *Second,* the authority of the man on whose testimony the individual accepts these theorems is an added proof of their truth. In this way, apart from a demonstration, the assent of an individual to a particular truth may be ultimately caused by "the wonted veracity of the speaker in other cases, or his supposed veracity in this."[44]

Locke also speaks of the "several degrees and grounds of probability,"[45] and insists that "probability is likeliness to be true. . . ."[46] As opposed to a "demonstration," Locke calls the act of the mind associated with probability either "belief, assent, or opinion," noting that in such probable knowledge we accept a certain proposition as true because of the "arguments or proofs that are found to persuade us to receive it as true, without certain knowledge that it is so."[47] Precisely because it fails to achieve that certain knowledge proper to a demonstration, Locke's "probability" admits of degrees.[48] There are some probable statements, he claims, which border so nearly on certainty that we entertain no real doubts about them, and proceed to act upon them as resolutely *as if* they were infallibly demonstrated and certain. At the same time, he admits that in this category the degrees of certainty can vary from "almost certain and demonstrated" to "improbability and unlikeliness," almost to "impossibility." And the assent will vary accordingly, reaching from full assurance and confidence (in regard to those things "almost demonstrated"), down to conjecture, doubt, or even distrust (in regard to matters considerably less certain).[49]

The chief point of agreement between Butler and Locke would seem to lie in Locke's admission that one can accept certain propositions as true simply because of the "arguments" or "proofs" associated with them, even though the individual would still have the consciousness that he does not possess a true demonstration (which alone, for Locke, "infallibly determines the understanding, and produces certain knowledge . . ."[50]). Similarly, there is an insistence in Locke that in many cases the upper ranges of probability are sufficiently certain to be acted upon with no serious doubts or hesitancies; in fact, for practical purposes, he feels that these states of mind leave us as little liberty to assent or not to assent as does a true demonstration.[51] Locke's reason for holding this is emphasized strongly by Butler, that is, that we have no other alternative than acting on what small evidence we possess, since it is necessary to act here and now.[52] As Locke states: "The conduct of our lives, and the management of our great concerns, will not bear delay; for those depend, for the most part, on the determination of our judgment in points wherein we are not capable of certain and demonstrative knowledge, and wherein it is necessary for us to embrace the one side or the other."[53]

Locke also speaks of analogy in a manner reminiscent of Butler's treatment. He claims that "in things which sense cannot discern, analogy is the great rule of probability."[54] By this, Locke indicates a type of knowledge which cannot arise from either observation or testimony, but can be known only by *comparing* certain things to other objects that we do know on the basis of observation and testimony; he cites, as examples of this, the existence of angels and microscopic beings. Thus, he points out that "analogy in these matters is the only help we have, and it is from that alone we draw all our grounds of probability."[55] The truth of what we know in this manner will be more or less "probably true" in the degree that it agrees with truths already established in our minds in other ways, and insofar as it fits proportionately into the entire complex of our knowledge.

While Butler makes this type of argument, based on analogy and probability, the ultimate basis for the assent of faith, Locke himself places faith on an entirely distinct level; had Butler followed Locke's lead in this regard, he might well have avoided the rationalistic pit into which his defense of Christianity fell. Locke fails to appreciate the role of a visible Church in the realm of faith, as included in Catholic teaching, and he casts aside any notion of a true faith existing within any church or community; in doing this, however, he does not reduce the assent of faith to the realm of reason.

It is true that for Locke the various communities represent only diverse religious opinions, and he criticizes not only Catholics but all others, Christian and non-Christian alike, who (from his point of view) pin their faith on nothing more secure than the variable opinions of their fellowmen: "And if the opinions and persuasions of others, whom we know and think well of, be a ground of assent, men have reason to be Heathens in Japan, Mahometans in Turkey, Papists in Spain, Protestants in England, and Lutherans in Sweden."[56]

What is of interest here is Locke's concern for the assent and certitude of faith. While Butler attempts to combine an assent of faith which would be based upon rational argument and proofs (chiefly miracles and prophecies) and at the same time be realized in the faith of the Established Church of England, Locke places the assent of faith and its corresponding certitude in a different category altogether:

> Besides those we have hitherto mentioned, there is one sort of proposition that challenges the highest degree of our assent upon bare testimony, whether the thing proposed agree or disagree with common experience and the ordinary course of things or no. The reason whereof is, because the testimony is of such a one, as cannot deceive, nor be deceived, and that is of God himself. This carries with it an assurance beyond doubt, evidence beyond exception.[57]

For Locke, this authority of God is perceived in a fashion distinct from all human proof and historical or rational arguments; the testimony is revelation, and our assent to it is called faith, which "absolutely determines our minds, and as perfectly excludes all wavering, as our knowledge itself; and we may as well doubt of our own being, as we can, whether any revelation from God be true."[58] In a statement almost diametrically opposed to the position of Butler, Locke warns against the danger of believing a false revelation, since in such a case "our assent can be rationally no higher than the evidence of its being a revelation. . . . If the evidence of its being a revelation, or that this is its true sense, be only on probable proofs, our assent can reach no higher than an assurance or diffidence, arising from the more or less apparent probability of the proofs."[59]

Had Butler been as anxious to avoid this danger as was Locke, his *Analogy* would have been considerably transformed to secure for the assent of faith the absolute certitude it demands. Locke distinguishes faith and reason entirely. *Reason,* he says, "as contradistinguished to faith," is "the discovery of the certainty or probability of such propositions or truths as the mind can deduce." *Faith,* on the other hand, "is the assent to any proposition, not thus made out by the deductions of reason, but upon the credit of the proposer, as coming from God, in some extraordinary way of communication."[60] In other words, the certitude of faith — the psychological act itself — cannot be ultimately reduced to some form of human reason (whether it be a deistic reduction of Christian truth to the level of reason, or some form of rational demonstration or argument from probability, such as Butler defends).

From a Catholic point of view, it is also noteworthy that, for Locke, reason must still "judge the truth of its being a revelation."[61] He would not propose any purely subjective type of faith, nor run the risk of subjecting faith to the terrors of false illuminationism or psychotic hallucination. His position here approaches far more the teaching of the Catholic Church in regard to the judgment of credibility and the reasonableness of faith.[62] Locke insists on a rational preparation for faith, but for him the assent of faith itself is something distinct and unique, and it is for this reason that its certitude far overreaches the limits of even the highest type of rational argumentation. The motive of faith in

Locke's view is rooted on the authority of God, perceived not in any purely natural manner, but in some supernatural manner that affects the act of faith even as a psychological act. On this point Locke approaches far more, in his own fashion, the Thomist-Saurezian theory of faith and its insistence that the motive of supernatural faith itself is believed; and for the same reason, his concept of the assent of faith is totally distinct from that of Butler, despite the similarity on other scores.

THE CHRISTIAN EVIDENCE SCHOOL

In England during the eighteenth century there arose the Christian Evidence School, which, following the lead of Locke as interpreted by Butler, emphasized above all the argument from probability and external evidence. It culminated in William Paley's *A View of the Evidences of Christianity* (1794), which Mossner describes as a "skilful redintegration of Butler's method with Lardner's data."[63] Nathaniel Lardner, a nonconformist, had written his *Credibility of the Gospel History* (1723–55) as an attempt to confirm the New Testament as pure history (in our more modern sense) by making an appeal to nonscriptural writers; it is something of a symbol of the antideistic reaction which led to an attempt to meet the deists and rationalists on their own terms by treating the Bible purely as a historical book.

In Paley, this historical approach of Lardner is coupled with Butler's appeal to analogy and probability, resulting in an extreme expression of what may not have immediately appeared so obvious in Butler, that is, a type of Christian faith that rests entirely on historical evidence. It is a form of the reduction of the assent of faith to the purely rational level, since it is only through the records of history that the believer comes to perceive both the fact of revelation and the authority of God associated with that revelation. Not unlike Butler, Paley avoids a discussion of the mysterious nature of the doctrines of Christianity, claiming that man is able to perceive the truth of the Christian system without going into such matters as the Trinity or the Incarnation: "The doctrine itself is by no means necessary to the belief of Christianity, which must, in the first instance at least, depend upon the ordinary maxims of historical credibility."[64]

In a similar fashion, Paley answers the objection that the proof of Christianity is not as clear and demanding as it might have been. He admits that we could imagine all other possible ways in which God might have dealt with men (such as personal revelation, intuition, and the like); but dealing with revelation as it has actually been given, and as it is known to us through historical evidence, Paley insists: "The question is not, whether Christianity possesses the highest possible degree of evidence, but whether the not having more evidence be a sufficient reason for rejecting that which we have."[65]

DAVID HUME

This type of appeal to historical evidence as the foundation for the assent of faith was destined to come under early attack by a man who had the greatest respect for Butler, but who nevertheless was instrumental in undermining Butler's philosophical position. This man was David Hume.[66] Hume had already written his *Essay on Miracles* before he published the *Treatise on Human Nature* (1739); it was originally a part of this work, but Hume cautiously excised it from the tract. Hume had hoped to submit the *Treatise* to Butler, but realizing, it would seem, the probable effect of the chapter on miracles, he suppressed it in hopes of receiving a better evaluation of his work; this is at least one of the probable reasons for this change in Hume's plans. Eventually his attempts to contact Butler failed, and he sent him only a copy of the *Treatise* when it was finally published.[67] On the advice of his friends, the essay on miracles was not restored to its place in the *Treatise* at this time, although Hume might also have been motivated by the thought suggested by Mossner, that is, "an indication that what he was counting on was serious consideration of his philosophy as philosophy, rather than as religious controversy."[68] The essay on miracles, however, was later included in Hume's *Philosophical Essays concerning Human Understanding* (a work which finally appeared in 1748 under a different title: *An Enquiry concerning*

Human Understanding). As might be expected, the essay on miracles at once stirred up strong religious controversy; this was four years before Butler's death.

Hume is not overmuch concerned with the question of probability, although he admits the notion and makes use of it. While Locke divides all arguments into demonstrative and probable, Hume urges a threefold distinction: demonstrations, proofs, and probabilities. By proofs he means "such arguments from experience as leave no room for doubt or opposition."[69] There is, however, a slightly different twist to the notion as it appears in Hume. Arguing from his basic position that "there be no such thing as Chance in the world," Hume understands probability only as the state of mind resulting from our ignorance of the real cause of any event.[70]

This notion of probability figures largely in his discussion of miracles. Hume's purpose in his *Essay on Miracles* is not to prove the philosophical impossibility of miracles, as is often thought; he is concerned throughout with showing merely that miracles cannot be used as a foundation for faith or any system of religion. His chief argument is that the fact of a miracle simply cannot be proved on the basis of testimony: "Upon the whole, then, it appears that no testimony for any kind of miracle has ever amounted to a probability, much less to a proof. . . and therefore we may establish it as a maxim that no human testimony can have such force as to prove a miracle, and make it a just foundation for any such system of religion."[71]

Hume's argument is that "it is experience only which gives authority to human testimony."[72] Thus, if a number of people testify from their experience that there has been a miracle, there will also be as many people who will testify that according to their experience there are only laws of nature. In this way the two contrary testimonies will cancel out one another. Hume does claim that there might be a "miracle" that could be proved by an unusual universality of testimony, but he goes on to add that "perhaps, it will be impossible to find any such in all the records of history."[73] He suggests a case where the testimony of all people, from all parts of the earth, agreed that from the first of January, 1600, there was a total darkness over the whole earth for eight days. Should that happen, Hume concludes that "our present philosophers, instead of doubting the fact, ought to receive it as certain, and ought to search for the causes whence it might be derived."[74]

In other words, Hume still feels that nothing happens either by "chance" or in any "miraculous" manner outside the fast and unchanging laws of nature. While he would accept such a "miracle" as this as certain, he still does not really think it is a miracle in the usual sense at all, and would want to set about investigating the laws which brought it about. As for a resurrection from the dead, Hume rejects this *a priori,* just as he rejects Christianity.[75] For him, such a thing simply could not happen, even by divine power; his skepticism is so strong that he feels that even God must deal with mankind through the testimony of other men, and this is quite untrustworthy.

Of concern for us here is the argument against religious assent that Hume levels at Christian theologians. He notes his pleasure at the type of reasoning he has proposed, "as I think it may serve to confound those dangerous friends or disguised enemies to the *Christian Religion,* who have undertaken to defend it by the principles of human reason."[76] The opening paragraph of the chapter on miracles is really an attack on the use of historical evidence as a proof for Christianity. Hume begins by recalling Tillotson's argument against the Real Presence, based on the assumption that "the authority, either of the scripture or of tradition, is founded merely in the testimony of the apostles who were eye-witnesses to those miracles of our Saviour, by which he proved his divine mission."[77] Hence, Tillotson concludes that the evidence for the truth of the Christian religion is less than the evidence for the truth of our senses. The apostles at least had this evidence of their senses, but we are reduced to nothing but testimony — indeed, a testimony that "must diminish in passing from them to their disciples. . . ."[78]

Tillotson uses this argument to reject the doctrine of transubstantiation as contrary to experience, but Hume goes on to apply the same argument to miracles in general. It is interesting to note, however, the picture of more orthodox theologians that is depicted here. Christianity is supposedly proved by an appeal to history and the testimony concerning it. Hume's presentation of the Christian faith exaggerates its dependence upon reason alone, but it must be admitted that the appeal to reason to which Hume objects had been overworked by the apologetes he had in mind, including Bishop Butler. Hume uses the same argument from probability and turns it into a tool for destroying the force of Butler's *Analogy,* by implication at least. Hume insists that the probability for the miraculous evidence of the truth of Christianity is outweighed by the probability that everything happens according to the unchanging laws of nature, and that the testimony concerning these miracles is therefore untrustworthy. A wise man, says Hume, "proportions his belief to the evidence. . . . He weighs the opposite experiments,"[79] and finally compares the two sides, subtracting the smaller evidence from the greater "in order to know the exact force of the superior evidence."[80]

Whatever type of faith Hume does retain, he sees at least that it should be something distinguished from reason. He notes that, in regard to Christianity, "mere reason is insufficient to convince us of its veracity."[81] This is true in every sense of the word, but the apologetes Hume had in mind were actually attempting to prove the truth of Christianity in this manner. Apparently Hume looks upon Christianity as subversive of the principles of understanding. Thus, his description of a believer is obviously cynical: "Whoever is moved by Faith to assent to it [Christianity], is conscious of a continued miracle in his own person, which subverts all the principles of his understanding, and gives him a determination to believe what is most contrary to custom and experience."[82] But if he fails to see the truth of Christianity, Hume does manage to perceive the weakness of that defense of Christian truth proposed by those who appeal to reason alone.

OTHER OBJECTIONS TO BUTLER

It is not surprising, in the light of such considerations, that similar objections were aimed more directly at the doctrine of Bishop Butler in the *Analogy*. In his *Autobiography,* John Stuart Mill (born in 1806) relates that he was brought up in an atmosphere devoid of any religious belief in the ordinary acceptance of the word. He recalls what his father had told him on this subject of religion:

> I had heard him say that the turning point of his mind on the subject was reading Butler's *Analogy*. That work, of which he always continued to speak with respect, kept him, as he said, for some considerable time, a believer in the divine authority of Christianity by proving to him that whatever are the difficulties in believing that the Old and New Testaments proceed from or record the acts of a perfectly wise and good Being, the same and still greater difficulties stand in the way of the belief that a Being of such a character can have been the Maker of the universe.[83]

This was hardly the purpose Bishop Butler had in mind in writing the *Analogy,* that is, to show that deism involved even greater difficulties than Christianity, so that one might as well remain a Christian; but it is a reading that can be given to it. In the case of James Mill, even this was only a temporary help; as his son records: "Finding therefore no halting place in Deism, he remained in a state of perplexity until, doubtless after many struggles, he yielded to the conviction that concerning the origin of things nothing whatever can be known."[84]

Tristram has remarked on the fact that while Butler's *Analogy* was successful if read by a deist from his own point of view, if we consider later nondeistic readers "we shall find ourselves forced to the conclusion that a considerable number had their faith, if not shattered, at least weakened rather than confirmed by Butler's apologetic."[85] Mossner cites additional witnesses to this fact. William Pitt, the younger, declared that "Butler's work raised in his mind more doubts than it had answered,"[86] and Thomas Huxley parodies Butler's argument in the *Analogy* thus: "There is no absurdity in theology so great that you cannot parallel it by a greater absurdity in nature."[87] The Unitarian James Martineau claims that he considered the *Analogy* of Butler to contain "the most terrible persuasives to atheism that have ever been produced."[88]

With such changes in view, it is not surprising that about 1860 the *Analogy* was dropped from the list of standard authors for the final examination at Oxford; it had been incorporated into the list in 1833. In the 1870's, the criticism of Butler's position appears in more extended fashion in the writings of Leslie Stephen and Matthew Arnold, both worthy of brief consideration.

In his *History of English Thought in the Eighteenth Century* (1876), Stephen gives a very rationalistic interpretation of Butler that is far from flattering to the Bishop of Durham. He notes that "though Butler is habitually described as amongst the ablest champions of Christianity, he has probably made few converts, and has clearly helped some thinkers towards scepticism,"[89] and it is Stephen's opinion that one can certainly discover a line of thought in the *Analogy* that "leads to Atheism."[90]

Despite the title, Stephen's work is not exactly a history but more his own personal reaction to the events and teachings of history, written in the spirit of the nineteenth-century essayist. But his parody of Butler's position is indicative of the manner in which such a mind would react to the *Analogy*. He feels that Butler's argument from probable evidence may simply be reduced to this:

> . . . the chances are so awful that we cannot afford to neglect them. If there is no presumption against the existence of heaven and hell, there is a presumption for it; or, at least, a plain reason for acting as though it were a fact. . . . In matters of health or money, we have to act upon insufficient evidence. Why not in matters of salvation? Hell is probable enough to be worth avoiding.[91]

Stephen views Butler's opinion that the need to act upon less than satisfactory evidence indicates a type of reasoning that "provokes the criticism most commonly directed against the 'Analogy.' It is an attempt to meet difficulties, by suggesting equal or greater difficulties. It should, therefore, lead to scepticism rather than to conviction."[92]

Like certain others, Stephen is willing to admit that Butler's argument is undeniable against the deists,[93] but this is not the point of view from which Stephen is writing. He sums up Butler's defense of Christianity by stating that "if *nature* is a riddle, how should the *message* of the God of nature be clear?"[94] This is not an unfair criticism of Butler's defense, although it is no criticism of Christianity itself. Had Butler rested the assent of Christian faith on something more solid than his argument from probable evidence, this criticism could never have been made; but Butler directed his thought entirely to the deistic principles, arguing from history and reason alone. Instead of giving the right answer, he actually gives a faulty one by admitting too much of his opponent's position. Stephen is entirely right when he states that "Butler fails to understand that his assertions read by the light of a different set of assumptions would lead to a totally different result."[95]

The evaluation of Butler given by Matthew Arnold is no more favorable than that of Stephen. Arnold delivered two lectures at the Edinburgh Philosophical Institution which were later published in 1876: "Bishop Butler and the Zeit-Geist." In them he chose to ask what might be the value of the *Analogy* for the nondeist audience of the nineteenth century.[96] Arnold's final answer is this: "Let us, then, confess it to ourselves plainly. The *Analogy,* the great work on which such immense praise has been lavished, is, for all real intents and purposes now, a failure; it does not serve."[97] It apparently had some force in the past, but it is totally ineffectual now.

Arnold's conclusion is based upon a number of considerations. One of them is the basic inability of the *Analogy* to help those who most need help in their religious life: "I say, a man who is looking seriously for firm ground cannot but soon come to perceive what Butler's argument in the *Analogy* really amounts to, and that there is no help to be got from it."[98] The reason why Arnold asserts this is that the nineteenth century was experiencing a new "Zeit-Geist." Remarking that Butler considered miracles and the fulfillment of prophecy to be the fundamental "proofs" of Christianity, Arnold appeals to the biblical criticism of his own age, and holds that this in itself has made the *Analogy* outmoded: "Neither could Butler now speak of the Bible-history being all of it equally 'authentic genuine history,' or argue in behalf of this thesis as he does."[99] Butler's approach belongs to a former age, never more to return.

It is true that Butler argues from the position of his own age; his argument faces difficulties along these lines today, even when confronted by the most conservative estimate of biblical criticism. Yet this is only a part of the argument formulated by Butler. The chief principle to which he appeals is that of the need of acting on only probable evidence, and it is interesting to note the reason why Arnold attacks Butler on this question: "The wonderful thing about the *Analogy*," he says, "is the poor insignificant result, even in Butler's own judgment — the puny total outcome — of all this accumulated evidence from analogy, metaphysics, and Bible-history."[100] Arnold complains that the most Butler's argument can do is indicate that something is "probably" true, and nothing more; nor is he satisfied with Butler's response that we must be content to act on similar evidence in other events of our daily lives. He sums up the agrument in favor of religion in this manner: "It ought, in all reason, considering its infinite importance, to have nearly the same influence upon practice, as if it were thoroughly believed."[101]

Arnold contrasts this unsettled state of mind with that which he ascribes to the Bible (and which he would refer to as proper to the assent of supernatural faith):

> How unlike, above all, is this motive to the motive always supposed in the book itself of our religion, in the Bible! After reading the *Analogy* one goes instinctively to bathe one's spirit in the Bible again, to be refreshed by its boundless certitude and exhilaration. 'The Eternal is the strength of my life!' 'The foundation of God standeth sure!' — that is the constant tone of religion in the Bible. 'If I tell you the *truth*, why do ye not believe me? — the *evident* truth, that whoever comes to me has life; and evident, because whoever *does* come, gets it!' That is the evidence to constrain our practice which is offered by Christianity.[102]

Had Butler managed to emphasize far better the certitude of faith, the truth that results on the authority of God directly perceived by the believer and not grasped by means of reason alone, this criticism would not be justified. As it is, we must admit that the contrast is well drawn. It is a great failing of the *Analogy* that it leaves faith rooted on so unstable and insecure grounds.

INFLUENCE ON NEWMAN

While the nineteenth century brought forth this criticism of Butler, it also witnessed the high praise accorded him by those involved in the Oxford Movement — Newman, above all. It was about 1823, Newman tells us, that he read Butler's *Analogy;* he was then twenty-two years of age, preparing for his ordination (in 1825) to the priesthood in the Church of England. Newman was greatly impressed by the work. From it he gained two points above all which became, according to his own admission, "the underlying principles of a great portion of my teaching."[103] One of these was Butler's general notion of an analogy between the separate works of God; the other was his "doctrine that Probability is the guide of life. . . ."[104]

It is important to note, however, that these served merely as starting points for Newman's later teaching; he did not accept Butler's position in an uncritical fashion. Thus, he notes that this doctrine of probability in Butler "led me, at least under the teaching to which a few years later I was introduced, to the question of the logical cogency of Faith, on which I have written so much."[105]

The later influences in Newman's life profoundly altered the manner in which he made use of Butler's argument from probability. Newman made the essential distinction we have criticized Butler for ignoring, that is, the distinction between the fact of revelation (the judgment of credibility) and the act of faith itself. Juergens sees a contrast here between Newman's approach and that of the so-called "traditional school":

> Newman's aim differs from that of the traditional school of apologists in this that, while the latter demonstrates that human reason has irrefragable proofs for its certitude in the divinity of Christianity, his sole object is to show that the aver-

age man has a proof sufficient for his own needs, though he ordinarily cannot analyze this proof, give it proper expression and skillfully defend it against attack.[106]

There is some truth to this, but the fault seems to lie more on the side of the "traditional school," which, in the light of the entire teaching of the Church, does not appear to be quite so "traditional." To seek "irrefragable proofs" for the divinity of Christianity would seem to be striving to root the certitude of faith on some form of historicorational argumentation; it would reflect the post-Cartesian theories of faith and their confusion of the judgment of credibility (the apologetic problem of the relationship between faith and reason) with the assent of faith itself. The moral certitude sufficient for the judgment of credibility would seem to be the chief concern of Newman when speaking of the preambles of faith.[107]

There should be no difficulty, therefore, in making use of Newman's notion of probable evidence to arrive at this judgment of credibility. Even in its unrevised form in Butler, the argument was claimed by its author to lead one to some sort of moral certitude, but Butler unfortunately made this the grounds for the certitude of faith; this was his failing. In Newman, however, the assent of faith is not grounded on this basis, as he himself reminds us: "Reason is one thing and faith is another, and reason can as little be made a substitute for faith, as faith can be made a substitute for reason."[108]

Just how far Newman eventually separated himself from Butler can be seen in his *Letter to the Duke of Norfolk* (1874), where he rejects entirely the notion of Christian truth proved from historical argument in a manner evident in Butler:

> For myself, I would simply confess that no doctrine of the Church can be rigorously proved by historical evidence; but at the same time that no doctrine can be simply disproved by it. Historical evidence reaches a certain way, more or less, towards a proof of the Catholic doctrines; often nearly the whole way; sometimes it goes only so far as to point in their direction; sometimes there is only an absence of evidence for a conclusion

contrary to them; nay, sometimes there is an apparent leaning of the evidence to a contrary conclusion, which has to be explained; — in all cases there is a margin left for the exercise of faith in the word of the Church. He who believes the dogmas of the Church only because he has reasoned them out of History, is scarcely a Catholic. . . . After all . . . in all cases the immediate motive in the mind of a Catholic for his reception of [these doctrines] is, not that they are proved to him by Reason or by History, but because Revelation has declared them by means of that high ecclesiastical *Magisterium* which is their legitimate exponent.[109]

An analysis of Newman's position on the assent of faith would take us too far afield, but it is generally conceded that he belongs to that school of thought which considers the grace of faith as having a psychological as well as an entitative effect in the believer.[110] Thus, when Newman says that "the absolute and perfect certitude of divine faith does not rest on reasoning or human motives, but solely on the fact that God, the Eternal Truth, who cannot deceive nor be deceived, has spoken,"[111] he is arguing along these lines. In this he is worlds apart from Butler and the *Analogy,* whatever similarity exists on other points.

NEWMAN MISUNDERSTOOD

It is quite easy to see the manner in which Newman could possibly have been misunderstood in much of what he wrote. He was a man whose thought-life was constantly evolving, and he wrote in a language and terminology that was sometimes difficult for others to grasp, especially for those who (unlike Newman) were trained in the atmosphere closer to Scholasticism. In many respects Newman is like Augustine, since the writings of each bear so strongly the changing imprint of the particular period of life in which they wrote, or the various debates they faced. Newman does not express himself in the coldly logical terms of the Scholastics, and this increases the difficulty. The similarity between some of Newman's phrases and those of Butler, plus his avowed respect for Butler, might easily have led to misunderstanding.

There is no indication, for example, that Cardinal Manning had Newman in mind in his work *The Grounds of Faith,* but he is surely opposing an approach to faith which would not represent Newman's more mature views, but is certainly that which we find in Butler's *Analogy:*

> We are told, indeed, that to be certain is inconsistent with faith, that probability is the atmosphere in which faith lives, and that if you extinguish probabilities, faith dies. Did the Apostles then believe the doctrine of the ever-blessed Trinity upon a probability? Did they believe the doctrine of the Incarnation upon conjecture? Was it because they walked in twilight that their faith in their Divine Lord was acceptable?
>
> To what are we come? In this Christian land, once full of light, once in unity with the Church of God, once replenished with truth — to what are we come? A new virtue is promulgated: to be uncertain of the truth and of the will of God; to hold our faith on probabilities. And yet, what is the very idea of Revelation but a Divine assurance of Truth! Where faith begins uncertainty ends. Because faith terminates upon the veracity of God; and what God has spoken and authenticated to us by Divine authority cannot be uncertain.[112]

This is precisely the fault found on all sides with Butler's defense of Christianity. Newman's position on faith, however, was eventually clearly separated from anything approaching this view. This difference in point of view is indicated in a letter dated February 8, 1861; it is cited by Robinson as taken from an unpublished notebook used in the preparation of the *Grammar of Assent:*

> Bishop Butler stopped the evil (of scepticism) only by lowering the pretensions of Christianity — for, without wishing to speak disrespectfully of a writer to whom I owe so much, as many others do, still it does seem as if the practical effect of his work was to make faith a mere *practical certainty,* i.e. a taking of certain statements of doctrine, not as true, but as safest to act upon.[113]

In his study of the notion of faith in Newman prior to his conversion to the Church of Rome in 1845, Elbert comes to a similar conclusion, that is, that "Newman's conception of faith must have undergone considerable change in the course of his life. . . ."[114] Prior to 1845, Newman apparently held to a theory of faith similar to that of Butler, in which faith is presented as "a discursive act just as is any other act of reason."[115] Yet Elbert insists that "in his Catholic days Newman was certainly dissatisfied with probability as the guide of life and required more than 'a mere balance of arguments.' For real and earnest practical religion he demanded certitude, at least in the premises."[116]

From his *Discussions and Arguments* it appears that by 1866 Newman had rejected this approach entirely, and had formulated a more profound theory of faith in which the assent does not rest on reason and historical argument, and in which certitude replaces mere probability:

> It is the very characteristic of the profession of faith made by numbers of educated Protestants, and it is the utmost extent to which they are able to go in believing, to hold, not that Christian doctrine is certainly true, but that it has such a semblance of truth, it has such considerable marks of probability upon it, that it is their duty to accept and act upon it, as if it were true beyond all question or doubt; and they justify themselves, and with much reason, by the authority of Bishop Butler.[117]

Newman goes on to add, however, that such a faith "does not rise to the level of the *sine qua non,* which is the condition prescribed for becoming a Catholic."[118] The entire approach of Newman to the assent and certitude of faith had progressed during these years. It is not too difficult, however, to imagine that some of those who read Newman failed to make the distinction between his earlier and his later positions (if, indeed, they read that much of him to begin with), and thus attributed to the Catholic Cardinal a position he himself had long since rejected. It may be in this way that the faulty notion of faith as an assent based on reason alone, and associated with mere probability, filtered down to the advocates of Modernism. These men did not in all likelihood read Butler anymore, but they did read Newman, failing, however, to understand his change of position on these essential points where he came to differ radically from Butler.

THE TEACHING OF MODERNISM

Thus we come to the proposition of Modernism condemned in 1907 under Pius X by the decree *Lamentabili,* issued by the Holy Office: "The assent of faith rests ultimately on an accumulation of probabilities."[119] There was an open attempt on the part of Alfred Loisy to associate Newman with this condemned proposition. After the appearance of the *Lamentabili,* Loisy claimed that the statement that the assent of faith rests on an accumulation of probabilities "was Newman's doctrine."[120] Loisy refers to an article he had published under the pseudonym of Firmin in the *Revue du clergé français* of March 15, 1900. The article itself has particular interest.

Like many others who fall into one extreme, Loisy was able to perceive the error of another school of thought very clearly. The article in question was occasioned by the appearance of Auguste Sabatier's *Outline of a Philosophy of Religion.* Sabatier criticizes the Scholastic approach as having rationalized dogma, and goes on to complain that "the intervention of miracle as a criterion or proof of doctrine does not remove the difficulties of the theory; it multiplies and aggravates them."[121] Sabatier holds that with the lapse of time, joined to the incertitude of the documents and the demands of modern thought, it is even more difficult to prove that these miracles are true than it is to prove the truth of the religion they are supposed to substantiate.

We can note in this the same confusion found in Butler, namely, the presumption that miracles and historical evidence are the proof upon which the certitude of faith rests: the doctrine is accepted as the result of a reasoning process. Thus, Sabatier complains that "faith, which, in the Bible, was an act of confidence and consecration to God, becomes an intellectual adherence to an historical testimony or to a doctrinal formula."[122]

Loisy rises to the defense of Catholic faith in this instance and launches out on something of an attack on what he (like Sabatier)

considered "traditional apologetics." Unfortunately, both of them
were concerned only with this faulty notion so evident in Butler,
but found even in the writings of Catholic apologetes in the nineteenth and early twentieth centuries. Loisy saw the error in this
approach and set out to solve the problem; but his solution was
another error — that of immanentism. While his complaint concerning faith and historical certitude in "traditional" apologetics
may have been justified, since the question might then have been
presented in so faulty a manner, his solution is just as unacceptable. But understanding the type of appeal given in Butler and
reflected elsewhere, we can see the justice of Loisy's comment that
"the most clear-sighted spirit, after having studied the most profound apologetic books, can still remain very undecided and per-
plexed if he has consulted only speculative reason and has limited
his investigation to a critique of the proofs, seeing that each particular proof leads only to a probable conclusion which does not
exclude absolutely the possibility of the opposite conclusion. . . ."[123]

This is a complaint in no way different from the many we have
recorded in regard to Butler. The solution suggested by Loisy,
however, is not the notion of the grace of faith exercising its influence on the psychological as well as the entitative level, but a
more subjective, immanent idea of faith associated with the thought
of Schleiermacher and similar writers of the post-Kantian era.
Loisy denies the value of external evidence as a foundation for
faith itself, noting that the full and decisive efficacy of these proofs
does not depend on the accumulation of probabilities "which
again creates for reason only the utmost probability, but on the
intimate experience that one has and on the vital rapport which
is established between the soul which seeks and the truth which
tenders itself."[124]

This immanent notion of faith is joined throughout the article
to Loisy's other doctrinal position regarding the variable expressions proper to religion, and "to the relativity of traditional
creeds."[125] His concept of faith is purely subjective: ". . . the profound and universal basis of faith is none other than the con-
formity of religion with the need and aspirations of man."[126]

In speaking of the role of reason leading to faith, however, Loisy remains quite orthodox, despite his aberrations on the notion of faith itself: "Reason shows the reasonableness of faith; but the moral certitude which it gives is not the absolute certitude of faith, a certitude which results from faith itself and which is an act of the soul in its entirety, aided by God to recognize Him in His revelation."[127] Loisy's definition of faith, of course, reflects his purely immanentist approach, but if we replace this with a truly Catholic concept, the statement expresses quite well the relationship between reason and faith.

Loisy notes that the enemies of religion have attempted to show how inane religion is by making an appeal to science and reason, but he complains that the apologetes have also made a great mistake by attempting to demonstrate the absolute truth of religion by these same arguments of reason and science.[128] It is not an unjust criticism. This represents another example of the weakness already demonstrated in Butler of attempting to meet the adversary on his own ground, only to end up by giving a totally unsatisfactory defense of one's own position.

In speaking of the *Lamentabili,* however, Loisy is anxious to indicate that the condemned doctrine of faith resting upon probabilities is really the doctrine of Newman. Benard has already shown that Loisy extracted a passage from the *Apologia* of Newman which describes his state of mind in 1843–1844, while still an Anglican. Considering the acknowledged appreciation Newman had for Butler, it is not difficult to see in this statement a doctrinal position in regard to faith which would reflect the *Analogy* of Butler. Nevertheless, Newman is careful to note in this precise section of the *Apologia* that he is recording attitudes which had been his in the past (and which he had by this time come to reject):

Let it be recollected that I am historically relating my state of mind, at the period of my life which I am surveying. I am not speaking theologically, nor have I any intention of going into controversy: but, speaking historically of what I held in 1843–4, I say that I believed in a God on a ground of probability, that I believed in Christianity on a probability, and that

I believed in Catholicism on a probability, and that these three grounds of probability, distinct from each other of course in subject-matter, were still, all of them, one and the same in nature of proof, as being probabilities — probabilities of a special kind, a cumulative, a transcendent probability, but still probability. . . .[129]

This is the Newman of 1843 speaking, but essentially it is the doctrine of Bishop Butler, who is further reflected in Newman's statement that at that time he felt that "He who has made us has so willed, that in mathematics, indeed, we should arrive at certitude by rigid demonstration, but in religious enquiry we should arrive at certitude by accumulated probabilities. . . ."[130] When Loisy attributed this position to the mature teaching of Newman as a Catholic, he did him an injustice — and undoubtedly he did so knowingly, since he purposely left out of his citation from Newman the important phrase indicating that he was "speaking historically." Many other things entered into Newman's experience before he escaped the trap unwittingly set for him by Butler and carefully distinguished between the judgment of credibility and the act of faith itself. For Newman the Catholic, as Benard points out, "the convergence of probabilities in itself, logically preceding faith, forms a sufficient argument for the rational certitude of that faith."[131] But this is not as yet faith; it is only the judgment of reason concerning the fact of revelation by which the act of faith is rendered reasonable, that is, an act in accord with reason, an act which does no violence to man's intellectual nature.

BUTLER AND THE CURRENT PROBLEMATIC

A consideration of the position of Butler in effect traces the argument of probability from the time of John Locke down to the *Lamentabili* of 1907, but it also offers insight into a number of questions debated at the present time. The relationship between ideas becomes an especially intriguing study when we can note the subtle manner in which one idea is reformed, rephrased, and refashioned throughout history by successive thinkers. In this instance we confront the background of a statement which began in the defense proposed by an eighteenth-century Anglican bishop against the deistic attacks of his age on the Christian system, but which eventually came to take its place in the long history of propositions condemned by the Church of Rome because of their unorthodox import. Butler surely never intended or envisioned the ultimate result, but the historical record is inescapable.

Out of this complex of concerns, there has emerged with ever increasing clarity a realization that faith has only too often been in danger of being falsely identified with theology, and that belief would be ultimately rooted upon a series of "proof texts" from Scripture, coupled with rational-historical arguments set forth in syllogistic fashion. Butler is a prime example of the dangers inherent in such a mentality; his mistakes point out a path to be avoided today.

Basically, one of the great problems of the present hour coincides in large measure with the question with which Bishop Butler struggled, that is, the relationship of history to the certitude of faith. For Catholic theologians, this problem centers chiefly on a question paramount in the two overall approaches to the assent of faith. What may be described as the "more recent" theory of the post-Cartesian era appears to offer no better solution to this question than the *Analogy* of Butler; indeed, in the light of the many objections made to it (chiefly in regard to the nondefinitive nature of historical certitude, and the shift in emphasis concerning the precise manner in which the Scriptures verify the notion of true history), it is difficult to see how such an approach can be defended at all today as an acceptable theory of faith.[132]

No one contests that this more recent theory gives an acceptable explanation of the *supernaturality* of the act of faith; its insistence upon an entitative (ontological) elevation of the act of faith to the supernatural level suffices for this purpose, since, in accord with the Tridentine emphasis upon the need to believe in a manner necessary for salvation, it is satisfactorily distinguished from a purely human, natural act.[133] It is in regard to the *certitude* of the assent of faith that this theory fails dismally, and it is here that the crux of the problem lies. Those who have defended this view in recent times (Billot, Van Noort, Lercher, Lennerz, de Aldama, among others) have universally admitted at least the possibility (though not always demanding the necessity) of a so-called act of "natural" or "scientific faith." If this assent differs in no way psychologically from the assent of supernatural faith, the conclusion must follow that supernatural faith is bogged down in the very problem associated with historical certitude; it is a perception of the authority of God revealing that rests on rational-historical arguments and cannot serve to explain adequately the absolute, unswerving certitude proper to the assent of Christian faith. No amount of "entitative elevation" of that act can strengthen or change the degree of certitude, since this rests on different grounds entirely.

In the past, the Thomist-Suarezian approach has generally defended its concept of faith by having recourse to the axiom that "acts are specified by their formal objects," so that the assent to a supernatural truth would demand an act which is supernatural psychologically and not merely entitatively. While accepting the validity of this axiom, it might seem that, for the reasons cited above, it would be more profitable to discuss the question from the opposite point of view, considering the degree of certitude possible in a psychological assent to Christian truth which — precisely as assent — is identical in "scientific" and "saving faith" (noting especially the present-day view of the Scriptures as books written by believers for believers, rather than purely historical accounts of past events).

Faith must possess a certitude surpassing even that of meta-physical certitude; it must be an *assensus essentialiter certus, firmissimus, super omnia firmus;* no Catholic could deny this.[134] The Thomist-Suarezian response to this problem is based largely on a clear distinction between the judgment of credibility and the assent of faith itself; for the judgment of credibility, moral certitude (proper to historical conclusions) will suffice, while the certitude of the assent of faith leaps beyond this level in that the very motive of faith (the authority of God revealing) is psychologically perceived in a supernatural manner, and thus pertains to that which is believed in Christian faith.[135] The act of faith will exist side by side with the judgment of credibility (since at each moment of his life of faith the believer must know that he is not acting contrary to reason); the two acts complement one another, despite the fact that they are psychologically distinct. As Alfaro expresses it, the judgment of credibility is a *conditio sine qua non* for making an act of faith (a condition involving priority of nature, if not of time).[136] This judgment of credibility, however, does not constitute "even partially" the logical motive for the assent of faith itself.[137]

Basically, this judgment of credibility treats of the *fact* of revelation and the "reasonableness" of man's going on to believe, thus avoiding a purely immanentist type of faith or one linked with the theories of fideism or traditionalism. Since this judgment is something preparatory in nature, nothing more than moral certitude is required, as all theologians agree; it is an act which fits into the general category of those things which men must do in the day-to-day routine of life and in which they must act on whatever certitude they have: in this regard, the principles of Locke and Butler are quite valid. In addition, it need not be held that each individual actually formulates such a judgment of credibility by the power of reason alone. We are concerned here merely with the root power found in mankind; this very same judgment, while remaining distinct from the assent of faith, may also be formulated with the aid of divine grace.

In the purely theoretical order, Alfaro would seem to be correct in stating that the absolutely essential, but at the same time the final, meeting place of reason and grace would be the "practical judgment of credibility."[138] The usual analysis of the genesis of faith is, of course, concerned with the abstract order; in practice, these steps are not so clearly delineated, and the adult approaching faith undoubtedly will most often be assisted by actual grace from the very start. Since the practical judgment of credibility involves a personal commitment to go on to believe, however, the help of grace would be absolutely necessary (had it not been granted previously). In addition, it would appear that it is in this practical judgment that the rational motives behind it exercise their psychological force for the last time, as far as the act of faith itself is concerned; the force of the judgment of credibility itself, of course, would continue throughout the life of the believer.

In the Thomist-Suarezian view, this judgment of credibility does not constitute the act of faith, or enter in any way into the act itself; beyond this point the absolute, unswerving assent of faith will result from the supernatural perception of the authority of God revealing (a perception which results from man's acceptance of and cooperation with the grace of faith itself, in which the entire process is terminated).[139] All of this implies, of course, a rejection of the very possibility of any so-called "natural" or "scientific faith." All that any individual without the grace of faith itself could possess would be a precise knowledge of *what* the Christian believes; but a true act of faith, a personal act of assent and a Christian commitment to the way of life unveiled through revelation, involves much more than simply *knowing* what others believe. Assuredly, the rational-historical type of argumentation of the "more recent" theory of faith, with all its syllogistic overtones, can lead to knowledge of *what* Christians believe, but it cannot result in that absolute, unswerving certitude proper to supernatural faith.

Those who attempt to defend this post-Cartesian theory of faith reflect its deficiencies in their very defense; they are obviously struggling to find some acceptable explanation for the absolute certitude required. An entitative elevation of the psychologically natural act will not suffice. Hence they seek to discover some other element associated with faith that will solve this problem. Lennerz, for example, distinguishes between two types of syllogisms, one presumably proper to scientific faith, the other connected with supernatural faith precisely because of the special note of obedience to the command of God to believe.[140] The attempt fails, however, since it shifts the essence of supernatural faith — that which is unique to it, as distinct from any so-called "scientific faith" — from an act of the intellect to an act of the will (something quite contrary to the teaching of St. Thomas and the Scholastics, made the authentic teaching of the Church at Vatican I, namely, that faith is essentially an act of the intellect).[141]

Apart from this, however, the emphasis upon the special note of obedience to God's command does nothing to explain the specific certitude proper to supernatural faith; certitude as such pertains to the intellect, and if the assent of faith is conceived of as possible on a purely human level, a mere entitative elevation of that psychological act cannot increase the degree of certitude, any more than an additional note of obedience to God's will could do so. While it is true that the authority of God is supreme and infallible, the precise question is the manner in which man *perceives* that authority. The mere fact that God revealed these truths does not suffice for attributing absolute and unswerving certitude to man's perception of that fact, if this is done by a psychologically natural act.

SCRIPTURAL QUESTIONS

As noted above, this more recent theory of faith also works under the supposition, accepted by Butler, that the Scriptures represent history in the strictly modern sense;[142] it was for this, among other things, that Matthew Arnold criticized the position of Butler.[143] Today, any acceptance by the Catholic of the principles of Form Criticism as set forth in the *Divino afflante Spiritu* of Pius XII and the 1964 Instruction of the Pontifical Biblical Commission destroys the very possibility of any purely "scientific" or "natural faith."[144] The Catholic does not, of course, deny the basic historicity of the Gospel accounts, and he does not interpret them in the context of a post-Kantian philosophical approach; this would be Modernism. To accept the teaching of Pius XII concerning literary criticism in the Bible, however, and still hold out for the possibility of a purely "scientific faith" would leave the Catholic with the alternative of giving no better interpretation than that associated with Protestant Liberalism or Modernism (since such a "scientific" or "natural faith" by its very nature must exclude the operation of the Holy Spirit either in formulating the manner of presentation of the scriptural message or its gradual clarification through the centuries by means of a divinely guided magisterium within the living Church; such a "scientific faith" demands a purely historical source).

The Thomist-Suarezian approach, however, experiences none of these difficulties when faced with the present view on the nature of the biblical writings. It can easily accept the Bible as what O'Keefe calls "the believing history of the primitive Church."[145] In fact, this theory of faith finds a natural counterpart in the present discussions concerning the intimate relationship between Scripture and tradition, and the role of the living magisterium in the presentation of revealed truth as well as its relationship to the authority of God as the one and only motive of faith.

As noted elsewhere,[146] it is not only the present-day Catholic theologian who is concerned with this problem of historical certitude and the assent of faith, but many crisis theologians and existentialist theologians of modern Protestantism as well. Forced by the findings of the Form Critics to admit a previous oral and written tradition which is reflected in the Bible, these theologians have had to abandon the extreme fundamentalist scriptural position of the sixteenth century. At the same time, they wished to cut themselves off from the Liberalism of the nineteenth century and its more anthropocentric religion, which made "religious experience" the center point of belief rather than God. As H. Richard Niebuhr puts it, these theologians are again seeking the God of faith, who had become a necessary "auxiliary" to this subjective experience and little more.[147]

The influence of Bultmann in this matter cannot be ignored, and it was precisely the question of history and faith which led him to work out his unique distinction between *Historie* and *Geschichte*, whereby *Historie* is concerned only with facts or events in the course of human life; in this sense the death of Christ upon the cross may be viewed as a historical fact, proved with historical certitude and based on historical sources. This is not, however, faith in Bultmann's eyes. In the light of God's revelation, this event in history takes on another, deeper meaning; it is associated with the entire redemptive plan of God, which came to fulfillment in Christ's death and resurrection. Henceforth the believer must personally become associated with that redeeming act, which now informs or fills, as it were, the events of history. It is this all-important divine element that brings forth what Bultmann calls *Geschichte*. This is revealed to man only through faith, and this alone has real importance for the Christian. The passing events of time, the life and function of the historic Church — *Historie* in general — must be looked on as of relatively little importance; faith is not a subject of history alone.[148]

Whatever may be said of Bultmann's distinction, it is interesting to note here one of the chief reasons which led him to adopt this theological approach. He had studied first of all in the liberal tradition of the nineteenth century, both at Tübingen and at Berlin; later, at Marburg, he became engrossed in the concerns of Form Criticism. In an age strongly effected by the trials of war and given over to far-reaching shifts in philosophical thought, Bultmann found himself drawn to the so-called "new theology" (initiated especially by Barth's *Römerbrief* in 1919); he was impressed by its emphasis on personal encounter and the further conclusion Bultmann saw in this approach, namely, that faith is not to be linked essentially to history:

> It seemed to me that in this new theological movement it was rightly recognized, as over against the "liberal" theology out of which I had come, that the Christian faith is not a phenomenon of the history of religion, that it does not rest on a "religious *a priori*" (Troeltsch), and that therefore theology does not have to look upon it as a phenomenon of religious or cultural history. It seemed to me that, as over against such a view, the new theology had correctly seen that Christian faith is the answer to the word of the transcendent God that encounters man and that theology has to deal with this word and the man who had been encountered by it.[149]

Eventually this approach came to be incorporated into his hermeneutical tool of demythologizing. For Bultmann, it is only through contact with the apostolic kerygma that the hearer is able to enter into the moment of salvation and encounter Christ. This message, however, has come down to us in writings in which men

necessarily attempted to express the "otherworldly," the transcendent and the divine, in phrases which are proper to this world:
human, tied to time, reflective of man's way of thinking. These
elements Bultmann describes as "myths": not in the sense of
pagan myths or of something unreal and untrue, but rather in
the sense of human modes of expression by which men strive to
give voice to the otherworldly and the transcendent.

Since these phrases were introduced by the biblical writers to
enable the men of their own time to understand the apostolic
kerygma, the exegete must now strip such phrases away so that
the pure kerygma might once again be uncovered in its original
import and then interpreted in terms of man's present concerns;
hence the term "demythologizing." Central in this approach to
faith, however, is the question of the relationship of faith to history. Bultmann does not deny some relationship between history
and the kerygma, but he insists that history and historical formulas are of secondary importance. Thus he rejects the attempt of
nineteenth-century liberalism to explain faith in terms of history
and historical method, but he does so not in the sense of condemning the method entirely, but rather of striving "to carry
further the tradition of historical-critical research as it was prac-
ticed by the 'liberal' theology and to make our more recent
theological knowledge fruitful for us."[150]

For Bultmann, there can be no attempt to "prove" the truth
of Christianity by such methods; he is anxious to avoid all such
approaches, and wishes to argue along his own lines precisely
because of this basic desire of extricating faith and the personal
encounter with God from the limitations of historical proof. He
feels that it is necessary to urge this, since otherwise, as Lengsfeld
explains, "the activity of God would be placed under that view
of man which establishes things historically, and thus faith would
no longer be a decision but a reasonable conclusion from historical premises."[151] The phrase "reasonable conclusion from historical
premises" certainly recalls the position of Butler and others, and
the dangers inherent in such an understanding of faith. Yet, as
has become more apparent today, Bultmann's escape from history

led to so radical a disregard for the historical facts of the life of Jesus that barely anything was left.[152] The desire of the post-Bultmannian school (represented by such men as Bornkamm, Fuchs, and Käsemann) to set forth on a new quest of the historical Jesus is a reaction to this position; they are confident that the historical negativism of Bultmann led to a gross exaggeration.[153] Yet the basic question remains dominant even here: What is the precise relationship between history and faith?

A similar concern can be noted in the writings of Paul Tillich, who has objected to "the attempt to give a foundation to Christian faith and theology through historical research. . . ."[154] He also views this attempt as a failure. Tillich's great question appears to be the problem of the certitude of the assent of faith. Thus he points out the fact that, by following the historical method, "the historian never can reach certainty in this way, but he can reach high degrees of probability. It would, however, be a leap to another level if he transformed historical probability into positive or negative historical certainty by a judgment of faith. . . ."[155] For this reason, Tillich considers the quest of the historical Jesus a failure precisely because it presumed that historical studies, research, or scholarship could serve as an adequate basis for Christian faith:

> The search for the historical Jesus was an attempt to discover a minimum of reliable facts about the man Jesus of Nazareth, in order to provide a safe foundation for Christian faith. This attempt was a failure. Historical research provided probabilities about Jesus of a higher or lower degree. On the basis of the probabilities, it sketched "Lives of Jesus." But they were more like novels than biographies; they certainly could not provide a safe foundation for the Christian faith. Christianity is not based on the acceptance of a historical novel; it is based on the witness to the messianic character of Jesus by people who were not interested at all in a biography of the Messiah.[156]

Granting the vastly different philosophical and theological basis on which Tillich works, it would appear clear enough that what he is striving to solve in this instance is the same problem which besets the Catholic theologian when discussing the effect of the grace of faith on the psychological level: he is in search of something that will remove the act of faith itself (as distinct from the preparation for faith) from the certitude bound by the limitations of the historical, critical, and rational order. Tillich even asks whether such a use of historical certitude as the foundation of faith is not dangerous for the believer: "Does not the acceptance of the historical method for dealing with the source documents of the Christian faith introduce a dangerous insecurity into the thought and life of the church and of every individual Christian?"[157] Tillich's statement in regard to historical proof and probability is essentially the same as the conclusion of the present study concerning faith and reason in the writings of Bishop Butler: "Whatever faith can do in its own dimension, it cannot overrule historical judgments. It cannot make the historically improbable probable, or the probable improbable, or the probable or improbable certain. The certitude of faith does not imply certainty about question of historical research."[158]

The ultimate solution must lie elsewhere, and while the Catholic will not detach the assent of faith from history altogether, he finds the point of contact in that historical certitude concerning the fact of revelation: the judgment of credibility is built upon historical analysis. The absolute, unswerving certitude of Christian faith, however, would appear to be defended adequately for the Catholic only within the general realm of the Thomist-Suarezian theories of faith. Christianity is rooted in history and in historical fact; even the Bible indicates this historical nucleus, although one may not always be able to single it out from the full context in which the Christian revelation eventually took shape in written form. Moreover, Christian faith has its close and necessary relationships with reason; it is not contrary to reason, and it may be approached through reason. The assent of faith itself, however, leaps beyond to a higher level, where the divine power becomes evident to the believer within the confines of the living, divinely guided Church. The specter of Bishop Butler lifts a warning hand to those who would ignore this approach, indicating that should faith become confused with historical certitude and rational argumentation, one or the other will suffer.

Butler's Argument in
The Analogy of Religion

It is not easy to summarize the entire thought of Bishop Butler in *The Analogy of Religion,* chiefly because of its length. The volume is written in the verbose style of eighteenth-century literature, and is divided into two parts. Part I (with eight chapters) deals with natural religion; Part II (with nine chapters) deals with revealed religion. In his edition of Butler's works, Gladstone sums up the chapters of the *Analogy* in this outline form:[1]

PART I: NATURAL RELIGION

1. A future life, I, i
2. Of reward and punishment, I, ii
3. For good and evil conduct, I, iii
4. This life a probation, I, iv
5. And discipline, I, v
6. Answers to objections:
   a) Objection of necessity, I, vi
   b) Objection to vagueness: scheme known only in part, I, vii
7. Conclusion, I, viii

PART II: REVEALED RELIGION

1. Sin, ruin, and a blinded sense, required a further plan, II, i
2. Proved by miracles, II, ii
3. Contents partly strange and unexpected, II, iii
4. Constituting a scheme or system, II, iv
5. Worked by the Messiah for our recovery, II, v
6. Partially revealed and with partial evidence, II, vi, vii
7. Answer to objections, II, viii
8. Conclusion, II, ix

INTRODUCTORY ARGUMENTS

In Part I, the starting point is the "constitution and course of nature" as we observe it on the purely natural level, considering both the laws of nature and the natural moral law.² Just as caterpillars pass from one stage into butterflies, we might see a presumption that our own conscious powers would continue on into a *future life;* at least Butler feels it ought to confirm in some fashion the possibility of such an afterlife.

Similarly, since what we do here and now accounts for the pleasure or pain we experience, it would seem probable that *in a future life* we would also have to *bear the burden* of our good or evil actions. This presupposes, of course, that God has established a certain moral law; yet He has also established the laws of the material universe, so this should not seem surprising. Our present state then appears clearly enough as a *state of trial.* This is true in general, Butler insists; life is not a state of settled security from birth to death; hence, in thinking of a future life, we can easily enough accept the notion that it is only in that distant future that this period of probation will cease.

If this be true, then we must view man as we do the other creatures in the universe, all of which have some specific purpose and are created for some particular way of life. If man's ultimate goal, however, is reserved for a future life, following a period of trial, it would seem that he also has a specific way of life, namely a *life of self-discipline and improvement:* a struggle for virtue. This would appear to be the ultimate explanation of the temptations, the pain, the sorrow we all experience in this life; just as animals and plants must struggle for existence, so must man in his attempt to achieve his ultimate goal.

At the end of Part I, Butler pauses to consider the *objections* that might be raised to all of this by the men of his times. One such objection would be that of the Fatalists who contended that men live out their lives under a blind necessity rather than by the exercise of freedom; to this, Butler simply argues that both experience and the history of the human race are opposed to such a conclusion. On the other hand, those objections concerning the lack of wisdom and goodness apparent in this whole scheme are rooted in an imprudent demand that we understand all that God has willed. We cannot even understand the mysteries of the *material* world in which we live, so that the fact that we face mysteries in this religious scheme is really not surprising. Thus considering the purely physical world, we can see that analogy would indicate we are also incompetent to judge the entire scheme of religion as well. Hence we ought to reject such objections, realizing that if we could perceive the entire plan of God, such difficulties would vanish.

With this said more by way of introduction (covering some 185 pages!), Butler proceeds in Part II to argue that we find a remarkable similarity between the scheme of natural religion discussed in Part I and the teaching of Christianity to be considered at present. For Butler, Christianity is not, as it was for the deists, a mere republication of natural religion. Revelation serves a dual purpose: it sets forth the doctrines of natural religion in a more clear fashion, and at the same time unfolds to mankind truths not at all discoverable by human reason (such as the doctrine of the Trinity, the need of baptism, and the like).[3] Butler fails, not in what he considers Christianity to be, but in the manner in which he proposes the act of faith in that revelation.

Since Butler admits these supernatural mysteries, he centers his attention on the obligation of investigating the *claims* of Christianity, of examining "most seriously into the evidence of it, supposing its credibility; and of embracing it, upon supposition of its truth."[4] If God has actually revealed such a system of belief, we may not treat it in a light manner; indeed, if its truth be proven, we are certainly obligated to accept it. Hence the basic spirit of natural religion should lead men to investigate the claims of Christianity, since it is contended, especially in Scripture, that such a Christian revelation has been given.

In Chapter 2 of Part II, Butler at once considers the usual objections raised against Christianity, beginning with that which objects to *miracles* being adduced as *proof* of the truth of revealed religion. In their rejection of the supernatural, many deists in the eighteenth century, even before the time of Hume, denied the very possibility of miracles; if God had no contact with the universe after the act of creation, such divine intervention as presupposed in miracles would have to be excluded. Their rationalism and skepticism would lead them to assert that it would be *more difficult* to prove the truth of such alleged miracles than the truth of the Christian religion they supposedly support.

Again, Butler argues that this objection rests on the *supposition* that man ought to be able to grasp the *entire divine scheme,* whereas our observation of the universe and our own human experience ought to lead us to expect that Christianity would also involve situations where things prove to be *unlike* one another. Hence man ought to admit quite readily the possibility of such extraordinary phenomena in relationship to Christianity.

So also, the objection that Christianity includes the role of a *Mediator* between God and man presents no real difficulty. On the contrary, the course of nature and human life would only lead us to expect this, since all living creatures, even though they come ultimately from God, are brought into the world and are protected and instructed by others. If we consider this fact, as well as the unfathomable wisdom of God, we must conclude that we simply "are not judges, antecedently to revelation, whether a mediator was or was not necessary. . . ."[5]

FINAL OBJECTIONS

Chapter 6 is given over to answering less theoretical and more practical objections against Christianity. There are those who complain about the *weakness of the "proof"* offered for the truth of Christianity, to whom Butler can only respond that such individuals should take a close look at the rest of their life and consider thoughtfully "what that evidence indeed is, which they act upon with regard to their temporal interests."[6] They will find that the evidence is no stronger than the proof from miracles and prophecies in support of Christianity; why, he then asks, ought we demand more proof in this instance?

Others argue that Christianity cannot be true if it is *not universally preached* nor universally *accepted,* yet here again a close look at life reminds us that men all are given various degrees of health and strength, particular talents, riches, and the like; hence such inequality being so universal, a similar situation in regard to Christianity ought not surprise us at all. And the fact that not all accept the Christian revelation is explained far more easily by recognizing that many men demand more proof than they ought; or that they refuse to gather together the varied evidence at hand:

> Thus, that religion is not intuitively true, but a matter of deduction and inference; that a conviction of its truth is not forced upon every one, but left to be, by some, collected with heedful attention to premises; this as much constitutes religious probation, as much affords sphere, scope, opportunity, for right and wrong behaviour, as any thing whatever does.[7]

In other words, the tedious process of following out the proof of Christianity is all a part of the trial, the period of probation. In Chapter 7, Butler gives an *outline* of his complicated "proof" for the truth of Christianity. Feeling that his earlier chapters have succeeded in answering the objections in regard to the possibility of revelation, as well as the theoretical or practical objections raised against Christianity itself, Butler is now ready to consider "what positive evidence we have for the truth of it. . . ."[8] This argument centers around *miracles and prophecies* at the beginning of the Christian era, noting that "Christianity obtained, i.e. was professed to be received in the world, upon the belief of miracles, immediately in the age in which it is said those miracles were wrought. . . ."[9]

The teaching of Christianity, and the testimony of those first witnesses, however, has come down to us, so that the *presumption* rests *in favor* of the Christian religion:

> Upon the whole: as there is large historical evidence, both direct and circumstantial, of miracles wrought in attestation of Christianity, collected by those who have writ upon the subject; it lies upon unbelievers to show, why this evidence is not to be credited.[10]

None of the other reasons adduced for the immediate conversion of such large numbers of people who, in fact, were inclined both by training and culture to reject Christian truth, can be regarded as a sufficient explanation.[11] Emotional enthusiasm is no answer to the question of why a large number of individuals even gave up their lives for this truth, men and women who gave every sign of being stable and intellectually demanding persons, who could not easily be deceived by others and whose entire approach would show how unthinkable it would be that they should themselves be deceivers.[12]

Butler's view of the entire argument is that it includes both "direct and circumstantial evidence," but that if all be considered together, the truth of Christianity cannot be denied.[13] He follows the account of the "Scripture-history"[14] from the Old Testament down to the New Testament era, evaluating the various types of evidence, and coming to the conclusion that unbelievers *must accept* the truth of Christianity "for though they may say, that the historical evidence of miracles wrought in attestation of Christianity, is not sufficient to convince them, that such miracles were really wrought; they cannot deny that there is such historical evidence, it being a known matter of fact that there is."[15] And if all the collateral evidence be considered, it will be apparent that there is a valid proof here "in the evidence of *probability, as distinguished in* nature, from the evidence of *demonstration.*"[16] It is at this point that Butler stresses one of the basic elements of his entire proof, insisting that "probable proofs, by being added, not only increase the evidence, but multiply it."[17]

Ultimately, it remains true for Butler that "the truth of our religion, like the truth of common matters, is to be judged of by all the evidence taken together."[18] He admits that it is easy for some "to show, in a short and lively manner, that such and such things are liable to objection," limiting their remarks to particular questions, so that those who oppose Christianity have an advantage. It is not quite possible, however, "to show, in like manner, the united force of the whole argument [in favor of Christianity] in one view."[19] Thus Butler's final argument is that, just as it has been shown that there is no presumption *against* a revelation as miraculous, and that the general scheme of Christianity is conformable to the order of things in the universe as we experience it, thus making it quite credible; *so also* the account of the positive evidence attesting to the truth of Christianity must lead one to the final conclusion that, even though the force of the proof might be *lessened,* its nature is such that it *cannot* be destroyed *entirely.*[20]

This is the same line of thought pursued further in the last two chapters of the *Analogy.* In Chapter 8, Butler attempts to meet the objection that it is a poor response to the difficulties involved in the Christian revelation to simply point out that there are similar difficulties in the scheme of natural religion and in the order of the universe in general. Butler's answer does not change at all: he continues to insist that man cannot demand that he comprehend the entire divine scheme, and that since religion is a *practical* matter, man *must be content* to work with that type of probable evidence by which he must also direct the conduct of his moral life in general.[21]

In this way, Butler reduces his argument to the question of *proof* and *certitude.* Though the proof may not be all that one might desire, he insists that it is all that man can possess, and that he must accordingly settle for whatever certitude it offers, seeing therein proof enough to justify his action in the practical order. He must recognize a *middle path* between a full satisfaction of the truth of Christianity and a conviction that there is no truth in it whatsoever: "The middle state of mind between these two consists in a serious apprehension, that it may be true, joined with doubt whether it be so."[22] For Butler, this is as far as one might go in the direction of "speculative infidelity" once the entire evidence for the truth of Christianity has been set forth; but, for him, the conclusion is still sufficiently strong to demand the acceptance of the Christian scheme in its entirety.[23]

THE APPROACH AND STYLE OF BUTLER

It is important to note that Butler purposely adopted a particular technique in presenting this entire argument. Though engaged in writing a polemical work, he did all that he could to avoid a polemic style or approach. He was ever aware of his opponents and of their objections to religion, but he hoped to lead them to an acceptance of these supernatural truths by a calm, objective argument based on his notion of analogy. In order to emphasize this spirit, he admits that in the *Analogy* he argues "upon the principles of others, not my own."[24] By this he does not mean that he would attempt to prove anything by *using* what he considered to be false principles; but that, *notwithstanding* them, that is, by not demanding that his opponents reject them, he would still make out his case for Christianity.[25]

This tactic, unrealistic as it may seem, is important for evaluating the argument of Butler. He himself recognized the effect it would have in lessening the force of his proof; indeed, he does not even expect to overwhelm his adversaries by his argument so as to turn the nonbeliever into a devout Christian. He is content to settle for a situation in which these others do no more than admit, as a result of his presentation, that there is more to revealed religion than they had suspected, and that their objections do not have the force they may at first have attributed to them.[26]

Butler deliberately understates his case and he was, in fact, criticized for this tactic later on by those whom Spooner describes as convinced that "what the age demanded was a vigorous and demonstrative proof of the Being and Attributes of God and of the plain obligations of morality. . . ."[27] This was not, however, the view of Butler. His aim was not to present the strongest possible case at all, strange as it may seem: ". . . in this Treatise, I have argued upon the principles of others, not my own: and have omitted what I think true, and of the utmost importance, because by others thought unintelligible, or not true."[28]

This rather strange approach for a polemicist — who might reasonably be presumed to set forth armed with his strongest forces and most blunt terms — can only be understood as an attempt at what we today might call "popular apologetics," aimed at gaining the good will of the adversary. Newman, who had been strongly influenced by Butler, frequently adopted this tactic in part, but without becoming involved in the confusion of tactic and objective truth such as we encounter in Butler. In the *Grammar of Assent,* as Flanagan explains, Newman "would in all consciousness enter on a discussion which at first sight seemed to have no connection with the point in dispute."²⁹ This was part of his tactic. He would write around the point, preparing the minds of his readers for the ultimate conclusion he wished to draw: ". . . he believed that a reader was far more likely to be convinced if he happened to stumble across the truth for himself than if it were forced on him from without."³⁰

As a psychological approach, there is much to be said for this; Butler, however, extended the tactic too far and — in his eagerness to please — cast aside basic positions in regard to the assent of faith without which his defense of Christianity was doomed to ultimate failure. A great part of the *Analogy* is devoted to this type of argumentation, but instead of simply noting the similarities between the natural universe, natural religion and Christianity, Butler actually ends up with a Christianity burdened with the difficulties and mysteries of the other two objects in the comparison, but with none of that unique evidence proper to Christian truth upon which the unswerving certitude of Christian faith must rest.

Apart from the diffuse style of the *Analogy,* which is liable to mislead the reader, Butler confuses the issue by writing — for the sake of argument — as a deist and a fatalist; or at least not as an express antideist or antifatalist. But he does not write precisely as a Christian bishop. He fights, therefore, with his best hand tied, and the *Analogy* ends up as a classic example of the futility of attempting to meet the adversary on his own terms when this means passing over the best — and in this case, the only — arguments in defense of one's own position.

For this reason, Butler proceeds to consider Christianity "merely as a question of fact. . . ."³¹ The result of this is that the Christianity of the *Analogy* emerges as a creed accepted not by any supernatural assent, but simply on the basis of arguments drawn from reason and history. Christian truth is to be accepted as a *fact of human life;* and its truth is seen to rest on arguments entirely proportioned to human reason. Thus, as Butler states, "it is obvious that Christianity, and the proof of it, are both historical."[32]

Butler admits that this "proof" is not demonstrative in itself, in the way in which metaphysical proofs demand assent; its force lies solely in the realm of *probability*. Discussing the ultimate question of reward or punishment, Butler admits that his argument is not as strong as it might have been, had he insisted upon "the principles of liberty and moral fitness," but he still contends that what he has presented is "a really conclusive practical proof of it, which is greatly strengthened by the general analogy of nature: a proof easily cavilled at, easily shown not to be demonstrative, for it is not offered as such; but impossible, I think, to be evaded or answered. And thus the obligations of religion are made out, exclusively of the questions concerning liberty and moral fitness. . . ."[33]

Later generations realized how unwise Butler's tactic was, for in assuming the position of his adversaries, he necessarily assumed all the weaknesses of their position. It is in this manner that the *Analogy* is seen in its true light, and that its author is not unjustly described as a rationalist apologist for Christianity, despite the fact that Butler had intended primarily to give a defense of the Christian religion as something revealed in the strict sense, and something essentially related to the supernatural.

There were limits, of course, beyond which even Butler would not go in this irenic spirit. He simply took for granted the fact of God's existence and that of divine providence.[34] As for that type of fatalist who would reduce all activity to purely biological or chemical functions, excluding any intelligence and design even in the necessary agent, Butler asserts simply that ". . . I shall not pretend to reason with them."[35] He also admits that the negligence and prejudice of individual men can hinder them from seeing, or at least from admitting, the evidence of religion; the problems in regard to accepting Christianity do not all lie on the side of the evidence. Nevertheless, Butler is convinced of the persuasive power of his argument and attempts to do what he can by discussing the evidence on hand in a totally objective fashion.[36]

MEANING OF ANALOGY

The key to an understanding of Butler's argument rests in the meaning given by him to the word "analogy." He is speaking in this instance of the "argument from analogy" or of "inference from analogy"; this is also referred to as "reasoning by resemblance." Thus in his *Analogy of Religion, Natural and Revealed, to the Constitution and Course of Nature,* Butler argues that certain similarities between the material universe, natural religion, and Christianity ought to be a form of proof for the deists of the eighteenth century of the acceptability of revealed religion, especially when this fact is joined to a consideration of the miracles and prophecies worked in testimony of the truth of the Christian religion.

This notion of "reasoning by analogy" must not be confused with the concept of analogical knowledge; these refer to two quite different things. Reasoning by analogy is an argument based upon a more or less accidental *resemblance* between two things; it results in a conclusion that if one thing known to us is true, that which is similar to it must also be true.

Analogical knowledge, on the other hand, presupposes, in the proper analogy of proportion, the existence of the identical attribute in both terms being considered: even in the virtual analogy of proportion there must be a true attribute in both terms, different though it may be in both. Thus we know the goodness of God analogically by means of our knowledge of the good in creatures; the "goodness" both in God and in creatures must be in some respect identical if we are to have valid knowledge of God. Such knowledge is based upon more than an argument by resemblance; it involves an *a posteriori* argument concerning the existence and being of God that leads to an absolutely certain conclusion. Thus we truly know God and His attributes, even though imperfectly.

In the virtual analogy of proportion, the attributes used in the comparison must also be known to us as absolute realities; otherwise the comparison itself could not even be made. We are dealing here with types of knowledge rather than with means of knowing; the relationship between things we know, rather than an intellectual process of learning.

BUTLER'S ARGUMENT FROM ANALOGY

In his *Analogy of Religion*, Butler is not speaking of analogy in the manner associated with Scholastic metaphysics. He wishes to stress the notion of analogy or similarity as a means of knowing: thus he makes of it the basis for a line of argumentation (rather than as a manner of speaking of two absolute terms known from other sources). Such an argument, however, can do no more than render the conclusion *probable*, and this is all that Butler seeks to achieve in his work. He would readily agree with Maritain's statement that "reasoning by analogy" (as distinct from analogical knowledge) "can furnish only probable knowledge, not certainty."[37] The entire foundation of Butler's response to those who complain that he achieves no real certitude in his argument is that this is, unfortunately, *true;* but we must be satisfied with what we have since nothing better is possible.

As used by Butler, analogy is perhaps best described, with Adamson, as "a mode of reasoning from what is known of nature to the probable truth of what is contained in religion."[38] Butler does tend to confuse the issue at times and, as Gladstone points out, he "passes from probability to analogy without describing the resemblance between them."[39] Actually, much of Butler's insistence upon probability is involved in his use of the proof from historical evidence. Since there is no metaphysical proof of the truth of Christianity (a fully rational demonstration), and no sense perception in regard to the truth of it (as associated with physical certitude), we are forced back upon historical evidence and the testimony of others. Even in the eighteenth century, Butler saw in some sense that this type of argument in defense of Christianity throws one back upon moral certitude and the question of probability associated with it.

Basically, Butler does little more than accept the notion of probable knowledge as outlined in the writings of others, chiefly John Locke. Gladstone contends that Dr. Fairbairn falls into a "casual mistake, when he holds that Butler borrowed his doctrine of probability from Locke."[40] This stricture is true in the sense that Butler does not simply repeat the words and ideas of Locke, but the fact remains that Locke is to a large extent the philosophical starting point for Butler's position.[41]

In the Introduction to the *Analogy*,[42] Butler explicitly refers to the story of the King of Siam and his inability to imagine the nature of ice, a story related in the well-known chapters on probability in Locke's *Essay on Human Understanding*.[43] As Mossner remarks, Butler might be content to accept on Locke's authority the proposition that "in things which sense cannot discern, analogy is the great rule of probability,"[44] even though "in practice the argument from probability not infrequently becomes [in Butler] the argument from possibility."[45] Butler weakens the argument accordingly, and argues not only from the position that true certitude comes only from what sense can perceive, but goes further and affirms the *merely possible* as evidence of the real.

The position of Butler was also influenced by other considerations, of course. As Mossner points out, "Butler's claim to originality — and of its kind it is a potent one — is in the carrying out in an eclectic manner and with great detail a truly ancient scheme."[46] Thus, Butler's commitment to the clerical life of the Established Church would account for such other influences as the passage cited in the Introduction to the *Analogy* taken from Origen's *Philocalia*: "He who believes the scripture to have proceeded from him who is the Author of nature, may well expect to find the same sort of difficulties in it as are found in the constitution of nature."[47] Whatever might have been the intent of Origen in saying this, Butler sees here an added indication for his overall response that since there are mysteries and difficulties in the entire constitution of nature as well as in the scheme of natural religion, one ought not be surprised to encounter similar problems in Christianity. As Butler views the problem, the argument ought to be turned against the deists themselves. If they insist on denying that the Scriptures came from God simply because they find difficulties in them, they ought logically to give up their deistic stand and claim that the world was not formed by God either, since there are obviously many mysterious elements associated with the universe as well.[48] This is typical of Butler's basic argument, and in it lies both the strength and the weakness of what he has to say.

PROBABLE EVIDENCE

As Butler begins his *Analogy* of Religion, he states his basic principle — a norm that will guide his thought throughout: "Probable evidence is essentially distinguished from demonstrative by this, that it admits of degrees; and of all variety of them, from the highest moral certainty, to the very lowest presumption."[49] All of these various degrees fall within the area of that which is considered "probably true," despite the greater or lesser degree of certitude involved. Butler rejects any suggestion that "one very slight presumption" would suffice as evidence of such probable truth, but he does contend that a *series* of such slight presumptions, added together, "will amount even to moral certainty."[50] Butler is frequently concerned with some such total argument, based on many different types of evidence, which together lead to a stronger conclusion than any individual point could engender.

According to Butler, a likeness or similarity between two things can be based on any one of three reasons: (1) one thing may be like the other "in itself," that is, in the intrinsic nature each possesses; (2) there may be a similarity arising from the fact that a number of circumstances are associated with both of the objects considered; (3) or a similarity may rest on the "evidence" or "external proof" given in support of the two notions.[51] The *probability* itself is constituted, in any event, by this element of "likeness" or "similarity" that can be perceived; thus analogical reasoning will beget probability.

In applying this principle, Butler considers such things as the sun rising tomorrow, the tide going out tonight, and so forth. Continual and repeated observation of these facts will build up a state of mind which, in different circumstances, can be described as "a presumption, opinion, or full conviction" that the event will come to pass again.[52]

The first step in this process is observation. If there were no observation of contrary facts, one would be led to conclude that what he had always observed would always take place, as in the example of the King of Siam (described by Locke), who, having never seen ice and having always observed water in its liquid state, "concluded in the way of analogy, that there was no such thing as water's becoming hard. . . ."[53]

Butler admits that such a method of arriving at truth by probable evidence is a very imperfect method and that it results in an imperfect kind of information. God does not see things in this fashion, of course; the infinite intelligence can know things absolutely either as "certainly true" or "certainly false." But creatures must be content to know things in a less perfect way, and most often in the manner associated with probable evidence. Hence Butler concludes that "to us, probability is the very guide of life."[54] This fundamental principle consistently sets the tone for his argument, and Butler is anxious that his reader accept it, with all its shortcomings, as the best we can do on the creaturely level.

Arguing on this basis, Butler goes on to say that there are even times when we must act, despite the fact that we have nothing but a very low degree of evidence, because "more satisfactory evidence cannot be had, or is not seen. . . ."[55] If there were any presumption even of the lowest degree, remaining on the *other* side, we would still have to ignore that presumption and any doubt it might suggest, and go on to accept the truth intellectually. This, he insists, is a daily requirement in many matters of importance, and it applies in regard to religion as well, where such a degree of presumption may also "lay us under an absolute and formal obligation, in point of prudence and of interest, to act upon that presumption or low probability, though it be so low as to leave the mind in very great doubt which is the truth."[56]

When Butler comes to apply this theory to the question of revealed religion, he considers the types of similarity that might exist between natural and revealed religion: in itself, in a number of circumstances, or in the evidence (or external proof) associated with them. He sees traces of all three. In themselves, both natural and revealed religion stress at times the same truths: the existence of God, a future life, rewards and punishments; this would seem to imply an inner identity of some sort, partial though it may be. Moreover, there are similar circumstances in both realities (such as the similar obscurities they each involve, or the same type of objections raised against them); this is the basis of a further likeness.

HISTORICAL PROOF

The heart of Butler's argument, however, lies in the third type of similarity based upon *evidence* or *external proof.* The historical evidence in favor of Christianity — miracles and prophecies, above all — firmly establishes its truth. Butler admits that natural religion might well be accepted because of its proportion to human reason; the "proper motives" for accepting such a religion would be associated with arguments drawn from the moral nature of man, the voice of conscience or man's natural knowledge of God.[57] Nevertheless, he points out that in the present historical order, even natural religion has been given additional external proof, over and above the arguments of reason alone. This proof lies in the fact that the system of natural religion, with minor variations, has been held by men in all ages and countries, so universally in fact, that Butler contends (in something which sounds very much like the Traditionalism of the nineteenth century), that "it is certain historical fact, so far as we can trace things up, that this whole system of belief . . . was received in the first ages," so that it was not merely reasoned out, but "was taught first by revelation."[58]

This line of argument is intensified when Butler discusses the historical proofs for the truth of Christianity. Just as we must "trust" our observation of the external world in order to understand nature, and just as we might view the universal acceptance of natural religion as an added proof of its truth; *so also* must we accept the honesty and reliability of the historic witnesses in regard to Christianity and admit that even if the evidence offered is not such that our assent is necessitated (as is the case, he admits, in historical certitude, where we must make a prudential judgment regarding the evidence), it at least establishes *so high a probability* of the truth of the Christian scheme that we cannot prudently cast it aside.

In dealing with revealed religion, Butler admits that the *content* of Christianity surpasses human reason; hence there can be no question of an acceptance of this scheme on the basis of any supposed proportion to unaided reason. Butler's concern is with the question of the *assent* of faith and the *certitude* attached to that assent, and for him the answer lies entirely in the external evidence which proves the truth of revealed religion. Such observable facts as miracles and prophecies (when viewed in conjunction with the argument that God would not perform them to attest to the truth of a religion if it were not what it claims to be) will become the basis of the assent to Christian faith. Butler admits that *de facto* the Christian revelation contains the truths of natural religion as well, so that these same miracles and prophecies attest to the truth of natural religion; but he is not too concerned with this facet of the question. As he explains in Part I of the *Analogy,* since the objections to this historical evidence "are chiefly urged against revealed religion," he will treat of them only once in Part II in order to avoid repetition of the same matter.[59]

While stressing the importance of this historical evidence (which is really only probable evidence for him — evidence leading to what is probably true), Butler freely admits that some doubt or hesitancy may yet remain. This is universally true of all probable evidence. Nevertheless, these historical proofs, as he sees them, lay upon us not only the obligation of accepting Christianity, but also of ignoring whatever doubts or hesitancies may be present because of the lack of more compelling evidence.[60] Thus when Butler speaks of the "evidence for Christianity" at the end of his treatise, he admits that there is no full proof or demonstration of its *truth;* but neither is there a full proof or demonstration of its *falsity.* We are dealing here with the question of probable evidence associated with analogy; it would be foolish, he insists, to demand anything more. He repeats his basic position that "there is a middle path between a full satisfaction of the truth of it, and a satisfaction of the contrary."[61] This middle ground is that of probable evidence and it will admit of degrees; but the very lowest degree (listed below as number 4: a conclusion that Christianity is not unlikely) can be described as "a serious apprehension, that it may be true; joined with doubt whether it be so."[62]

Whatever doubts remain must give way to the more persuasive evidence that has resulted from a consideration of *all* the evidence — the various miracles and prophecies (which are the chief signs, the direct and fundamental proofs),[63] as well as other less obvious, though related, signs. Different men will react in different ways to this total proof, but a serious-minded person who investigates all the evidence will, Butler insists, discover that the various arguments put together "amount to a much higher degree of proof, upon such a joint review, than could be supposed upon considering them separately, at different times...."[64] He adds this often-quoted statement accordingly: "For probable proofs, by being added, not only increase the evidence, but multiply it."[65] It is by giving these proofs their full force that a type of moral certainty concerning the truth of Christianity can be achieved.

In his edition of Butler's works, Gladstone appends a somewhat longer classification of the states of mind resulting from various considerations of a proof; it helps illustrate the mind of Butler:[66]

(1) Demonstrated as true   (5) Neutral
(2) Moral certainty   (6) Improbable
(3) Likely   (7) Demonstrated as false
(4) Not unlikely

Gladstone notes that "Butler's arguments for religion will range from (2) down to (4)," that is, from *moral certainty* to not *unlikely*.[67] Butler does not consider a full demonstration of the truth of Christianity at all (1); and he rejects with no less vigor the possibility of a full demonstration of its falsity (7). He feels that the evidence set forth is so strong that it would be impossible for anyone examining it to any degree to consider that Christianity is improbable (6) or to assume a neutral attitude toward it (5).

Using this more elaborate classification, we would have to say that, for Butler, a serious-minded person could achieve — at best —

no more than moral certainty in regard to the truth of Christianity after having investigated the evidence (2); this is the highest degree of certitude here possible. Some individuals might give the evidence less consideration or grasp its import less clearly, and thus conclude that Christianity is likely (3); such a state of mind would indicate some positive persuasion in favor of its truth. But Butler would insist that even the most skeptical of men who would consent to consider the evidence at all, with an open mind, could go no further in the direction of "speculative infidelity," than the conclusion that Christianity is *not unlikely* (4).[68] Beyond that point, he feels sure that only a failure to have the full evidence set before one, or else blind prejudice and a refusal to recognize facts, could result in a lesser degree of certitude.

NOTES

Introduction

1. John Dillenberger and Claude Welch, *Protestant Christianity* (New York: Scribner's Sons, 1954), p. 43.
2. *DS* 1532. The English translations of Denzinger are taken, whenever possible, from Van Ackeren (ed.), *The Church Teaches* (St. Louis: Herder, 1955).
3. *DS* 1525.
4. *Constitution on the Sacred Liturgy* (Dec. 4, 1963), par. 59.
5. Cf. Karl Barth, in Hans Küng, *Rechtfertigung* (Einsiedeln: Johannes Verlag, 1957), p. 11. Eng. translation, *Justification* (New York: Nelson, 1965).
6. *Ibid.*, p. 12.
7. *Ibid.*
8. Cf. Josef R. Geiselmann, "Das Konzil von Trient über das Verhältnis der Heiligen Schrift und der nicht geschriebenen Traditionen," in Michael Schmaus, *Die mündliche Überlieferung* (Munich: Max Hueber, 1957), p. 169.
9. Cf. Burkhard Neunheuser, "La teologia protestante in Germania," in *Problemi e orientamenti di teologia dommatica,* edited by the Pontifical Theological Faculty of Milan (Milan: Marzorati, 1957), I, 627.
10. Karl Barth, *Church Dogmatics,* trans. G. T. Thomson (Edinburgh: T. & T. Clark, 1936), I–1, p. x (Foreword).
11. Cf. Neunheuser, *Problemi e orientamenti,* I, 624–629. Barth states (*Church Dogmatics,* II–I, 84) that he rejects the teaching of Vatican I on the knowledge of God by reason "because it is a construct which obviously derives from an attempt to unite Yahweh with Baal, the triune God of Holy Scripture with the concept of being of Aristotelian philosophy." What he has in mind is the truth that the God of Christian faith reveals Himself as much more than reason can demonstrate; Catholic teaching quite agrees. Thinking along this line, however, Barth remarks (p. 84) that "to affirm that the true, whole God, active and effective, the Head and Shepherd of the Church can be knowable [through reason] is only possible if He has already been identified with that false god [of pagan thought]."
12. Gottlieb Söhngen, "Analogia fidei. I. Gottähnlichkeit allein aus Glauben. II. Die Einheit der Glaubenswissenschaft," *Catholica,* 3 (1934), 113–136, 176–208; 4 (1935), 38–42.
13. Barth, *Church Dogmatics,* II–I, 82.
14. *Ibid.*, I–1, 389 (No. 8, 3).
15. For a longer discussion of the adaptations required in these areas, cf. John L. Murphy, "Seventy-five Years of Fundamental Theology," *AER,* 150 (1964), 385–404; 151 (1964), 21–40.
16. *DS* 3000 ff.
17. *DS* 3425.

CHAPTER I: MAN AND GOD

1. Friedrich Nietzsche, *Die fröhliche Wissenschaft* (Leipzig: E. W. Fritzsch, 1887), No. 125, p. 153. (For translation by Walter Kaufmann, cf. *The Portable Nietzsche* [New York: The Viking Press, 1954], pp. 95–96.)
2. *Ibid.*, pp. 154–155 (Kaufmann, p. 96).
3. Friedrich Nietzsche, *Also Sprach Zarathustra*, Part IV, no. 73, 2: On the Higher Man (Kaufmann, pp. 389–399).
4. Pius XI, *Divini Redemptoris: On Atheistic Communism* (New York: Paulist Press Edition, 1937), par. 9.
5. Karl Marx, "Towards the Critique of the Hegelian Philosophy of Right," in *Selected Writings in Sociology and Social Philosophy*, edited by T. Bottomore and M. Rubel (London: Watts, 1956), p. 27.
6. In still another fashion, this optimistic hope for the unending progress of mankind found expression in the positivism of Auguste Comte, in which "humanity" replaces "God." Cf. Henri de Lubac, *The Drama of Atheist Humanism*, trans. E. Riley (New York: Sheed and Ward, 1949), pp. 77–159.
7. Jean-Paul Sartre, *L'être et le néant*, 4 ed. (Paris: Libraire Gallimard, 1953), p. 708.
8. Cf. below, pp. 49–56.
9. *DS* 2730 ff., 2751 ff., 2811 ff.
10. *DS* 3004 ff., 3026 ff.
11. *DS* 3004.
12. *DS* 3005.
13. Ludovicus Billot, *De Deo uno et trino*, 7 ed. (Rome: Universitas Gregoriana, 1935), Quaestio II, p. 23.
14. *Ds* 3005.
15. Billot, *De Deo uno et trino*, pp. 23–24.
16. *Ibid.*, pp. 19–20.
17. Ludovicus Billot, *De virtutibus infusis*, 4 ed. (Rome: Universitas Gregoriana, 1928), pp. 182–203; 292; 313–321. Cf. below, pp. 74–75.
18. Josef Trütsch, "Glaube," in *Lexikon für Theologie und Kirche*, 2 ed. (Freiburg: Herder, 1960), IV, 922. — Abbreviated as *LThK*.
19. I, q. 1, art. 1, c.
20. II–II, q. 2, art. 4, sed contra.
21. II–II, q. 2, art. 4, objectiones.
22. II–II, q. 2, art. 4, c.
23. II–II, q. 1, art. 5, c: "Potest tamen contingere ut id quod est visum vel scitum ab uno, sit creditum ab alio . . . ut id quod est visum vel scitum ab uno homine, etiam in statu viae, sit ab alio creditum, qui hoc demonstrative non novit."
24. II–II, q. 1, art. 5, ad 3: "Praeterea, ea quae demonstrative probantur sunt scita: quia demonstratio est *syllogismus faciens scire*. Sed quaedam quae in fide continentur sunt demonstrative probata a philosophis: sicut Deum esse, et Deum esse unum, et alia huiusmodi. Ergo ea quae sunt fidei possunt esse scita. — *Ad tertium* dicendum quod ea quae demonstrative probari possunt inter credenda numerantur, non quia de ipsis sit simpliciter fides apud omnes: sed quia praeexiguntur ad ea quae sunt fidei, et oportet ea saltem per fidem praesupponi ab his qui horum demonstrationem non habent."

25. II–II, q. 2, art. 4, ad 3.
26. *Collectio Lacensis: Acta et decreta sacrorum concilorum recentiorum* (Freiburg: Herder, 1890), VII, 507, d (Caput II: Condemnatio rationalismi). — This work is cited hereafter as *CL*.
27. *DS* 3004. (*CL*, VII, 250, d.)
28. *CL*, VII, 520, c–d.
29. *Ibid.*
30. *Ibid.* — It might be noted that while Vatican I is concerned always with a *complete* knowledge of God, with no admixture of error, this is not necessarily the type of knowledge spoken of when theologians discuss the salvation of the pagan who has absolutely no contact with divine revelation. Yet even an obscure knowledge of God does not solve the entire problem, since this also may be difficult for some to obtain. Moreover, the pagan must also establish contact with supernatural faith, the root and foundation of all justification; mere rational knowledge of God, even obscure knowledge, is not the entire solution. This is assuredly one of the most difficult problems facing theologians today, but it is not an acceptable solution to claim, as some tend to do, that a clear knowledge of God by reason is a comparatively easy task.
31. *CL*, VII, 129, d.
32. *CL*, VII, 521, b. There still remains room for further investigation as to whether the various Traditionalists or Fideists in their teaching envisioned a natural tradition (or faith), or a supernatural revelation — even Christian revelation. This is by no means clear in the writings of the individual theologians.
33. *DS* 3004: "Eadem sancta mater Ecclesia tenet et docet, Deum, rerum omnium principium et finem, naturali humanae rationis lumine e rebus creatis certo cognosci posse; 'invisibilia enim ipsius, a creatura mundi, per ea quae facta sunt, intellecta, conspiciuntur' [*Rom.* 1:20]: attamen placuisse eius sapientiae et bonitati, alia eaque supernaturali via se ipsum ac aeterna voluntatis suae decreta humano generi revelare, dicente Apostolo: 'Multifariam multisque modis olim Deus loquens patribus in Prophetis: novissime diebus istis locutus est nobis in Filio' [*Heb.* 1:1 sq.]" — *DS* 3026: "1. Si quis dixerit, Deum unum et verum, creatorem et Dominum nostrum, per ea, quae facta sunt, naturali rationis humanae lumine certo cognosci non posse: anathema sit." (Cf. also *CL*, VII, 72, a; 76, b.)
34. *CL*, VII, 86, c: "Capitis principium dirigitur contra traditionalistas, sed etiam dirigitur contra illum errorem, qui late in Germania propagatus est, eorum nempe qui dicunt rationem per se nihil cognoscere sed tantum percipere."
35. *Ibid.*
36. *CL*, VII, 127, d.
37. *CL*, VII, 148, b.
38. *CL*, VII, 125, c.
39. *CL*, VII, 149, b.
40. *CL*, VII, 153, c.
41. *CL*, VII, 215, a. (Congregatio 45: *CL*, VII, 739, a).
42. *CL*, VII, 232 ff. (Congregatio 46: *CL*, VII, 739, d).
43. *CL*, VII, 224, d.
44. *CL*, VII, 225, a; 236, b.
45. *CL*, VII, 236, c.
46. *CL*, VII, 236, d; 238, a.

47. *CL*, VII, 238, b.
48. *CL*, VII, 121, a (no. 5).
49. *CL*, VII, 131, c.
50. *CL*, VII, 509, b: "Verumtamen in iis etiam, quae de Deo et de lege naturali humanae rationi per se impervia non sunt, agnoscendum est supernaturalis revelationis maximum beneficium; siquidem pro praesenti humani generis conditione, huic supernaturali revelationi debetur harum quoque veritatum propositio omnibus accommodata ita, ut ad earundem cognitionem debito tempore, sufficienti amplitudine, firma certitudine et absque errorum admixtione perveniri possit."
51. *CL*, VII, 524, d: "Attamen pro genere humano in praesenti conditione ad has veritates debito tempore, sufficienti claritate et plena certitudine, sine admixtione errorum assequendas eae sunt difficultates, ut potentia physica generatim non perducatur ad actum sine speciali adiutorio. Difficultates ita comparatae constituunt *impotentiam moralem*, cui respondet *moralis necessitas* adiutorii. Hoc autem adiutorium speciale in communi providentia praesentis ordinis naturae elevatae consistit in ipsa supernaturali revelatione. Ergo haec *revelatio* quoad illas quoque *veritates per se rationales* in praesenti ordine censeri debet humano generi *moraliter necessaria*."
52. *CL*, VII, 524, d.
53. *CL*, VII, 525, a: "Videlicet per ipsam revelationem tollitur *moralis impotentia*, atque adeo redditur humano generi cognitio *moraliter possibilis*."
54. I, q. 1, art. 1; II–II, q. 2, art. 4. Also: *C.G.*, I, 4; *De veritate*, q. 14, art. 10.
55. *DS* 3005: "Huic divinae revelationi tribuendum quidem est, ut ea, quae in rebus divinis humanae rationi per se impervia non sunt, in praesenti quoque generis humani condicione ab omnibus expedite, firma certitudine et nullo admixto errore cognosci possint. Non hac tamen de causa revelatio absolute necessaria dicenda est, sed quia Deus ex infinita bonitate sua ordinavit hominem ad finem supernaturalem, ad participanda scilicet bona divina, quae humanae mentis intelligentiam omnino superant; siquidem 'oculus non vidit, nec auris audivit, nec in cor hominis ascendit, quae praeparavit Deus iis, qui diligunt illum' [*I Cor.* 2:9]." (Cf. also *CL*, VII, 251, a).
56. *CL*, VII, 135, a.
57. *DS* 3005 (*CL*, VII, 72, b): also Bishop Gasser's comments on Emendatio 18: *CL*, VII, 136, a.
58. *CL*, VII, 135, b (italics ours). While in its solemn decrees Vatican I did not use the term "moral necessity" in regard to revelation of natural truths, the phrase does appear in the encyclical of Pius XII, *Humani generis* (*DS* 3876; N.C.W.C. ed., par. 3): "It is for this reason that divine revelation must be considered morally necessary so that those religious and moral truths which are not of their nature beyond the reach of reason in the present condition of the human race, may be known by all men readily with a firm certainty and with freedom from all error." ("Quapropter divina 'revelatio' moraliter necessaria dicenda est. . . .")
59. *CL*, VII, 121, d (no. 17).
60. *CL*, VII, 225, b (nos. 55½, 56).
61. *CL*, VII, 238, c; 239, b.
62. Etienne Gilson, *Christianity and Philosophy* (New York: Sheed & Ward, 1939), pp. 74–75.
63. *Ibid.*, p. 74.

64. *DS* 3008, 3032 (*CL*, VII, 166, a).
65. *CL*, VII, 510, d (Caput VII).
66. Gilson, *Christianity and Philosophy*, p. 75.
67. *Ibid.*, pp. 75–76.
68. *Ibid.*, p. 76.
69. *Ibid.*, p. 74.
70. St. Augustine, *Confessions*, trans. John K. Ryan (New York: Image Books, 1960), Book 5, chap. 14 (p. 132).
71. *Ibid.*, Book 6, chap. 1 (p. 133).
72. *Ibid.*, Book 1, chap. 1 (p. 43).
73. Ps. 142:6–7.

CHAPTER II: KIERKEGAARD

1. Cf. below, pp. 75–79.
2. H. F. Lovell Cocks, "Foreword" to H. V. Martin's *The Wings of Faith* (London: Lutterworth Press, 1950), p. 5.
3. Cf. James Collins, *The Mind of Kierkegaard* (Chicago: Henry Regnery, 1953), pp. 214–220; Regis Jolivet, *Introduction to Kierkegaard*, trans. W. H. Barber (London: Frederick Muller, 1950), pp. 30–42, 206–218; Martin, *The Wings of Faith*, pp. 82–84.
4. Jolivet, *Introduction to Kierkegaard*, p. 223.
5. Martin, *The Wings of Faith*, p. 19.
6. Cf. below, pp. 211–256.
7. Martin, *The Wings of Faith*, p. 88.
8. *DS* 3008.
9. *DS* 1525.
10. *DS* 3010.
11. *DS* 3035.
12. Henri Vignon, *De virtutibus et donis vitae supernaturalis* (Rome: Universitas Gregoriana, 1948), pp. 239 ff. Cf. below, pp. 54, 76–77, 202.
13. *DS* 2738.
14. Cf. Jolivet, *Introduction to Kierkegaard*, p. 212.
15. Cf. Walter Lowrie, in "Introduction" to Søren Kierkegaard, *Attack Upon "Christendom,"* trans. Walter Lowrie (Boston: The Beacon Press, 1956), p. xiv: "S. K.'s contemporaries, though of course this source of information was closed to them, were disposed to conjecture that, if S. K. had lived longer, he must have felt compelled to take refuge in the Church of Rome, as some of the readers of the *Instant* did. That was only a guess, but it was at least more plausible than the guess of Georg Brandes, that he would have 'leapt over' to free thought. Perhaps, if S. K. had lived to become a Catholic, he might have written another satire, dealing especially with Catholicism, and more especially with Rome. For all that, he may have been *essentially* a Catholic in his way of thinking. That is what Father Przywara makes out in *Das Geheimnis Kierkegaards*, by which he was able to convince Karl Barth that, as he put it, 'If I were to follow Kierkegaard, I might as well go over there,' pointing, as he wrote these words near his window in the Hotel Hassler on the Pincian Hill, to the Vatican on the other side of the Eternal City."
16. Collins, *The Mind of Kierkegaard*, p. 216.

17. *Ibid.*
18. *Ibid.*
19. We may well ask today if the entire movement associated with "keryg-matic theology" did not arise out of a faulty theory of faith and the false notion of the work of so-called scientific theology associated with it. In opposing "scientific theology" to "kerygmatic theology," the defenders of this view seem to look upon scientific theology as a stepped-up phi-losophical science of some sort, completely vitiating the role of theology as outlined by Pius XII in *Humani generis*. F. Lakner, for example, in his article, "Das Zentralobjekt der Theologie," in *Zeitschrift für katholische Theologie*, 62 (1938), 1, 15 speaks of the "wissenschaftlichen Theologie" and "die streng logische und analytische Wissenschaftsmethode" used in scientific theology. Thus (p. 31) he speaks of the formal object of *scientific* theology as the "demonstrabilitas ex verbo Dei revelato (et magisterio Ecclesiae custodito)," and that of *kerygmatic* theology or "Verkündigungs-theologie" as the "praedicabilitas ex verbo Dei (et missione Ecclesiae)." — At the basis of this distinction there seems to be a concept of theology as a strictly scientific labor, into whose essence the role of the magisterium does not enter. Possibly it is not by accident that this "kerygmatic" ap-proach arose, in large measure, at the University of Innsbruck, which is always associated with a theory of faith which admits the possibility of a "natural" or "scientific faith," and denies any psychological effect of the grace of faith itself. (Cf. Ludovicus Lercher-F. Schlagenhaufen, *Institu-tiones theologiae dogmaticae*, 5 ed. [Innsbruck: Rauch, 1951], I, 396 ff.) It may well be that a different approach to the act of faith and the role of the theologian more along Thomistic lines might have eliminated the supposed — and quite unfounded — opposition between "scientific theology" and "kerygmatic theology." It is always the magisterium itself which proposes for belief the truths revealed by God, and both preachers and theologians who are not bishops share in this work only by virtue of a mandate. In no case does it become their task in so-called "scientific theology" to attempt to "prove" or to "demonstrate" the truths of revela-tion, as if to prove that the infallible magisterium has not, *de facto*, fallen into error. This would be tantamount to an attempt to demonstrate that God is right.
20. It must be noted that the phrase "traditional" or "classical" apologetics is very deceptive. Apologetics is a quite recent tract within the framework of Catholic dogma, showing its first clear beginnings in the seventeenth century. Few would agree that this particular tract has even yet com-pleted its period of formation, even though the debates and the solemn definitions of the past three centuries have established clearly and defini-tively a number of essential elements that must always be included in any apologetic. Central to this tract is the relationship between faith and reason, and until other questions in regard to the tract *De fide* are further clarified, there is hardly any possibility of setting forth a "final" apologetic tract — which is what the phrase "traditional" or "classical" apologetic seems to indicate. Indeed, one may question whether *any* theological tract assumes such a final stage, this side of heaven. It remains true, nevertheless, that any further formulation of the tract must necessarily include those elements settled by the magisterium beyond dispute. Cf. Joseph C. Fenton, "The Case for Traditional Apologetics," *AER*, 141 (1959), 415: "This portion of theological science can be rearranged. It can

and should be improved and advanced. Substantially it can never be abandoned, unless a man is willing to abandon the teaching set forth in our chapter of the *Dei Filius.*" Cf. *DS* 3000–3020.

21. Cf. below, pp. 65–68.
22. Søren Kierkegaard, *The Journals of Søren Kierkegaard*, edited and translated by Alexander Dru (London: Oxford University Press, 1938), no. 1052. — This is cited hereafter as *Journals* (Dru), with the appropriate entry number.
23. Kierkegaard, *Journals* (Dru), no. 1050.
24. Jolivet, *Introduction to Kierkegaard*, p. 207.
25. Kierkegaard, *Journals* (Dru), no. 1084.
26. *Ibid.*
27. Kierkegaard, *Sickness Unto Death,* trans. Walter Lowrie (New York: Doubleday Anchor Books, 1954), p. 235 (Appendix to I).
28. *Ibid.,* p. 230.
29. *Ibid.*
30. Cf. below, pp. 49–56.
31. Kierkegaard, *Sickness Unto Death,* p. 218.
32. Kierkegaard, *Training in Christianity,* trans. Walter Lowrie (Princeton: Princeton University Press, 1944), p. 222.
33. *Ibid.,* p. 225.
34. Cf. below, pp. 132–143.
35. Jolivet, *Introduction to Kierkegaard,* p. 171. In regard to Kierkegaard's tendencies toward Catholic principles, besides Lowrie (above, note 15), cf. also, Collins, *The Mind of Kierkegaard,* p. 219; Martin, *The Wings of Faith,* p. 82 ff.
36. Jolivet, *Introduction to Kierkegaard,* p. 99.
37. Kierkegaard, *Journals* (Dru), no. 847.
38. In regard to the sixteenth-century Protestant mentality, cf. John T. McNeill, *The History and Character of Calvinism* (New York: Oxford University Press, 1954), pp. 40, 142; Roland H. Bainton, *Here I Stand: A Life of Martin Luther* (New York: Abington Press, 1950), p. 367; Dillenberger-Welch, *Protestant Christianity,* pp. 45 ff., 189 ff. (in regard to the Liberal approach to Scripture), and 226 ff. (in regard to the approach of present-day Protestant Fundamentalism).
39. As to the mentality of the theologians of the Classical era, cf. Josef R. Geiselmann, in Schmaus, *Die mündliche Überlieferung,* pp. 176, 182–187. — Geiselmann mistakenly views John Driedo (d. 1535) as a forerunner of the classical spirit (*loc. cit.,* pp. 176, 186); on this point, cf. John L. Murphy, *The Notion of Tradition in John Driedo* (Milwaukee: Seraphic Press, 1959), pp. 273–280.
40. Kierkegaard, *Training in Christianity,* pp. 143–144.
41. *Ibid.*
42. *Ibid.,* pp. 28–29.
43. *Ibid.,* p. 29.
44. *Ibid.*
45. Cf. below, pp. 196–206.
46. Cf. below, pp. 65–68.
47. Kierkegaard, *Training in Christianity,* p. 30.
48. *Ibid.*
49. *Ibid.,* p. 29. In regard to his Nominalism, cf. Jolivet, *Introduction to Kierkegaard,* p. 157.

50. Kierkegaard, *Training in Christianity*, p. 33.
51. *Ibid.*, p. 34.
52. *Ibid.*, p. 98.
53. *Ibid.*
54. *DS* 3886 (N.C.W.C. ed., par. 21).
55. *Ibid.*
56. DS 3887 (par. 22).
57. Karl Rahner, *Schriften zur Theologie* (Einsiedeln: Benziger, 1954), I, 10; Eng. trans. by Cornelius Emit, *Theological Investigations* (Baltimore: Helicon, 1962), I, 12.
58. A good example of this is the teaching of St. Thomas on the moral necessity of revelation (II–II, q. 2, art. 4) which is obviously the source of inspiration for the pertinent decree on this matter in Vatican I. (Cf. above, pp. 10–17.) The Council proposes this teaching on its own authority, however, and not simply because St. Thomas said it. As it happened, St. Thomas expressed well what the magisterium wished to propose, and hence it used his concepts; but the binding force of the decree derives from the divinely guided magisterium alone. In regard to the faith presumed by the theologian, and the special contribution of exegetes and dogmatic theologians, cf. Eduard Schillebeeckx, "Exegesis, Dogmatics and the Development of Dogma," in Herbert Vorgrimler (ed.), *Dogmatic vs. Biblical Theology* (Baltimore: Helicon, 1964), pp. 115–145.
59. Cf. St. Thomas, *Summa*, I, Prologus, especially the phrase ". . . secundum ordinem disciplinae," which would be the *ordo doctrinae* as distinct from the actual historical unfolding of the truths — the *ordo inventionis*, in which the Church, under the guidance of the Holy Spirit, "found" or "came to understand" the deeper implications of revelation. — This is treated at some length by Bernard J. Lonergan, *Divinarum personarum conceptio analogica* (Rome: Universitas Gregoriana, 1957), pp. 7–51, esp. 20–21; also John L. Murphy, "The Development of Mariology," *AER*, 138 (1958), 89–103, esp. 99, 103. — Cf. Vatican I on the comparison of the natural and supernatural orders as an aid for understanding the truths of faith: *DS* 3016.
60. It is for this reason that theologians have rejected the distinction between "kerygmatic" and "scientific" theology, mentioned above in note 19. In the 1930's a number of European theologians who held to the "more recent" theories of faith suggested this distinction, which unfortunately is still proposed in the United States at this late date. (E.g., Joseph B. Collins, "Kerygmatic Catechesis and Education," *AER*, 147 (1962), 365: "Theology texts upon which priests have been trained for many centuries were both deductive and scholastic in nature. The great truths of religion were first expressed in formal propositions and theses and then expertly analyzed and proved from scripture, tradition, and reason.") — In point of fact, the distinction is not valid in itself. In Europe this has been recognized, and what should have been done at the start is now being accomplished, that is, the very notion of "scientific" or "natural" faith is being rejected, along with the concept of a "scientific theology." As Karl Rahner points out, the distinction "rightly met with no approval" for the simple reason that *all* theology is necessarily kerygmatic: "All theology must be salvation-theology; there neither can nor may be a theology that is basically only 'theoretical' and not personally engaged" (Karl Rahner, "Kerygmatische Theologie," *LThK*, 2 ed., VI, 126). The

notion of "scientific theology" in this sense arose with the more recent theories of faith, and it has been set aside along with them.

61. When Thomas asks (III, q. 2) whether the hypostatic union took place in the nature or in the person, he refers to Chalcedon in the *Sed contra* of art. 1 and art. 2; he refers to Ephesus in the corpus of art. 3. These are his "telling" arguments; they indicate what *faith* accepts, thus necessitating him, as a believer, to come to these particular conclusions. In q. 2, art. 6 he speaks in the corpus of the Monophysites and the Nestorians, and refers to II Constantinople and the "Three Chapters" in order to uphold his views; his arguments appeal to history, but their force is derived from the fact that they represent the official teachings of the Christian faith. The problem of the two wills in Christ (q. 18) centers entirely around the errors of the Monothelites, especially of the patriarch of Constantinople, Sergius; and the teaching defended by Thomas is supported by the letter of Pope Agatho and the decrees of II Constantinople (q. 18, art 1; art. 6). This is a consistent approach used by St. Thomas, and reflects his basic intention in teaching. What he proposes is the "faith" which we must "accept"; the *Summa* is thus a *proclamation* of the faith in the truest sense. While Thomas presents this faith in an orderly fashion, he is not attempting to "prove" it, despite any superficial appearances to the contrary. Like the Church itself, he is proclaiming the revealed message, albeit in a scholastic framework.

62. Cf. *Contra gentiles*, I, cap. 6.

63. *Ibid.*, cap. 7–8. Cf. also *Summa theologiae*, I, q. 1, art. 8.

64. Cf. Hermann Lais, "Apologetik," in *LThK*, 2 ed., I, 723; also below, p. 204.

65. Lercher-Schlagenhaufen admit (*Institutiones theologiae dogmaticae*, I, 45; no. 90) that St. Thomas would appear to discuss the necessity of revelation more as a doctrinal matter in the *Contra gentiles;* he does not seem to have written an apologetic treatment of the topic. They express the opinion, on the other hand, that in the *Summa* (II–II, q. 2, art. 3) Thomas approaches a discussion of this topic that is more in line with the "more recent" philosophical treatment. It seems difficult to admit the validity of this opinion. Thomas approaches more closely the position which treats the matter in a more dogmatic fashion. He asks, "Utrum credere aliquid supra rationem naturalem sit necessarium ad salutem" (art. 3), and his response moves entirely in line with the thought that man, in his present historic state, cannot be saved unless he accepts truths which surpass unaided reason. His emphasis in the *Sed contra* is not upon any philosophical argument, but on an appeal to Scripture (citing Heb 11:6 — "Without faith it is impossible to please God"); indeed, the entire article stresses the supernatural goal of the beatific vision. Thomas refers here to earlier statements (I, q. 12, art. 1; I–II, q. 3, art. 8) that the ultimate happiness of man consists in a supernatural vision of God, and then goes on to note that no man can achieve that vision unless he accepts the role of one who is taught by God. Unless man is willing to accept God as a Teacher in the supernatural order — in faith — he will simply fail to reach this one and only goal of mankind: II–II, q. 2, art. 3: "Unde ad hoc quod homo perveniat ad perfectam visionem beatitudinis praeexigitur quod credat Deo tanquam discipulus magistro docenti." This is emphasized all the more in his response to the second objection, where he states that the man who possesses the *infused virtue of faith* is thereby enabled to judge what does

or does not pertain to revelation, just as his natural reason immediately recognizes the basic principles of thought. This is accomplished by the "light of faith" infused into the believer through the power of God Himself. Hence, this article stresses the *opposite* of that with which present-day apologetic works are concerned; it stresses, that is, the need of faith for salvation, rather than the preparation of the part of reason for faith.

66. Cf. *Contra Gentiles,* I, cap. 3–4, where St. Thomas insists (as also in the *Summa,* II–II, q. 2, art. 4) that it is fitting that God reveal even such things as the fact of His existence (of themselves truths which could be known by unaided reason), and that God accordingly command that such *natural truths* be believed by an act of supernatural faith. — As to Vatican I, cf. above, pp. 17–20.

67. Jolivet, *Introduction to Kierkegaard,* p. 176.

68. Collins, *The Mind of Kierkegaard,* p. 227.

69. Cf. Jolivet, *Introduction to Kierkegaard,* p. 55 ff.; Collins, *The Mind of Kierkegaard,* pp. 227–229.

70. Martin, *The Wings of Faith,* p. 76.

71. Bultmann's distinction between *Historie* and *Geschichte* also seems to be concerned with a very similar problem. In order to avoid holding that faith is a conclusion deduced from historical premises, Bultmann appears to seek a solution by subtracting all that is earthly, historical, on this side of eternity (the *Historie*), so that the believer might come into contact directly with that which is entirely "other," beyond history and the earthly: the *Geschichte.* The believer personally encounters the redeeming acts of Christ as *geschichtlich,* quite distinct from the particular historical circumstances which surrounded the individual events. — Cf. below, pp. 252–255; also, Peter Lengsfeld, *Überlieferung: Tradition und Schrift in der evangelischen und katholischen Theologie der Gegenwart* (Paderborn: Verlag Bonifacius-Drückerei, 1960), pp. 236, 239, 244, 248; P. Joseph Cahill, "Rudolf Bultmann and Post-Bultmann Tendencies," *CQB,* 26 (1964), 153–178.

72. Jolivet, *Introduction to Kierkegaard,* pp. 225, 226.

73. *Ibid.,* p. 226.

74. *DS* 3020.

CHAPTER III: THEORIES OF FAITH

1. II–II, q. 2, art. 9: "Ipsum autem credere est actus intellectus assentientis veritati divinae ex imperio voluntatis a Deo motae per gratiam. . . ."

2. Faith is always and necessarily an act involving the entire man in his personal encounter with God and his commitment to the Christian way of life. The decree of Vatican I (*DS* 3008) includes an act of the intellect in its description of the essential elements of faith, but its equal insistence on grace and free will emphasizes the commitment of the entire man, the human totality (*DS* 3010, 3035). The distinction concerning the motive of the intellectual act in the natural order ("propter intrinsecam rerum veritatem naturali rationis lumine perspectam") and in faith ("propter auctoritatem ipsius Dei revelantis") does not exclude these other essential elements from the notion of faith, which, as Pius XII explained even more clearly in *Mystici corporis Christi,* always involves the "personal freedom, responsibility and principles of conduct" in each believer (*DS* 3817). It is

in this sense that one may perceive the pertinence of Philbin's objection to a statement that Vatican I "canonized" the notion that faith is to be viewed "purely as belief" — that is, as a cold, intellectual, depersonalized assent to the truths of revelation presented in propositional form (R. G. Philbin, review of E. D. O'Connor, *Faith in the Synoptic Gospels*, in *TS*, 23 [1962], 649).

3. As appears from the *Acta*, the intention of Vatican I was to reject the position of those nineteenth-century philosophers and theologians who would exclude the use of reason in the total process of coming to believe (e.g., the immanentism of Schleiermacher; the reduction of faith to reason, as with Hermes; or the acceptance of the Kantian principles and the denial of a rational preparation for faith, as with the fideists and traditionalists). Cf. *CL*, VII, 87; VII, 186; VII, 191; VII, 528.

4. Cf. Trent, *DS* 1532.

5. *DS* 3035. — This statement was also directed against Hermes' ultimate conclusion that the "faith of knowledge," being something purely rational, required no grace, since it resulted from the necessitating and convincing arguments of reason alone. Cf. *CL*, VII, 528–530. — Much of this same line of thought is also found in Kant's late work, *Religion Within the Limits of Reason Alone*. Cf. below, pp. 176–179.

6. Vatican II, "Summary of Declaration on Religious Liberty," in *The Catholic Messenger*, 83 (Oct. 7, 1965), 5.

7. *DS* 1525.

8. Cf. *DS* 3008, 3032.

9. Rom 10:17, 14.

10. Cf. *DS* 3009, 3033, 3034, 3539, 3892.

11. *DS* 3013. — An article in *Life* magazine for July 6, 1963 (p. 28) contains a paragraph reminiscent of this decree: "But Pope Paul's reign promises progressive change, not revolution. In a world where the transmission of power from one regime to the next is seldom accomplished without a major upheaval, the Roman Church achieves a marvelous and mysterious continuity."

12. *DS* 3009.

13. *DS* 3033, 3009. — The form of canon 3 *de fide* (*DS* 3033) as originally suggested adds insight to the version finally approved: "Si quis dixerit, fieri non posse, ut *revelatio* divina externis signis reddatur credibilis, ideoque sola interna cuiusque experientia homines ad fidem moveri: a.s," (*CL*, VII, 77). The verb *reddatur* indicates the purpose of the signs; they manifest the fact that one can honestly believe this revelation on the authority of God revealing, without doing violence to one's intellectual nature.

14. *DS* 3034.

15. *DS* 3892. — The teaching on this point emphasizes always that the Church values human reason highly, since it is capable of proving the *fact* of divine revelation. It does not indicate, however, that every single individual either can or must prove this fact by reason alone, as an existential prerequisite for faith. Vatican I rejected an emendation (no. 102) to canon 3 *de fide* (*DS* 3033) which would change it to: "Si quis dixerit, Deum externis signis non reddidisse Revelationem divinam vere credibilem *omnibus* . . ." (*CL* VII, 163). The reason for this rejection, as explained by the relator *de fide*, Bishop Martin, is that the canon is not concerned with the *fact* that this is done, but merely with the *possibility* of human reason perceiving the credibility of divine revelation (*CL*, VII, 186). By the vote of the

assembled bishops, the emendation was accordingly rejected (*CL*, VII, 191).
— The case is similar to Vatican I's decree on the basic power of human
reason to know the existence of God, coupled with its teaching that most
men will need revelation and will accept this truth on faith. Cf. above,
pp. 13–20. As to the possibility of grace aiding in the formation of the
judgment of credibility, cf. Juan Alfaro, *Adnotationes in tractatum de
virtutibus* (Rome: Universitas Gregoriana, 1959), p. 200 ff.; Guy de Broglie,
"La vrai notion thomiste des 'praeambula fidei,'" *Gregorianum*, 34 (1953),
341–389.

16. Cf. Michael Nicolau, *De revelatione christiana*, in *Sacrae theologiae summa*
(Madrid: Biblioteca de autores cristianos, 1952), I, 115 ff.; Sebastian Tromp,
De revelatione christiana, 6 ed. (Rome: Universitas Gregoriana, 1950),
propositio V, p. 92 ff.; J. M. Hervé-C. Larnicol, *Manuale theologiae
dogmaticae* (Paris: Berche et Pagis, 1962), I, 67 ff. (no. 94); Lercher-
Schlagenhaufen, *Institutiones theologiae dogmaticae*, 5 ed., I, 35 ff. (no. 74);
Albert Lang, *Fundamentaltheologie: Die Sendung Christi* (Munich: Max
Hueber, 1962), p. 97 ff.

17. Cf. Lang, *Die Sendung Christi*, p. 98: "Wir glauben Gott nicht auf unser
Suchen hin, nicht wegen der Zeichen und Kriterien, die seine Gegenwart
anzeigen, sondern wir glauben ihm, ihm allein, auf sein Wort hin, weil er
Licht und Wahrheit, Quelle und Burgschaft aller Wahrheit ist. Umgekehrt
behält der Glaube seine absolute Gewissheit, auch wenn dem Glaubwür-
digkeitsurteil nur moralische Gewissheit zukommt. Die Glaubwürdig-
keitsgründe weisen ja nur den Weg zum Glauben, machen kund, dass das
Glaubensmotiv zu Recht der christlichen Offenbarung gegenüber in
Anwendung gebracht werden kann und muss. Sie liefern keinen Beitrag
zu der inneren Tragkraft des Glaubensmotivs, das seine einzigartige Gewissheit
von der unfehlbaren und untrüglichen Wahrheit Gottes hat."

18. Alfaro, *De virtutibus*, p. 198 (Thesis XI, corollarium II).

19. Vatican I merely indicated, of course, that the one and only motive of
faith is the authority of God revealing; it said nothing about the further
question as to the precise manner in which the believer perceives this
divine authority — whether as a result of a logical process of reasoning (as in
the "more recent" theories of faith), or as an object of faith, believed in the
act of faith itself (as in the Thomist-Suarezian theories). In any event, all
theories must show how faith truly possesses a certitude surpassing even
that of metaphysical certitude — an *assensus essentialiter certus, firmissimus,
super omnia firmus*. It is difficult to see how the "more recent" theories can
actually do this. Cf. below, pp. 195–200, 246–251.

20. *DS* 1532.

21. Cf. *DS* 222 ff., 248 ff., 375 ff., 1526, 1553, 3008, 3010.

22. Cf. Ludovicus Billot, *De virtutibus infusis*, 2 ed. (Rome: Universitas
Gregoriana, 1905), pp. 198–348; *De ecclesia*, 5 ed. (Rome: Univeritas
Gregoriana, 1927), II, 25–55.

23. Cf. Joseph de Aldama, *De virtutibus infusis*, in *Sacrae theologiae summa*
Madrid: BAC, 1953), III, 775 ff. (no. 116).

24. *Ibid.*, p. 777: "Consequenter ad ea quae diximus, admittimus possibilitatem
actus *fidei naturalis*, cuius motivium sit ipsa auctoritas Dei revelantis,
cuius tamen principium elicitivum sit *solus intellectus* cum concursu Dei
naturali." (Italics ours.)

25. Lercher-Schlagenhaufen, *Institutiones theologiae dogmaticae,* I, 396 ff. (no. 632): "Actus fidei non ut supernaturalis [hic] spectatur, sed ut actus vitalis et proinde rationalis. . . . Quaestio igitur hic tractanda est, utrum assensus fidei resolvi possit in suum objectum formale, quod est auctoritas Dei loquentis, et si id, num in hoc motivo sistat resolutio, ita ut auctoritas Dei loquentis sit unicum motivum formale fidei, an ipsa quoque *auctoritas Dei* in *alia principia logica* resolvi possit. Si ultimum, resolutio actus fidei in forma syllogistica fieri potest in hunc modum: Quidquid Deus revelat, verum est. Atqui Deus revelavit se esse trinum. Ergo (credo) Deus est trinus. Si hoc fit tribus actibus, fides est *discursus formalis,* si unico actu, fides est *discursus virtualis.*"

26. *Ibid.,* I, 399 (no. 639): "Teste conscientia veritas revelata affirmatur propter auctoritatem Dei loquentis. Atqui motiva credibilitatis per judicia fidem antecedentia affirmata teste eadem conscientia impellunt tanquam ratio objectiva ad auctoritatem Dei loquentis affirmandam. Ergo motiva credibilitatis seu revelatio passiva sunt motiva ipsius actus fidei."

27. H. Lennerz, *De virtutibus theologicis* (Rome: Universitas Gregoriana, 1947), p. 187 (no. 339): Thesis 12): "Actus fidei in linea assensus intellectualis resolvitur ut in motivum suum internum in solam auctoritatem Dei revelantis, certo quidem, sed non fide divina cognitam."

28. *Ibid.,* pp. 188–189 (no. 340): italics ours: "Actus fidei est actus honestus, libere a voluntate imperatus. Ut voluntas rationabiliter et honeste assensum fidei super omnia firmum imperare possit, praerequiritur certa cognitio, firmissimum hunc assensum esse rationabilem. Haec cognitio motivis credibilitatis innititur, ita ut in his fundetur, quod actus fidei sit rationi conformis. Cognitio certa, actum voluntatis imperantis praecedens et dirigens, sequenti syllogismo exhiberi potest: *Certum est,* me posse ea, quae testis sciens et verax testatur, tanta firmitate ei credere, quanta est ipsa auctoritas testis; atqui certum est, Deum esse testem summae auctoritatis, qui nec falli nec fallere potest, eumque revelasse se esse trinum; ergo certum est, me posse propter summam auctoritatem Dei revelantis assensu super omnia firmo Deo credere eum esse trinum."

29. *Ibid.,* I, 189 (no. 340), note 1: "Hic syllogismus, qui perducit ad credibilitatem veritatis revelatae, bene distinguendus est a syllogismo qui ad ipsam veritatem concludit, uti subest fidei scientificae: Id quod testis sciens et verax testatur, est verum; atqui Deus est testis sciens et verax, qui testatur se esse trinum; ergo Deus est trinus."

30. *Ibid.* — Lennerz confuses the issue here by speaking of the certitude which the believer can have as being proportioned to the authority in the one revealing. Granted that God has the supreme authority, the certitude of the individual's act of faith is still determined by his ability to know *that* this Supreme Authority has spoken, and *what* He has said. As a human act, such a conclusion must necessarily remain on the human, rational level, and cannot explain the certitude of faith *super omnia firma.* There is, in Lennerz' thinking, an invalid transposition of the absoluteness of the Revealer to the assent of the believer. No amount of "obedience" to the divine command can change the nature of that intellectual assent. — Cf. below, pp. 247–251.

31. *Ibid.,* p. 190 no. 342); p. 194 (no. 346).

32. Cf. below, pp. 196–202.

33. De Aldama, *De virtutibus infusis,* III, 779 (no. 120).

34. Cf. Billot, *De virtutibus infusis*, p. 287 (Thesis 16) where Billot explains that faith is rooted in the authority of God revealing, but an authority known by means of a prior intellectual knowledge. He insists that faith would not thus rest on the knowledge itself, which he considers merely a means or a prerequisite for knowing the authority of God itself. Billot obviously wants to eliminate the notion of faith as terminating in a *knowledge* of the authority of God rather than the authority itself; but he has a difficult time explaining how such a "prerequisite" knowledge will not somehow affect the believer's adherence to the divine authority.

35. *Ibid.*, Prolegomenon, III: De ratione distinctionis supernaturalium habituum (no. 2), p. 68.

36. *Ibid.* (no. 3), pp. 72–73, where Billot explains the supernaturality of a saving act of faith in his approach: "Quod in actibus supernaturalibus virtutum viae, formalitas supernaturalitatis faciens ut actus sint proportionati conditioni obiectorum secundum se, *non* provenit ex obiecto prout quoad nos munere obiecti fungitur, videlicet, neque ex obiecto materiali quod creditur, quod speratur, quod diligitur, *neque ex obiecto formali* propter quod creditur vel speratur vel diligitur, *sed unice* ex principio gratiae *qua elevatur operativa potentia* ad eum ordinem perfectionis, cuius ultima consummatio est in unione per lumen gloriae ad divinam essentiam ut ad formam intelligibilem." (Italics ours.)

37. DS 376, 396, 1553, 1525.

38. Cf. Juan Alfaro, *Adnotationes in tractatum de virtutibus* (Rome: Universitas Gregoriana, 1959); Roger Aubert, *Le problème de l'acte de foi* (Louvain: E. Warny, 1958); *idem*, "Questioni attuali intorno all'atto di Fede," in *Questioni e orientamenti di teologia dommatica* (Milan: Marzorati, 1957), I, 655–708; Guy de Broglie, *Pour une théorie rationnelle de l'acte de foi* (Paris: Institut catholique, 1955); Joseph Falcon, S.M., *La crédibilité du dogma catholique* (Paris: Emmanuel Vitte, 1952); Reginald Garrigou-Lagrange, *De virtutibus theologicis* (Rome: Institutum Angelicum de Urbe, 1948); *idem*, *De revelatione per ecclesiam catholicam proposita* (Rome: Institutum Angelicum de Urbe, 1950); L. L. Guérard des Lauriers, *Dimensions de la foi* (Paris: Les Éditions du Cerf, 1952); Louis Monden, *Le miracle, signe de salut* (Bruges: Desclée De Brouwer, 1959); Josef Trütsch, "Glaube," in *Lexikon für Theologie und Kirche*, 2 ed. (Freiburg: Herder, 1960), IV, 922; *idem*, "Glaube und Erkenntnis," in Feiner, Trütsch, Böckle, *Fragen der Theologie Heute* (Einsiedeln: Benziger, 1957), pp. 45–68; Henri Vignon, *De virtutibus et donis vitae supernaturalis* (Rome: Universitas Gregoriana, 1948). — In English, the following less technical works prove very helpful: Martin C. D'Arcy, *Belief and Reason* (Springfield, Ill.: Templegate, 1947); *idem*, *The Nature of Belief* (St. Louis: Herder, 1958); Jean Mouroux, *I Believe* (New York: Sheed & Ward, 1959); Illtyd Trethowan, *The Basis of Belief* (New York: Hawthorn, 1961).

39. Trütsch, "Glaube," *LThK*, IV, 922.

40. On this point we find ourselves in disagreement with de Aldama, *De virtutibus infusis*, III, 792 (no. 142); and Hervé, *Manuale theologiae dogmaticae*, III, 287 (no. 271), who hold that the proposition by the Church is only a *condition* of some sort, although absolutely necessary. Considering the difficulties involved in any historical study of Scripture, much less in a simple reading of the Bible, it seems that absolute certitude in regard to what Christian revelation actually teaches would demand some divine assurance, as given here and now in the living Church, of the

precise content and meaning of that revelation. The same would also be true, *mutatis mutandis*, of the former decrees of the Church; it is not *any* understanding of them that is correct, but only the understanding authoritatively proposed by the Church Teaching. To limit this role of the magisterium to that of a mere condition would seem to open the door to subjectivistic interpretations of all sorts, in which the individual would lay claim to accepting the teaching of the Church, but only too easily come to think of *himself* as the Church — that is, as the authoritative teacher, thus possibly undermining his own faith. On the other hand, if what the Church proposes is not more intimately related to faith itself, it is difficult to understand faith at all, since in practice the Catholic *does* believe that which the Church teaches as revealed. This is true, certainly, of dogmas in the strict sense, as singled out by Vatican I as the objects of faith (*DS* 3011). — On this point, cf. Vignon, *De virtutibus*, p. 214 ff.

41. Although he rejects this concept personally, the Protestant theologian, Gerhard Ebeling, gives a uniquely clear and straightforward statement of the Catholic position — one far surpassing that offered by many Catholic theologians. Cf. Gerhard Ebeling, *Wort und Glaube* (Tübingen: J. C. B. Mohr, 1960), p. 21.

42. Cf. de Broglie, "La vraie notion thomiste des "praeambula fidei," " *Gregorianum*, 34 (1953), 346: "When St. Thomas speaks of the 'praeambles of faith,' he intends to speak solely of certain truth which *can* be known by natural reason before faith; but he does not contend — indeed he even expressly denies — that it is indispensable to know any of these before believing, under the pain of not being able to believe reasonably." — As we have noted above, the individual is even able to believe supernaturally in the existence of God; the same would be true of the preliminary judgments associated with faith. Cf. above, pp. 20–24.

43. Alfaro, *De virtutibus*, p. 198 (Thesis XI, corollarium II).

44. Ebeling, *Wort und Glaube*, pp. 3, 36, 74, 87.

45. Vincent Lerins, *Commonitorium*, 2 (*RJ* 2168).

46. *DS* 3020.

CHAPTER IV: TRADITION

1. Cf. J. L. Murphy, *The Notion of Tradition in John of Driedo* (Milwaukee: The Seraphic Press, 1959), Appendix III: "Faith and Morals" at Trent, pp. 292–300.

2. *DS* 1501.

3. Cf. Murphy, *The Notion of Tradition*, Appendix II: "Traditions" and the Council of Trent, pp. 288–291.

4. Cf. the Letter of the Cardinal Legates to Cardinal Farnese (7/8 Feb. 1546), in *Concilium Tridentinum diariorum, actorum, epistularum, tractatuum nova collectio* (ed. Görresgesellschaft: Freiburg, 1901 ff.), X, 373, lines 20–21: "Il qual punto [the existence of an extra-scriptural element in Revelation] è di tanta importantia, che hoggi il heretici non hanno cosa, quale più cerchino di sbattere, che questa." — *Note:* All references to this edition of the *Acta* of the Council of Trent will be cited thus: *CTr.*

5. *CTr*, V, 4, line 4: "Quod in futura sessione suscipiantur libri sacrae scripturae et qua via et modo sint recipiendi: an praevia aliqua conquisitione

292 *Notes*   TRADITION

vel examinatione facienda per theologos deligendos a Rmis. Dmis. legatis, ut responderi possit rationibus adversariorum. Item proponendum, quod ultra scripturas novi testamenti habemus traditiones apostolorum, de quibus est facienda aliqua mentio in concilio. . . ."

6. Cf. Murphy, *The Notion of Tradition*, p. 288; Yves M.-J. Congar, *La tradition, et les traditions: essai historique* (Paris: Librairie Arthème Fayard, 1960), pp. 207–232; Josef R. Geiselmann, *Die heilige Schrift und die Tradition* (Freiburg: Herder, 1962), pp. 274–281.

7. *CTr*, X, 377, line 34–378, line 3: "Fatto questo [*the mention of Scripture*], segue il stabilire la traditione della chiesa; della quale ci pare necessario, che nel medemo decreto si faccia mentione, almento in genere et indeffinitamente, perchè sarà un gran ponto questo, che non ci possa esser detto: 'la tal cosa non si trove nella scrittura, adunque non è vera.'"

8. *CTr*, V, 7, lines 34–36. Cf. also *CTr*, I, 30, line 5; 435, line 6.

9. *CTr*, V, 10, line 29. Cf. also *CTr*, I, 484, line 8.

10. *CTr*, V, 11, lines 18–27: "Laudavitque, post sacros libros statim recipi traditiones, cum istae ab illis non differant nisi tantum, quod ill scripti sunt, hae non, sed ab eodem spiritu et illos et istas descendisse; declaravitque, tria esse principia et fundamenta nostrae fidei: primum libros sacros, qui scripti sunt dictante Spiritu Sancto, secundum esse evangelium, quod Christus Dominus Noster non scripsit, sed ore docuit et in cordibus illud plantavit, cuius evangelii nonnulla postea evangelistae scripto mandarunt, multa quoque relicta sunt in cordibus hominum. Tertium, quia non semper filius Dei corporaliter nobiscum mansurus erat, misit Spiritum Sanctum, qui in cordibus fidelium secreta Dei revelaret et ecclesiam quotidie et usque ad consummationem saeculi doceret omnem veritatem, et si quid in mentibus hominum dubii occurrisset, declararet."

11. *Acta*, in *CTr*, V, 11, lines 18–27; *Diarium III*, in *CTr*, I, 484, lines 47–485, line 16.

12. The historical records of these early sessions are quite defective. Massarelli was not present at the General Sessions until April 1, 1546, although he did attend the *classis* held under Cardinal Cervini from February 2 on. Thus Massarelli's account of the General Sessions in the *Acta* are largely dependent upon the Commentary of Ercole Severoli, who was present as a representative of the Roman Curia. Cf. Merkele's discussion of these sources in *CTr*, I, lxvi ff.

13. *CTr*, I, 484, line 53.

14. *CTr*, I, 485, lines 1–2.

15. *CTr*, I, 485, lines 4–5.

16. *CTr*, V, 11, lines 21–23. A similar line of thought is evidenced in a formula suggested by Thomas Caselli, the bishop of Bertinoro: *CTr*, I, 524, lines 29–34.

17. *CTr*, V, 11, lines 24–27. Cf. also that statements of Robert Filheul, the bishop of Aix: *CTr*, I, 483, line 24; and the letters to Cardinal Farnese (No. 306, 311): *CTr*, X, 386, lines 8–12; 394, lines 1–5, 15.

18. Cf. Murphy, *The Notion of Tradition*, pp. 73–97, 292–300; Congar, *La tradition*, pp. 210–214; Geiselmann, *Die heilige Schrift*, pp. 161–165, 274–281.

19. Cf. Geiselmann, "Das Konzil von Trient . . . ," in Schmaus, *Die mündliche Überlieferung*, pp. 176, 188–193; *Idem, Die heilige Schrift*, pp. 40–52; Congar, *La tradition*, pp. 244–249; Murphy, *The Notion of Tradition*, pp. 277–280.

20. Cf. above, p. 80.
21. Cf. August Deneffe, *Der Traditionsbegriff: Studie zur Theologie* (Münster i. W., 1931), p. 126; Murphy, *The Notion of Tradition*, pp. 239–240.
22. *CTr*, V, 14–15, gives these scriptural passages as indications of this: Jer 31:33; John 20:30; 21:25; 16:12; 2 John 12; 3 John 13; 1 Cor 11:2, 34; 2 Cor 3:2; Phil 3:15; 4:8; 2 Thess 2:14; 1 Thess 4:1.
23. *CTr*, V, 15–18. Some of these citations are difficult to locate. They were evidently drawn from the sources at hand which attributed the works to those writers mentioned, not always with complete accuracy. Similarly, the wrong books are cited at times as well.
24. Gratian, *Decretum*, pars I, dist. xi, cap. 8: *Catholica* . . . ; dist. xii, cap. 11: *Illa*. . . .
25. *DS* 782.
26. *CTr*, V, 15, line 32. Cf. Geiselmann, "Das Konzil von Trient . . . ," in Schmaus, *Die mündliche Überlieferung*, p. 140.
27. *CTr*, V, 17, line 23.
28. *CTr*, V, 16, lines 23–28, 36–39; 17, lines 1–6. Cf. also the small work of Ludovicus Nogarola, *Apostolicae institutiones in parvum libellum redactae* (Venetii: apud Andream Arrivabenum, 1549), which was prepared for use at the time of Trent, and which contains a very similar list of such traditions.
29. *CTr*, V, 13, lines 33–36. (Acts 15:19–20.)
30. *CTr*, V, 14, line 6.
31. *CTr*, V, 31, lines 24–25. For the sake of comparison, we give here the rest of the decree as originally suggested, placing in parentheses the changes made in the final version: ". . . perspiciensque, hanc veritatem [*add:* 'et disciplinam'] partim [*omitted*] contineri in libris scriptis, partim [*omitted,* and 'et' *added*] sine scripto traditionibus, quae vel [*omitted;* and 'ab' *added*] ipsius Christi ore ab apostolis acceptae vel [*omitted; and* 'aut' *added*] ab ipsis Apostolis Spiritu Sancto dictante quasi per manus traditae ad nos usque pervenerunt: orthodoxorum patrum exempla secuta omnes libros tam veteris quam novi testamenti, cum utriusque unus Deus sit auctor, necnon traditiones ipsas [*add:* 'tum ad fidem tum ad mores pertinentes'] tamquam vel oretenus a Christo vel a Spiritu Sancto dictatas et continua successione in ecclesia catholica conservatas, quibus par pietatis debetur affectus summa cum reverentia pro sacris et canonicis [*the phrase:* 'quibus par pietatis . . . pro sacris et canonicis' *was omitted; in its place was added:* 'pari pietatis affectu ac reverentia'] suscipit et veneratur suscipique ab omnibus Chrïstifidelibus statuit et decernit [*the words from* 'suscipique' *to* 'decernit' *were omitted*]."
32. *CTr*, V, 14, lines 17–20. Cf. also *CTr*, I, 490, lines 45 ff.
33. *CTr*, V, 14, lines 20–21.
34. *CTr*, V, 14, lines 20–21. Cf. Gratian, *Decretum*, I, dist. 11, cap. 5: *Ecclesiasticarum*. . . .
35. *CTr*, I, 35, lines 15–18: ". . . nam abusus scripturarum sub se continent ordinem et modum predicandi verbi Dei et libros ipsos interpretandi, traditionum vero abusus totam pene disciplinam ecclesiasticam respicere videntur. Nam et confessiones et omnes ceremonie nostre ad ipsas traditiones respiciunt."
36. *CTr*, V, 41, lines 36–39: "An placeat dici, quod in decreto est scriptum, cum de libris sacris et traditionibus apostolorum fit mentio: *quibus par debetur pietatis affectus;* an vero haec verba sint expungenda et alia

illorum loco addenda, quae debitam utrisque reverentiam adhibendam exprimant."

37. *CTr*, V, 39, 34 ff. Cf. also *CTr*, V, 34, 21 ff.; I, 523, lines 1 ff.
38. Cf. the remarks of Salvatore Alepo, the archbishop of Sassari: *CTr*, V, 18, lines 23–26; and those of Lejay: *CTr*, V, 35, line 23; as well as the letter of Cardinal Farnese to the legates on March 4, 1546: *CTr*, X, 406, lines 11–15.
39. The six bishops were Salvatore Alepo, the archbishop of Sassari; Giov. Michele Saraceni, the archbishop of Matera; Robert Vauchop, the archbishop of Armagh; Tommaso Campeggio, the bishop of Feltre; Giacomo Giacomelli, the bishop of Belcastro; and Francisco de Navarra, the bishop of Badajoz. This decision was reached on February 26. Cf. *CTr*, V, 21, lines 27–28.
40. Cf. the objection raised by Alepo before the formulation of the decree: *CTr*, V, 18, lines 24–26; and the answer of Campeggio and Giacomelli to a similar objection raised, after the decree was formulated, by Marco Vigerio della Rovere, the bishop of Sinigaglia: *CTr*, V, 33, lines 8–10, 22–28.
41. *CTr*, V, 53, lines 11–12. (In favor of retaining the phrase, 33; preference for "similis pietatis affectus," 11; preference for "reverentia debeatur," 3; doubtful, 3; displeased with the phrase, 2.)
42. *CTr*, V, 42, lines 1–4: "An vero illis verbis suo loco manentibus ille modus loquendi temperari debeat, addendo aliqua verba, quae hunc sensum exprimant, ut illis traditionibus, *quae ad dogmata* pertinent, par pietatis affectus debeatur, qui illis dogmatibus, quae in scriptis exprimuntur. Et eodem modo proportione in iis, *quae ad mores* pertinent, singula singulis referendo."
43. *CTr*, V, 53, lines 24–30.
44. *DS* 1501. Cf. note 31 above.
45. *CTr*, X, 413, lines 1–3: ". . . et le traditioni non scritte erano di sorte impugnate, che a nessuna cosa s'attendeva più che ad anihilarle con dare ad intendere, che tutto quello che era necessario alla salute era scritto. . . ."
46. *CTr*, X, 413, line 5.
47. *CTr*, V, 14, line 1.
48. *CTr*, V, 14, line 18.
49. *CTr*, I, 524, lines 12–14.
50. *CTr*, V, 40, lines 1–7.
51. *CTr*, V, 55, lines 24–27.
52. *CTr*, V, 57, lines 34–36.
53. Cf. Hubert Jedin, *Papal Legate at the Council of Trent: Cardinal Seripando*, trans. Frederic C. Eckhoff (St. Louis: Herder, 1947), p. 277.
54. *CTr*, XII, 517, line 28.
55. *CTr*, XII, 518, lines 1–9. Regarding those traditions (practices) contained in Scripture, he cites these passages: Acts 15:29; Titus 1:6; 1 Cor 11:15; 1 Tim 2:9; 1 Cor 7:12; 1 Tim 5:4; 1 Cor 1:20; 1 Cor 6:1; 1 Cor 14:1; Acts 16:4. — They are all concerned with some facet of liturgical or disciplinary life among the members of the primitive Church.
56. *CTr*, XII, 518, lines 21 ff.
57. *CTr*, XII, 518, lines 50–519, line 5. (Cf. *RJ*, 1419.)
58. *CTr*, XII, 521, lines 47–52. No source is given for this statement in the writings of Augustine, although it would represent his mentality as evidenced in his *De doctrina christiana*, 2:9 (*ML* 34:42): "In iis enim quae

aperte in Scripturis posita sunt, inveniuntur illa omnia quae continent
fidem, moresque vivendi, spem scilicet atque charitatem."
59. Cf. Murphy, *The Notion of Tradition*, pp. 98–137.
60. Cf. the pertinent remarks of Robert Guelluy, "L'évolution des methodes
théologiques à Louvain d'Érasme à Jansénius," *Revue d'histoire ecclési-
astique*, 37 (1914), 31–144.
61. *CTr*, XII, 522, note 1.
62. *CTr*, XII, 522, lines 1–17, 22 ff.
63. *CTr*, XII, 523, lines 17–18. (Italics ours.)
64. *CTr*, XII, 524, note 2.
65. *CTr*, XII, 523, lines 37–38.
66. Cf. Murphy, *The Notion of Tradition*, p. 118 ff.
67. *CTr*, XII, 523, lines 46 ff.
68. *CTr*, XII, 523, lines 6–16.
69. *CTr*, XII, 524, lines 9–11.
70. Cf. E. Amann, "Pères de l'Église," *DTC*, XII, 1, col. 1196–1197.
71. *CTr*, XII, 524, lines 12–24. The editor of these tracts, Schweitzer, notes
that he has sought out the citation from Innocent II in vain.
72. *CTr*, XII, 524, lines 35–525, line 5.
73. *CTr*, XII, 525, lines 6 ff.
74. *CTr*, XII, 525, line 51.
75. *CTr*, XII, 526, lines 5–7.
76. *CTr*, XII, 526, lines 31–35. Cf. also *CTr*, XII, 527, lines 35–39.
77. *CTr*, XII, 526, line 35.
78. *CTr*, XII, 527, lines 24–30.
79. Cf. Lengsfeld, *Überlieferung*, pp. 120–124.
80. Cf. Geiselmann, "Das Konzil von Trient . . . ," in Schmaus, *Die mündliche Uberlieferung*, p. 194 ff.; Shillebeeckx, in Vorgrimler, *Dogmatic vs
Biblical Theology*, pp. 126–148.
81. Henrich Lennerz, "Scriptura Sola?" *Gregorianum*, 40 (1959), 38–53; "Sine
scripto traditiones," *Gregorianum*, 40 (1959), 624–635; "Scriptura et tradi-
tio in decreto 4. sessionis Concilii Tridentini," *Gregorianum*, 42 (1961),
517–522.
82. In discussing this point, Geiselmann cites a statement of Congar, and
indicates his personal endorsement of it: Geiselmann, *Die heilige Schrift*,
p. 151: "Gewiss könne kein Katholik sich zum Prinzip der scriptura sola
bekennen. Denn es gebe keinen einzigen Punkt der christlichen Lehre, der
sich auf die alleinige Schrift gründe. Vielmehr schliessen alle Schrift und
Tradition zugleich und untrennbar in sich, wobei die beiden sich in
einem lebendigen Austausch aufeinander beziehen. In Wirklichkeit beziehe
die Kirche keine Wahrheit allein von der Schrift, auch keine allein von
der Tradition." – Cf. Congar, *La tradition*, p. 217, from which these statements are derived.
83. Cf. our discussion of Lennerz' theory of faith above, pp. 72–74; also Geiselmann, "Scripture, Tradition and the Church: An Ecumenical Problem," in
Daniel J. Callahan, *et al.*, *Christianity Divided* (New York: Sheed and
Ward, 1961), pp. 39–72; *idem*, "Die Tradition," in Feiner, *et al.*, *Fragen
der Theologie Heute*, pp. 69–108.
84. Cf. note 31 above.
85. Cf. René Draguet, "Le maître louvaniste Driedo inspirateur de décret de
Trente sur la Vulgate," *Miscellanea historica in honorem Alberti de Meyer*
(Louvain, 1946), II, 836–854; Beniamino Emmi, "Il posto del 'De ecclesiasticis

scripturis et dogmatibus' nelle discussioni Tridentine," *Ephemerides theologicae Lovanienses,* 25 (1949), 585–597.
86. Cf. Murphy, *The Notion of Tradition,* pp. 98–137.
87. Cf. Lengsfeld, *Überlieferung,* pp. 120–124; Johann Beumer, "Das katholische Schriftprinzip in der theologischen Literatur der Scholastik bis zur Reformation," *Scholastik,* 16 (1941), 24–52; Paul de Vooght, *Les sources de la doctrine chrétienne d'après les thélogiens du XIVᵉ siècle et du début du XVᵉ.* (Bruges, 1954).
88. Cf. Francis de Vitoria, *Comm. in IIam — IIae,* q. 1, art. 10: "Ecclesia [*after the death of the apostles*] non habet potestatem determinandi nisi ex scriptura . . . habet suas regulas ex scriptura sacra et ex his quae derivata sunt ad nos ex apostolis et factis Christi."
89. Cf. Lengsfeld, *Überlieferung,* p. 120, notes 123–128.
90. *CTr,* V, 18, 28–29.
91. *CTr,* I, 494, line 18; 495, line 17.
92. *CTr,* X, 399, line 11.
93. *CTr,* X, 399, line 12.
94. *CTr,* V, 71, lines 16–17, 32–34.
95. *CTr,* V, 72, line 9.
96. *CTr,* I, 525, lines 16–18.

CHAPTER V: SCHLEIERMACHER

1. Denz. 2105. — We will cite the encyclical from the old Denzinger-Bannwart-Umberg-Rahner edition of the *Enchiridion symbolorum* (Freiburg: Herder, 1954), since the new Denzinger-Schönmetzer edition has chosen to leave many sections of the encyclical out of the volume. The English translations are from *All Things in Christ,* edited by Vincent A. Yzermans (Westminster, Md.: Newman, 1954); it is cited simply as "Yzermans." In this instance: Yzermans, p. 117.
2. *EB* 548 (N.C.W.C. ed., par. 18).
3. *EB* 557 (N.C.W.C. ed, par. 33).
4. *EB* 558 (N.C.W.C. ed., par. 35).
5. The preceding chapter and its discussion of the meaning of *traditiones,* or of the phrase "tum ad *fidem,* tum ad *mores*" as used at the Council of Trent is but one example of the need of understanding the words in the historical context proper to them. Any number of similar examples could be adduced.
6. Cf. *Instruction On Bible Research,* (N.C.W.C. ed.), par. 11–21.
7. *Ibid.,* par. 8.
8. Denz. 2096 (Yzermans, p. 109).
9. Denz. 2097 (Yzermans, p. 111).
10. *Ibid.*
11. Denz. 2098 (Yzermans, p. 111).
12. Denz. 2099 (Yzermans, p. 112).
13. Denz. 2101 (Yzermans, p. 113).
14. Denz. 2101 (Yzermans, p. 114).
15. *Ibid.*
16. Denz. 2072 (Yzermans, p. 91).

17. Denz. 2074 (Yzermans, p. 92).
18. Denz. 2079 (Yzermans, p. 95).
19. *Ibid.*
20. Denz. 2079 (Yzermans, p. 96).
21. Denz. 2080 (Yzermans, p. 96).
22. Denz. 2087 (Yzermans, p. 101).
23. Richard B. Brandt, *The Philosophy of Schleiermacher* (New York: Harper, 1941), pp. 307–308.
24. It may be noted that the term "liberalism," like the word "liberal," has been used in many different senses during the past few centuries. As used in present-day theological circles, it may have a variety of meanings; but as used in *Pascendi* (Denz. 2093; Yzermans, p. 106), it indicates chiefly that type of post-Kantian thought which came to life in the writings of Schleiermacher and similar-minded men. It must be distinguished from such uses of the word "liberal" as would indicate the opposite of "conservative," as well as from the "liberalism" spoken of in some other nineteenth-century writings, such as those of Newman. In his *Lectures on the Prophetical Office of the Church* (1837), Newman uses the word "liberalism" to refer more properly to deism or eighteenth-century rationalism rather than the type of philosophic thought discussed in the *Pascendi*. (Cf Romuald A. Dibble, *John Henry Newman: The Concept of Infallible Doctrinal Authority* [Washington, D. C.: Catholic University of America Press, 1955], *passim*.) This is another of the many examples of the same word meaning many different things theologically.
25. Cf. Dillenberger-Welch, *Protestant Christianity*, p. 182; McNeill, *The History and Character of Calvinism*, p. 406.
26. *CL*, VII, 528, d (note 2).
27. Felix Flückiger, *Philosophie und Theologie bei Schleiermacher* (Zollikon-Zürich: Evangelischer Verlag, 1947), p. 9.
28. *Ibid.*, pp. 9–17, 174 ff.
29. Brandt, *The Philosophy of Schleiermacher*, p. 261.
30. Friedrich D. E. Schleiermacher, *The Christian Faith*, trans. Mackintosh and Steward (Edinburgh: Clark, 1928), p. 44 (No. 10, 1). Cited simply as *The Christian Faith* hereafter.
31. *The Christian Faith*, p. 45.
32. Schleiermacher, *Werke*, Part One, II, 586: in Brandt, *The Philosophy of Schleiermacher*, p. 280.
33. Cf. Flückiger, *Philosophie . . .* , p. 184; Brandt, *The Philosophy of Schleiermacher*, pp. 4–5.
34. Brandt, *The Philosophy of Schleiermacher*, p. 217 ff.
35. Dillenberger-Welch, *Protestant Christianity*, p. 159.
36. Friedrich D. E. Schleiermacher, *On Religion: Speeches to its Cultured Despisers*, trans. John Oman (London: Kegan Paul, Tranch, Trübner, 1893), pp. 12–13. Cited simply as *On Religion* hereafter.
37. *On Religion*, p. 14.
38. *Ibid.*
39. *Ibid.*
40. *Ibid.*, p. 15.
41. *Ibid.*, p. 18.
42. *Ibid.*, p. 27. (Italics ours.)
43. *Ibid.*, p. 31.
44. *Ibid.*, p. 33.

45. *Ibid.*, p. 36.
46. *Ibid.*, 1 ed.: in the Oman translation, pp. 278, 277.
47. Cf. Brandt, *The Philosophy of Schleiermacher*, pp. 155, 175 ff.
48. *Ibid.*, p. 313.
49. Oman, "Introduction" to his translation of *On Religion, p. xliii.* (Italics ours.)
50. Brandt, *The Philosophy of Schleiermacher*, p. 179. (Italics ours.)
51. *Ibid.*, p. 180.
52. Flückiger, *Philosophie* . . ., p. 121.
53. *Ibid.*, p. 126.
54. *Ibid.*, p. 128.
55. *Ibid.*, p. 125.
56. *The Christian Faith*, p. 612 (No. 133, 1).
57. Dillenberger-Welch, *Protestant Christianity*, p. 189.
58. *The Christian Faith*, p. 5 (No. 3, 1).
59. *Ibid.*, p. 12 (No. 4).
60. *Ibid.*, p. 18 (No. 5).
61. *Ibid.*, p. 26 (No 6).
62. *Ibid.*, p. 37 (No. 8, 4).
63. *Ibid.*
64. *Ibid.*, p. 38. (No. 8, 4).
65. *Ibid.*
66. *Ibid.*, p. 52 (No. 11).
67. *Ibid.*, p. 68 (No. 14).
68. *Ibid.*, p. 52 (No. 11, 1). (Italics ours.)
69. *Ibid.*, p. 53 (No. 11, 1).
70. *Ibid.*, p. 76 (No. 15). (Italics ours.)
71. Flückiger, *Philosophie* . . ., p. 128.
72. *The Christian Faith*, p. 88 (No. 19).
73. *Ibid.*, p. 89 (No. 19, 2).
74. *Ibid.*
75. *Ibid.*
76. *Ibid.*, p. 89 (No. 19, 1).
77. *Ibid.*, p. 90 (No. 19, 3).
78. *Ibid.*, p. 677 (No. 148, 2).
79. *Ibid.*, p. 678 (No. 149, 1).
80. *Ibid.*, p. 690 (No. 154, 2).
81. *Ibid.*, p. 90 (No. 19, 3).
82. *Ibid.*
83. *Ibid.*, p. 690 (No. 154, 2).
84. *Ibid.*
85. *Ibid.*, p. 691 (No. 154, 2).
86. *Ibid.*
87. *Ibid.*, p. 593 (No. 128, 3).
88. *Ibid.*, p. 593 (No. 128, 2).
89. *Ibid.*, p. 594 (No. 129).
90. *Ibid.*, p. 50 (No. 10, postscript).
91. *Ibid.*, p. 594 (No. 129, 1).
92. *Ibid.*, p. 595 (No. 129, 1).
93. *Ibid.*, p. 596 (No. 129, 2).
94. *Ibid.*
95. *Ibid.*

96. Flückiger, *Philosophie* . . ., p. 98.
97. Dillenberger-Welch, *Protestant Christianity*, p. 188.
98. *Ibid.*, p. 196.
99. Cf. below, p. 175.
100. Cf. Dillenberger-Welch, *Protestant Christianity*, pp. 217 ff.
101. Denz. 2001 ff. (Yzermans, p. 223, no 1 ff.). — *DS* 3401 ff.
102. Denz. 2009, 2011 (Yzermans, p. 224, no. 9, 11).
103. Denz. 2012 (Yzermans, p. 224, no. 12).
104. Denz. 2020 (Yzermans, p. 225, no. 20).
105. Denz. 2021 (Yzermans, p. 225, no. 21).
106. Denz. 2027 (Yzermans, p. 225, no. 27).
107. Denz. 2054 (Yzermans, p. 227, no. 54).
108. Denz. 2062 (Yzermans, p. 228, no. 62).
109. Denz. 2065 (Yzermans, p. 228, no. 65).
110. Cf. above, pp. 115–119.
111. Dillenberger-Welch, *Protestant Christianity*, p. 274. Cf. also p. 255 ff.
112. Cf. Flückiger, *Philosophie* . . ., p. 185.
113. Cf. Karl Barth, "Schleiermacher," in *Die Theologie und die Kirche: Gesammelte Vorträge* (Zollikon, 1930); *Die protestantische Theologie in 19. Jahrhundert* (Zollikon-Zurich, 1947).
114. *The Christian Faith*, p. 67 (No. 13, postscript).
115. Cf. Brandt, *The Philosophy of Schleiermacher*, Appendix II: "Schleiermacher and Hegel," pp. 322–326.
116. Gustave Weigel, "A Survey of Protestant Theology in Our Day," *Proceedings: CTSA*, 1953 (Yonkers, N. Y.: St. Joseph Seminary), p. 59.
117. *Ibid.*, p. 52.
118. H. Richard Niebuhr, "Reformation: Continuing Imperative," *The Christian Century*, 77 (March 2, 1960), 249, 250.
119. Cf. Nels F. S. Ferre, *Searchlights on Contemporary Theology* (New York: Harper & Brothers, 1961), pp. 89–91.

CHAPTER VI: HISTORICAL METHOD

1. G. J. Garraghan, *A Guide to Historical Method* (New York: Fordham University Press, 1946), p. 33. (Italics ours.)
2. As we noted above (p. 109) the dogmatic theologian, no less than the Scripture scholar, must also avoid detaching the various conciliar and papal decrees from the specific historic milieu which brought them forth. Cf. Paul VI, *Mysterium Fidei*: "The Church, with the long labor of centuries and, not without the help of the Holy Spirit, has established a rule of language and confirmed it with the authority of the councils . . . [which formulas] express concepts which are not tied to a certain form of human culture, nor to a specific phase of human culture, nor to one or other theological school."
3. Cf. Henri-Irénée Marrou, *De la connaissance historique*, 4 ed. (Paris: Éditions du Seuil, 1962), p. 48.
4. *Ibid.*, p. 89.
5. *Ibid.*, p. 60 ff. — As Marrou rightly holds (p. 279) "research is of itself indefinite, historical truth is never definitive, it is always still becoming. . . ."

6. Garraghan, *A Guide to Historical Method*, p. 33. — It is for this reason that Marrou *(De la connaissance historique*, p. 32) defines history as "la connaissance du passé humain," placing the emphasis upon the process of knowledge: "Nous dirons *connaissance* et non pas, comme d'autres, 'recherche' ou étude (bien que ce sens d' 'enquête' soit le sense premier du mot grec ἱστορία), car c'est confondre la fin et les moyens; ce qui importe c'est le résultat atteint par la recherche: nous ne la poursuivrions pas si elle ne devait pas aboutir; l'histoire se définit par la vérité qu'elle se montre capable d'élaborer."

7. Cf. R. P. Phillips, *Modern Thomistic Philosophy* (Westminster, Md.: Newman, 1935: reprint), II, 3: "This study [epistemology] has only come into great prominence, in its entirety, in modern times; for though there have always been men who doubted the possibility of arriving at certainty, and discussed this question, it is far from clear that, as is sometimes maintained, they approach it by the modern road, viz. by critical examination of the validity of our knowledge of the extra-mental world. It certainly seems that attention was first definitely concentrated on this question by the enquiries of Kant."

8. McNeill, *The History and Character of Calvinism*, p. 40.

9. *Ibid.*, p. 75.

10. *Ibid.*, p. 142.

11. Bainton, *Here I Stand*, pp. 256–264, 266–267, 319, 375–378.

12. *Ibid.*, pp. 257–258.

13. These terms refer to the tendency of seventeenth-century Protestantism to make the various Protestant Creeds the norm for the interpretation of the Bible. Cf. Dillenberger-Welch, *Protestant Christianity*, p. 97.

14. Cf. P. Godet, "Érasme," *DTC*, V, 1, 389.

15. We ought not ask too much nor be too critical of these manuals; they serve a purpose, even though they are not intended to be flying wedges of theological investigation. As Karl Rahner reminds us *(Schriften zur Theologie*, I, 10): "Die Schulbücher sind — Schulbücher. . . . Es ist aus dem Wesen der katholischen Glaubenswissenschaft heraus und durch ihre Absicht, sich an Theologen zu wenden, die die Lehre der Kirche zum erstenmal gründlich studieren wollen, gegeben, dass solche katholische Schulbücher nicht den Ehrgeiz haben dürfen, um jeden, Preis 'originell' zu sein." As he also indicates, they can be improved and need not be mere repetitions of past attempts, but their primary function will still remain the same at heart. John Courtney Murray sets forth a similar practical conclusion: "The Thesis Form as an Instrument of Theological Instruction," *Proceedings: CTSA* (1956), p. 224: "Fourth, given the ordinary limitations of time, and the hardly less ordinary limitations of knowledge, to which the teacher is subject, the best hope would seem to be that the teacher should intersperse pieces of genuine theologizing with stretches of what really amounts only to indoctrination in theses."

16. Cf. Engelbert Klüpfel, *Institutiones theologiae dogmaticae* (Wien, 1789), I, c. 53 (p. 104, A. 3). It would be useful to know more about the meaning of the phrase *Patres* at the Council of Trent, particularly the phrase "contra unanimen consensum Patrum" *(DS* 1507). The first *Patrologies* appeared only in the seventeenth century, so that we might question if the Tridentine phrase had the meaning given to it later, indicating a unanimous consent of the Fathers of the Church associated with the study of patrology. Could it have meant simply the teaching of the *bishops* in

earlier centuries? This would seem to be a better understanding; it would refer actually to the living tradition itself, in that function of it which is proper to the magisterium.

17. Cf. Geiselmann, "Das Konzil von Trient . . .," in Schmaus, *Die mündliche Überlieferung*, p. 183.
18. *Ibid.*, p. 188 ff.
19. Erich Przywara, *Analogia Entis: Metaphysik. I. Prinzip* (Munich: Josef Kösel & Friedrich Pustet, 1932), p. 41.
20. Jacques Maritain, *Education at the Crossroads* (New Haven: Yale University Press, 1943), p. 74.
21. Cf. Etienne Gilson, *God and Philosophy* (New Haven: Yale University Press, 1941), p. 105, note 32.
22. *Ibid.*, p. 106.
23. Cf. Gerald R. Cragg, *The Church and the Age of Reason* (Baltimore: Penguin Books, 1960), p. 76.
24. Theodore M. Greene, "Introduction" to Immanuel Kant, *Religion Within the Limits of Reason Alone* (New York: Harper Torchbooks, 1960), p. ix.
25. A more complete outline of Butler's views is to be found in the Appendix (p. 257 ff.), and his influence on later religious thought is the subject matter for Chapter VII.
26. Joseph Butler, *The Analogy of Religion, Natural and Revealed, to the Constitution and Course of Nature* (1736), II, 6, 11 (in W. E. Gladstone, ed., *The Works of Joseph Butler, D.C.L.*, [Oxford: Clarendon Press, 1896], I, 285). — We will cite from this edition throughout; the numbers given in parentheses indicate the volume and page in the Gladstone edition (the text of the Analogy is found in Vol. I, 1–383). Thus the present citation: *Analogy*, II, 6, 11 (I, 285).
27. *Analogy*, II, 6, 11 (I, 285).
28. It would be extremely helpful to have a detailed investigation of the way in which the use of the Bible as a purely historical work was introduced into the realm of Christian thought in the manner so frequently accepted in the past few centuries. Above all, a worthwhile investigation might be made into the influence of these rationalist debates on the development of the historicorational argument associated with much of Catholic apologetics and the "more recent" theory of faith discussed in Chapter III. At present we have many varied indications of what this influence was, but we do need a more definitive study of the question.
29. Cf. below, pp. 224–229.
30. *Analogy*, I, Intro., 4 (I, 5).
31. Cf. below, pp. 233–238.
32. J. M. Levasseur sums up the general conclusions thus: *Le lieu théologique "histoire"* (Trois-Rivières: Éditions du bien public, 1960), p. 166: "Mais, si l'histoire peut avoir d'une certain façon tous les degrés de certitude comme tous les degrés de probabilité, il faut reconnaître que la certitude propre à l'histoire est la certitude morale, c'est-à-dire une certitude qui, bien qu'elle n'exclut pas toute possibilité du contraire, en exclut cependant toute crainte prudente; et, comme l'histoire ne porte pas sur la règle des actes humains présents ou futurs, mais sur les faits passés, elle aboutit à une *certitude morale spéculative* et même *critique*, parce qu'une telle certitude arrive au terme de la critique historique." Cf. this entire section, pp. 158–166; see also Garraghan, *A Guide to Historical Method*, p. 74 ff.;

Marrou, *De la connaissance historique,* pp. 116–117, 133–136; Martin C. D'Arcy, *The Meaning and Matter of History* (New York: Meridian Books, 1961), p. 46. D'Arcy notes (p. 61) his general agreement with Marrou on the purpose of historical research and the certitude it engenders, despite a slight difference in their respective approaches.

33. Garraghan, *A Guide to Historical Method,* p. 76. — He adduces the principle of sufficient reason to explain the reduction of historical certitude to metaphysical certitude: "The alleged historical fact A is reported by several independent witnesses. But their agreement cannot possibly be explained except by the objective truth of the fact reported (principle of sufficient reason). Consequently the alleged fact A is metaphysically certain." Without adopting a completely skeptical attitude, we might ask if this is not pushing the principle of sufficient reason too far. Do we, after all, actually have anything more than moral certitude as to the truth of the statement that such agreement of independent witnesses must be true? It hardly seems that we could.

34. Cf. A. Molien, "Richard Simon," *DTC,* XIV, 2, 2094–2118; Jean Steinmann, *Richard Simon et les origenes de l'exegèse biblique* (Bruges: Desclée de Brouwer, 1960).

35. Cf. G. Raveau, "Spinoza," *DTC,* XIV, 2, 2501–2503.

36. John M'Clintock and James Strong (ed.), *Cyclopaedia of Biblical, Theological and Ecclesiastical Literature* (New York: Harper & Brothers, 1881), III, 1019. Also Remigius Bäumer, "Hugo Grotius," *LThK,* 2 ed., *IV,* 1243–1244.

37. Cragg, *The Church and the Age of Reason,* pp. 48–49; cf. also Friedrich Maliske, "Pierre Bayle," *LThK,* 2 ed., II, 81–82.

38. Cf. Pius XII, "Discours au Xeme congrés international des sciences historiques" (Sept. 7, 1955), *AAS,* 47 (1965), 682: "Il n'existe pas de science, du moins pas de science positive, que se passe réelement de présupposés. Chacune postule au moins certaines lois de l'être et de la pensée, qu'elle utilse pour se constituer Si au lieu de dire: 'libre de présupposés,' on avait dit 'impartiale'! Que la science dans sa poursuite de la vérité ne se laisse pas influencer par des considérations subjectives — voilà une proposition su) laquelle tous auraient pu tomber d'accord." Cf. also Rudolf Bultmann, "Ist voraussetzungslose Exegese möglich?" *Theologische Zeitschrift,* 13 (1957), 409–417.

39. Cf. Marrou, *De la connaissance historique,* pp. 13–14, 97.

40. *Ibid.,* p. 13.

41. Cf. Francis J. McCool, "The Preacher and the Historical Witness of the Gospels," *TS,* 21 (1960), 531, note 21: "These hypotheses are composed of a series of prejudgments which express the best solution which the previous study of the history has uncovered for the various problems of the Gospel texts. Inasmuch as they are *judgments,* these solutions are firmly held, because a great number of individual texts converge to support them. Inasmuch as they are *pre*judgments, which have been made antecedently to and independently of the detailed analysis of the text under investigation . . . these solutions are considered to be highly probable but not definitive. They have enough support in the Gospel texts to provide a reasonable starting point for serious investigation. However, the historian is ready to modify them, or to abandon them in part or *in toto,* if further study of his texts imposes either of these decisions on him."

42. Paul Tillich, *Systematic Theology* (Chicago: University of Chicago Press, 1951), II, 113. — Reinhold Niebuhr expresses a similar concern in his

evaluation of Catholic belief in *Faith and History* (New York: Charles Scribner's Sons, 1949), p. 170: "If the truth of faith merely becomes a 'fact' of history, attested by a miracle, or validated by ecclesiastical authority, it no longer touches the soul profoundly. If it is made into a truth of reason which is validated by its coherence with a total system of rational coherence, it also loses its redemptive power."

43. Cf. above, pp. 115–116.
44. Denz. 2099 (Yzermans, pp. 111, 112).
45. Cf. Edward F. Siegman, "Teaching in Parables," *CBQ*, 23 (1961), 164; "Form Critics refer to this as the 'life-situation' of the pericope (*Sitz im Leben*). So far no one would quarrel with them. But all too often they resorted to the *Sitz im Leben* to account for not merely the *preservation* of certain deeds and sayings of Our Lord, but for the *creation* of these incidents by the 'primitive community' to justify the existing situation. Thus, the Caesarea Philippi incident is created to vindicate Peter's exercise of authority in the early Church." — In note 7, he cites Rudolf Bultmann, *Die Geschichte der synoptischen Tradition*, 3 ed. (Göttingen: Vandenhoeck and Ruprecht, 1957), pp. 147–150, 156, as one of those writers who would place Mt 16:18–19 among the sayings "created by the community." — Cf. also Lang, *Die Sendung Christi*, p. 184.
46. Pius XII, "Discours au Xᵉᵐᵉ congrès international des sciences historiques," *AAS*, 47 (1955), 673.
47. Cf. Greene, "Introduction" to Kant, *Religion Within the Limits of Reason Alone*, p. xxix, note 1.
48. Cf. above, pp. 33–38.
49. Kant, *Reason* . . . , Book Three, V (p. 98).
50. *Ibid.*, Title (p. 94).
51. *Ibid.*, Book Two, B (p. 56); cf. also General Observations, p. 79.
52. *Ibid.*, Book Three, Division Two (p. 120); cf. also Book Four, Part Two, 3 (p. 169).
53. *Ibid.*, Book Four, Part One, Section Two (pp. 151, 152).
54. *Ibid.*, Book Three, VI (p. 105).
55. *Ibid.*, Book Four, Part Two, 4 (p. 175).
56. Albert Schweitzer, *The Quest of the Historical Jesus*, trans. W. Montgomery (New York: Macmillan Paperbacks, 1961), p. 10. — Schweitzer's own position in regard to the divinity of Jesus is obvious from his own statement (p. 3): "This dogma had first to be shattered before men could once more go out in quest of the historical Jesus, before they could even grasp the thought of His existence. That the historic Jesus is something different from the Jesus Christ of the doctrine of the Two Natures seems to us now self-evident."
57. An interesting summary of Renan's approach can be found in Eugene J. Ahern, "Ernest Renan: The Man and his Work," *AER*, 143 (1960), 361–375.
58. McCool, in *TS*, 21 (1960), 525. Schweitzer had formulated the same conclusion in regard to disproving the historicity of Mark as did others: *The Quest of the Historical Jesus*, p. 330: ". . . so it is again now, when, retaining the assumption of the priority of Mark, the historicity of the hitherto accepted view of the life of Jesus, based upon the Marcan narrative, is called in question."
59. Rudolf Bultmann, *Jesus and the Word*, trans. L. P. Smith and E. H. Lantero (New York: Charles Scribner's Sons, 1958), pp. 8–9. Cf also Lengsfeld, *Überlieferung*, p. 247: "Man wird beim Studium Bultmanns den

Eindruck nicht los, als wäre Christus Jesus für ihn im Grunde nur ein Mensch, durch den Gott zwar spricht und handelt, der aber nicht selbst göttliche Person in menschlicher Daseinsweise (Natur) genannt werden kann." Bultmann's concern for the message alone, and his disregard of *who* proclaims that message is, for Lengsfeld, the source of the greatest confusion in Bultmann's thought.

60. Myles M. Bourke, "Review of Ernst Fuchs, *Zur Frage nach dem historischen Jesus*," *TS*, 23 (1962), 277–278, has this interesting comment: "The correspondence [of the kerygma with the words and conduct of Jesus] will be principally on what J. M. Robinson calls 'the deeper level of meaning' below the 'terminological level' (cf. *A New Quest of the Historical Jesus* [Naperville, 1959] p. 120). For when the expressions used in the kerygma are found in the Gospels on Jesus' lips, there rises the well-nigh insoluble problem of whether they represent what Jesus said, or what the early Church attributed to Him. But from the Gospel material which bears least terminological resemblance to the Christian kerygma it is possible to find that Jesus' understanding of His own existence corresponds to the understanding of existence which is found in the kerygmatic formulas. Thus, the historical Jesus may be encountered in the Gospels via modern historiography, as opposed to that of the nineteenth and early twentieth centuries. . . . The purpose of the new quest is not to prove that the kerygma is true but to 'test the validity of the kerygma's identification of *its* understanding of existence with *Jesus'* existence' (so Robinson, *op. cit.*, p. 94)." A valuable discussion of this question, indicating the direction that might be followed in the construction of apologetic tracts in the future, can be found in Franz Mussner, "The Historical Jesus and the Christ of Faith," in Vorgrimler, *Dogmatic vs. Biblical Theology*, 197–239.

61. David Friedrich Strauss, *The Life of Jesus, Critically Examined* (1835), trans. M. Evans (New York: Calvin Blanchard, 1860), I, 28.

62. *Ibid.*, I, 21–22. (Italics ours.)

63. *Ibid.*, I, 32.

64. *Ibid.*, I, 35. — Karl A. Hase, *Das Leben Jesu zunächst für akademische Studien* (1829), had also rejected what he called the "legends of the Childhood." Cf. Schweitzer, *The Quest of the Historical Jesus*, p. 60.

65. Strauss, *The Life of Jesus*, I, 65–66. He cites the Midrash Koheleth, f. 73, 3 (in Schöttgen, *Horae hebraicae et talmudicae*, 2, p. 251 ff.), singling out such comparisons between Moses and the Messiah as these: Ex 4:20: "So Moses took his wife and his sons, and started back to the land of Egypt with them riding the ass"; and Za 9:9: "See, your king shall come to you; a just savior is he, meek, and riding on an ass. . . ." — Ex 16:4: "I will now rain down bread from heaven for you"; and Ps 72 (71): 16: "May there be an abundance of grain upon the earth. . . ." — So also, just as Moses brought forth water from a rock (Ex 17:6), so the Messiah: Jl 4:18: "A fountain shall issue from the house of the lord, to water the Valley of Sattim." — Strauss also discusses *Tanchuma*, f. 54, 4 (in Schöttgen, p. 74).

66. Strauss, *The Life of Jesus*, I, 66–67.

67. *Ibid.*, I, 76.

68. Schweitzer emphasizes this point when speaking of Schleiermacher: *The Quest of the Historical Jesus*, p. 67: "On these premises it is possible to write a Life of Christ; it is not possible to write a life of Jesus. It is, therefore, not by accident that Schleiermacher regularly speaks, not of Jesus, but of Christ."

69. Cf. Heinrich Fries, "Mythos und Offenbarung," in Feiner, *et al.*, *Fragen der Theologie Heute*, pp. 11–19; Jean Danielou, "La démythisation dans l'école d'Alexandrie," in *Il problema della demitizzazione* (Padua: Cedam, 1961), pp. 45–49.

70. Cf. Strauss, *The Life of Jesus*, I, 39.

71. Adolf Harnack, *What is Christianity?* trans. T. B. Saunders (New York: Harper Torchbooks, 1957), p. 51.

72. *Ibid.*, p. 6.

73. Alfred Loisy, *The Gospel and the Church*, trans. C. Home (New York: Charles Scribner's Sons, 1909), pp. 6, 4.

74. *Ibid.*, p. 6.

75. *Ibid.*, p. 7.

76. *Ibid.*, p. 8.

77. *Ibid*

78. *Ibid.*, p. 9.

79. *Ibid.*, pp. 17–18.

80. Pius XII, *Mystici corporis Christi* (1943) and *Mediator Dei* (1947).

81. A good example of this would be the use by Vatican I (*DS* 3005) in its decree on the knowledge of God by reason of those arguments and terms proposed by Thomas Aquinas in the *Summa:* cf. above, Chap. 1. Another example would be the use of the words of Peter Lombard regarding the doctrine of the Trinity in the definition of IV Lateran (*DS* 803).

82. *DS* 3886 (N.C.W.C. ed. par. 21).

83. *Ibid.*

84. We have a good example of this in the discussions concerning the proper meaning of the Tridentine decree on Scripture and tradition: cf. above, Chap. 4; or the analysis of the "purpose of creation" as defined by Vatican I: cf. Philip J. Donnelly, "The Vatican Council and the End of Creation," *TS*, 4 (1943), 3–33.

85. Cf. above, pp. 100–102. — There are those who speak of a "one source theory," but it would seem better to describe it as a "unified source theory," in that Scripture and tradition are distinct elements, but there is an intimate union, an interpenetration, as it were, of the two. It is only in conjunction with tradition, therefore, that Catholic theologians will defend the statement today that "All truths necessary for salvation are somehow contained in Scripture."

86. *DS* 3886 (N.C.W.C. ed., par. 21); he goes on to explain: "For together with the sources of positive theology God has given to His Church a living Teaching Authority to elucidate and explain what is contained in the deposit of faith only obscurely and implicitly."

87. *DS* 3887 (N.C.W.C. ed., par. 22).

88. Yves J.-M. Congar, *Vraie et fausses reforme dans l'église* (Paris: Éditions du Cerf, 1950), p. 498; cf. also Charles Journet, *Esquisse du développement du dogme marial* (Paris: Alsatia, 1954), p. 33 ff.

89. Congar, *Vraie et fausses reforme*, p. 499.

90. Cf. Ebeling, *Wort und Glaube*, esp. pp. 3, 36, 74, 87.

91. It is assuredly in this sense that the words of Pius XII in the definition of the Assumption of the Blessed Mother must be understood: *DS* 3900: "All these proofs and considerations of the holy Fathers and the theologians [concerning the doctrine of the Assumption] are based upon the Sacred Writings as their ultimate foundation (Sacris Litteris tamquam ultimo fundamento nituntur)." There is no clear reference to

the Assumption in Scripture, but it is not for that reason an "unscriptural" dogma. The "starting points" would go back first to the doctrine of original sin, whereby (as stressed in Rom 5) two things came into the world: sin and death. The redemptive activity of Christ was directed at triumphing over sin and death, and He did so chiefly by His passion, resurrection, and ascension. Scripture, as Pius XII goes on to point out, always portrays Mary as most intimately joined to her Son in the divine plan. In this way, it directed the Church toward an understanding of Mary's unique privileges. Like all of mankind, she also was to share in Christ's victory, but she did so in a more profound manner. Through the Immaculate Conception she was redeemed by Christ, triumphing over sin by His power; and through the Assumption she triumphed over death, again through Christ. In this Mary is the model of the Church, whose members are also called to triumph over sin and enter heaven, triumphing even over death at the day of the final resurrection of mankind at the Second Coming of Christ. Thus, in the unfolding and clarification of this dogma, it was neither Scripture nor tradition alone, which was at work, but the combination of the two; they were intended to complement one another in this fashion. This is true even of seemingly explicit scriptural statements. *Hoc est enim corpus meum* would, on the surface, seem clear enough, but the debates between Lutheran and Zwinglian parties (as to whether *est* means "is" or "represents") showed the need of some extra-scriptural authority to settle definitively even such an apparently simply question.

92. Vignon, *De virtutibus*, p. 233.
93. Charles Davis, "Faith and Reason," in John J. Heaney (ed.), *Faith, Reason, and the Gospels* (Westminster, Md.: Newman, 1961), p. 16. — Cf. above, pp. 70–75, for a more detailed discussion of this subject.
94. Herve, *Manuale theologiae dogmaticae*, III, 335 (no. 316).
95. E.g., the condemnation of the teachings of Hermes (*DS* 2738), and Günther (*DS* 2829).
96. *DS* 1553.
97. Denz. 3493–3498.
98. Marrou, *De la connaissance historique*, p. 108. Marrou also points out p. 107) the nature of the documents in question: "The Gospels are not a direct testimony concerning the life of Christ; they are a primary document, and one of incomparable value, concerning the primitive Christian community. We do not encounter Christ except through this image which His disciples fashioned of Him. This is not to say that this image is deceptive, even though it is not that which the historian of events might wish that it had been." — Cf. also the statement of Bourke above (note 60) concerning "the well-nigh insoluble problem of whether they [the words in Scripture] represent what Jesus said, or what the early Church attributed to Him."
99. Cf. above, p. 80. — This view also stresses the importance of not confusing revelation and inspiration. The inspired books record that which was revealed, but it would seem that they rarely constitute that revelation itself; the revelation existed in the oral tradition before the books were written. Linked to this is Deneffe's useful distinction between *constitutive* and *continuative* tradition. The first refers to the apostolic era of the Church, in which period the whole deposit of revelation was given to mankind and entrusted to the guardianship of the Church; it was entirely constituted at

that time, and nothing more can later be added nor anything taken away. The Church in successive centuries (*living tradition,* understood not merely as the magisterium but as the entire Christian community, one in faith and preaching) is to continue this faith and teaching: hence the phrase *continuative* tradition in regard to later generations. — Cf. Deneffe, *Traditionsbegriff,* p. 126; Murphy, *The Notion of Tradition,* pp. 47, 253, note 11; Geiselmann, *Die heilige Schrift,* p. 15 ff., as well as our review of this work: *TS,* 24 (1963), 484–490.

100. Cf. above, pp. 30, 54, 76–77.
101. Vincent Lerins, *Commonitorium: RJ,* 2168.
102. Cf. Vignon, *De virtutibus,* p. 214 ff.
103. Cf. Hermain Lais, "Apologetik," *LThK,* 2 ed., I, 723.
104. Cf. above. pp. 61–69.
105. Phillips, *Modern Thomistic Philosophy,* II, 13. — Cf. below, pp. 247–251.
106. *EB,* 4 ed., 116 (Italics ours.)
107. *EB,* 118–123.
108. Cf. Murphy, *AER,* 150 (1964), 385–404; 151 (1964), 21–40.
109. Cf. above, note 42.
110. Cf. below, pp. 252–255.
111. Rudolf Bultman, "Introduction" to Harnack, *What is Christianity?* (Harper Torchbooks, 1957), pp. xv–xvi.
112. 1 Cor 13:12; Heb 1:1–2.

CHAPTER VII: BISHOP BUTLER

1. Matthew Spinka, *Christian Thought from Erasmus to Berdyaev* (New York: Prentice-Hall, 1962), p. 82.
2. Cf. Ernest Campbell Mossner, *Bishop Butler and the Age of Reason* (New York: Macmillan, 1936), for a lengthy list of biographical references in regard to Butler. Also: R. Adamson, "Joseph Butler," in *Encyclopaedia Brittanica,* 9 ed. (Boston: Little, Brown & Co., 1876), III, 582–587; W. E. Gladstone, *Studies Subsidiary to the Works of Bishop Butler* (Oxford: Clarendon Press, 1896); W. A. Spooner, *Bishop Butler* (London: Methuen & Co., 1901); Leslie Stephen, "Joseph Butler," in *The Dictionary of National Biography,* edited by L. Stephen and S. Lee (Oxford University Press, 1917 –), III, 519–524.
3. Cf. *Analogy,* I, Advertisement, 2 (I, 1). Cf. above, p. 501, n. 26.
4. Butler's *Sermons* (fifteen preached at the Rolls Chapel; six preached upon various public occasions) are found in Volume II, 1–396, of the Gladstone edition of Butler's *Works,* together with his *Charge to the Clergy of the Diocese of Durham.*
5. It is interesting for the historian of religion to note how frequently this tactic of meeting the adversary on his own grounds has led to misunderstandings and confusion, even apart from any danger of clearly heretical teaching that might result. It is the spirit of "eirenism" of which Pius XII spoke in *Humani generis,* a desire to please that leads one into defending unacceptable doctrines (*DS* 3880). In our present discussion concerning the act of faith, it seems clear that the desire to answer the objections of the

rationalists of an earlier century on their own grounds led some Catholic theologians to formulate what we have termed the "more recent" theory of faith — basically a very rationalistic explanation of the assent of faith, but one which for a time enjoyed such great favor that it supplanted the older Thomist-Suarezian explanation in large areas of theological thought, only to be greatly lamented by the theologians of our own century. Thus too the "liberal" views of one generation become the "antiquated" teachings of the next.

6. A more detailed discussion of Butler's complete argument in the *Analogy* is given in the Appendix to this volume, pp. 257–275.
7. *Analogy*, I, Intro., 4 (I, 5).
8. Cf. *ibid.*, II, 6, 2 (I, 277); 7, 1 (I, 302).
9. *Ibid.*, 7, 60 (I, 350–351).
10. Cf. the remarks of Tillich above, pp. 173–174.
11. *Analogy*, II, 7, 2 (I, 303).
12. *Ibid.*, 33 (I, 330); cf. also 8, 25 (I, 368): ". . . it is obvious, that Christianity and the proof of it, are both historical."
13. *Ibid.*, 7, 45 (I, 340); cf. 33–39 (I, 330–337) for his longer description of this "scripture-history."
14. *Ibid.*, 3 (I, 304).
15. *Ibid.*, 3–7 (I, 304–309).
16. *Ibid.*, 10–21 (I, 312–320).
17. *Ibid.*, 22 ff. (I, 320).
18. *Ibid.*, 32 (I, 330); 1, 16 (I, 196); 1, 4 (I, 188); 4 (I, 242–252); 1, 18 (I, 197); 1, 17 (I, 197); etc.
19. *Ibid.*, 8, 14 (I, 361).
20. *Ibid.*: "Then, fourthly, though objections against the reasonableness of the system of religion cannot indeed be answered without entering into consideration of its reasonableness; yet objections against the credibility or truth of it may. Because the system of it is reducible into what is properly matter of fact: and the truth, the probable truth, of facts, may be shown without consideration of their reasonableness." — By "facts," in this instance, Butler means the doctrine as stated: II, 8, 13 (I, 360): ". . . for instance again, the fact last mentioned, that God will reward and punish men for their actions hereafter. . . ." Such doctrines as the Trinity or the Incarnation would also be considered simply as "facts." The acceptance of them (the assent of faith) rests purely on one's perception of the probative force of the various proofs which attest to the truth of these "facts."
21. *Ibid.*, II, 7, 50 (I, 343).
22. *Ibid.*
23. *Ibid.*, 1, 19 (I, 198).
24. Mossner, *Bishop Butler*, p. 166.
25. John Wesley, *Journal*, ed. Nehemiah Curnock, II, 256–257 n., in Mossner, *Bishop Butler*, p. 166.
26. John Wesley, "Sermon: June 11, 1738," in Mossner, *Bishop Butler*, p. 170.
27. *Analogy*, II, 7, 6 (I, 307).
28. *Ibid.*, 2, 6 (I, 213).
29. *Ibid.*, 3, 3 (I, 223).
30. Mossner, *Bishop Butler*, p. 233.
31. *DS* 3009; so also Pius XII, *Humani generis: DS* 3876.
32. Cf. above, pp. 66–67.
33. Cf. above, pp. 49–52.

34. Cf. *Analogy*, II, Concl., 15 (I, 380); 3, 28 (I, 240); 7, 62 (I, 352); 7, 60 (I, 350); 7, 9 (I, 359); 7, 30 (I, 328).
35. Cf. *ibid.*, 6, 2 (I, 277); 6, 10 (I, 284); 7, 1 (I, 302); 7, 59 (I, 350); 7, 60 (I, 350–351); 8, 9 (I, 359).
36. *Charge to the Clergy of Durham* 11 (II, 404); cf. also *Fifteen Sermons*, No. 15, 10 (II, 266); *Six Sermons*, No. 1, 16 (II, 290).
37. *Six Sermons*, No. 5, 9 (II, 367).
38. *Ibid.*, 11 (II, 369).
39. Søren Kierkegaard, *Training in Christianity*, p. 98.
40. *Analogy*, II, 6, 11 (I, 285). It is not difficult to perceive the skepticism implied in many of Butler's statements, such as in *Analogy*, II, Concl., 17 (I, 381): "It is certain, that doubting implies a degree of evidence for that of which we doubt; and that this degree of evidence as really lays us under obligations as demonstrative evidence."
41. Mossner, *Bishop Butler*, p. 186.
42. *Ibid.*, p. 205.
43. *Ibid.*, p. 227, n. 67; p. 225.
44. John Locke, *Essays on Human Understanding*, Book IV, chap. 15, 1 (cf. *The Works of John Locke*, printed for J. Johnson *et al.* [London, 1801], III, 88–89). This emphasis upon external "proof" in relationship to probable evidence is clearly reflected in Butler.
45. *Ibid.*, 2 (Johnson edition: III, 89).
46. *Ibid.*, 3 (III, 89).
47. *Ibid.*
48. *Ibid.*, 15, 2 (III, 89); IV, 16, 6–9 (III, 96–98).
49. This thought is reflected in Butler as well. Cf. *Analogy*, I, Intro., 1 (I, 3): "Probable evidence is essentially distinguished from demonstrative by this, that it admits of degrees, and of all variety of them, from the highest moral certainty, to the very lowest presumption."
50. Locke, *Essay on Human Understanding*, IV, 15, 5 (III, 90).
51. *Ibid.*, 16, 9 (III, 98).
52. E.g., *Analogy*, II, 8, 8–9; II, Concl. 15 (I, 358, 359, 380): "For it is said that the proof of religion is involved in such inextricable difficulties, as to render it doubtful; and that it cannot be supposed, that, if it were true, it would be left upon doubtful evidence. . . . Now the observation, that, from the natural constitution and course of things, we must *in our temporal concerns*, almost continually, and in matters of great consequence, act upon evidence of a like kind and degree to the evidence of religion, is an answer to this argument; because it shows, that it is according to the conduct and character of the Author of Nature to appoint we should act upon evidence like to that. . . . And, as the force of this answer lies merely in the parallel, which there is between the evidence for religion and for our *temporal conduct;* the answer is equally just and conclusive, whether the parallel be made out, by showing the evidence of the former to be higher, or the evidence of the latter to be lower. . . . And it is so far from being the method of Providence in other cases, to afford us such overbearing evidence, as some require in proof of Christianity; that, on the contrary, the evidence upon which we are naturally appointed to act in *common matters,* throughout a very great part of life, is doubtful in a high degree." (Italics ours.)
53. Locke, *Essay on Human Understanding*, IV, 16, 3 (III, 94).

54. *Ibid.*, 16, 12, title (III, 100).
55. *Ibid.*, 16, 12 (III, 101). Locke is obviously thinking here of a "proof" of the existence of angels from the philosophical point of view; and his notion of microscopic beings reflects an earlier period of scientific development. Our concern here, however, is solely with the principles he set forth.
56. *Ibid.*, 15, 6 (III, 91).
57. *Ibid.*, 16, 14 (III, 102–103). The importance of viewing the Church as the living Body of Christ and the divinely guided magisterium as the extension of Christ's authority in time and space escaped Locke entirely. What he rejects is the teaching of any church or community, since he feels that it can represent nothing more than the purely personal and entirely human "opinions and persuasions of others." Such a detached "teaching body," quite distinct from God, however, is entirely foreign to the Catholic view of faith, but Locke perceived nothing of this approach to Christianity.
58. *Ibid.* (III, 103).
59. *Ibid.*
60. *Ibid.*, 18, 2 (III, 126).
61. *Ibid.*, 8 (III, 132).
62. Cf. above, pp. 64–65.
63. Mossner, *Bishop Butler*, p. 146.
64. William Paley, *A View of the Evidences of Christianity* (Philadelphia: Thomas Dobson, 1795), p. 436.
65. *Ibid.*, p. 412.
66. Cf. Ernest Campbell Mossner, *The Life of David Hume* (Austin, Tex.: University of Texas Press, 1954), p. 110.
67. Mossner, *Bishop Butler*, p. 157.
68. Mossner, *David Hume*, p. 112.
69. David Hume, *An Enquiry concerning Human Understanding*, ed. L. A. Selby-Biggs (Oxford: Clarendon Press, 1902), Section 6: "Of Probability," no. 46 (p. 56).
70. *Ibid.*
71. *Ibid.*, Section 10: "Of Miracles," Part 2, n. 98 (p. 127).
72. *Ibid.*
73. *Ibid.*, no. 99 (p. 127).
74. *Ibid.* (p. 128).
75. *Ibid.* (pp. 128–129); cf. Mossner, *David Hume*, p. 174.
76. Hume, *Enquiry*, Section 10, Part 2, no. 100 (p. 130).
77. *Ibid.*, Part 1, no. 86 (p. 109).
78. *Ibid.*
79. *Ibid.*, no. 87 (pp. 110, 111).
80. *Ibid.* (p. 111).
81. *Ibid.*, Part 2, no. 101 (p. 131).
82. *Ibid.*
83. *The Autobiography of John Stuart Mill*, ed. J. J. Coss (New York: Columbia University Press, 1924), p. 27.
84. *Ibid.*, p. 28.
85. Henry Tristram, "Bishop Butler's Analogy: A Persuasive to Popery," *Dublin Review*, 199 (1936), 126.
86. R. I. and S. Wilberforce, *Life of William Wilberforce* (1838), I, 89–90, 94, 95: in Mossner, *Bishop Butler*, p. 200.

87. Leonard Huxley, *Life and Letters of Thomas Henry Huxley* (New York, 1901), I, 239–240; in Mossner, *Bishop Butler*, p. 220.
88. James Martineau, *Studies of Christianity* (1858), pp. 93–94: in Mossner, *Bishop Butler*, p. 213.
89. Leslie Stephen, *History of English Thought in the Eighteenth Century* (New York: Peter Smith, 1949 reprint), I, 280.
90. *Ibid.*, 301.
91. *Ibid.*, 287, 304.
92. *Ibid.*, 303.
93. *Ibid.*, 307.
94. *Ibid.* (Italics ours.)
95. *Ibid.*, 305–306.
96. Matthew Arnold, "Bishop Butler and the Zeit-Geist," in *The Works of Matthew Arnold* (London: Macmillan, 1904), IX, 317.
97. *Ibid.*, 333.
98. *Ibid.*, 322.
99. *Ibid.*, 329.
100. *Ibid.*, 331.
101. *Ibid.*, 331–332.
102. *Ibid.*, 332–333.
103. John Henry Newman, *Apologia pro vita sua* (London: Longmans, Green and Co., 1905), chap. 1, p. 10.
104. *Ibid.*
105. *Ibid.*, p. 11.
106. Sylvester P. Juergens, *Newman on the Psychology of Faith in the Individual* (New York: Macmillan, 1928), p. 148.
107. Cf. above, pp. 65–68.
108. John Henry Newman, *Discourses to Mixed Congregations* (London: Longmans, Green and Co., 1906), p. 189.
109. John Henry Newman, *A Letter Addressed to His Grace, the Duke of Norfolk, on the Occasion of Mr. Gladstone's Recent Expostulation*, in *Difficulties of Anglicans* (London: Longmans, Green and Co., 1896), II, 312, 313.
110. Cf. Philip Flanagan, *Newman and Faith* (Rome: Universitas Gregoriana, 1945), pp. 119–138.
111. John Henry Newman, "Cardinal Newman's *Theses de fide* and his Proposed Introduction to the French Translation of the University Sermons," ed. Henry Tristram, *Gregorianum*, 18 (1937), 235 (thesis 9).
112. Henry Edward Manning, *The Grounds of Faith* (London: Burns and Oates, Ltd., 1881), Lecture 1, p. 11. Cf. a similar statement by Newman, below, note 117.
113. John Henry Newman, *Letter of February 8, 1861*, in J. Robinson, "Newman's Use of Butler's Arguments," *Downside Review*, 76 (1958), 170, n. 32.
114. John Aloysius Elbert, *Newman's Conception of Faith Prior to 1845* (Dayton, Ohio: University of Dayton, 1932), p. 73.
115. *Ibid.*, p. 57.
116. *Ibid.*, p. 74.
117. John Henry Newman, *Discussions and Arguments* (London: Longmans, Green and Co., 1899), pp. 391–392.
118. *Ibid.*
119. *DS* 3425.

120. Alfred Loisy, *Simples réflexions sur le décret du Saint-Office Lamentabili sane exitu et sur l'encyclique Pascendi dominici gregis* (Paris: Ceffonds, 1908), p. 64.

121. August Sabatier, *Outlines of a Philosophy of Religion Based on Psychology and History*, anonymous English translator (New York: James Pott & Company, 1902), Book I, chap. 2, 3 (p. 48).

122. *Ibid.*, p. 46.

123. A. Firmin (pseudonym of A. Loisy), "Les preuves et l'économie de la révélation," *Revue du clergé français*, 23 (15 mars, 1900), 140. In his book *Simple réflexions . . .* Loisy refers (p. 64) to this article as having been written by him.

124. *Ibid.*

125. *Ibid.*, p. 152.

126. *Ibid.*, p. 142. Cf. above, pp. 137–140.

127. *Ibid.*, p. 145.

128. *Ibid.*, p. 141.

129. Newman, *Apologia*, chap. 4, 2 (p. 199).

130. *Ibid.*

131. Edmond Darvil Benard, *A Preface to Newman's Theology* (St. Louis: Herder, 1945), p. 188.

132. Cf. above, pp. 196–200.

133. *DS* 1553: "Si quis dixerit, sine praeveniente Spiritus Sancti inspiratione atque eius adiutorio hominem credere, sperare et diligere aut paenitere posse, *sicut oportet,* ut ei iustificationis gratia conferatur: A.S." — As the corresponding chapter indicates (*DS* 1525), the phrase "credere . . . sicut oportet" emphasizes the total supernaturality of the act of faith. This was also the sole concern associated with the use of the phrase "sicut oportet" in II Orange's condemnation of Semipelagianism (*DS* 376, 396). Neither II Orange nor Trent was concerned with the current debate over the effect of the grace of faith on the psychological level. Billot does refer to these decrees as arguments in favor of his distinction between "scientific faith" and a saving faith; he interprets them as indicating that since there is a way of believing *sicut oportet,* it is implied that man can also make an act of "natural" or "scientific faith" which would be a true act of faith, but not a saving one. Billot surely reads more into these decrees than the historical context would allow: cf. Billot, *De virtutibus infusis,* Prolegomenon, 3: "De ratione distinctionis supernaturalium habitum," no. 1, sectio 2, p. 70.

134. The theological note attached to this statement varies, although no Catholic could safely deny the proposition. De Aldama's contention that it is *De fide divina et catholica,* at least from the ordinary magisterium, appears to be the best-founded response; cf. de Aldama, *De virtutibus infusis,* III, 754 (no. 83). Thomas Aquinas also implies a direct and unique certitude resulting from faith, entirely distinct from the certitude generated by arguments from history and reason; one of the clearest of such statements is in the *Summa,* I, q. 1, art. 5: ". . . haec [fides: sacra doctrina per revelationem] autem *certitudinem* habet *ex lumine divinae scientiae,* quae decipi non potest," and this certitude is here contrasted with that certitude "ex naturali lumine rationis humanae."

135. Cf. above, pp. 65–68, 77–79.

136. Cf. Alfaro, *De virtutibus,* p. 200.

137. *Ibid.*, p. 194.

138. *Ibid.*, p. 198.
139. Cf. *DS* 3008, 3032.
140. Cf. above, pp. 72–74.
141. Cf. above, pp. 58–59, 287, n. 3.
142. Cf. above, pp. 198–200.
143. Cf. note 99 above.
144. Cf. above, pp. 108–113.
145. Vincent T. O'Keefe, "The Gospels Read as Gospels," in Heaney, *Faith, Reason and the Gospels,* p. 241.
146. Cf. above, pp. 172–174, 182–183.
147. Cf. H. Richard Niebuhr, *The Meaning of Revelation* (New York: Macmillan Paperbacks, 1960), p. 28. A similar comment is made by Dillenberger-Welch, *Protestant Christianity,* p. 271: "For liberalism, God became essentially the counterpart of religious experience, and revelation tended to become identical with history (Ritschl) or religious experience (Schleiermacher). The primary reality, the one directly known, was religious experience. . . . The point of this is that, as it seems to more recent thought, a terrible inversion had taken place. Religion had been substituted for God."
148. This notion is not unlike the docrine of the "Instant" or "Moment" so central in the thought of Kierkegaard: that type of synthesis of time and eternity in which the believer becomes contemporaneous with Christ. Cf. above, pp. 52–53, 286, n. 71.
149. Rudolf Bultmann, "Autobiographical Reflections," in *Existence and Faith: Shorter Writings of Rudolf Bultmann,* trans. S. M. Ogden (New York: Living Age Books, 1960), p. 288.
150. *Ibid.*
151. Lengsfeld, *Überlieferung,* p. 236. Cf. also pp. 239, 244, 248.
152. Cf. above, p. 182.
153. Cf. James M. Robinson, *A New Quest of the Historical Jesus* (Naperville, Ill.: Allenson, 1959).
154. Tillich, *Systematic Theology,* II, 107.
155. *Ibid.*, 104.
156. *Ibid.*, 105.
157. *Ibid.*, 113. Cf. above, pp. 173–174.
158. *Ibid.*, 108.

APPENDIX

1. *Analogy,* I, Intro., 16, note 1 (I, 16). — Cf. chapter 6, note 26 for the manner of citing from the *Analogy of Religion.* (We have somewhat adapted Gladstone's outline to make it more complete.)
2. *Ibid.*, Advertisement, 1 (I, 1).
3. In this, Butler's position resembles greatly the teaching of Thomas Aquinas and the decree of Vatican I on the content and need of revelation: cf. above, pp. 10–17, chap. 1, No. 19 ff.
4. *Analogy,* II, 1, 25 (I, 202).
5. *Ibid.*, 5, 20 (I, 270).
6. *Ibid.*, 6, 2 (I, 277).
7. *Ibid.*, 6, 11 (I, 286).
8. *Ibid.*, 7, 1 (I, 302).

9. *Ibid.*, 7, 8 (I, 309).
10. *Ibid.*, 7, 10 (I, 312).
11. *Ibid.*, 7, 9 (I, 312).
12. *Ibid.*, 7, 20 (I, 319).
13. *Ibid.*, 7, 30 (I, 329).
14. *Ibid.*, 7, 48 (I, 341).
15. *Ibid.*, 7, 58 (I, 349).
16. *Ibid.*, 7, 59 (I, 350). Italics ours.
17. *Ibid.*, 7, 60 (I, 350).
18. *Ibid.*, 7, 62 (I, 352).
19. *Ibid.*, 7, 63 (I, 353).
20. *Ibid.*, 7, 64 (I, 353).
21. *Ibid.*, 8, 9 (I, 358).
22. *Ibid.*, 9, 20 (I, 381).
23. *Ibid.*
24. *Ibid.*, 8, 23 (I, 366).
25. *Ibid.*, footnote.
26. *Ibid.*, 8, 27 (I, 370).
27. W. A. Spooner, *Bishop Butler*, p. 213.
28. *Analogy*, II, 8, 23 (I, 367).
29. Philip Flanagan, *Newman and Faith*, p. 8. Cf. also, Sebastian Tromp, *De revelatione christiana*, p. 17; John L. Murphy, *The Mass and Liturgical Reform* (Milwaukee: Bruce, 1956), p. 50.
30. Flanagan, *Newman and Faith*, p. 8.
31. *Analogy*, II, 8, 25 (I, 367–368); cf. II, 8, 23 (I, 366): "I have argued upon the principles of the Fatalists, which I do not believe and have omitted a thing of the utmost importance which I do believe, the moral fitness and unfitness of actions, prior to all will whatever; which I apprehend as certainly to determine the Divine conduct, as speculative truth and falsehood necessarily determine the Divine judgment."
32. *Analogy*, II, 8, 25 (I, 368).
33. *Ibid.*, 8, 26 (I, 369).
34. *Ibid.*, I, Intro., 10 (I, 12).
35. *Ibid.*, 6, 4 (I, 141).
36. *Ibid.*, II, 6, 21 (I, 298).
37. Jacques Maritain, *Formal Logic*, trans. Imelda Chocquette (New York: Sheed & Ward, 1946), p. 286.
38. R. Adamson, "Joseph Butler," in *Encyclopaedia Britannica*, 9 ed., III, 584.
39. Gladstone (ed.), *The Works of Joseph Butler*, I, 8, note 2. (The note refers to *Analogy*, I, Intro., 7.)
40. *Ibid.*, 5, note 1 (*Analogy*, I, Intro., 4).
41. Butler had also interested himself in other aspects of Locke's thought; in fact, his works include a dissertation that attacks Locke's notion of personal identity: cf. Butler, *Dissertation I: Of Personal Identity* (in Gladstone edition: I, 387–396).
42. *Analogy*, I, Intro., 3 (I, 5); cf. note b.
43. John Locke, *Essay on Human Understanding*, IV, 15, 5 (Johnson edition: III, 91).
44. *Ibid.*, 16, 12, title (Johnson edition: III, 100).
45. Mossner, *Bishop Butler*, p. 101. — Cf. *Analogy*, I, Intro., 7 (I, 7, 9) where Butler sidesteps the more difficult question of the ultimate "nature, the

foundation and measure of probability; or whence it proceeds that *likeness* should beget that presumption, opinion, and full conviction . . ." which the human mind takes from it. He admits that "reasoning from analgoy" is liable to certain errors if misused, but he does not concern himself with a discussion of the means of avoiding them. This, he claims, belongs to the subject of logic, and he would prefer to leave such theoretical matters to the logicians, noting that this question "is a part of that subject [logic] which has not yet been thoroughly considered." For his part, he is satisfied that this manner of arguing, in its general outline, is "evidently natural, just and conclusive," so that he need not enter into these further questions.

46. Mossner, *Bishop Butler,* p. 79.
47. Origen, *Philocalia,* p. 23, ed. Cant., in *Analogy,* I, Intro., 8 (I, 9).
48. *Analogy,* I, Intro., 8 (I, 10).
49. *Ibid.,* 1 (I, 3).
50. *Ibid.,* 1, 2 (I, 3).
51. *Ibid.,* 3 (I, 4).
52. *Ibid.*
53. *Ibid.* (I, 5).
54. *Ibid.,* 4 (I, 5).
55. *Ibid.,* 5 (I, 6).
56. *Ibid.*
57. *Ibid.,* Concl., 14 (I, 184).
58. *Ibid.,* 6, 18 (I, 154): line 3 of par. 18 has the phrase "so there is *no* express historical or traditional evidence, as ancient as history, that it was taught first by revelation"; however, the word "no" was added erroneously in the Gladstone edition.
59. *Ibid.,* 3, 3, note b (I, 65).
60. *Ibid.,* Intro., 5 (I, 6).
61. *Ibid.,* II, 9, 20 (I, 381–382).
62. *Ibid.* (I, 382).
63. *Ibid.,* 7, 2 (I, 302).
64. *Ibid.,* 7, 60 (I, 351).
65. *Ibid.*
66. Gladstone, *The Works of Joseph Butler,* I, 383, note 1 (*Analogy,* II, Concl., 22).
67. *Ibid.*
68. *Analogy,* II, Concl., 20 (I, 382).

Index of Names

(Raised numbers refer to notes.)

Topical Index

(Raised numbers refer to notes.)

Act of Will, faith and, 58 ff, 73 ff, 250 ff, 289[30]
Agnosticism, Butler and, 211 ff, 222 ff; faith and, 256; Modernism and, 117
Age of Reason, theology and, 49, 164 ff
Anabaptists, Luther and, 161; Zwingli and, 160
Analogia entis, invention of Antichrist (Barth), xiii
Analogia fidei, theology and, xiii
Analogical knowledge, meaning of, 267 ff
Analogy, argument from (Maritain), 267 ff; threefold basis of (Butler), 270; of proportion, 267; and analogical knowledge, 267; probability and 268; existence of angels and (Locke), 226; Paley on, 229
Analogy of Religion, cf. **Butler**
Annotationes, of Vatican I Schema, 13 ff
Antiquity, argument from, cf. **Theology:** Classical Era
Apologetics, origin of (17th century), 170 ff, 204, 282[20]; basic problem of, 239; moral certitude and, 203; and faith, 204, 207; and proof of Christianity, 239; manual theology and, xvi; Modernism and, 116; Scripture and, 301[28]; "traditional," "classical," 282[20]; and *Apologie,* 49, 204; popular (pastoral), 204, 264; future approach of, 304[60]; Aquinas and, 48, 285[65]; Bayle and, 171; de Elizalde and, 170; Grotius and, 170 ff; Kierkegaard and, 33; Leo XIII and, 207; Loisy and, 244; Newman and, 264 ff
Apologie, meaning of, 49, 204
Apostles, and close of revelation, 80
Aristotelianism, not basis of Catholic belief, 110, 277[11]

Assent of faith, cf. **Certitude**
Assumption, scriptural basis of, 194, 305[91]
Atheism, and Communism, 5
Aufklärung, cf. **Enlightenment**
Augsburg Confession, 133, 141 ff
Authority, argument from, 225, 231
Authority of God, cf. **Faith:** *Theoretical Discussion*
Avant-garde, theology and, 32

Barth, Catholic faith and, xi–xiv; existentialism and, 153 ff; *Römerbrief,* 152, 186, 253; on teaching of Vatican I, 277[11]
Bible, cf. **Scripture**
Biblical Commission, On Bible Research (1964), 111 ff, 148
Bultmann, life of, 253; *Historie* and *Geschichte,* 209, 252 ff, 286[71]; historical pessimism of, 182, 255; demythologizing and, 182, 253 ff; rejects Protestant Liberalism, 254; post-Bultmannians and, 182, 255
Butler: *Life and Teachings,* early history, 211 ff; methodology of, 212; originality of, 269; sources of, 269; core of teaching, 222; natural religion and, 258 ff, 272; revealed religion and, 259 ff; rationalist defense of Christianity, 222, 266; meets adversary on his terms 265; sets aside own principles, 264; limited goal of argument, 264; understates case, 264; avoids debating atheists, 266; weakness of argument, 213, 236, 238, 265 ff; warning lesson of, 222; peak and decline of fame, 223 ff; early reactions to, 223; on and off Oxford reading list, 223, 235; later interpretations of, 222, 234 ff; parodies of argument, 235 ff; influence on disparate groups, 224; Oxford Movement and,

321

nature of, 173, 183, 201, 214, 247, 255 ff, 302⁴¹; reductively metaphysical, 168, 302³³; Butler and, 214 ff, 272 ff

Christ: General Questions: *Quest for Historical Jesus,* 179 ff, 182–183, 255, 304⁶⁰; Scripture and historical, 196 ff; as new Moses, 184; known only through primitive church, 306⁹⁸; *ipsissima verba* not in Scripture, 198; development of doctrine on, 194; man's encounter with, 210; and Christian faith (Schleiermacher), 131 ff; and redemption of Mary, 306⁹¹; resurrection, fact, and mystery, 208; Christ of faith, 116; Christ of history, 112–113, 116, 173–174, 210, (Bultmann) 182, 209, (Tillich) 173 ff, 255

Christ: Divinity of, not "proved," 43, 203 ff; object of belief, 208; Bultmann on, 304⁵⁹; Leo XIII on, 206 ff; Schweitzer on, 303⁵⁶

Christ: Lives of, infancy narrative, 184; "legends of Childhood" (Hase), 304⁶⁴; midrash and, 184, 304⁶⁵; fictitious lives, 179; rationalistic lives, 179 ff; Renan and, 180; Schweitzer and, 179 ff; Schleiermacher and, 304⁶⁸; Strauss and, 180 ff; Liberal Protestantism and, 180 ff

Christianity, always proclaimed, not proven, 285⁶¹; not demonstrated, 154 ff; not easily proven or disproven (Butler), 262–263, 273; probable evidence for, 213; and deductive proof, 166 ff; miracles a proof of, 64 ff, 166 ff, 177 ff, 213 ff, 230 ff, 236, 243, 259 ff, 272 ff, 287¹³; as a fact of human life, 265; reason shows only *what* it proclaims, 250; apologetes of (Hume), 233; deism and, 164; ethical goals of (Ritschl), 147; essence of (Harnack, Loisy), 185–189; *das Gefühl* and, 134; Locke's view of, 310⁵⁷; highest form of monotheism (Schleiermacher), 135; witnesses to, 272

Christianity: *History and,* historical religion, 157 ff; Tillich on, 255;

historical certitude and, 239; historical skepticism and, 214, 219, 256, 263, 309⁴⁰

Christianity: *Proof of,* Arnold and, 236; Bultmann and, 254; Butler and, 211 ff, 259 ff; Harnack and, 186; Juergens and, 238; Kant and, 177 ff; Loisy and, 188; Paley and, 229 ff

Christian Evidence School, 229 ff

Christology, Aquinas on, 48 ff, 285⁶¹

Church, as perpetual miracle, 64; as motive of faith, 64, 201, (*Life* magazine) 287¹¹; Scripture and primitive, 143 ff; Scripture judged by (Schleiermacher), 144; no creative function in, 140, 175, 303⁴⁵; historical method and primitive, 200; "no salvation outside," 202; authentic teachers in, 190, 200; as created testimony, cf. **Faith:** more than condition for faith, 290⁴⁰; conciliar decrees, Scripture and, 194; faith of non-Catholics and, 202; Schleiermacher's concept of, 134–145; role of community (Schleiermacher), 140 ff; role of Church in proclaiming revelation, 76 ff, 96, 186, 189 ff, 209 ff, 290⁴⁰

Classes, at Trent, 82 ff

Classical Era, antiquity and, 41, 161, 283³⁹

Communism, atheism and (Pius XI), 4 ff

Community, cf. **Church**

Conciliar decrees, interpretation of, xii, 109 ff, 208, 291⁴⁰; theologians quoted in, 190, 305⁸¹; scriptural teaching and, 194; Schleiermacher on, 142 ff

Contemporaneity, cf. **Instant**

Created testimony, cf. **Faith**

Credendity, judgment of, i.e, practical judgment of credibility, 67

Credibility, Church as motive of, 64, 201, 287¹¹; reasonableness of faith and, 61 ff

Credibility: *Judgment of,* faith and, 22, 66 ff, 71 ff, 77 ff, 205 ff; purpose of, 288¹⁷; history and, cf. **Certitude,** *Historical;* reason and, cf. **Certitude,** *Types of,* moral; a con-

Pietism, Kant and, 177; Schleiermacher and, 122
Positivism, historical, cf. **Historical Method**
Post-Cartesian Theories of Faith, 70 ff, 195 ff, 203, 217 ff, 229, 238 ff, 248 ff, 282[19], 284[60], 285[65], 288[19], 301[28]; Butler and, 219 ff, 247 ff; an innovation (Davis), 195; Juergens and, 238 ff; Locke and, 229
Practical Judgment of Credibility, 67 ff
Preaching, kergyma and, 30, 63, 77, 186, 210, 282[19], 284[60]; of metaphysics, 20 ff
Preambula fidei, Aquinas and, 291[42]
Probability (and Faith), accumulation of probabilities, 243; argument from, 166 ff, 174, 222, 241, 268; argument from analogy and, 268; certitude and, 205 ff; probable evidence and, 270 ff; guide of life, 167, 271; probable proofs and, 274 ff; weakness of argument from, 222, 241; Arnold and, 237; Butler and, 167 ff, 213 ff, 222, 262, 266 ff; Hume and, 231; Locke and, 224 ff; Loisy and, 244; Manning and, 241; Newman and, 239, 242, 245; Paley and, 229; Tillich and, 255 ff
Proofs, theological, Christianity and, 238 ff, 254; divinity of Christ and, 48, 203, 206 ff, 285[61]; evidence multiplied by probable proofs, 214, 262, 274; faith and, 22, 247; Scripture and, 161 ff; theology and, 191 ff; Aquinas and, 48, 285[61]; Hume and, 231; Locke and, 226; cf. also, **Christianity:** *Proof of;* **Faith; Miracles**
Prophecies, cf. **Miracles**
Protestantism, existentialism and, 152 ff; on historical certitude, 252 ff; Neo-Liberalism, 154 ff; Neo-Orthodoxy, 154 ff; cf. also **Reformation, Trent, Vatican I**
Protestant Liberalism, biblical criticism and, 147, 174 ff, 180 ff, 251 ff; three causes of, 146 ff; lives of Christ and, 180 ff; Darwinian thought in, 149 ff; evolutionary nature of, 149 ff; "experience" re-

places God in, 252, 313[147]; notion of faith in, 58, 146 ff; Modernism and, 118, 151; Neo-Orthodoxy, Neo-Liberalism and, 154 ff; Reformation and, 119 ff; religious experience, center of, 146, 313[147]; Schleiermacher, father of, 146; social gospel and, 147; Barth and, 152; Bultmann and, 253 ff; Harnack and, 146 ff, 186 ff; Kierkegaard and, 50; Niebuhr and, 155; Ritschl and, 146; Schleiermacher and, 146 ff
Protestant Orthodoxy, 125, 134, 161, 176, 300[13]
Protestant Scholasticism, cf. **Protestant Orthodoxy**
Providence, Romanticists and, 126

Quest for the Historical Jesus, cf. **Christ**

Rationalism, rise of, 159 ff; influence of Descartes on, 163 ff; effect on theology, xvi ff, 76 ff, 162 ff; theories of faith and, 76 ff; Butler and, 218, 221 ff; Schleiermacher and, 124; cf. also **Deism, Vatican I**
Reason and faith, cf. **God:** *Known by Reason;* **Faith; Age of Reason**
Reasonableness of faith, 61 ff; also cf. **Credibility:** *Judgment of*
Reformation, Humanism and, 159 ff; Scripture and, 114, 160 ff, 193 ff, 198; faith and reason in, 58, 160 ff; argument from antiquity and, 200; naïvete of Zwingli, Calvin, 160–161; Liberal Protestantism and, 119 ff; Kierkegaard and, 27 ff, 32, 40; Schleiermacher and, 134, 137, 142 ff; cf. also **Trent; Faith; Scripture:** *Scriptura sola*
Religion, natural, cf. **Natural Religion**
Religion: *Schleiermacher and,* essence of, 127; as chiefly subjective, 130; as ethical system, 126 ff; as feeling (Gefühl), 130 ff; as experience, 128; as intuition and feeling, 129
Resurrection, as historical fact and as mystery, 208
Revelation: *Notion of,* reasons for,